Islamic and European Expansion   THE FORGING OF A GLOBAL ORDER

In the series
CRITICAL PERSPECTIVES
ON THE PAST
edited by
Susan Porter Benson,
Stephen Brier,
and Roy Rosenzweig

Islamic & European Expansion

THE FORGING OF A GLOBAL ORDER

Edited by
MICHAEL ADAS
for the
American Historical
Association

TEMPLE
UNIVERSITY
PRESS
Philadelphia

Temple University Press, Philadelphia 19122
Copyright © 1993 by Temple University. All rights reserved
Published 1993
Printed in the United States of America

The paper used in this publication meets the minimum
requirements of American National Standard for Information
Sciences—Permanence of Paper for Printed Library Materials,
ANSI Z39.48-1984 ∞

Library of Congress Cataloging-in-Publication Data
Islamic and European expansion : the forging of a global order /
edited by Michael Adas for the American Historical Association.
    p. cm. — (Critical perspectives on the past)
    Includes bibliographical references.
    ISBN 1-56639-067-2—ISBN 1-56639-068-0 (pbk.)
1. Historiography.   I. Adas, Michael, 1943– .   II. American
Historical Association.   III. Series.
D13.I76 1993
907'.2—dc20   92-43872
                                                        CIP

CONTENTS

vii   Introduction
MICHAEL ADAS

1   *Islamic History as Global History*
RICHARD M. EATON

37   *Gender and Islamic History*
JUDITH TUCKER

75   *The World System in the Thirteenth Century: Dead-End or Precursor?*
JANET LIPPMAN ABU-LUGHOD

103   *The Age of Gunpowder Empires, 1450–1800*
WILLIAM H. MCNEILL

141   *The Columbian Voyages, the Columbian Exchange, and Their Historians*
ALFRED W. CROSBY

165   *The Tropical Atlantic in the Age of the Slave Trade*
PHILIP D. CURTIN

199   *Interpreting the Industrial Revolution*
PETER N. STEARNS

243   *Industrialization and Gender Inequality*
LOUISE A. TILLY

311   *"High" Imperialism and the "New" History*
MICHAEL ADAS

345   *Gender, Sex, and Empire*
MARGARET STROBEL

377   The Contributors

INTRODUCTION

Until the past two or three decades, world history has been a neglected and often disdained stepchild within the historical profession. Although of ancient lineage—Herodotus, after all, ranged across civilizations and aspired to a global perspective—world history had fallen on hard times by the late nineteenth century. The popularity that it had enjoyed in Western intellectual circles in the cosmopolitan and eclectic age of the Enlightenment, as perhaps best evidenced by Voltaire's grand survey of civilized development, was rapidly eroded by the late eighteenth-century revolutions and the growing importance of the nation–state. In the nineteenth century, national histories—often blatantly chauvinistic and usually informed by exceptionalist assumptions—were favored at the expense of general surveys of the human experience. These trends were reinforced by the concurrent professionalization of historical writing, which was grounded in an insistence on empiricism and the consequent use of primary data. History in the grand style, which ranged across centuries and civilizations and probed for general patterns, became suspect. It possessed neither the scientific attributes that national specialists claimed for their own work nor did it lend itself to the thick, narrative style that aspired, in Leopold von Ranke's often-quoted adage, to reconstruct the human past *"wie es eigentlich gewesen."*

Following World War I, largely precipitated by the great power rivalries represented in the national histories of the nineteenth century, world history enjoyed a brief revival. But the search for an encompassing teleology or underlying laws that informed the writings of Oswald Spengler and Arnold Toynbee, the leading exponents of world history in this period, was strongly resisted by the great majority of empirically minded area specialists who dominated the historical profession. Few read more than bowdlerized summaries of Spengler and Toynbee, and most were dubious about the feasibility or even the advisability of attempting to generalize across vast swaths of time and space. Among professional scholars at least, world history came to be seen as a pastime for dilettantes or popularists.

Even among teachers, it was increasingly equated with unfocused social studies courses at the secondary school level.

In view of these developments, the growth of interest among professional historians in writing and teaching global and comparative history since the 1960s is truly remarkable. The appearance of numerous works by prominent scholars on transcultural interaction; the critical roles comparative studies have played in the development of leading fields of historical inquiry such as slavery, protest, and the study of racism; and the appearance of several journals on world history and at least four university press series devoted to comparative works—all attest to the importance of these approaches to historical research and scholarship. The great proliferation at both college and secondary school levels of courses on world history and numerous textbooks to teach them, and the formation in the early 1980s of the World History Association, an affiliate of the American Historical Association, testify to the new emphasis given to cross-cultural and global perspectives in educational curriculums at a variety of levels.

The publication of this volume of essays on comparative and global history—as well as the issuing of the essays as individual pamphlets by the American Historical Association—is intended to provide both professional historians and interested readers with overview assessments of developments within a revitalized field of study. These essays also represent a response to the demands of educators and policymakers for cross-cultural perspectives in history instruction in contemporary societies that are increasingly ethnically mixed, multicultural, and more and more linked to the rest of the world. One of the central purposes of this collection is to make available much needed background information on the sources and methods essential for effective teaching and writing on cross-cultural history. Each of the essays is aimed at providing secondary and college teachers facing the formidable task of preparing courses that are global or comparative in scope with a sense of some of the main issues and findings that have emerged from historical research in these fields in the past few decades. Individual essays may also prove useful to those embarking on research projects with a cross-cultural dimension.

Focusing on areas and issues where their own work has been concentrated, each author explores selected themes and interpretations that have emerged from cross-cultural and comparative historical studies undertaken in the past three or four decades. Though there are differences in approach, none of the authors attempts a comprehensive survey of all the works that have appeared in her or his field of concentration. Instead, each writer seeks to chart the advances in our understandings of different aspects of world history that research and writing in this period has brought about, as well as to identify significant gaps in our knowledge that have yet to be filled and interpretive problems that remain to be solved. Each author deals with both specific findings and the broad patterns that cross-cultural study has revealed. All the essays are thematically oriented, and each is organized around a particular historical era, such as the age of Islamic expansion or the centuries of the industrial revolution. Though all the essays provide references to key works and further readings, some are a good deal more bibliographically oriented than others. Contributors were intentionally given considerable latitude on this issue as well as on the approach they took to the different topics considered.

Taken together, the essays in this collection exemplify some of the key features of recent writing on world history that distinguish it in fundamental ways from earlier work, including the multivolumed tomes of the eighteenth-century *philosophes* or the equally lengthy disquisitions of Toynbee and Spengler in the 1920s. Recent writers and teachers of global history have been less concerned than their predecessors with comprehensiveness or providing a total chronology of human events—though these concerns are often evidenced in world history textbooks or mandated by state school boards. In the past two or three decades global and comparative history has tended to be thematically focused on recurring processes, such as changes in military organization and patterns of colonization, or on such cross-cultural phenomena as the spread of disease, technology, and trading networks. In approaching these topics, recent scholars have more consciously employed techniques of comparative analysis than earlier writers, who tended to forage rather erratically and randomly across cultures and civilizations. In fact, one of the key advances in the writing of cross-cultural history in the past few decades has been the rigorous application of the comparative method. In contrast to virtually all earlier works on global history, where case evidence from different cultures was juxtaposed but rarely systematically compared, recent scholarship has often thoroughly integrated the techniques of comparative analysis that have been refined mostly by practitioners of the other social sciences.

Here it is important to stress that though they are routinely conflated, world and comparative history represent quite distinct approaches. Both are cross-cultural; both aim at identifying larger historical trends and recurring patterns. But while world history involves mainly questions of perspective, genuinely comparative history requires the application of a distinct methodology. Central to the comparative technique are the systematic selection of case examples and the mastery of the historical materials relevant to each of these. As Theda Skocpol and Margaret Somers have argued,[1] case selection involves testing to determine that the case contexts are in fact comparable, the identification of constants to link the different parts of the comparison, and the determination of independent (or causal) and dependent (or outcome) variables. Care must be taken that the variables are consistently employed across each of the cases—a process that involves further choices regarding the specific method of comparison an author wishes to employ. As Skocpol and Somers implicitly illustrate, historians tend to favor the contrast-of-contexts approach, which reflects a disciplinary stress on the importance of empirical evidence, often at the expense of grand theorizing. But as numerous and influential works written on cross-cultural phenomena in the past two or three decades have shown, historians can deal effectively with macrocausal issues, develop meaningful typologies, and test hypotheses. As in the other social sciences, analytical payoff provides the main rationale for the application of the comparative technique. The key contributions that comparativists have made in recent decades to debates over slavery and revolution, for example, which have preoccupied social scientists in a variety of fields, are alone sufficient to justify the serious application of the comparative technique by professional historians.

The great proliferation of studies by area specialists in the post–World War II era has in many ways facilitated serious comparative history and cross-cultural analysis. Area specialists' monographs have provided contemporary scholars with a good deal more data on different cultures and societies throughout the globe than was available to earlier writers who attempted comparative or world history. As a result, the best recent works in these fields have displayed far greater sensitivity than earlier, more comprehensive, world surveys to cultural nuances and to the intricacies of the internal histories of the societies they cover. Sensitivity to the diversity and complexity of the human experience deters most contemporary cross-cultural and comparative historians from the search for universal laws or attempts to discern an overarching teleological meaning in world history. Their main concerns are the identification of patterns and recurring processes, and the study of the dynamics and impact of cross-cultural interaction.

As the essays in this collection demonstrate, much of contemporary work on global and comparative history has been focused on non-Western cultures and societies, or the regions lumped together as the Third World before the recent collapse of the Second World and with it the credibility of Cold War ideology. The spread of Islamic civilization, European overseas expansion, the rise and decline of the South Atlantic slave trade, industrialization and the completion of Europe's drive for global hegemony, all have key European (or North American) components. But each of these processes has been grounded in the historical experiences of non-Western societies, and each in turn has been profoundly influenced by the responses of African, Asian, Latin American, or Oceanic peoples. As the references to key historical works considered in the following essays suggest, practitioners of the new world history have very often adopted this perspective because they see it as the most effective way of bringing the experience of the "people without history" into the mainstream of teaching and scholarship. Over the past two or three decades, global and comparative history have proved compelling vehicles for relating the development of Europe to that of the rest of the world and of challenging the misleading myth of exceptionalism that has dominated much of the history written about the United States.

The overall focus of this first of three projected volumes of essays on global and comparative history to be published by Temple University Press is the epoch of world history that began in the seventh century and extended into the early 1900s. Because of the unprecedented increase in cross-cultural contacts and global integration that occurred in this era, it provides a fitting starting point for this series. The essays by Richard Eaton, Judith Tucker, and Janet Abu-Lughod explore key themes in the spread of Islamic civilization, which was the first to bring together the continents of the "Old World" ecumene—Africa, Asia, and Europe. Abu-Lughod's and William McNeill's contributions tackle key questions concerning the reasons for the rise of western Europe as the civilization that would supplant Islam as the mediator of the process of global unification. Together they cover a wide range of social and economic and military—political issues that were central to the great transitions that occurred between the fourteenth and sixteenth centuries. Alfred Crosby provides a trenchant survey of the impact of the "Columbian" exchanges that accompanied the integration of the Americas into the developing global order during this period, while Philip Curtin's exploration of key themes in the Atlantic slave trade reveals another key dimension of this process. The essays by Peter Stearns and Louise Tilly provide detailed assessments of the abundance of historical studies that have appeared on yet another era of profound transformations that distinguished this epoch, those set in motion by the industrial revolution. As the contributions by Michael Adas and Margaret Strobel illustrate, the decisive advantages that industrialization brought to the nations of western Europe and North America made possible the establishment of Western hegemony throughout the globe. Beginning with the rise of Islamic civilization, which was the first to encompass numerous centers of the Old World ecumene, and ending with the processes by which the nation-states of the West attained domination over all other civilizations and culture areas, the epoch covered in these essays was truly a watershed era in world history and thus a fitting focus for the first collection of essays in the Temple–American Historical Association global and comparative history series.

In selecting the topics and authors of these essays, a conscious effort was made to include representatives of each of the major schools of world history that have emerged in recent decades. The contributions of William McNeill and Albert Crosby are characteristic of an approach to world history pioneered by McNeill, which focuses on key cross-cultural processes—the spread of disease or military technology, the consequences of the incorporation of previously isolated areas like the Americas into the global order—that are examined over broad swaths of time. The more systematically comparative work of what has been called the Wisconsin School is reflected in the essays of Philip Curtin, who has for decades been the leading practitioner of this approach, and of Richard Eaton and Michael Adas. Though both are prominent comparativists, Louise Tilly and Peter Stearns come from a rather different tradition. Both are European social historians who have sought in recent years to extend the range of their analysis to key North American and Asian case examples of industrialization. As their essays in this volume illustrate, Tilly, Tucker, and Strobel have all been leading advocates of the comparative approach to gender issues. Abu-Lughod's contribution provides a superb introduction to the structuralist, world-systems framework that the writings of Immanuel Wallerstein have done the most to advance in recent decades. As she and Wallerstein readily acknowledge, this mode of analysis owes much to the work of Fernand Braudel and the French *Annales* school.

The authors of the essays included in this volume have also been key, and in some cases controversial, exponents of some of the innovative approaches that have revolutionized the writing of history since the early 1960s. Virtually all the essays deal extensively with questions informed by the "new" social history. Those by Crosby, McNeill, Stearns, and Curtin tackle underlying demographic trends; Abu-Lughod, Eaton, and Curtin examine the vital roles played by traders and trading networks in forging a global order; and Crosby, Stearns, and Adas explore some of the ecological consequences of the rise of the capitalist world system. Gender issues are central to the essays by Tucker, Tilly, and Strobel and are treated more selectively in the contributions by Eaton, Stearns, and Adas. Tucker's essay also reflects the growing importance of the use of legal documents to explore gender relationships in the context of family and community history. Technological and organizational change is central to McNeill's account of the shift of military and political power to the West, and it figures prominently in the arguments of Eaton, Abu-Lughod, Crosby, Stearns, Tilly, and Adas. Curtin's essay on the slave trade as well as those on industrialization and imperialism survey the findings in fields in which debate, analysis, and research agendas have been critically shaped by comparative historical work.

Because there are many approaches to world history, the contributions to this collection vary widely in format and content, from ones that are argumentative and highly interpretive to others that are more heavily bibliographic or concentrate on providing an overview of major patterns and processes in global development. Each essay, however, suggests some of the most effective ways of dealing with the topics and eras covered, given the current state of our knowledge. The first of three volumes on global and comparative history, this collection will be followed by a volume that explores themes in early and classical history; the third volume will be devoted to world history in the twentieth century.

NOTE

1. "The Uses of Comparative History in Macrosociological Inquiry," *Comparative Studies in Society and History* 22 (1980): 174–97.

Islamic and European Expansion THE FORGING OF A GLOBAL ORDER

Islamic History as Global History

RICHARD M. EATON

The Legacy of Europe's Encounter with Islam

Some years ago, Harold Isaacs wrote *Scratches on Our Minds*, a book probing the images that ordinary Americans held about China and India. Subjecting his informants to the techniques of psychoanalysis, the author also wanted to learn where, when, and how such images as "inferior" Chinese and "fabulous" Indians had been formed. If Isaacs had written another book scratching American minds respecting Islam or Islamic history, one suspects he would have uncovered some fairly lurid images: of grim fanatical clerics seizing political power in the contemporary Middle East, of generals amputating the hands of thieves in the name of religion, or of women held in a state of permanent domestic bondage. Had he scratched a bit more, he might have found images, informed perhaps by youthful readings of *The Arabian Nights*, of Arab princes lavishly entertained by sensuous women, of sumptuous banquets, or of genies and lamps—all set in an atmosphere of Oriental splendor and decadence. He might also have dredged up from the minds of his informants images of medieval violence: of fierce warriors on horseback wielding broad scimitars or of caliphs delivering swift and arbitrary justice via the executioner. Finally, well embedded in the subconscious of his hypothetical subjects, Isaacs may also have found some hazy notion of Islam as a religious heresy or of Muhammad as a false prophet.

Such images are part of the legacy of Europe's long and often hostile encounter with Muslim societies. For here was a religion that affirmed the one God of the Jews and Christians yet denied the Trinity; that accepted Jesus as sent to humankind and born of the Virgin Mary, yet rejected his divinity; that accepted the Torah and the Gospels and their adherents, the Jews and Christians, as "people of the Book," yet rejected the claims to exclusivity made by the former and the worship of Jesus as practiced by

1

the latter. Unlike Hinduism or Buddhism, which were rendered relatively innocuous by their geographical and theological distance from Europe and Christianity, Islam was simply too close to Europe—both geographically and theologically—to be treated with anything like equanimity. Hence the Crusades: the Europeans' forcible attempt to reconquer Palestine for the Cross and, by extension, to uproot the so-called heresy that Arabo-Islamic civilization supposedly represented. Contemporary impressions of Arab Muslims are vividly reflected in the *Chanson de Roland*, the French epic poem, crystalized in the eleventh century, that depicts Muslims as idolaters, polytheists, and, above all, as the archvillains of Christendom; while the Emperor Charlemagne is portrayed as the snowy-bearded defender of Christendom who leads the French into a mighty struggle waged in the name of the Christian God.[1] The poem thus expresses a worldview rigidly split into a we–they opposition that is about as absolute as any to be found in Western literature.

Since the eleventh century, it was the fate of Islamic civilization to serve in the European imagination as a wholly alien "other," a historic and cosmic foil against which Europeans defined their own collective identity as a world civilization. Gradually, however, Western scholars became aware of the primary textual sources on which Islamic civilization was built. Beginning with the Crusades and continuing throughout Europe's medieval period, a handful of scholars learned Arabic and began editing, translating, interpreting, and publishing the immense corpus of primary texts that had accumulated during the rise and expansion of Islamic civilization. Some wished to refute the religious claims of what they saw as a Christian heresy; others sought to recover for classical scholarship those texts translated into Arabic by Muslims that had been lost in the Greek original. Then, in the late eighteenth century, when much of the Muslim world began falling under European colonial rule, institutional foundations such as the Asiatic Society of Bengal and the French Asiatic Society were established for the serious study of Islamic civilization, while in European universities chairs in Arabic language and literature were founded. From these developments emerged a new cadre of scholars in the nineteenth and early twentieth centuries—people like Ignaz Goldziher, D. B. McDonald, J. Wellhausen, Carl Brockelmann, C. H. Becker, Theodor Nöldeke, Louis Massignon, Edward G. Brown, and Reynold Nicholson—who studied Islamic civilization as their primary field and not just as a subject ancillary to some other discipline.

These scholars' strength was their mastery of philology and the principal languages of Islam: Arabic, Persian, and Turkish. Many were veritable pioneers who ransacked obscure private collections all over Europe and Asia in search of original manuscripts, which were then edited, collated, or translated. Those who analyzed and published these texts more or less consciously endeavored to give definition to Islam as a civilization, that is, as a unified body of beliefs, ideas, and values elaborated and transmitted in literature. And perhaps somewhat less consciously, these same scholars saw themselves as interpreters of that civilization to "the West," their home audience. But there was a darker side to this intellectual enterprise. In their attempt to give definition to Muslim civilization, many of these scholars tended to present Islam as a "tradition" that was static, timeless, and uniform, and by implication, impervious to the dynamics of change or historical process. Moreover, recent critics have sensed a political motive in much of this scholarship. Scholarly concentration on the classical texts of Islam, and especially on those produced during the formative eighth to eleventh centuries, encouraged the belief that this particular period represented some sort of "golden age," after which Islamic civilization was doomed to a slow and painful decline. The notion of a declining Islamic civilization suggested, in turn, that Europe's relatively easy conquest of Muslim societies in the eighteenth and nineteenth centuries, and the continued European domination over them into the twentieth, had been not only inevitable but justified.

The Rise and Growth of Islam and Its Historians

For most Europeans and North Americans, the vision of Islam as a static monolith or as a mysterious, exotic "other" remained dominant until the mid-twentieth century. In the decades after World War II, however, and especially since the 1960s, American and European universities experienced a historiographical revolution that considerably expanded the conceptual framework within which Islamic history was studied. Whereas classical Islamicists had asked, "What can the *text* tell us of the *civilization?*" a new generation of historians began asking, "What can the *data* tell us of the *societies?*" Implicit in these very different questions was a whole range of issues, both conceptual and methodological, asked not only by historians of Muslim civilization but by historians throughout the profession who had been influenced by new intellectual currents, particularly the pioneering work of Marc Bloch and the *Annales* school of historical scholarship in post-World War I France. The new approach also signaled the influence of anthropology on history and all the social sciences.

To say that societies replaced civilization as the principal object of study implied a shift in focus from the literate elite classes from whose milieu the authors of the classical texts usually came, to those many other communities whom Eric Wolf has called the "people without history." The new emphasis also recognized that Islamic civilization was not the monolithic entity that many had thought it to be but that, on closer examination, it broke down into a diffuse plurality of communities that differed vastly over time and space. Many, in fact, rejected the concept of civilization altogether as a useful category in social analysis, since any reconstruction of Islamic history based primarily on the Muslim literary tradition would likely give undue importance to the normative social vision conveyed by Muslim literate elites. Furthermore, as the object of historical analysis changed, so did the questions asked. Earlier Islamicists had concentrated on political and intellectual history largely because classical Islamic texts were themselves preoccupied with these topics. But the new generation of historians began asking questions that ranged considerably beyond the political or intellectual, embracing such subdisciplines as economic history, the history of technology, historical demography, urban history, social history, political economy, nomadic history, microhistory, and historical linguistics.

The methodological techniques employed for addressing these questions also expanded. Truly, the immense corpus of Arabic and Persian texts on which older generations of Islamicists relied almost exclusively remains indispensable for any sort of inquiry into Muslim history. But such texts were frequently formal works written by Muslim chroniclers—many of them in the pay of political leaders—who were self-consciously writing about their own present or recent past with a view to posterity. Hence the texts such authors produced were deliberate constructions or reconstructions of people or events, carrying the same risks of bias, judgment, perspective, or interest that can accompany the endeavor of any author. What the new historians wanted to do was to supplement such texts with information that had not already been self-consciously packaged for them as "history" by intermediaries, that is, by the authors of the texts who stood between them and the events or processes they wished to describe. Once the principle of paying attention to sources other than primary texts was accepted, as increasingly has been the case among historians working since the 1950s, the search was on for contemporary literary sources generated outside the Islamic corpus or for *any* sort of contemporary artifact produced by the society in question that had survived into our own times. The new generation of historians thus uncovered an impressive variety of sources: commercial documents, tax registers, official land grants, administrative seals, census records, coins, gravestones, magical incantations written on bowls, memoirs of pilgrims, archeological and architectural data, biographical dictionaries, inscriptional evidence, and more recently, oral history.

We may illustrate some of the new questions and techniques for addressing these sources by examining specific issues that have occupied modern historians. These issues include some of the most remarkable movements in Islamic history and indeed in global history: the rise of Islam among the tribes of seventh-century Arabia; the eruption of Arab Muslims out of the Arabian peninsula and their defeat of the two largest and culturally most advanced empires in western Asia, Sasanian Persia and Byzantine Rome; and the integration of most of the population of the Middle East into a newly constituted Islamic society that had become by the tenth century a world civilization.

THE RISE OF THE ISLAMIC RELIGION IN ARABIA

There is a cliché that Islam, because it appeared in the seventh century, long after other world religions, arose "in the full light of history," as if news reporters were on hand to record for posterity exactly what happened. But the widely differing historical interpretations of this event would suggest more obscurity than light, at least as concerns the earliest phase of Islamic history. In our day, three principal kinds of interpretations prevail: the traditional Muslim account based on Arabic sources that appeared in the early centuries of Islam; modern Western accounts that tease sociologically rational explanations out of those same materials; and modern Western accounts that look outside the corpus of Arabic sources.

Traditional Muslim accounts of Islamic history generally commence with the Prophet of Islam, Muhammad ibn Abdullah, whose prophetic career began in the early decades of the seventh century. A western Arabian belonging to a mercantile clan, Muhammad often retreated to meditate on a mountain near his native city of Mecca. On one such occasion he was startled to hear a voice identified as that of the angel Gabriel, who addressed him with the command, "Recite!" Muhammad soon realized that he had in fact received a command from God:

> Read: In the name of thy Lord Who createth,
> Createth man from a clot.
> Read: And thy Lord is the Most Bounteous,
> Who teacheth by the pen,
> Teacheth man that which he knew not.[2]

On subsequent occasions Muhammad received further revelations, which were committed to memory by the small band of followers to whom he began preaching in Mecca and who were known later as Muslims, meaning those who had "submitted" to God. Several decades later Uthman (644–56), the third "successor" or caliph (*khalīfa*) to Muhammad as leader of the growing community of believers, ordered that these verses be collected into the canonical scripture that constitutes the Qur'an. For Muslims, these revelations represent the last of several occasions on which God, through the medium of successive prophets, had broken through from the divine realm, where he alone resides, to the human realm. Thus

Muhammad is connected prophetically with Abraham, Moses, Jesus, and other prophets; yet because he came after the Hebrew prophets, his revelation was believed to have superseded those of his predecessors.

Initially, according to traditional accounts, the oligarchs who dominated Mecca rejected Muhammad's prophecy as a threat to their position. But the nearby city of Medina, which was at that time split into contentious factions, invited Muhammad to come and arbitrate their internal disputes. In the end they accepted not only Muhammad the arbiter but Muhammad the Prophet of God, and thus the first Muslim community emerged in Medina in the year 622. That Muslims date the beginning of Islam from this event indicates that it was not so much God's breakthrough to humankind that distinguished Islam from other world events. Rather, the year 622 was significant because it represented humanity's response to God's message, humanity's willingness to undertake the moral obligation of obeying God by forming a new human society—the community of believers called the *umma*—constructed around the divine message.

Since the late nineteenth century, Western scholars have developed interpretations of the rise of Islam using the same body of classical Arabic texts as those used by Muslim traditionalists, but they have done so with a view to finding in those texts explanations that conform to Western models of social development. Thus scholars like Montgomery Watt or M. A. Shaban, current representatives of this trend, have viewed the emergence of the new religion as a function of deeper socioeconomic changes held to have been occurring in sixth- and seventh-century western Arabia. During the half century or so before the emergence of Muhammad, Meccan merchants are said to have become long-distance traders who entered and even dominated international trade routes connecting Yemen to the south with Syria to the north and ultimately India with Europe. The rise of Mecca as the hub of an expanding international trade network, according to this view, was the cause of any number of social problems for Mecca and western Arabia generally: greater social stratification, greater social inequities, greater dependence of poorer clans on wealthier ones, general social disruption, and even spiritual malaise. In this situation the Prophet Muhammad emerged proclaiming a message intended to dissolve the tribal units altogether and replace them with a single pan-Arab community to be guided by a new and much higher authority—God. Since the new movement declared all people to be equal before God, converted communities whose aspirations had previously been blocked by social inequities now acquired, or expected to acquire, much greater socioeconomic mobility. Likewise, the movement's heavy emphasis on social justice and its rejection of all forms of hierarchy or privilege is said to have found a receptive audience among the disenfranchised classes of Arab society, especially the poor, slaves, and women—Muhammad himself had been an orphan—for whom the message guaranteed specific rights and forms of protection.

Thus the emergence of Muhammad and the success of his preaching is interpreted in terms of the Prophet's solutions to specific, contemporary socioeconomic problems. But the premise on which these arguments rest—that the problems of Muhammad's day arose from the rapid wealth that accrued to Mecca as a result of its rise in international trade—has been seriously challenged by several scholars. In particular, Patricia Crone has recently published considerable evidence showing that far from occupying the hub of a vast and expanding commercial network, Mecca at the time of Muhammad was quite peripheral to world trade and in fact occupied an economic backwater on the fringes of the world's two superpowers, Sasanian Persia and Byzantine Rome. If Mecca was not the thriving commercial center that most social historians had alleged it to be, then the entire sequence of sociological arguments that rest on that assumption, and which are used to explain the rise of Islam, collapses.

A third cluster of scholars has sought to move beyond exclusive reliance on the vast body of Arabic commentaries, histories, biographies, and other texts that developed within the early tradition of Islamic scholarship and to study early Islamic history on the basis of contemporary literary materials written by non-Muslims in Greek, Hebrew, Syriac, Coptic, and Armenian.[3] The discovery and use of such literary sources have truly revolutionized the field. The editor of a volume arising from a 1975 conference on early Islam that included a paper on Syriac sources wrote: "For the first time in our lives many of us became acquainted with the outlook of non-Arab, non-Muslim historians on the conquests and [their] perpetrators."[4] By comparing the non-Arabic with the Arabic sources, or by combining both, scholars are now beginning to replace earlier, oversimplified views with more refined interpretations of early Islamic social history. It is as though a generation of World War II historians who had previously used only German sources for writing about the war suddenly discovered the mountains of wartime sources written in English, Russian, Japanese, and French.

If some historians wish merely to supplement Arabic sources with non-Arabic ones for the study of early Islam, others, such as Patricia Crone and Michael Cook, are more skeptical of the reliability of the Arabic sources altogether. For, apart from the Qur'an itself, these sources did not begin to appear until several centuries after the death of Muhammad, meaning that the primary materials historians had been using for writing the early history of Islam are far from contemporary. On crucial issues, moreover, these primary sources are ambiguous or even self-contradictory. By contrast, many non-Arabic sources were contemporary or nearly contemporary with the events they described, though as outside sources they also carried the possibility of anti-Muslim bias. It is hardly surprising, then, that scholars who have been most skeptical of the Arabic literary tradition and most receptive to using non-Arabic sources have reached extremely controversial conclusions—for example, that the earliest Muslims considered themselves descendants of Abraham through Hagar and Ishmael, that the movement originated in northern Arabia and not Mecca, and that Palestine and not Medina was the movement's principal focus.[5] Moreover, whereas the traditional Muslim position sees Islam as having appeared fully developed in the form of Muhammad's revelations in Mecca and Medina, contemporary non-Muslim sources depict the slow evolution in the centuries before Muhammad of a monotheistic cult that, heavily influenced by Jewish practice and Jewish apocalyptic thought, absorbed neighboring pagan cults in Arabia in the time of Muhammad.[6]

In sum, the Muslim scholarly tradition generally postulates a dramatic break between the age of pre-Islam (the *jâhilîya*, or "age of ignorance") and that of Islam. In contrast, modern Western interpretations, influenced by nineteenth-century European notions of social evolution, have come to regard the origins of Muslim history in distinctly organic terms, that is, as having logically grown out of earlier socioreligious structures. The important division among Western historians is between those whose work is confined to the traditional Arabic sources and those who have begun tapping into the contemporary non-Muslim sources, resulting in interpretations of Islam's origins and early development that are more complex, and in some instances far more controversial, than earlier understandings.

THE EARLY CONQUESTS IN THE MIDDLE EAST

During the ten years immediately following the Prophet's death, from 632 to 642, Arab Muslims erupted out of the Arabian peninsula and conquered Iraq, Syria, Palestine, Egypt, and western Iran. The movement did not stop there, however. To the west, Arab ships sailed into the Mediterranean Sea, previously a "Roman lake," taking Cyprus (649), Carthage (698), Tunis (700), and Gibraltar (711), before conquering Spain (711–16) and raiding southern France (720). Sicily, Corsica, and Sardinia suffered repeated pillaging during those years. Meanwhile, Arab armies during the 650s marched eastward across the Iranian plateau and completed the destruction of the Sasanian Empire, forcing the son of the Persian "king of kings" to flee to the Tang court in China. By 712 Arab armies had seized strategic oases towns of Central Asia—Balkh, Samarqand, Bukhara, and Ferghana—and would soon be meeting Chinese armies face to face. To the south, Muslim navies sailed to the coasts of western India where in 711 they conquered and occupied the densely populated Hindu–Buddhist society of Sind. Thus began the long and eventful encounter between Islamic and Indic civilizations, during which time Islamic culture would penetrate deeply into India's economy, political systems, and religious structure.

While Arab rule in Sind was being consolidated, other Arab armies continued the overland drive eastward. Requested by Turkish tribes to intervene in conflicts with their Chinese overlords, Arab armies in 751 marched to the westernmost fringes of the Tang Empire and engaged Chinese forces on the banks of the Talas River. The Arabs' crushing victory there, one of the most important battles in the history of Central Asia, probably determined the subsequent cultural evolution of the Turkish peoples of that region, who thereafter adopted Muslim and not Chinese civilization. Although Muslims would never dominate the heartland of China or penetrate Chinese civilization as they would India, their influence in Central Asia gave them access to the Silk Route, which for centuries to come served as a conduit for Chinese civilization into the Muslim world. Moreover, Muslim Arabs had already established maritime contact with China, having begun trading along the Chinese coast in the late seventh century.

Thus, within 130 years of Islam's birth, Arab armies and navies had conquered a broad swath of the known world from Gibraltar to the Indus delta and had penetrated both China and Europe by land and sea. How to explain it? Whence came the energy that had propelled Arab Muslims out of the Arabian peninsula, laying the groundwork for the establishment first of an Arab empire and then of a world civilization? Traditionalist Muslim sources generally accounted for these momentous events in terms of a miraculous manifestation of Allah's favor with his community, an interpretation consonant with Islamic understandings of the relationship between divine will and the historical process, but one that tells us more of Islamic theology than of Islamic history.

Theories of the Muslim conquests advanced by many nineteenth- and early twentieth-century European Islamicists are hardly more helpful. The general tone is captured in the following lines penned in 1898 by Sir William Muir, a Scot, whose interpretation of the Arab conquests sounds rather like the screenplay for a Cecil B. De Mille film, complete with technicolor, panoramic vision, and stereophonic soundtrack:

> It was the scent of war that now turned the sullen temper of the Arab tribes into eager loyalty. . . . Warrior after warrior, column after column, whole tribes in endless succession with their women and children, issued forth to fight. And ever, at the marvellous tale of cities conquered; of rapine rich beyond compute; of maidens parted on the very field of battle "to every man a damsel or two" . . . fresh tribes arose and went. Onward and still onward, like swarms from the hive, or flights of locusts darkening the land, tribe after tribe issued forth and hastening northward, spread in great masses to the East and to the West.[7]

In the end, though, after the thundering hooves have passed and the dust has settled, in attempting to explain the conquests, Muir leaves us with little of substance, apart from simply asserting the Arabs' fondness for the "scent of war," their love of "rapine," or the promise of "a damsel or two." Muir's vision of a militant, resurgent Islam gone berserk reflected, in addition to the old European stereotypes, colonial fears that Europe's own Muslim subjects might, in just such a locustlike manner, rise up in revolt and drive the Europeans back to Europe. Sir William, after all, was himself a senior British official in colonial India as well as an aggressive activist for the Christian mission there. But his was no fringe school concerning the rise of Islam or the subsequent conquests; indeed, his understanding dominated for decades to follow and, like the traditionalist Muslim interpretation, tells us more about the narrator than the subject.

In the early twentieth century, scholars introduced the thesis that around the time of the Prophet's death, Arabia's grazing lands had suffered from a severe, short-term desiccation that drove the nomadic Arabs to search, literally, for greener pastures. Although it lacked convincing evidence, this theory found plenty of advocates then, as it continues to do today. Variations on the desiccation theory, also lacking firm evidence, held that poverty, overpopulation, or other such social miseries had driven the Arabs out of their homeland. Still other historians shifted attention from the Arabs themselves to Byzantine Rome and Sasanian Persia, the two great empires of western Asia, whose domains included, respectively, Syria and Iraq. These empires were portrayed as "exhausted" from several hundred years of mutual warfare, thus enabling the more "vigorous" Arabs to walk over both with ease. But this thesis likewise lacked empirical evidence, and, above all, failed to account for the Arabs' continued expansion into lands far beyond the domain of either empire. Meanwhile, the notion of the Arabs' supposed militancy, legitimized by the religious doctrine of *jihâd*, or holy war, generally still informs popular sentiment about Muslims and has continued to find its way into history textbooks to the present day, though in a somewhat less lurid version than Muir's portrayal.

Whereas older theories saw the invasions as a random or unorganized influx of ragtag hordes pushed out of the peninsula by population pressure or drawn by the love of rapine, recent research has revealed methodically planned and well-executed military maneuvers directed by a central command in Medina and undertaken for quite rational purposes. There was the economic need to provide the growing community with material support—accomplished by the movement's capture of lucrative trade routes and new surplus-producing regions—which the relatively meager economic resources of Arabia could not provide. And there was the political need to contain and channel the tremendous energies released by the Prophet's socioreligious revolution. In this latter sense, the initial Arab conquests resemble the French or Russian revolutions, in which socioideological energies generated in the process of consolidating the original movement proved so intense that they could not be contained geographically and spilled over into adjacent regions.

Above all, what is missing from earlier explanations is any mention of Islam itself. One does occasionally come across references to the lure of an Islamic paradise filled with dark-eyed beauties awaiting the frenzied believer who would martyr himself in battle, but such romantic allusions appear to be holdovers from older stereotypes associating Islam with sex and violence. By and large, Western historians of the nineteenth and early twentieth centuries displayed a chronic inability to accept the possibility that the religion itself could have played a fundamental, as opposed to a supportive, role in the movement. In recent years, however, there has been an effort to bring religion back into the discussion by focusing on the Muslim community's social fragility during the earliest years of its formation, and especially the volatility of divine revelation as the basis of its authority. Thus the death of Muhammad in 632 confronted the community of believers, then confined to the population of western Arabia, with their first genuine crisis: How would the charismatic authority of the Prophet, who for ten years had provided both spiritual and political leadership to the growing *umma*, be sustained or channeled when he was no longer present? Some tribes, apparently supposing that with the loss of the Prophet the continuing authority of revelation had ended, simply withdrew from the community altogether. Others began following rival prophets—at least two men and one woman sprang up in the Arabian interior—who claimed to be receiving continuing revelations from God.

With both the political and the religious basis of the fledgling community thus threatened, Muhammad's first successor as leader of the community, Abu Bakr, moved vigorously to hold the volatile movement together. First, he forbade any tribe to leave the community once having joined; and second, in order to prevent the movement from splintering into rival communities around rival prophets, he declared that Muhammad had been the last prophet of God. These moves amounted, in effect, to a declaration of war against those tribes who had abandoned the *umma* or subscribed to other self-proclaimed prophets. Thus the initial burst of Muslim expansion after the Prophet's death was directed not against non-Muslims but against just such Arab tribes within the peninsula. In the process of suppressing these rebellions, however, Abu Bakr made alliances with tribes on the southern fringes of Iraq and Syria, and as the circle of such alliances widened, Muslim Arabs soon clashed with client tribes of the Sasanians and Byzantines and eventually with Sasanian and Byzantine imperial forces themselves.

Once launched, the movement continued to be driven by powerful religious forces. Islam had derived its initial power from Muhammad's ability to articulate the collectivization of Arabia's deities into a single supreme God, together with the collectivization of its tribes into the single, corporate *umma* under the direct authority of God. After the Prophet's death, these movements gained momentum as the masses of Arab soldiery participating in the expansion came to regard the movement's social ideals as immediately attainable. Hence, for them the distribution of the riches of conquered lands among members of the community, which looked to the rest of the world like senseless plunder, served to actualize the ideal, preached by the Prophet, of attaining socioeconomic equality among all believers. The importance of this factor is underscored by the fact that one of the first and most serious dissident movements in Islam, the Kharajite movement, was spearheaded in conquered Iraq by men of piety whose military stipends had just been reduced. Leaders of the revolt, which resulted in the assassination of the Caliph Uthman in 656, justified their actions by emphasizing the radical egalitarianism, including social equality for women, that had been preached by the Prophet. In short, recent explanations of the early Arab conquests, unlike earlier European theories, have focused on social processes rather than social stereotypes, and on the internal dynamics of early Muslim society and religion.

Early Islamic Civilization and Global History

From the perspective of global history, perhaps the most significant theme of early Islam is the evolution of a relatively parochial Arab cult into a world civilization, indeed history's first truly global civilization. For the Arab conquests inaugurated a thousand-year era, lasting from the seventh to the seventeenth century, when all the major civilizations of the Old World—Greco-Roman, Irano-Semitic, Sanskritic, Malay-Javanese, and Chinese—were for the first time brought into contact with one another by and within a single overarching civilization. What is more, Muslims synthesized elements from those other civilizations—especially the Greek, Persian, and Indian—with those of their Arabian heritage to evolve a distinctive civilization that proved one of the most vital and durable the world has ever seen. At work here were several factors: the emergence of state institutions and urban centers that provided foci for the growth of Islamic civilization; the conversion of subject populations to Islam; the ability of Muslim culture to absorb, adapt, and transmit culture from neighboring civilizations; and the elaboration of socioreligious institutions that enabled Islamic civilization to survive, and even flourish, following the decline of centralized political authority.

ISLAMIC STATES AND ISLAMIC CITIES

In the early years of the Islamic venture, the community had been ruled from Medina by an Arab merchant aristocracy led by four consecutive successors to Muhammad. By the second half of the seventh century, however, political power had shifted outside Arabia and into the hands of two successive imperial dynasties—the Umayyad, which governed a de facto Arab empire from Damascus between 661 and 750; and the Abbasid, which overthrew the Umayyads and reigned, if not always ruled, from its splendid capital city of Baghdad until 1258. Thus while Mecca and Medina remained the spiritual hubs of Islamic civilization, reinforced by the annual pilgrimage to the Ka'ba shrine, the Arab rulers in Syria and Iraq inherited from the Persian and Roman empires traditions and structures that facilitated their own transition to imperial rule. These included notions of absolute kingship, courtly rituals and styles, an efficient bureaucratic administration, a functioning mint and coinage system, a standing army, a postal service, and the kind of land revenue system on which the political economies of all great empires of the Fertile Crescent had rested. Even the Iwan Kisra, the famous royal palace of the Persians on the banks of the Tigris River, had been conveniently vacated by the last Sasanian emperor, Yazdegird III, as if to beckon its new Arab occupants to embark on and fulfill their own imperial destiny.

This they certainly did. Earlier historians, writing under the spell of Arabic narratives dwelt on the swiftness and thoroughness of the conquests, emphasized the sense of discontinuity between the old and the new orders. More recent historians, however, especially those drawing on non-Arabic as well as Arabic sources, have tended to see more continuity between the two orders. In fact, recent research suggests that the Arabs' rapid transition from a life of desert nomadism to one of imperial rule resulted largely from the expectations of their non-Muslim subjects. In Egypt, the earliest Arab governor ratified the appointment of church patriarchs just as Byzantine governors had done; in Iraq, the Arab governors adjudicated disputes among Nestorian Christians at the insistence of the Nestorians themselves, for that was what the Sasanian government had done. For the first fifty years of their rule, the Arabs even continued to mint coins in the fashion of the Sasanians, complete with a portrait of the Persian shah on one side. The Persian office of *wazîr*, or chief minister of state, was carried over into Abbasid government. And the caliphs, though technically the successors (*khalîfa*) to the Prophet's leadership, adopted the regalia, the majestic court ceremonies, and the mystique of absolutism of their Sasanian predecessors, even adopting the titles "Deputy of God" and "Shadow of God on Earth." The caliphs also carried over the Sasanian practice of patronizing a state religion, substituting Islam for Zoroastrianism. They appointed *qâdîs*, or Muslim judges, and promoted the construction of mosques, just as the Persian shahs had appointed Zoroastrian priests and built fire temples. Moreover, having acquired the taste for urban life that their Sasanian predecessors had cultivated, the caliphs lavishly supported the whole gamut of arts and crafts that subsequently became associated with Islamic culture: bookmaking, carpet weaving, pottery, calligraphy, ivory carving, wood carving, glassware, and tapestry, among others. Thus the centralized, imperial caliphate, though strictly speaking a violation of Islamic notions of the equality of believers, served as a vehicle for the growth of Islamic civilization in its widest sense.

As the social historian Ira Lapidus has shown, all of this growth took place in the context of the extraordinary urbanization that soon followed the conquests, which became one of the hallmarks of Islamic civilization. While older cities like Damascus, Jerusalem, Isfahan, Merv, and Cordova were simply occupied, others, like Cairo and Basra, began as garrison cities for Arab soldiers, a development resulting in part from a policy of settling and urbanizing otherwise potentially turbulent nomads. Cities, both new and old, also grew in response to the caliphate's need for administrative centers, and these, once in place, drew in and absorbed the surrounding population as urban proletariat classes. The most spectacular such case was that of Baghdad. Established in 756, the new Abbasid capital rapidly swelled to a population of about half a million, or ten times the size of nearby Ctesiphon, the former Sasanian capital. Everywhere from Cordova to Delhi there sprang up great cities, which, stimulated by the appetite of the ruling classes for luxury goods, became burgeoning centers and markets for the production and consumption of numerous crafts and industries. Also, by spatially dividing functionally autonomous communities into separate quarters, these cities projected a social vision, inherited ultimately from the Sasanians' policy toward their own minority communities, whereby the Islamic ruler extended to the communities recognition, tolerance, and protection in return for political loyalty and taxes. By virtue of such arrangements a Muslim city such as eleventh-century Toledo, Spain, could absorb a community of ten thousand Jews without experiencing the sort of anti-Semitic hostility typical of Christian cities of late medieval Europe.

CONVERSION TO ISLAM

Another dimension to the entry of Islamic civilization into global history was the mass conversion of Middle Eastern sedentary communities to Islam. Unlike other great conquests in which the foreign conqueror merely came and went—or perhaps came and assimilated—by the tenth and eleventh centuries Islam was well on its way to becoming the dominant religion in the Middle East. The dynamics of this movement have been fruitfully explored in Richard Bulliet's *Conversion to Islam in the Medieval Period: An Essay in Quantitative History*, a book whose subtitle illustrates the entry of new social science techniques into a field that had formerly been the exclusive preserve of classical, textual scholarship. Bulliet's concern was to plot the pace and direction of conversion by tabulating the patterns of change in personal names recorded in biographical dictionaries for selected Middle Eastern communities.

Other recent studies have emphasized the striking extent of cultural continuity amid the conversion process. In an important study of the cultural effects of the conquests in Iraq, Michael Morony argued that non-Muslims found it easier to accept Islam when ideas, attitudes, or institutions already present in their own cultures shared affinities with those imported from Arabia. For example, the Muslims shared animal sacrifice with pagans and Zoroastrians and ritual slaughter with Jews; they shared circumcision with Jews and Christians; they institutionalized charity, like Jews and Christians; they covered their heads during worship, like Jews; they had a month-long fast followed by a festival, like many other groups; they practiced ritual ablutions, as did Zoroastrians; and their ritual prayer resembled that of Nestorian Christians. Studies like Bulliet's and Morony's thus show a distinct shift away from earlier and cruder models of religious conversion, which, in the tradition of William Muir, tended to conflate the conquests and the conversion of non-Muslims into a single process, thereby reducing Islam to a "religion of the sword."

Moreover, we are now beginning to see that by the late seventh century Muslims were regarding themselves as carriers of a global civilization and not just members of an Arab cult. In their newly won empire they found themselves ruling over a plurality of autonomous and self-regulating religious communities—Greek Orthodox Christians, Monophysites, Nestorians, Copts, Zoroastrians, Manicheans, Jews—as well as a plurality of linguistic and literary traditions, including Greek, Coptic, Syriac, Armenian, Middle Persian, and various dialects of Aramaic. In forging an independent Islamic identity amid these older religious communities, Muslims faced a critical choice: Either they could constitute themselves as one more autonomous community modeled on those they ruled—thereby preserving Allah as an Arab deity, Islam as an Arab cult, and Arabic as the language of the ruling class—or they could try to bring all these diverse communities and traditions together into a new cultural synthesis. During the initial decades after their conquest of the Fertile Crescent and Egypt, Muslim rulers generally opted for the former alternative, as Islam remained the proud emblem of the Arab ruling elite. But by the eighth century they had turned to the latter alternative, a move that may have been decided as much on practical as on religious grounds. Convinced of the political imprudence of a tiny ethnic minority ruling indefinitely over an enormous non-Muslim majority, the caliphs openly encouraged their non-Arab subjects to convert. Henceforth the Arabic language and the Islamic religion would provide a sense of civilizational coherence by uniting hitherto separate religious and linguistic communities into a single ethnoreligious identity, initially transcending and ultimately supplanting all other such identities. Because

Muslims chose this second option, Islam became a world civilization and not just one more parochial, ethnic cult.

That Muslims quite self-consciously saw themselves as playing this unifying role seems to be the import of the Qur'an's passages exhorting Jews and Christians to leave aside their differences and return to the pure, unadulterated monotheism of Abraham, their common ancestor. Verses to this effect were inscribed around Islam's earliest surviving monument, Jerusalem's magnificent Dome of the Rock, built in 691:

> O mankind! The messenger hath come unto you with the Truth from your Lord. Therefor believe; [it is] better for you. . . .
>
> O People of the Scripture! Do not exaggerate in your religion nor utter aught concerning Allah save the truth. The Messiah, Jesus son of Mary, was only a messenger of Allah, and His word which He conveyed unto Mary, and a spirit from Him. So believe in Allah and his messengers, and say not "Three"— Cease! (it is) better for you!—Allah is only One God. Far is it removed from His Transcendent Majesty that He should have a son. His is all that it is in the heavens and all that is in the earth. And Allah is sufficient as Defender.[8]

As an invitation clearly intended for the Jews and Christians of Jerusalem, and of Palestine generally, these words point to the unifying, integrative role that Muslims saw themselves as playing amidst the older religious traditions of the Middle East.

ISLAMIC CIVILIZATION AND CULTURAL DIFFUSION

Islamic civilization also became a global civilization because of its ability to receive and absorb culture from one end of the world and then pass it on to other parts of the world. Consider, for example, the art of papermaking. The Islamization of Central Asia was only one consequence of the Arabs' defeat of Chinese armies in the mid-eighth century. The other consequence was that the victors learned from their Chinese prisoners of war the technology of papermaking, which then rapidly diffused throughout the Abbasid Empire. By the end of the eighth century Baghdad had its first paper mill; by 900 Egypt had one, and by the twelfth century paper was manufactured in Morocco and Spain, whence it spread to Europe. Papermaking technology also traveled southeastward. Having learned the technology from the Abbasids, Turks introduced it in North India in the thirteenth century, and for the next several centuries it gradually spread throughout the subcontinent, everywhere replacing the much less efficient palm leaf, just as in Europe paper replaced the Egyptian papyrus. Moreover, since paper is the bureaucrat's stock in trade, papermaking technology greatly contributed to the expansion and consolidation of the Indo-Muslim bureaucratic states from the fifteenth century onward.

The diffusion of paper technology would have religious as well as political consequences. Since Muslims believe that the Qur'an—every syllable of it—is the actual Word of God, the diffusion of the Qur'an, vastly accelerated by the new technology, contributed to the growth of the religion as well. Indeed, when one considers the power of literacy and the role of literate communities in articulating and preserving the substance of law, religion, or education, the spread of papermaking technology must be seen as having played an enormously important role in the post-eighth-century history of the globe, and especially in the expansion of Islamic civilization with which the initial diffusion of paper was most clearly associated.

One of the most exciting areas of recent research is the study of the worldwide diffusion of agricultural products to, through, and from the early Muslim world. In terms of the number of species and the geographical scope involved, this was probably the most dramatic agricultural event in world history prior to the meeting of the peoples of the Western and Eastern hemispheres in the fifteenth century. In a superbly documented study, Andrew Watson has recently laid to rest the myths that the Arabs, because of their desert, pastoral background, were somehow disinclined to agriculture and that early Islamic times had witnessed a decline in agriculture. Watson shows, to the contrary, that between the eighth and thirteenth centuries, while Europeans remained unreceptive to agricultural innovation, Muslims both actively promoted such innovations and vastly expanded agricultural production everywhere they went.

A key event in Watson's analysis was the Arab conquest of Sind in 711, which established a direct and regular contact between India and the Fertile Crescent, the heartland of the Umayyad and Abbasid governments. This conquest in turn threw open western Asia, Africa, and Europe to the agricultural treasures of India, effectively incorporating all these regions for the first time into a single agricultural universe. Between the eighth and tenth centuries Arabs had brought back from India and successfully begun cultivating staples such as hard wheat, rice, sugarcane, and new varieties of sorghum; fruits such as banana, sour orange, lemon, lime, mango, watermelon, and the coconut palm; vegetables such as spinach, artichoke, and eggplant; and the key industrial crop, cotton. From Iraq, these crops (except the mango and coconut) then spread westward all the way to Muslim Spain, which was transformed into a veritable garden under Muslim rule. Other crops passed by ship from southern Arabia to East Africa, and reached as far south as Madagascar, while still others moved by caravan from northwest Africa across the Sahara to tropical West Africa. This was especially true for cotton, whose diffusion in Africa directly paralleled the spread of Islam itself. Finally, beginning in the thirteenth century, most of these crops were introduced into Europe via Spain, Sicily, and Cyprus, but at a comparatively slow rate owing to the Europeans' inferior agricultural skills, their more limited irrigation technology, and their lower population density, which made it unnecessary to maximize their soil productivity.

Everywhere they were cultivated, the new crops contributed to fundamental social changes. Since the traditional crops of the pre-Islamic Middle East and Mediterranean area had been winter crops, the fields of those regions generally lay fallow in the summertime. But as most of the newly introduced crops were summer crops, adapted to India's hot, monsoon climate, their spread into western Asia vastly increased agricultural productivity by adding, in effect, another growing season for each calendar year. Moreover, since the Indian crops were adapted to high rainfall regions, they required more water than could be provided by the irrigation systems already present in the pre-Islamic Western world. Hence the Arabs' successful diffusion of the Indian crops also involved an intensification of existing irrigation technology (e.g., underground water canals, water-lifting devices) and the invention of still others (e.g., certain types of cisterns). All these innovations, in addition to systems of land tenure and taxation that encouraged land reclamation and a more intensified use of older fields, contributed to a significant increase in food production in the eighth to eleventh centuries, making possible the population increases and urbanization so characteristic of Muslim societies in this period.

Just as they had borrowed, assimilated, and diffused Indian agriculture, Muslims did the same with Greek and Indian knowledge. By the seventh century the Byzantine Greeks had long neglected the classical intellectual tradition of Aristotle, Ptolemy, and Galen, the cultivation of which migrated eastward when religious persecution drove Syriac-speaking Nestorian Christians into Iran. There the Nestorians continued to teach Greek sciences under the late Sasanians. In the eighth and ninth centuries this submerged intellectual tradition resurfaced when the Abbasids established their capital, Baghdad, in the heart of the old Sasanian Empire. Eager for what they deemed practical knowledge—for example, keeping themselves physically well, measuring the fields, predicting the agricultural seasons from heavenly bodies—the caliphs opened a "house of wisdom," in essence a translation bureau for rendering Arabic versions of Greek, Syriac, Sanskrit, and Persian works dealing with a broad spectrum of foreign thought, especially medicine, astronomy, and mathematics. By the ninth, tenth, and eleventh centuries, Muslim scientists, most of whom were Arabic-writing Iranians, were no longer merely translating but were creatively assimilating this foreign knowledge. From the Greeks they accepted the notion that behind the apparent chaos of reality lay an underlying order run by laws that could be understood by human reason. In addition to this imported rationalist tradition, scholars evolved their own empiricist tradition that developed especially rich knowledge in the field of medicine. Representing the more mature phase of Muslim knowledge, both al-Razi (d. 925) and Ibn Sina (d. 1037) compared and contrasted what the Greeks had written about certain medical problems with what they had learned directly from their own medical observations. The resulting syntheses were translated into Latin in the twelfth century and remained major medical texts in Europe for the next five hundred years.

We also see this combining of various intellectual traditions in mathematics and astronomy. Around 770, Indian scholars brought to Baghdad treatises on astronomy that the caliph promptly ordered translated into Arabic. Some decades later, the translations fell into the hands of Khwarizmi (d. ca. 850), the famous astronomer and mathematician, who then combined and harmonized Greek, Iranian, and Indian systems with astronomical findings of his own. The Indians had also brought works on mathematics to Baghdad, and it was from these that Muslim scientists assimilated what was to them, and would be for the rest of the world, a revolutionary system of denoting numbers, including the concept of zero. Called by Muslims "Indian (*Hindî*) numerals," they were known as "Arabic numerals" when subsequently received by Europeans via Spanish Arabs. Building on this knowledge, Khwarizmi combined principles of Greek geometry and Indian arithmetic to evolve the system of mathematics known as algebra, itself an Arabic word taken by Europeans from the title of one of his works, *Hisâb al-Jabr wa'l-Muqâbala.*

The accumulation of this sort of knowledge thus had a compounding effect that moved Islamic science considerably beyond the merely imitative or eclectic. Indeed, one may rightly challenge the popular contention that in the eleventh century Christian Europe "rediscovered" classical Greek knowledge in the libraries of Toledo or Granada in conquered Muslim Spain. This is in reality a Eurocentric view, as it implies that Muslims played a strictly passive role, in which their historic destiny was to put early European knowledge into cold storage until such time as it could be reclaimed by subsequent Europeans. With greater truth one could say it was Indian thought that Christian Europeans discovered in those Spanish libraries; or more correctly still, an integrated alloy of Greek, Indian, and Iranian knowledge.

Islamic Socioreligious Institutions

Between the tenth and thirteenth centuries, the Abbasid caliphs began to lose their grip on power when Turkish military slaves, recruited to guard the caliphs and the empire, began taking control into their own hands. The caliphate was thus reduced to a mere figurehead office, while real power devolved among various sultanates throughout the Muslim world. The final blow came in 1258 when Mongol armies, having moved from East to Southwest Asia in the early thirteenth century, entered, sacked, and destroyed the Abbasid capital of Baghdad. What is more, they executed the last Abbasid caliph and abolished his office, thus severely undermining the symbolic unity of the Muslim world. In recent centuries many Western scholars came to understand these events as signaling the beginning of a protracted period of decline for Islamic civilization. But it now seems apparent that such an interpretation of gloom and decline confused the destiny of Islamic civilization as a whole with that of Muslim rulers and their states—a perception that in turn reflects an earlier historiographical emphasis on dynastic and political–military history.

Over the past several decades, historians have cast their vision far beyond the political careers of the caliphs, sultans, shahs, and amirs that had figured so prominently in earlier studies of Islamic history. In part, this shift in emphasis reflects a more general trend, prevalent throughout the historical profession, from political to social history. Moreover, students of Islamic history had to address an apparent contradiction that political history could not resolve: In the post–thirteenth-century period, the very time that it fragmented politically, Islamic civilization not only maintained its internal cohesiveness but achieved its highest cultural florescence. Moreover, at that time, Islamic civilization also embarked on a career of worldwide diffusion even more impressive in scope than the Arab conquests of the seventh and eighth centuries. Hence, much recent scholarship has focused on individuals or institutions that provided Muslim societies with internal cohesion and spiritual direction when Islamic civilization lost its political coherence. These included, above all, the scholars, saints, and mystics who, from the eighth century forward, elaborated an immense corpus of rituals, dogmas, legal structures, social forms, mystical traditions, modes of piety, aesthetic sensitivities, styles of scholarship, and schools of philosophy that collectively defined and stabilized the very core and substance of Islamic civilization. Because of the vitality of that core, Islamic civilization was able to survive and even expand amid adverse political fortunes.

The role played by scholars, or 'ulamâ, in Muslim societies came from basic religious assumptions. Since Muslims have always understood Islam as the response of the community of believers to divine command, it became essential that ordinary Muslims know exactly how they should act both toward their fellow humans and toward God. This entailed the elaboration of the Sharî'a, or Islamic Law, and hence the emergence of specialists to interpret and implement that law. Based mainly on the Qur'an and the remembered words and deeds of the Prophet, the Sharî'a is understood as a completely comprehensive guide to life. Not at all priests, the 'ulamâ constituted a class that included judges, interpeters for judges, Qur'an reciters, prayer leaders, and preachers. For their training, there were of course formal colleges and state-supported theological schools, but most *'ulamâ* were trained through informal networks of teachers whose competence was certified not by any government board of education but by the more personalized means of popular acclaim. Hence Muslims placed especially high value on a peripatetic tradition of education, whereby people seeking knowledge would travel from one renowned *shaikh* to another, studying until given "permission" (*ijâzat*) to teach by their *shaikh*. In this way, informal schools of law and scholarship grew up around especially famous teachers, and in time, informal schools crystalized into formal schools. Yet the tradition of informal scholarly networks has persisted throughout the history of Islam, providing the community of believers with remarkable cohesion and stability whatever the fortunes of the rulers and their armies.

If it was the vocation of the *'ulamâ* to inform ordinary Muslims how to live their lives before God and humanity, it was the calling of mystics, known as Sufis, to know God in their hearts and to assist others in doing so. Although it grew alongside Islamic legal and scholastic traditions, Sufism addressed a different and complementary side of human consciousness. Like many scholars, Sufis often lived itinerant lives searching for renowned masters who could help in their personal quest for God. There also emerged various schools of mysticism oriented around particular modes of spiritual discipline. Named after their founders, these schools soon coalesced into stable organizations, or orders, whose networks crisscrossed the Muslim world and beyond, knitting together widely scattered communities with shared literatures and spiritual genealogies. Perhaps most significant of all, the great Sufi orders appeared in the thirteenth and fourteenth centuries, precisely at the time when the community's political unity had shattered, suggesting that the loss of political unity prompted Muslim communities to seek legal and spiritual direction closer to home.

Pioneered by J. S. Trimingham's *Sufi Orders in Islam* (1971), a growing literature has appeared in recent years analyzing the rise and growth of institutionalized Sufism, focusing on the role that the orders and individual Sufis played in the growth of the global Muslim community. In fact, in areas far from the reaches of Muslim states the first seeds of new Muslim communities often began with the appearance of anonymous, itinerant holy men whom the local population might associate with miraculous powers. Typical is the following extract from the medieval folk literature of eastern Bengal:

> At that time there came a Mahomedan *pîr* [Sufi] to that village. He built a mosque in its outskirts, and for the whole day sat under a fig tree. . . . His fame soon spread far and wide. Everybody talked of the occult powers that he possessed. If a sick man called on him he would cure him at once by dust or some trifle touched by him. He read and spoke the innermost thoughts of

a man before he opened his mouth. . . . Hundreds of men and women came every day to pay him their respects. Whatever they wanted they miraculously got from this saint. Presents of rice, fruits, and other delicious food, goats, chickens, and fowls came in large quantities to his doors. Of these offerings the *pîr* did not touch a bit but freely distributed all among the poor.[9]

It is apparent here that the Sufi's widespread popularity rested on his perceived supernatural, healing, and psychic powers, and the simple generosity he displayed to the poor. Moreover, we can detect here an early phase of Islamization. The humane qualities of the Sufi would be associated with his mosque, which would remain after the Sufi's departure and continue to provide the local community, at this point not yet formally Muslim, with some rudimentary religious focus. What was happening in Bengal was occurring in many corners of the globe, a theme to which we now direct closer attention.

Islam in the Wider World

As the accompanying table illustrates, more than two-thirds of the world's 900 million Muslims live outside the Middle East. Furthermore, over four-fifths of all Muslims are non-Arabs, with the majority of the worldwide community living in South and Southeast Asia. Indonesia has the largest Muslim population of any country in the world, followed by Pakistan, Bangladesh, and India. Yet scholarly work on Islamic history in Asia and Africa has lagged far behind that done in the Middle East. As recently as 1976 a college-level textbook entitled *Introduction to Islamic Civilization* neglected to discuss—citing "practical reasons"—the two-thirds of the Muslim world that resides beyond the Middle East.[10] The reason for this unfortunate blindness probably lies in Europe's historic confrontation with its neighbors across the Mediterranean Sea, as a consequence of which the Muslim world *is* the Arab world for many European Islamicists. It is an association that dies very hard.[11]

Research in the past several decades, however, has gone far in redressing this scholarly imbalance. Especially noteworthy is Marshall Hodgson's three-volume *Venture of Islam* (1974), which remains today the most sympathetic and comprehensive history of Islam on the market. In three important respects—conceptual, geographical, and chronological—Hodgson's work broke decisively with most earlier scholarship. First, he endeavored to understand Islamic history on its own terms and not view it through the tinted lenses of European bias. Even before Hodgson wrote, the era had passed when the caliph was casually termed Islam's pope, the Qur'an its Bible, the mosque its church, or Shi'ism its Protestant sect. But the

WORLDWIDE DISTRIBUTION OF MUSLIMS, 1983

Country or Region	Percentage of Worldwide Total (country)	Percentage of Worldwide Total (region)
China		2(?)
Southeast Asia		17
Indonesia	15	
Malaysia, Philippines, and mainland countries	2	
South Asia		30
Pakistan	11	
Bangladesh	10	
India	9	
Central Asia		6
Middle East		32
Turkey	6	
Iran	5	
Afghanistan	2	
Egypt	5	
North Africa and Sudan	8	
Arabian Peninsula and Fertile Crescent	6	
West Africa		9
Nigeria	5	
Remaining West Africa	4	
East Africa		3
Ethiopia	1	
Remaining East Africa	2	
Balkans		1

Source: Richard V. Weekes, *Muslim Peoples: A World Ethnographic Survey*, 2nd ed. (Westport, Conn.: Greenwood Press, 1984). Compiled from data in Appendix 1.

Venture of Islam goes further and persistently challenges the reader's unconscious terminological assumptions, themselves legacies of a thousand years of Europe's mystification of the Islamic "other." Second, Hodgson refused to confine his study geographically to the Middle East or ethnically to the Arabs but insisted instead that the only proper unit for the study of Islamic history is the entire belt of agrarian lands stretching from the Mediterranean basin to China. It was by virtue of this vision, which in fact accords with the worldwide demographic distribution of Muslims (as seen in the table), that Hodgson could appreciate Islam's truly global character and its capacity to integrate far-flung civilizations. And third, Hodgson broke with most earlier Islamic historiography by not treating the post-Abbasid history of Islam as one of protracted decline. It was of course true that the Abbasids had developed a high, cosmopolitan culture that touched on and communicated with all the older world civilizations, and that with the destruction of Baghdad and the caliphate in 1258, Muslims had lost their central political focus. But Hodgson more than most historians emphasized the coincidence of and relationship between political fragmentation and cultural florescence in Islamic history. Above all, he understood that it was only in the centuries after 1258 that the Islamic religion, as a belief system *and* as a world civilization, grew among the peoples of Asia and Africa.

If Marshall Hodgson's work broke new ground conceptually, it has been followed by a good deal of empirical research on Islamic history—the spadework on which historical generalists depend—that has vastly expanded our understanding of Islam as a global phenomenon. One of the most pervasive concerns of this new research has been the historical formation and growth of new Muslim communities, or Islamization, in Asia and Africa. No single book has pulled together all the complex elements of this process, but a volume edited by N. Levtzion, *Conversion to Islam* (1979), remains perhaps the best summary. The dominant trend among scholars studying the Islamization process appears to be the effort to see it not as an expansion, which implies imposition, which in turn implies the use of force, an old European stereotype; but rather to view it as an assimilation. Thus, instead of adopting the perspective of one standing in Mecca, looking out upon an ever-widening, ever-expanding religious tide that is uniform and monolithic, one adopts the perspective of someone standing in a remote and dusty village, incorporating into one's existing religious system elements considered useful or meaningful that drift in from beyond the ocean, from over the mountains, or simply from the neighboring village. This shift in perspective has dramatically changed the way in which scholars think not only about Islam but also about the dynamics of religious change. With this in mind, let us look more closely at the growth of Islam beyond the Middle East and at the state of historical scholarship concerning that growth.

Where India is concerned, two lines of historical inquiry are discernible, one of them intellectual, the other social. The former consists of efforts to unravel the complex and fascinating ways that Muslims hailing from points to the west came to grips intellectually with India's highly developed Hindu–Buddhist systems of religion and thought. Arab rule in eighth-century Sind having weakened and died, it was left to Persianized Turks to establish a permanent Muslim presence in India from the thirteenth century. But what would the new ruling class, itself only recently converted to Islam in Central Asia, make of the land of the Buddha, Shiva, and the marvelous incarnations of Vishnu? And to what extent would Islam adapt or change in order to find for itself a niche in India's rich cultural universe? Lurking behind these apparently innocent questions were fundamental issues, both for modern historians looking back over the past seven centuries and for Indian Muslims living in any one of them. In its manifold accommodation with India's culture, was Islam becoming diluted? Or was it simply growing with the times, adapting to new circumstances, building on what was already there? These were urgent questions, because in coming to terms with India's formidable cultural legacy, Muslims were also compelled to come to terms with their own. As recent research suggests, Indian Muslims felt a deep-seated ambivalence toward Indian culture, with responses ranging from an enthusiastic embrace of Hindu philosophy (for example, by Prince Dara Shikoh, d. 1659) to an outright rejection of Hindus as "worshippers of idols and cow-dung" (Zia al-Din Barani, d. 1357).[12]

Whatever urban intellectuals may have felt about Indian culture, however, at the folk level millions of Indians were converting to Islam, or more precisely, assimilating Islamic rituals, cosmologies, and literatures into their local religious systems. Beginning in the fourteenth century and continuing through the Mughal period (1526–1858), converted Indian Muslims became the majority community in the eastern and western wings of the subcontinent. Regarding these regions, as elsewhere in the Muslim world, scholars are developing understandings of the conversion process far more refined than earlier, cruder stereotypes of Islam as a warrior religion. Recent research suggests that the growth of sedentary agriculture in lightly Hinduized regions of India will tell us more about conversion than will the movement of medieval armies. For in both wings of India that became Muslim-majority regions—Bengal in the east, Punjab and Sind in the west—the growth of Muslim societies correlated with the adoption of sedentary agriculture. And both regions were still frontier societies where Hindu religious values and the hierarchic social ideals of Brahmin priests had not yet deeply penetrated.

Thus in the west, Punjab and Sind shrines of great Sufis attracted and integrated preagrarian and non-Muslim pastoral clans into their ritual, socioeconomic, and political orbits. Descendants of such Sufis then established marriage alliances with the leaders of the pastoralist clans, while the Delhi sultans and Mughal emperors granted huge tracts of rich land for the support of the ritual ceremonies performed at the shrines. The shrines thus served as important mediating agencies—both with the state and with Islamic cosmology—at the very moment that these communities were passing from a life of pastoral nomadism to one of settled wheat agriculture. Also involved here was the expansion of irrigation technology, which, as noted earlier, typically accompanied Islamic civilization and, in this case, permitted a rapid growth in wheat production. A similar thing happened at the other end of India, in Bengal, where Muslim pioneers acquired grants from the Mughals to clear virgin forests for expanding the empire's area of rice cultivation. These pioneers also constructed mosques that functioned as magnets integrating non-Muslim forest peoples both into an agrarian way of life focused on the mosques and into a locally structured style of Islam heavily inflected with the culture of saints and saint veneration. As a result of such processes, by the eighteenth century large communities of Muslim peasants had appeared in both Punjab and Bengal. In contrast, in India's heartland, where both agriculture and a sedentary Hindu society were well established, conversion to Islam was far less significant.

Malabar, India's southwestern coastal region, also saw the dramatic growth of local Muslim communities. Unlike Punjab or Bengal, Malabar lay beyond the orbit of Mughal imperial influence and the Persianized culture associated with it. Rich in pepper, cardamom, and ginger, and strategically located at the midpoint of Indian Ocean trade routes, Malabar did, however, fall within the orbit of Arab maritime commercial influence. From at least the ninth century, when the oldest surviving mosque appeared, Arab merchants had established a fixed residence in port cities along the spice-rich coastline. By the fourteenth and fifteenth centuries, when the pace of this trade quickened and the entire Indian Ocean came alive with Arab dhows loaded with spices and textiles, a substantial resident community of Arab traders appeared in Malabar, living under the protection of Hindu kings (who profited handsomely from the trade). Eventually, a sizable Muslim community emerged through Arab intermarriage with the local population. In the sixteenth century, the appearance of the Portuguese, aggressively hostile rivals for the pepper trade, dramatically solidified the Malabar Muslims, transforming a loosely knit body of merchants and their local affiliates into an armed community with fixed social boundaries. Of great significance for Indian history, the confrontation also illustrates an important theme of global history: the clash of two expanding and ideologically hostile trade diasporas, each adhering to a universal religion.

In many respects Islamization in Southeast Asia resembled that of Malabar: As a spice-exporting region it was integrated into a maritime trade network under Islamic hegemony; it had hinterlands of rice-cultivating peasants informed by Hindu religious culture; and at a crucial phase in its cultural evolution it was challenged by aggressive European commercial powers hostile to Muslim traders. But the source materials for reconstructing the growth of Islam in Southeast Asia—fragments of Sufi poetry, barely decipherable gravestones, highly stylized court chronicles—are not only sparse but are so elusive that the line dividing mythology from history (a line whose presence is perhaps problematic in any historical writing) appears to vanish completely. Nevertheless, it is certain that by the end of the thirteenth century a Muslim city-state appeared at Pasai, in the northern tip of Sumatra. This was followed in the fourteenth and early fifteenth centuries by other predominantly Muslim city–states along the coasts of Sumatra and North Java, and most important, at Malacca in the Straits of Malacca. When Malacca was captured by Portuguese captains in 1511, Muslim trade shifted to Aceh on Sumatra's northern coast. When Dutch power arrived a century later, Muslim merchants again shifted, this time to Makassar on the southwest coast of Celebes (Sulawesi).

Modern historians have focused on two main lines of argument in explaining the penetration of Islam in Malay-speaking Southeast Asia. One centers on the extraordinary expansion of regional and international maritime trade in the Indian Ocean during the fourteenth and fifteenth centuries. This activity resulted in turn from the diminished use of land-based trade routes following the Mongol invasions of Central and West Asia, together with increased demand in Europe for Southeast Asian spices. Thus there emerged in the Straits of Malacca and the Java Sea an exceptionally cosmopolitan atmosphere that was multiethnic—with traders from south China, Gujarat, Tamil Nadu, Bengal, Malabar, and the Arabian Peninsula—but ideologically unified around Islam, with the proliferation everywhere of Persian and Arabic literature. A century of heated scholarly controversy aimed at identifying from where Islam came and who brought it—South India and south China are currently leading contenders—probably missed the point. The whole Indian Ocean had become so culturally fused, its port cities so imbued with an overriding Islamic ethos, that the ethnic identity of particular merchants mattered little. Although historians agree on a clear correlation between Islamization and expanding trade networks in the Malay world, the precise links between the two still seem to elude their grasp.

A second line of argument focuses not on the quickened pace of commerce as such, but on the intellectual and spiritual networks that emerged as a consequence of, or along with, the commercial diaspora. In 1512–15, the Portuguese traveler Tome Pires noted that foreign merchants in Southeast Asian port towns were accompanied by "chiefly Arab *mullâs*," a category that could have included scholars and Sufis as well as preachers. Seizing on this clue and building on the fragmentary writings that Sufis and scholars themselves have left, historians such as Anthony Johns have attempted to reconstruct the intellectual and spiritual milieu of the commercial port towns in the sixteenth and seventeenth centuries and the nature of their contacts both with their Sumatran or Javanese hinterlands and with scholars in India or Arabia. By painstakingly identifying who studied with whom, where, when, and under whose (if anybody's) patronage, the hope is that we may one day be able to make more meaningful statements about the process of Islamization in the Malay world.

Coinciding with the developments described above, from the late fifteenth century, Muslim city-states of Java's north coast—notably Denmak—began expanding into the interior of Java, Southeast Asia's richest and most densely populated island. Here Muslims confronted, not European merchant captains, but ancient Hindu–Buddhist civilizations possessing hierarchically organized social structures, refined literati, elaborate court rituals, revenue-collecting aristocracies, and dense populations of rice-cultivating peasants. In the early sixteenth century, a coalition of Muslim kingdoms defeated the Hindu–Buddhist kingdom of Madjapahit, which was replaced by several new Muslim states, the most important being the Sultanate of Mataram in central Java. The history of this state, which reached its height of power under Sultan Agung (1613–1646), was marked by the appearance of enormously influential Javanese Sufis (*kiyayi*)—shadowy figures about whom fantastic legends have been embroidered—who seem occasionally to have assisted sultans to power and occasionally to have used their considerable influence with the rural masses to undermine the sultans' power. Despite state persecution and their own tenuous historicity, however, the *kiyayi* have survived in the collective memory of the Javanese peasantry as vivid cultural heroes. Cut off from regular exposure to the wider Islamic world of the port cities, the *kiyayi* cultivated forms of Islamic mysticism that were heavily tinged with Hindu–Buddhist and native Javanese conceptions. Hence, if the Islamization of the outer islands was linked to the rise of international trade and its spiritual and intellectual offshoots, the patterns of Islamization in the more densely populated interior of Java are associated with the activities of countless roaming saints whose luminous quasi-mythological lives have served, for subsequent generations, to connect Hindu Java with Muslim Java.

In sub-Saharan Africa, as in Southeast Asia, Muslim communities rose most typically with the growth of trade. Unlike the Romans or Byzantines, who had drawn fortified lines between themselves and the native Berber pastoralists of North Africa whom they considered "barbarian" (hence Berber), the Arabs endeavored to incorporate these peoples into the Muslim community after their conquest of the region in the early eighth century. In fact, the Arab expedition across Gibraltar to Spain was in reality a joint

Arab–Berber endeavor. To the south, one branch of Berbers, the Sanhajah, had already expanded across the Sahara Desert and established commercial contact with the black peoples of the broad east–west Sudanic belt. Their camel caravans carried salt down from North Africa in exchange for gold brought up from West Africa, which ultimately wound up in Europe. Sometime in the tenth century, the Sanhajah Berbers nominally converted to Islam, and toward the end of that century, the kingdom of Ghana expanded far enough north to meet them, thereby inaugurating a process that has continued for the past thousand years: the gradual Islamization of West Africa.

Although the commitment of the Sanhajahs to Islam was initially tentative, this changed when one of their chiefs, Yahya ibn Ibrahim, made the pilgrimage to Mecca in 1035. As is typical for pilgrims coming from the edges of the Muslim world, the experience of joining in ritual solidarity with Arabs, Turks, Indians, Persians, and Egyptians conveyed to this chief a sense of the truly global scope of Islam, in contrast to the more particularistic cults familiar to him in his native land. Inspired to impart such a religious vision to his own people, Yahya ibn Ibrahim brought back with him an educated Arab teacher, Abdullah ibn Yasin, for instructing the Sanhajah on the finer points of the faith. More than that, this teacher, on the model of the Prophet Muhammad's original movement in western Arabia, revitalized the Berbers in the name of Islam and sparked a military expansionist movement, the Almoravid, that swept over all Morocco and Spain in the eleventh and twelfth centuries.[13]

To the south, meanwhile, Arab and Berber merchants continued to open up trade routes, which crisscrossed the Saharan and Sudanic belts of Africa and linked Cairo, Tripoli, Tunis, and Fez in the north with Lake Chad, Mali, and Ghana in the south. Consequently, the earliest Muslims to appear in places like eleventh-century Ghana were foreign traders from the north who lived in separate town quarters under pagan kings. Islamization began only after agricultural peoples became drawn into expanding commercial networks of such traders, as happened to the Soninke, a former agricultural group that took up trading between the Ghanian goldfields and Muslim merchants from the north. As African communities such as the Soninke became detached from their peasant way of life, their attachment to local deities diminished; as their association with foreign merchants increased, they gradually incorporated Muslim rituals. So tight was the fit between trade and Islam, in fact, that when this process was reversed, as is documented in several cases of converted merchant groups that returned to a peasant life, they reverted to their former pagan cults.

As long as West African rulers remained pagan, however, mass conversion among the peasantry did not occur. And despite the presence of influential Muslim merchant classes in their midst, the rulers tended to remain at least nominally pagan, since their political legitimacy rested on rituals and beliefs associated with local cults popular among the peasantry on whose loyalty they depended. In these circumstances, the physical expansion of kingdoms and the consequent conversion of their kings often led to Islamization. For example, as thirteenth-century Mali expanded from a small chiefdom to a vast empire, in the process incorporating peoples of varying ethnic backgrounds attached to various cults, the religious orientation of its rulers aligned with Muslim merchants, the only community whose territorial reach spanned the whole empire. Hence, by the fourteenth century, Mali was internationally recognized as a Muslim state. But in the fifteenth century when it shrank back to its nuclear polity and was abandoned by many of its Muslim merchants, Mali's rulers reverted to the kingdom's former cults.

If merchants first introduced the religion of Allah and kings patronized it when politically expedient, it was left to scholars to stabilize it. For unlike the indigenous cults whose authority was based on mortal priests, Islamic authority was based on written scripture, giving Islam a status among West African cults that was by comparison immortal and unchallengeable. Moreover, in West Africa as in India, Muslims first introduced paper and papermaking technology. And with paper came the knowledge of writing and a class of scholars expert in applying the Sacred Law. In this way networks of teachers and students, together with the corps of literate jurists and judges the teachers produced, came to provide the sturdy scaffolding that would hold together a permanent Muslim community. In the thirteenth and fourteenth centuries, centers of learning sprang up all over West Africa, by far the most illustrious being Timbuktu. Strategically located on the bend of the Niger River and at the juncture of the desert and the savanna, Timbuktu had emerged around 1100 as an important commercial center, but by 1400 its mercantile wealth was visibly converted into scholarship. Indeed, Timbuktu is West Africa's finest example of the mutual interdependence of mercantile activity and the maintenance of Islamic educational institutions. So in West Africa it was not Sufis who played the initial roles in Islamization—they appeared in the eighteenth century with reformist movements—but mercantile and scholar classes. Nonetheless, in West Africa as in Bengal and much of Southeast Asia, the Islamic religion was accepted and assimilated as part and parcel of the broader world civilization into which Islam had evolved by the thirteenth century.

Dâr al-Islâm *as a World System*

In recent years there has been much talk in historical circles of *world systems theory* as an approach to global history. This theory is concerned with the expansion of economic networks, especially capitalist networks, that historically have cut across political boundaries in efforts to incorporate peoples into uniform structures. Whatever may be the validity of such an approach for students of global history, historians of Islam are beginning to realize that in the post–thirteenth-century period, Muslims also constructed a world system, but one radically different from that modeled on *Homo oeconomicus*. It was, rather, a world system linking men and women through informal networks of scholars and saints, built on shared understandings of how to see the world and structure one's relationship to it. Above all, it was a world system constructed around a book, the Qur'an, and of humanity's attempt to respond to its message by fulfilling both its external project of building a righteous social order and its internal project of drawing humans nearer their Maker.

Nowhere is this Islamic world system more vividly captured than in the genre of what can best be described as "travel literature" that emerged in the post–thirteenth-century period. The Qur'an itself enjoins its community to "journey in the land, then behold how He originated creation" (29:20). From the earliest days of Islam, pious Muslims followed this injunction; indeed the tradition of peripatetic scholars and saints is traceable in part to this verse. In the fourteenth and fifteenth centuries yet another purpose for "journeying in the land" appeared when increased European demand for spices and Mongol disruptions of overland routes triggered trade diasporas throughout the Indian Ocean and Sahara Desert. For both pious and commercial reasons, Muslims during these two centuries began moving through the known world in unprecedented numbers, also recording their experiences. The most famous of the travel genre is doubtless the *Rihla* of Ibn Battuta (d. 1368–69), the fourteenth-century cosmopolitan Moroccan and man-for-all-seasons: pilgrim, judge, scholar, devotee of Sufism, ambassador-at-large, connoisseur of fine foods and elegant architecture, and honored guest of Muslim princes and merchants everywhere.

It has been Ibn Battuta's fate to be repeatedly referred to in Western literature as the Marco Polo of the Muslim world. But the comparison is badly misleading. First, having for thirty years crisscrossed North and West Africa, the Middle East, the steppes of Central Asia, India, Southeast Asia, and China, for an estimated total of 73,000 miles, Ibn Battuta traveled much farther and visited many more places than did Marco Polo. Second, unlike the hard-nosed Venetian, Ibn Battuta emerges as a far more engaging fellow who shares with us just about everything he sees, learns, or feels—his severe culture shock on first disembarking in China, the altercations between rival Sufi brotherhoods in Anatolia over which one would have the honor of hosting him, the sexual customs of the Maldive Islanders, the techniques of coconut harvesting in Arabia, and the ritual ceremonies of the kings of Mali.

The two travelers differed most profoundly in their relationship to the societies they visited. Marco Polo, who died in 1324, the year before Ibn Battuta embarked from Morocco, had been a stranger everywhere he went, and he knew it. Indeed, his fame derives from his having introduced Europe, which in the thirteenth century was just emerging from being a global backwater, to a fabulous but utterly alien world of which it had only the haziest impressions. In contrast, Ibn Battuta, in his intercontinental wanderings, moved through a single cultural universe in which he was utterly at home. Most of his travels took place within what Muslims have always called *Dâr al-Islâm*, the "abode of Islam"; that is, the inhabited earth where Muslims predominated, or failing that, where Muslim authorities were in power and could uphold the *Sharî'a*. Everywhere he went he found the civilized company of merchants, scholars, Sufis, or princes; and with them he would converse, in Arabic, on topics ranging from mysticism to jurisprudence, and especially on events taking place elsewhere in *Dâr al-Islâm*. Overall, his book conveys a self-assured tone in which the cultural unity of *Dâr al-Islâm*, from Spain to China, was not even an issue; it was simply taken for granted. This was a world in which a judge learned in the Sacred Law could expect to find employment serving the Muslim community wherever he went. Indeed, the Moroccan traveler spent many of his thirty years away from home doing just that.

If Ibn Battuta intuitively understood that the Muslim world of his day constituted a truly global civilization, even a "world system" (though he would have taken offense at such social science jargon), it has taken Western historians some considerable time to understand it as such. To be sure, in just the past generation historians have sharply refined both their conceptual and geographical understandings of Islamic history. Conceptually, Europe's nineteenth-century mystification of Islam, and more broadly, of Orientalism, though still alive in a few dusty corners, has for the most part given way to newer approaches. Social scientists, for their part, have been collecting data on the history of Muslim societies, while historians of religion have been exploring systems of meaning embedded in the indigenous conceptions and the discourses of Muslims themselves. Thus far, both approaches have yielded rich harvests.

Geographically, too, the field has expanded. Although the study of Islam in China and the Soviet Union remains the most serious deficiency in historical scholarship today—even estimates of the current population of Chinese Muslims are only guesses, ranging from 15 million to 50 million—major regions such as West Africa, South Asia, and Southeast Asia are beginning to be integrated into larger surveys of Islamic history. At the same time, the study of Islam is gradually extricating itself from the grip of Near Eastern studies and the easy equation of Islam with Arab culture. We have also witnessed a burst of research monographs covering almost every corner of the Muslim world. But just adding discussion of more Muslim nations to our courses and our textbooks—a lecture here or a chapter there—is not enough: The key is to understand the global nature of the *umma*, and above all that the nation-state, Muslim or otherwise, is itself a very recent European political category having no roots in Islamic history. Indeed, as the political expression of an ethnic community, the nation-state concept is fundamentally hostile to the Islamic vision of the *umma*, the community of believers, the "abode of Islam."

If this fact seems less obvious to us today than it would have to Ibn Battuta, it is because in recent times the Islamic *umma* has been split asunder into modern nation-states—the long-term legacy of the French Revolution. Nationalist sentiments have even infected Muslims themselves, as recent conflicts between Islamic "nations" repeatedly demonstrate. Hence the challenge facing historians is to transcend perspectives rooted in recent times and appreciate the centrality of Islamic history in global history. Chronologically, Islamic history is the link between the ancient and modern worlds. Spatially, having originated in the heart of the Afro-Eurasian land mass, Islamic civilization grew to serve as history's first bridge connecting the agrarian belt stretching from Gibraltar to China. Historians have come far in appreciating this much, but we have far to go in grasping its full implications.

NOTES

1. See Dorothy L. Sayers, trans., *The Song of Roland* (Baltimore: Penguin Books, 1957), pp 175–76.
2. Marmaduke Pickthall, trans., *The Glorious Koran* (London: Allen & Unwin, 1976), Sura 96: verses 1–5, p. 813.
3. Among these are Claude Cahen, Michael Morony, J. Wansbrough, Elton Daniel, S. P. Brock, G. R. Hawting, Patricia Crone, and Michael Cook. While all these authors have utilized literary materials beyond the Arabic sources, they nonetheless differ sharply on points of interpretation.
4. G.H.A. Juynboll, ed., *Studies on the First Century of Islamic Society* (Carbondale: Southern Illinois University Press, 1982), p. 2.
5. For example, a fifth-century Greek source, written two hundred years before Muhammad, reported Arab communities in northern Arabia practicing a primitive form of monotheism, which, though corrupted by the influence of their pagan neighbors, was identical to that practiced by the Hebrews up to the days of Moses. The same source added that these Arabs had come into contact with

Jews from whom they learned of their descent from Abraham through Ishmael and Hagar. Syriac sources dating from the 640s, which were contemporary with the Arab conquests, identified Arab Muslims as "descendants of Hagar"; while the earliest biography of Muhammad, an Armenian chronicle dating from the 660s, described the Arabian Prophet as a merchant who had restored the religion of Abraham among his people and had led his believers into Palestine to recover the land God had promised them as descendants of Abraham.

6. Such an evolutionary interpretation is consonant with the growth of Allah from the particular deity of a second-century Arab tribe to, in Muhammad's day, the high God of all Arabs as well as the God of Abraham. From the Qur'an itself we know that before Muhammad's mission the tribes of western Arabia had already acknowledged Allah as their high god and were paying increasing attention to him at the expense of lesser divinities or tribal deities. At the time Muhammad began to preach, Allah was already identified as the "Lord of the Ka'ba" (Qur'an 106:3), and hence the chief god of the pagan divinities whose idols were housed there. In some Qur'anic passages the existence of lesser divinities and angels is affirmed, but their effectiveness as intercessors with Allah is denied (36:23, 43:86, 53:26); while in another passage Arab deities are specifically dismissed as nothing "but names which ye have named, ye and your fathers, for which Allah hath revealed no warrant" (53:23). This would indicate that these gods were altogether nonexistent, a position consonant with the first half of the Muslim credo, "There is no god but Allah, and Muhammad is his Prophet."

7. William Muir, *The Caliphate, its Rise, Decline, and Fall* (London, 1898; reprinted Beirut: Khayats, 1963), p. 45.

8. Pickthall, *Glorious Koran*, Sura 4: verses 170–71, p. 131.

9. D. C. Sen, trans. and ed., *Eastern Bengal Ballads*. 3 vols. (Calcutta, 1923), vol. 1, pp. 219–20.

10. R. M. Savory, ed. (New York: Cambridge University Press, 1976).

11. Factors internal to Islam may also be relevant here, as Muslims themselves have always accorded special prestige to the place of Arab culture in Islam. The Qur'an, revealed in Arabic, repeatedly refers to itself as "an Arabic Qur'an" (12:2, 42:7, 43:3), and therefore Muslims consider that it cannot properly be translated into any other language. Islamic liturgy remains exlusively Arabic. The five daily prayers are directed toward Mecca, and Islam's central ritual, the pilgrimage to the Ka'ba in Mecca, continuously reinforces the religion's Arab roots. This aspect of Islamic identity would therefore tend to reinforce European associations of Islam with the Arab world.

12. Mohammad Habib, *The Political Theory of the Delhi Sultanate* (Allahabad, India: Kitab Mahal, n.d.), p. 47.

13. Marilyn R. Waldman, "The Islamic World," *The New Encyclopaedia Britannica*, 15th ed. (Chicago: University of Chicago Press, 1991), 22: 122–23.

BIBLIOGRAPHY

GENERAL

Arberry, Arthur J., trans. *The Koran Interpreted*. New York: Macmillan, 1955.

Dunn, Ross. *The Adventures of Ibn Battuta: A Muslim Traveler of the 14th Century*. Berkeley: University of California Press, 1986.

Grabar, Oleg. *The Formation of Islamic Art*. New Haven: Yale University Press, 1973.

Hodgson, Marshall G.S. *The Venture of Islam: Conscience and History in a World Civilization*. 3 vols. Chicago: University of Chicago Press, 1974.

Lapidus, Ira. *A History of Islamic Societies*. Cambridge, England: Cambridge University Press, 1988.

Levtzion, Nehemia, ed. *Conversion to Islam*. New York: Holmes & Meier, 1979.

Michell, George, ed. *Architecture of the Islamic World: Its History and Social Meaning*. London: Thames and Hudson, 1978.

Robinson, Francis. *Atlas of the Islamic World since 1500*. Oxford: Phaidon, 1982.

Trimingham, John S. *Sufi Orders in Islam*. Oxford: Oxford University Press, 1971.

Waldman, Marilyn R. "The Islamic World," *The New Encyclopaedia Britannica*, 22: 102–35. 15th ed. Chicago: University of Chicago Press, 1991.

MIDDLE EAST

Bulliet, Richard. *Conversion to Islam in the Medieval Period: An Essay in Quantitative History*. Cambridge: Harvard University Press, 1979.

Cahen, Claude. *Pre-Ottoman Turkey: A General Survey of the Material and Spiritual Culture and History, c. 1071–1330*. Trans. J. Jones-Williams. New York: Taplinger, 1968.

Cook, Michael. *Muhammad*. New York: Oxford University Press, 1983.

Crone, Patricia. *Meccan Trade and the Rise of Islam*. Princeton: Princeton University Press, 1987.

Crone, Patricia, and Michael Cook. *Hagarism: The Making of the Islamic World*. Cambridge, England: Cambridge University Press, 1977.

Donner, Fred. *The Early Islamic Conquests*. Princeton: Princeton University Press, 1981.

Hitti, Philip, trans. *An Arab-Syrian Gentleman and Warrior in the Period of the Crusades: Memoires of Usamah Ibn-Munqidh*. New York: Columbia University Press, 1929; reprinted Princeton: Princeton University Press, 1987.

Inalcik, Halil. *The Ottoman Empire: The Classical Ages, 1300–1600*. Trans. N. Itzkowitz and C. Imber. New York: Praeger, 1973.

Lapidus, Ira. *Muslim Cities in the Later Middle Ages*. Cambridge: Harvard University Press, 1967.

Morony, Michael. *Iraq After the Muslim Conquest*. Princeton: Princeton University Press, 1984.

Mottahedeh, Roy. *Loyalty and Leadership in an Early Islamic Society*. Princeton: Princeton University Press, 1980.

Peters, F. E. *Allah's Commonwealth: A History of Islam in the Near East, 600–1100*. New York: Simon and Schuster, 1973.

Watson, Andrew. *Agricultural Innovation in the Early Islamic World: The Diffusion of*

Crops and Farming Techniques, 700–1100. Cambridge, England: Cambridge University Press, 1983.

Watt, W. Montgomery. *Muhammad: Prophet and Statesman*. Oxford: Oxford University Press, 1961.

SUB-SAHARAN AFRICA

Fisher, Humphrey. "The Western and Central Sudan and East Africa." In P. M. Holt, Ann K.S. Lambton, and Bernard Lewis, eds., *Cambridge History of Islam*. Vol. 2. Cambridge, England: Cambridge University Press, 1970.

Lewis, I. M., ed. *Islam in Tropical Africa*. 2nd ed. London: International African Institute, 1980.

Saad, Elias N. *Social History of Timbuktu: The Role of Muslim Scholars and Notables, 1400–1900*. Cambridge, England: Cambridge University Press, 1983.

Willis, John Ralph, ed. *Studies in West African Islamic History*. 3 vols. London: Frank Cass, 1979.

SOUTHEAST ASIA

De Graff, H. J. "South-East Asian Islam to the Eighteenth Century." Pp. 123–54 in P. M. Holt, Ann K.S. Lambton, and Bernard Lewis, eds., *Cambridge History of Islam*. Vol. 2. Cambridge, England: Cambridge University Press, 1970.

Geertz, Clifford. *Islam Observed: Religious Development in Morocco and Indonesia*. New Haven: Yale University Press, 1968.

Johns, Anthony H. "Islam in Southeast Asia: Reflections and New Directions." *Indonesia* (Ithaca) 19 (1975): 33–55.

———. "From Buddhism to Islam: An Interpretation of the Javanese Literature of the Transition," *Comparative Studies in Society and History* 9 (1966–67): 40–50.

CHINA AND INNER ASIA

Grousset, R. *The Empire of the Steppes: A History of Central Asia*. Trans. Naomi Walford. New Brunswick: Rutgers University Press, 1970.

Israeli, Raphael. *Muslims in China: A Study in Cultural Confrontation*. Copenhagen: Scandinavian Institute of Asian Studies, 1978.

Rossabi, Morris. "The Muslims in the Early Yuan Dynasty," in John D. Langlois, ed., *China under Mongol Rule*. Princeton: Princeton University Press, 1981.

SOUTH ASIA

Ahmad, Aziz. *Studies in Islamic Culture in the Indian Environment*. Oxford, England: Clarendon Press, 1964.

Dale, Stephen Frederic. *Islamic Society on the South Asian Frontier: The Mappilas of Malabar, 1498–1922*. Oxford, England: Clarendon Press, 1980.

Eaton, Richard M. *Sufis of Bijapur: Social Roles of Sufis in Medieval India*. Princeton: Princeton University Press, 1978.

Ikram, S. M. *Muslim Civilization in India*. New York: Columbia University Press, 1965.

Wink, Andre. *Al-Hind: The Making of the Indo-Islamic World*. Vol. 1, *Early Medieval India and the Expansion of Islam, 7th–11th Centuries*. Leiden: E. J. Brill, 1990.

Gender and
Islamic History

JUDITH TUCKER

Problems in the Study of Gender

Harems and bellydancers, the odaelisque and the aging master puffing on his waterpipe, shadowy black forms gliding through hostile public space, men who rule and women who submit—these are but a few of the many powerful images we confront in the more popular Western vision of gender and Islam. In recent years, most scholars have come to understand that such images have far more to do with the historical process of Westerners constructing and exploring their own gender system than with dominant realities in Islamic history. Edward Said's work on Orientalism,[1] while it did not address the question of gender in any detail, did help promote a more critical consciousness in the study of Islamic history in general by warning that our study of Islam has been, in part, the construction of the "other" in a specific political context.

In modern times, that political context has been one of outright domination. Lord Cromer, British consul general and de facto ruler of Egypt for twenty-four years at the turn of the century, liked to link "advancement" of the "peoples of the East" to change in the sorry position of women. For Cromer, and for French colonial officials in Algeria who similarly decried the indigenous gender system, the degradation of Muslim women was to be remedied only by enlightened rule and the introduction of Western patterns of gender relations. As Rosemary Sayigh has pointed out, the Egyptian and Algerian colonial periods both saw the proliferation of Western studies on women and gender that emphasized the exotic and alien nature of the gender system fostered by Islam.

Even when such bald justification of Western political control was not at issue, the theme of Western superiority and dominance has dogged the study of gender. Most primary sources authored by Westerners—travelers, consular officials, and scholars who were resident in the area—reflect a relationship of tension and distance. The imagined depravities of the harem, the stray misogynist proverb about how women are valued below donkeys, and the focus on where women are absent or missing in the society constitute an alarming proportion of the standard historical sources on gender. In recent years, scholars have become much more leery of using such sources because they tell us, in general, far more about the individual author's views on gender in his or her own society, and the attempt to validate these views, than about gender in the society under study.

The standard indigenous sources for historical study present their own set of problems. Government records, histories, biographical dictionaries, works of jurisprudence, and literature (especially poetry and the stories and folktales that were put into written form) were almost exclusively authored by members of a male elite of government officials and *'ulama* (members of the dominant intellectual group created by the Islamic educational system). Many of these accounts are essentially prescriptive in nature and detail the normative gender system that existed in the minds of an urban male educated elite, not the lived experiences of men as men and women as women. In working with these sources, historians have grown increasingly aware of the necessity to treat them with caution and handle them as a form of discourse about gender that reveals vested interest rather than records actual practice.

Much of the historical material we have to work with is putatatively "Islamic." It is far from clear, however, whether we can actually speak of an Islamic gender system. The core Islamic texts—the Qur'an, the *hadith* (authenticated collections of stories about the life and times of the Prophet Muhammad), the *shari'ah* (the body of codified Islamic law based, in principle, on the Qur'an and *hadith*)—have much to say about gender insofar as they describe gender relations in the early and most revered period of Islamic history and lay down rules for the interaction of men and women in the family and society. Most historians now agree, however, that the study of these texts should not be confused with the study of historical society. Islamic literature is not a descriptive account of how things happened, nor can we assume that Muslims throughout history have organized their lives to conform to the particular injunctions of their religion. In addition, of course, the scriptural literature itself is open to a variety of interpretations; there is no one essential Islamic view of gender.

Any discussion of gender in Islamic history must take into account the varieties of historical experience, across time and place, that we encounter in the Islamic world. The historical world of Islam was a world of rich cultural interaction, of Arab, Persian, Turkic, African, and South Asian cultures. As Richard Eaton demonstrates in his essay in this volume, the spread of Islam as a religion and of the Arabs as a people brought them into contact with a number of different cultures and societies; cultural inter-action and synthesis is a central hallmark of Islamic history. The ways in which an Islamic discourse on gender was received, understood, and elabo-rated in places as diverse as Muslim Spain, Egypt, India, or sub-Saharan Africa certainly varied enough to render most generalizations about an Islamic gender regime suspect. It is not surprising that many historians now working in the field of gender choose to focus their research rather narrowly, and to locate their discussion of gender in a specific time and place in order to deal with the complexities not only of cultural interaction but also of class and regional differences.

Historians of gender in Islamic history also share a growing conscious-ness of the problematic nature of cross-cultural gender studies. The his-torical study of gender has been strongly influenced by a feminist theory developed in the West, and its methodological approaches, central lines of investigation, and research techniques bear the stamp of peculiarly West-ern concerns. An earlier belief in the universalism of such concerns has given way to a realization that we must address the issue of "difference" and our role in the creation of that difference as we attempt to develop approaches that will allow us to pay close attention to the specificities of the historical, socioeconomic, and political context of gender in different parts of the Islamic world. The field is in the process of examining its basic notions about gender-based oppression and feminist agendas for cultural bias and is groping toward analytical approaches that will not employ the Western experience of gender as the template for the rest of the world.

In the light of these problems, does the concept of Islam or Islamic history constitute an analytical category of any use to the study of gen-der? Historians have arrived at different conclusions based, in part, on the period they study. In general, discussions of gender in the period pre-dating the nineteenth century tend to give a prominent place to Islam, as an ideology and a culture, whereas scholarship on gender in the nineteenth and twentieth centuries often dismisses the analytical relevance of Islam altogether. Some of the discontinuties in the field become apparent as we explore the ways in which Islam has and has not informed the development of a particular gender system in the regions where it has predominated.

Gender and the Rise of Islam

Islamic historiography recognizes the central roles of two towering female personalities in the early history of the Muslim community: Khadijah, the first wife of the Prophet Muhammad, who helped him believe in the call to prophesy he first received in A.D. 610 and remained his faithful supporter throughout her life, and 'Ayshah, the later child bride of Muhammad, who was to become his most beloved wife and play a key part in the development of the Muslim community after his death. The biographies of these two women, familiar figures revered by Muslims throughout the centuries, reveal the scope of female activities in the early Islamic period as well as the female qualities later biographers felt were worthy of emulation.

Khadijah was a Meccan widow of social standing and wealth who hired Muhammad, before his call to prophesy, to look after her business in trade. She proposed to and married this young man some fifteen years her junior and bore him children. She supported him in his mission from the beginning, believing in his revelations even when his own strength faltered and becoming the first convert to the new religion of Islam. As long as she lived, Muhammad took no other wives. She emerges in the histories of the period as a strong woman, who decided to place her wealth and her reputation in the service of the new religion. The young 'Ayshah led a rather different life, bethrothed, as she was, at age six to Muhammad after he had become an established prophet and had been widowed at age eighteen. As a girl bride, she secured the love and respect of Muhammad, who preferred her company to that of the other women he married and chose to die in her arms. She was also the first Muslim woman to observe the customs of veiling and seclusion, which did not prevent her from becoming an important source of information on the life of Muhammad after his death, particularly on his home life. Many of the *hadith* that give us information about how the Prophet treated his wives and how he thought about male–female relations are attributed to her. She was also involved in the politics of the early Muslim community. In the succession dispute that followed the death of the third caliph, or leader, of the Muslim community, 'Ayshah rode into battle on a camel to support one of the contending factions.

The biographies of these prototypical Islamic women, discussed and analyzed in some detail by Leila Ahmed, emphasize their virtues of strength, bravery, and intelligence and assign them a pivotal role in the birth and survival of Islam. Admittedly, their position was derivative: It was as wives of Muhammad that they came to prominence. But their importance in his life, the respect in which he clearly held them, and, certainly in the case of 'Aishah, the evidence of influence and wit, suggest that there was far more to the good Muslim woman than cheerful obedience to her husband.

Among the many other women who appear in the pages of early Islamic history, the intriguing figure of Hind bint 'Utba deserves special attention. She joined her father and her husband, both powerful members of the Quraysh tribe in Mecca, in their opposition to Muhammad and the new religion. After her father was killed in conflict with the new Muslims, she nurtured her grief until the Meccans defeated the Muslims in the battle of Uhud in 625. Hind, present on the field of battle, threw herself on the corpse of one of the Muslims, Muhammad's uncle Hamza, cut open his chest, and ate his liver as an act of vengeance. She was converted to Islam only when the Meccans made their final surrender and then, so the story goes, accepted the new religion only grudgingly. Female qualities of strength and independence could also be very threatening, as the stories about the intransigent and vengeful antihero Hind demonstrate.

In addition to the biographies of early Muslim women, the Islamic textual material that originated in this period and gradually (over the first few centuries of Islam) assumed final written form contributed to the development of an Islamic view of gender. The Qur'an, the book of revelations Muhammad had received from God, contained both general exhortations and specific regulations. The exhortations concerning relations between men and women, and the proper roles for women, tend to be open to varying interpretations. Although all women are to "cover their adornments," only the Prophet's wives are to seclude themselves and cover their faces in the presence of other men (33:32). Men "are a degree higher than women" primarily because men are the providers, responsible for financial support (2:228). In the spiritual realm, however, it is clear throughout the Qur'an that women's religious duties, rewards, and souls are the equal of men's. Specific rules include the laws of inheritance—women must inherit set portions from the estates of close relatives, although their share is only one-half of the corresponding male relative's share (4:11–13). A man has unrestricted rights of divorce, although he owes a divorced wife a certain amount of material support (2:228). Other Qur'anic passages regulate concubinage, condemn female infanticide, and allow limited polygyny (a man can marry up to four wives at one time, provided he can treat them equally).

This and other material from the Qur'an, combined with the *hadith*, which were collected and authenticated in the first few centuries after the death of Muhammad, formed the basis for the *shari'ah*, the religious law, which was also codified in the first formative centuries of Islam. The *shari'ah* regulated gender relations in a number of ways. It defined marriage as a relationship of reciprocity, in which a man owed his wife material support and a woman owed her husband obedience. It undergirded a patrilineal system of descent by granting a mother only temporary custody of young children after the termination of a marriage and vesting ultimate custody in the father or father's family. It enshrined the male right of unilateral repudiation of his wife while granting to a woman only the ability to try to bargain with her husband to end an unwanted marriage (*khul'*) or to ask the judge to end a marriage with serious defects. It reiterated the male right of polygyny and elaborated the meaning of equal treatment of wives. The presence of four major legal schools in Sunni Islam allowed for some differences on points of law, but the overall character of the laws regulating male–female relations point to a patrilineal social order that assigns men a dominant role.

Scholars have employed these biographies and textual materials from the early Islamic period to support strikingly different interpretations of the meaning of the rise of Islam for gender issues. First, we can distinguish a group that stresses the very positive and revolutionary nature of the rise of Islam for women. In this view, the benighted age of the *jahiliyya* (the "age of ignorance" that preceded the prophetic mission of Muhammad) incorporated a gender system in which women were subject to the arbitary power of their tribe, their husbands, or both, and lacked basic human rights. Lamya' al Faruqi focuses on the marriage arrangements of *jahiliyyah* Arabia, which included the *sadiqah* marriage in which a woman remained with her own clan, and the *ba'al* marriage in which she moved to her husband's clan. *Sadiqah* marriage, in turn, was of two kinds: temporary (*mut'a*) and permanent (*benna*). In either case, the husband acquired very few responsibilities toward his wife and children, who remained part of the wife's clan. Indeed, in the case of *mut'a* marriage, after the usually brief period of the contracted marriage was over, the man had no recognized relationship at all with his ex-wife and children, who remained in the care and control of the maternal clan in a period when individual rights were very much subsumed by the rights and interests of the larger family group. *Ba'al* marriage was also apparently of two types: marriage by capture and marriage by contract. Whether captured in war or married off by a contract in which the groom paid a bride price to the bride's father, *ba'al* marriage, according to al Faruqi, did not entail the consent of the bride. Other aspects of the marriage regime, including unregulated polygyny and concubinage, emphasized female subservience to men. The practice of female infanticide in parts of the Arabian penninsula further contributes to this view of a *jahiliyyah* in which women were devalued and lacked basic human rights.

Scholars who see Islam as a positive social revolution stress that the reforms Islam introduced into the marriage regime provided new rights and security to women. The *shari'ah* recognized only marriage by contract; insisted on the consent and outlawed the coercion of the bride; made the bride and not her father or family the recipient of the bridal gift; and prohibited *mut'a* marriage (except in Shi'a Islam). Islamic law also spelled out very clearly the responsibilities of the husband and father for the material support of his wife and children. Polygyny was not outlawed but was regulated by imposing a limit of four wives and requiring that all receive equal treatment. Slave concubines were permitted but were accorded certain rights should they bear children to their master. Overall, the vision of Islam as a positive social revolution rests on the idea that such reforms went a long way toward modifying existing social practice for the benefit of women. By endowing women with religious rights and duties equal to those of men, Islam takes a clear position on the ultimate equality of men and women before God. It is no mistake, in this view, that women feature prominently among the early followers of Muhammad and in the life of the early community.

A second and diametrically opposed view of Islam and gender also makes a net distinction between the gender system of the *jahiliyyah* and the gender system introduced by Islam. In this interpretation, however, many of the freedoms and much of the power accorded to women in the *jahiliyyah* were stifled by the rules and regulations of Islam. Fatima Mernissi, for one, points out that evidence exists that the diversity of pre-Islamic Arabian marriage practices included the possibility of female-initiated marriage, of polyandry (or multiple husbands), and of unilateral divorce by women, a practice prohibited under Islam. Rather than stress the kinds of abuse a woman might suffer at the hands of her male relatives in the less regulated pre-Islamic system, this line of argument points out that matrilocal marriages held real advantages for women, including the right of a woman to remain in her own clan and keep her children with her in the event of divorce. Islam, by institutionalizing patrilocal and patrilineal marriage as the only acceptable form, by granting only men the right of unilateral divorce, by assigning children to the father's family, and by recognizing polygyny and concubinage as legitimate practices for men while imposing monogamous marriage on women, ushered in a marital regime of distinct disadvantage to women.

In this interpretation, the women of the early Muslim community are vital figures precisely because they are not yet fully Muslim women. Khadijah, who had lived most of her life as a *jahiliyyah* woman, owed her independence and wealth to these *jahiliyyah* roots. Hind, another *jahiliyyah* woman, remained defiant and mistrustful of the new religion even after defeat had wrung a grudging conversion from her. When asked to take the oath of submission to the new religion, which included a pledge to refrain from adultery, Hind reportedly bridled and queried, "Does a free woman commit adultery?" a response taken to mean that any sexual relationship a free woman entered of her own accord could not be understood as adultery.[2] 'Aisha is the transitional figure whose marriage as a minor and eventual seclusion were part of a new Islamic regime. Other aspects of her life, however, including her active role in the transmission of *hadith*, some of which convey criticism of Muhammad, and her political maneuvers suggest that the legacy of the *jahiliyyah* was not extinguished overnight. One of Muhammad's own great-granddaughters purportedly supported the view that Islam had dampened women's activities. When she, Sukayna, was asked why she was so merry and charming while her sister Fatima was quiet and pious, she replied that she had been named after her pre-Islamic great-grandmother and her sister had been named after her Islamic grandmother.

A third distinct interpretation minimizes the impact of the rise of Islam on the prevailing gender system. Guity Nashat argues that much of what came to be called Islamic was actually rooted in pre-Islamic cultural traditions and customs of the region, particularly those that evolved in Mesopotamia. As early as the Code of Hammurabi (1792–50 B.C.), a woman could be punished by death if she refused her husband sexual intercourse and could be divorced by her husband but enjoyed no reciprocal rights. Assyrian kings (fourteenth to eleventh centuries B.C.) secluded the women of their households, and all women with the exception of prostitutes were legally required to veil in public. The Byzantine and Sasanian empires, in which patterns of female veiling, seclusion, and female legal disability can be discerned, were the heirs to this earlier Mesopotamian gender regime.

In contrast, pre-Islamic Arabia was relatively free of these cultural patterns; the dominant culture of the nomadic pastoralists of the penninsula granted considerable social power to women, who were involved in tribal decision making, enjoyed at least limited power to marry and divorce men of their choice, and made recognized contributions to the important local tradition of oral poetry. Nashat suggests that much of the material on gender in the Qur'an that emphasizes the spiritual equality of women, as well as the biographies of early Islamic women of the penninsula, must be located in this bedouin milieu. The penninsula itself was undergoing change at the time of the rise of Islam, however, as new wealth and the weakening of tribal values were beginning to erode social equality of various kinds, including gender equality. Born in an era of flux and change in gender arrangements, the new Islamic Empire then rapidly expanded (within four decades) into the lands of the Sasanian and Byzantine empires where it came more into contact with the cultural patterns of the region's settled urban peoples. The compilation of the *hadith* and the codification of the *shari'ah* were therefore accomplished under the influence of long-standing gender patterns of Mesopotamian heritage. The Islamic gender system, then, was novel only in the sense that it merged a tribal penninsular tradition with that of the settled, and imperial, states of the Middle East.

All three interpretations recognize the centality of gender to an Islamic vision. With the exception of Muslim apologists, however, most scholars now locate the development of this vision in changing economic, political and historical contexts. The elaboration of Islam and its view of gender took place in the context of an expanding Islamic Empire that was incorporating new lands and peoples. We do not reach a moment when we can say that this elaboration has been accomplished and we have arrived at a crystallization of the Islamic tradition. Although the foundations of an Islamic social order were laid in the first three centuries of Islam, intellectual exploration, economic developments, and political change continued to modify gender systems across both time and space.

The Classical Age

The period of the 'Abbasid caliphate (750–1258) represents, in both Arab and Western historiography, a kind of Islamic golden age. From their capital in Baghdad, the 'Abbasid dynasty ruled over an Arab empire that stretched from the Iberian penninsula to the Indus delta. Although the initial period of direct rule was gradually replaced by a more formal suzerainty over large parts of this territory, these five-hundred years saw the forging of a distinct Islamic culture. Even from the tenth century on, when the 'Abbasids effectively lost their political grip and the empire harbored a number of warring sultanates, Islamic scholars continued to push forward frontiers of knowledge in mathematics, medicine, and astronomy. Literature, especially poetry, flourished, and the putatively religious sciences, including law and philosophy as well as theology, acquired new substance and depth. Court patronage and the emergence of a group of *'ulama*, religiously educated scholars who completed their education by traveling from one center of learning to the next to study under renowned *shaykhs* (religious teachers), contributed to the development of a distinct body of Islamic learning. This cultural florescence, along with the initial successes of the empire in establishing an efficient bureaucracy, overseeing a period of economic prosperity based on agricultural production and trade, and imposing a *pax Islamicus* over a huge and varied territory, defined the imperial golden age.

Recent scholarship on the Athenian golden age has raised serious questions about who, exactly, participated in and benefited from the achievements of ancient Greece (certainly not women or the many slaves) and has served to warn historians about evaluating a historical period on the basis of the experience of the few. Indeed, as soon as we focus our attention on the historical experience of women and the construction of gender in the 'Abbasid period, new elements emerge. Certainly among the ruling elite, the veiling and seclusion of women became a standard and widespread practice. Women no longer played the public roles on the battlefield or in ruling councils that seemed to be open to the women of the early Islamic community. The 'Abbasid upper-class woman was a woman of the *harim*, the secluded section of the household, from which she only ventured completely veiled. As Nashat has pointed out, the wealth of the empire enabled the ruling group to construct lavish palaces and houses in which each wife was assigned a separate apartment and the women's quarters were complete with their own courtyards, gardens, and baths. Poorer houses imitated this design with a closed inner courtyard that was off-limits to male visitors. The caliph Mansur (754–75) officially sanctioned sexual separation by ordering that a separate bridge over the Euphrates for women be constructed in the new capital of Baghdad.

Adoption of the practices of veiling and seclusion may well have been an inevitable part of the Sasanian heritage that figured so prominently in the 'Abbasid court, but it soon found justification in Islamic writing. The philosopher and theologian Abu Hamid al-Ghazali (d. 1111) equated seclusion with piety and warned of female contact with outsiders:

> It is not permissible for a stranger to hear the sound of a pestle being pounded by a woman he does not know. If he knocks at the door, it is not proper for the woman to answer him softly and easily because men's hearts can be drawn to [women] for the most trifling [reasons] and the greatest number of them. However, if the woman has to answer the knock, she should stick her finger in her mouth so that her voice sounds like that of an old woman.[3]

Other respected Islamic thinkers, such as Nasir al-Din Tusi (d. 1274), also recommended seclusion as the Islamically prescribed way to avoid sexual temptation and ensure social peace.

In upper-class circles, the seclusion of women did indeed remove them from the public life of the empire. In contrast to accounts of early Islam, which abound in female personalities, the chroniclers of the 'Abbasid period rarely mention women at all: Tabari (d. 923) records information about the wives of various caliphs, for example, but they are flat portraits, limited in subject to their parentage and philanthropic works. Less official accounts of life in the period suggest that elite women, despite the prevailing social ideology, might use their wiles and wits to gain access to power and influence. *The Thousand and One Nights*, the popular collection of tales set primarily in 'Abbasid times, abounds in intriguing female figures whose schemes lie at the heart of many of the stories. Although the earliest extant written version of the tales dates from the fifteenth century, the different Arabic versions contain many tales clearly of 'Abbasid origin.

The frame story, the familiar one of Sharazad, the highly educated and accomplished young woman who marries King Shahriyar in an attempt to put an end to his practice of marrying each night and executing his new wife the following morning in revenge for the unfaithfulness of his first wife, underscores Shahrazad's qualities of courage and resourcefulness. The many tales she tells Shahriyar constitute her strategy of keeping him interested enough in the outcome of a story to put off her execution each morning until his vengefulness against women can be dissolved by the love and respect he comes to feel for her. Her stories also feature many women, like herself, whose cleverness allows them to assume a dominant and controlling role. In contrast, female infidelity and treachery in the form of women who trick their husbands or other innocent men continually remind us that such power can be very threatening indeed. The tales of *The Thousand and One Nights* suggest that women were at least thought to wield a hidden power within the *harim* world of the elite, but such power, when used for purposes other than the faithful support of one's husband, was the illegitimate power of the schemer.

We have at least one well-known example of a *harim* woman who emerged at a critical moment in Islamic history to play a highly public role. Shajar al-Durr was the wife of the 'Ayyubid sultan who reigned in Cairo in the mid-thirteenth century when the Seventh Crusade, led by Louis IX, invaded Egypt. At the moment when the sultanate was threatened, the sultan died, and his son and heir was abroad and unable to assume power. Shajar al-Durr concealed the news of her husband's death for some six months and ruled in his name. When the male heir was killed by political rivals before he could ascend the throne, Sharjah al-Durr became sultan in her own right and reigned for a few months until her marriage to a military commander, who then took the title of sultan, while she retired, we can only assume, to the *harim*. She achieved heroic stature, however, in indigenous history as the woman who staved off a serious threat from implacable enemies; at the same time, her rule is clearly seen as an aberration, as a desparate measure for a desparate situation. Soon all returned to their proper places.

Both Shajar al-Durr and her second husband were of slave origin; indeed, the structure and functions of the elite household in this period are not comprehensible without some attention to the subject of slavery. For the 'Abbasid ruling class and most of the sultanates that grew up in the empire's territory, slaves served a number of vital functions, primarily as soldiers, servants, and concubines. Throughout Islamic history, slaves play these roles, with a few notable exceptions such as the Zanj, who worked as agricultural laborers in the area of southern Iraq. Female slaves were commonly members of elite households where they worked as servants in the *harim* and as concubines. The *shari'ah*, as it came to be codified during this period, regulated the treatment of these women, allowing male owners sexual access to their slaves but specifying that any child born of a master–slave union would be both legitimate and free, with all the rights of a child born to a free wife. Once she was pregnant by her master, a slave acquired *umm walad* status: She could no longer be sold and would be automatically manumitted on the death of her master.

The importance of these women, although juridically unfree, to the elite household raises some intriguing questions about the nature of slavery as well as the construction of gender in this period. Female slaves, brought from outside the *Dâr al-Islâm* (the "house" or territory of Islam) lived alongside free Muslim wives and could rise to positions of security and influence. A slave woman, Khayzuran, married the Caliph al-Mahdi, and two of her sons, al-Hadi and Harun al-Rashid, succeeded to the caliphate. For the majority who did not marry their masters, the future might still be very bright. Many slave women were manumitted while still in their childbearing years and given in marriage to members of the ruling elite. Often endowed with property, educated, and well connected to a *harim* of importance, they were sought as wives. The ease with which some of these women moved from enslavement to freedom and maintained a privileged position within wealthy elite circles suggests that the condition of enslavement was viewed as a temporary one with little long-term impact on an individual's status. It also suggests that the qualities prized in a female slave—beauty, intellectual and artistic accomplishments, connections to the powerful, and, no doubt, sexual appeal—were indistinguishable from the qualities prized in a wife.

Just as historians of gender in the region no longer think of the *harim* as, primarily, a reservoir of passive women in the sexual service of their master, ideas about views of female sexuality in general have changed considerably. Basim Musallam's study of birth control in this period draws on a wide array of sources—legal materials, pharmacopoeia, erotica—to demonstrate what sophisticated knowledge about human procreation was available among legal, medical, and popular circles, as well as how open people were to the use of various forms of birth control. In legal discussions about the permissibility of birth control in marital sex, we repeatedly encounter the idea that the male and female make equal contributions to the creation of a child, an idea very much in advance of the then prevailing Western view of the female as vessel for the development of the male seed. Even more striking is the consistent position that women and men enjoy equal sexual drives and can claim equal rights to sexual fulfillment within the legally and socially sanctioned institution of marriage. Indeed, men are cautioned that they should not use such birth control practices as *coitus interruptus* in a way that interferes with the sexual pleasure of their wives. The recognition of female sexuality as a biological given and a social concern could also lead to rather more negative conclusions, as Fatna Sabbagh points out. The female drive could also be seen as destabilizing and dangerous: Some Muslim writers of the period clearly link powerful female sexuality to seclusion; the unbridled lust of women could lead to *fitna* (social chaos) in the Muslim community, and therefore women's movements and appearance must be strictly controlled. Whether for good or evil, however, Islamic thought clearly recognized and validated female sexuality.

Such views of sexuality may have reinforced the growing strength of the ideology of female seclusion in upper-class circles. We have far less information about the lives of ordinary women, whether urban or rural, although we can safely assume that strict seclusion was not economically feasible. In one case where we have solid and detailed information on the roles of men and women in a particular community, that of the Jewish community in Cairo, the range of the ordinary woman's activities was considerable. S. D. Goitein, basing his work on a rich collection of personal and business papers found in a Cairo synagogue (the Geniza documents), found women of means who invested in real estate and commerce, and poorer women who worked at a variety of jobs in the fields of petty trade and services. At least some of these women enjoyed basic literacy skills and evinced a familiarity with the public world of business that could only be the product of experience. Goitein and others feel certain that gender arrangements permitting women at least limited access to the market and a social world outside the family were not peculiar to the Jewish community. The shared cultural patterns of all the major religious communities of the period—Muslim, Jewish, and Christian—allow us to assume that middle- and lower-class women of other communities played similar roles. The upper-class *harim* may well have been an ideal, but it was an ideal difficult of attainment among classes of society where all contributions were essential. In the absence of other evidence, we can only speculate that the powerful image of the "guarded woman" did translate into greater modesty of dress and restriction of movement among lower-class women, but not into the disappearance of women from public life.

Differences in class and region make it very difficult to generalize about the development of an Islamic gender system in the 'Abbasid period. We can identify dominant patterns of thought, at least among the ranks of establishment *'ulama*, that argue for separate gendered space and underscore the social imperative of sexual segregation. On the other hand, the distinctions between men and women as spiritual and sexual beings were not that apparent: Society works best when males and females are separated and assigned distinct roles, but such separation does not always imply inferiority. The lived experience of a gendered social order in the 'Abbasid period also undermines any notion that a monolithic Islamic gender system emerged in this period. Ongoing discussion about gender and the wide variety of practices we encounter across class and region caution us against any sweeping generalization.

The Age of the Ottomans

In the twelfth and thirteenth centuries, the human geography of the Islamic heartland was transformed by the arrival in the region of first Turkish and then Mongol peoples who migrated westward from central Asia. Small groups of Turks had been coming into the area, primarily as slaves intended for military service and concubinage, since the ninth and tenth centuries, and some of them had managed to establish sultanates of their own within 'Abbasid territory. During the eleventh and twelfth centuries, this trickle became a flood as Turkish tribal groups moved into the area. One of these groups, the Seljuqs, took Baghdad in 1055 and became the successors to the 'Abbasid dynasty with the establishment of the Seljuq sultanate in much of the territory previously ruled by the 'Abbasids as well as large parts of Anatolia newly taken from the Byzantines.

The internal problems of the Seljuq state led to considerable disintegration, a process capped by the thirteenth-century arrival of the Mongols. In two separate waves of invasion, one in the early thirteenth century under Genghis Khan and one in mid-century under his grandson, Hulagu, the Mongols managed to destroy the Seljuq state and sacked and burned Baghdad in 1258. Only internal succession disputes drew the Mongols again eastward, where they eventually founded the Ilkhanid state in the area of present-day Iraq, Iran, and parts of Afghanistan and central Asia. In their wake, a number of principalities, controlled in the main by Turks and slave soldiers of Turkish origin, emerged to compete for power in the region. The Turkish Ottoman principality of Anatolia was to reunite large parts of the old Islamic Empire with new territories in the Balkans. From its base in western Anatolia, the Ottoman Empire expanded into Byzantine lands into the rest of Anatolia and the Balkans, conquered Constantinople in 1453, and, in the course of the sixteenth century, extended its sovereignty over most of the present-day Arab world—from Iraq and the coastal regions of the Arabian penninsula to Syria and Egypt and across North Africa.

There is considerable debate about what these political developments meant, if anything, for the elaboration of gender in the region. Guity Nashat has shown how both Turkish and Mongol societies, at least when these societies were composed primarily of nomadic pastoralists, exhibited gender patterns quite distinct from those prevailing in the settled parts of the Middle East in the 'Abbasid period. Ibn Battuta, an Arab traveler who in the fourteenth century visited Turkish tribes living on the fringes of the Islamic world, was struck by the novelty (to him) of the ways in which women participated in tribal councils and, occasionally, in warfare. The daily activities of women appear to have resembled those of other pastoralists, including those of the pre-Islamic Arabian peninsula. Women tended animals, the main wealth of the tribe, and were responsible for the production of most essential goods as well as the organization of tribal migration.

Among the Mongols as well, the pastoral nomadic heritage seems to have made an impact on views of gender. The constitution of the Mongol Empire, the Yasa, granted rights and status to women equal to those of men. When the Muslim historian Rashid al-Din included a discussion of the Mongol Il-Khans in his *Universal History*, he justified considerable discussion of royal women, usually left out of Islamic histories, by reference to the high regard in which they were held and their active participation in the society.

Did the arrival of Turkish and Mongol nomads in the Islamic world, and their subsequent incorporation into Islamic society, mean that their views on gender transformed or at least revised the views that had prevailed during the 'Abbasid period? There is little evidence to suggest any wrenching discontinuity. The process of the consolidation of the Ottoman Empire was also a process of the Islamization of Turkish elements and the Turkification of an already sedentary population in Anatolia and surrounding areas. As successors to the former great empires of the region—whether Arab, Persian, or Turkish—the Ottomans fell heir to a tradition of settled statecraft in which exclusively male succession, a male administration and military, and the institution of the *harim* were not modified in any obvious way. With the conquest of the Arab lands in the early sixteenth century, the Ottomans also incorporated many of the major seats of learning and the *'ulama* that were the repository of the Islamic intellectual tradition. Although the culture of the Turkish nomad may have involved much less sexual segregation and more fluid gender roles, these distinctive patterns persisted, by and large, only among the small nomadic groups of various ethnic origins that survived in the geographical redoubts of the region.

This is not to say that the Ottoman period inherited a cystalized and immutable Islamic tradition that imposed uniform gender arrangements impervious to change. As historians have increasingly come to appreciate the dynamism of the Ottoman Empire throughout its history, they have moved away from the assumption that the Ottoman state simply served to transmit a fixed Islamic tradition. In the field of law, for example, Islamic jurists continued to shape their thoughts and judgments in response to the issues of their day. We also cannot assume that the existence of particular institutions, the elite *harim*, for example, necessarily implies that the structure and function of these institutions remained the same. Fortunately, when we come to the Ottoman period, we have access to far more detailed information on gender arrangements, especially among the elite ruling group, than for previous periods. Biographical material on the lives of many of the women residing in the palace *harim* and copious records from the Islamic courts that detail the economic and social life of women of all classes provide material for exploring both the images and realities of the gender system.

One of the most illustrious sultans in the long history of the Ottoman dynasty was Suleiman I (1520–66), known as the "Lawgiver" in recognition of his achievements in setting a rapidly expanding empire on a solid administrative and legal footing. Europeans, impressed by the ongoing conquests of his reign and the opulence and sophistication of his court, dubbed him "the Magnificent" and the "Grand Turk." Some of Suleiman's glory must surely be shared with his wife, Hurrem Sultan, originally a concubine of Russian origin, who gained his affections and trust and rose to the position of legal wife. Much of the internal politics of Suleiman's reign are incomprehensible without close attention to the interventions of this woman, putatively enclosed within the *harim*. Hurrem Sultan worked tirelessly, often in league with one grand vizier or another, to shape the policies of the empire. In her support or opposition to key administrative personnel and her promotion of her own sons as successors to their father, she could use her privileged access to the ear of the sultan to further personal ends. Are we simply dealing here with classic palace intrigue and the petty squabbles of a hermetically sealed ruling group? Although historians have, until recently, tended to disparage *harim* politics, it seems that Hurrem Sultan, at least, was involved in some of the most critical policy decisions of her day. How best to manage the perenially troubling issue of succession, whether to focus military energies on the eastern or western fronts, and how to eliminate administrative corruption were among some of her concerns.

The career of Hurrem Sultan highlights the political role some *harim* women might play in the empire, despite the prevailing view that politics was a male affair. The ideological position that women did not belong in the political sphere was reflected in the tendency of Ottoman historians of the time to equate women's political interventions with decay and decline, an attitude inherited by many modern interpreters of the period as well. The late sixteenth and early seventeenth centuries, for instance, came to be known as the "sultanate of the women" because of the very obvious and persistent exercise of power by certain women of the palace *harim*. Was this the outward manifestation of a decline in the inherent qualities of the reigning sultans, or was it instead the continuation of a tradition of female involvement in the affairs of the empire? Historians are now beginning to rethink the phenomenon of *harim* politics and the entire role of gender in the Ottoman political system as a result.

Certain aspects of Islamic law provided other avenues for the exercise of influence by well-placed Ottoman women. Fanny Davis, in a study of the lives and activities of elite Ottoman women, collected information on the ways in which the women of the sultan's *harim* acquired wealth and then used this wealth to build mosques, schools, fountains, hospitals, and other buildings of social value. The security of female property under Islamic law, and the absolute right of women to the personal disposal of their property, allowed women to acquire wealth through inheritance, gifts, and bridal payments and to invest this wealth in income-producing properties and business activities. Property so acquired and increased was then available for good works: Many *harim* women used the institution of the *waqf*, the endowment of a property for a specific religious or charitable purpose, to underwrite substantial building programs. Besem-i Alem (d. 1853) exemplifies the ways in which a woman of the *harim* might make her mark. She was a concubine of Sultan Mahmud II and mother of the Sultan Abd al-Majid, and she put her money and influence behind the reform policies of the period. She commissioned the Dolmabahce mosque in Istanbul, a building in a strikingly modern style; provided a building for a school with a reformed curriculum; established a hospital; replaced one of the city's major bridges; and built some eight fountains for the use of the city's residents. Although particularly energetic, Besem-i Alem was not atypical: Over the centuries, women of the royal *harim* infused Istanbul's infrastructure with needed capital and left an impressive legacy of public works as well as private buildings such as palaces and tombs.

It was not only the women of the royal *harim* who amassed wealth and participated in the urban economy. All recent studies of urban property, particularly real estate, in Ottoman cities, including Istanbul, Aleppo, Bursa, Damascus, and Cairo, conclude that wealthy women were important holders of urban land.[4] The Islamic court records of the period, which include property deeds, *waqf* endowments, estate partitions, and merchant activities, demonstrate how women managed their property by buying, selling, and renting urban land and buildings, by endowing *waqf* property in such a way as to benefit themselves and chosen dependents, and by investing in business enterprises. These women were not very likely to own productive property such as workshops and the tools of a trade, and when they invested in business ventures, such as the lucrative long-distance trade, they often acted as the "silent partner" who provides the capital and takes a share of the profits but does not actually conduct the business.

Operating under Islamic law, women also found the *waqf* institution particularly congenial to the need to secure a hold over their property. The "family" *waqf* was commonly used in the Ottoman period as a way of consolidating and safegarding family property. In a family *waqf*, the founder may endow a piece of property for an eventual religious or charitable purpose but may designate individuals—family members or others—as beneficiaries of the *waqf* revenues for an interim period, a time that might extend until the extinction of a family line. The founder also appoints a *waqf* administrator who is responsible for overseeing the property, and collecting and distributing the revenues. The family *waqf* thus supplied a way for people to evade the strictures of Islamic inheritance law and safeguard their property against state encroachments: Once the property was endowed as *waqf*, it became inviolable. In many urban areas, anywhere from one-third to one-half of urban *waqfs* were founded by women. These female founders often appointed themselves as administrators of the property during their lifetimes and tended to name female as well as male descendents as the future administrators. Women founders were also more likely than men to choose other women—their daughters, sisters, mothers, or female slaves—as the beneficiaries of *waqf* income. As a great deal of urban land and real estate was tied up in *waqf*, the ways in which women used the *waqf* institution and the gendered pattern of that use are keys to our understanding of the urban economy and the Islamic institutions that lent it order.

The activities of poorer women in the period—women of the urban poor and peasantry—also belie the image of the sequestered female. Although some urban crafts appear to have been closed to formal female participation, women worked on the margins of many crafts, spinning yarn at home, for instance, for male weavers. Certain other trades were strongly identified with women: In Ottoman Cairo, women monopolized the sale of milk and pancakes, worked as attendants in the public baths, and performed as musicians and dancers at both male and female parties. Lower-class women also provided services to the upper-class women of the *harims*; entering the *harim* as entertainers, peddlers, cosmologists, and midwives, they linked the *harim* to the commerce, know-how, and gossip of the urban throroughfare. The well-documented presence of these poorer women in the Islamic court, where they often presented their own grievances against husbands, neighbors, and business partners, testifies to their presence in public space as well as their knowledge of, and belief in the efficacy of, the public institution of the court.[5] The custom of sexual segregation was surely not absent from the lower-class urban milieu; women and men worked in separate trades, and most guild organizations, as far as we know, were sex segregated. Nevertheless, women and men met in the quarters and markets of Ottoman cities in shared public space. In the countryside, where the majority of the population resided in Ottoman times, women were agricultural laborers who worked alongside men in the fields, most often farming in a cooperative family unit.

The Islamic *'ulama* of the Ottoman period, including the practicing judges of the court system and the more reflective juristic thinkers who wrote legal treatises, recognized these realities and were ready, up to a point, to oversee the development of Islamic law in response to social and economic pressures. Until quite recently, most historians of Islamic law have tended to view the Ottoman period as one of transmission of Islamic law, but not of change and innovation. On the contrary, the prevailing opinion was that the various schools of Islamic law cystalized in the late ninth century and that the following periods, especially the Ottoman period, were marked by a fairly rote application of standard rules and principles.

Recent research has suggested, however, that judges and jurisconsults (*muftis*) were responsive to the social problems of their day and found various ways to resolve tensions between legal norms and changing gender realities. The ability of women, for example, to obtain a divorce if their husband is not present and in agreement is extremely limited in the Hanafi school of law, the official legal school under the Ottomans: A woman can obtain a decree of divorce from a judge only if her husband is insane or impotent. But faced in the eighteenth century with the not uncommon problem of husbands who left home for private or official business and then failed to return as planned, leaving their wives in an awkward position, judges and jurisconsults agreed to allow a judge of the Shafi'i legal school, which had a more liberal attitude toward female-initiated divorce, to come to the Hanafi court as needed to grant such women a divorce. The court records of eighteenth-century Damascus and Jerusalem record numerous instances of this rather creative accommodation of a social problem, an accommodation that amounted to a decisive shift in the Hanafi recognition of the woman's power to divorce her husband. The *'ulama*, whom we would expect to serve as the upholders of an Islamic gender regime, were apparently willing to adjust the law to social need.

During the centuries of Ottoman Islam, overt discussion of gender that defined political and economic power as male and idealized the cloistered and guarded woman thinly masked a political system that allowed for female power and influence, economic structures that enabled women to acquire property and wealth, and a legal environment that proved to be fairly flexible on gender issues. The rich historical sources of this period have allowed historians to begin to explore the meaning of gender not only in terms of official pronouncements but also as an evolving set of ideas and practices that structured both women's and men's lives.

The Nineteenth Century

Although most historians of the Islamic world see the nineteenth century as a period of sweeping transformation as an expanding Europe first disrupted and then came to dominate indigenous economies and polities, the place of gender in this transformation has been little addressed. Many historians have simply assumed that a preexisting gender system, in which women remained in the inviolate world of the *harim* or in the confines of a "traditional" peasant family, isolated women and rendered the gender system impervious to change. Only in the late nineteenth century, according to this view, did the accumulated weight of modernization and Westernization began to move women into new positions in the modern working class and the professions, to bring them into contact with Western ideas of gender equality, and to introduce the kinds of female training and education that were to make significant change possible. This version of change has come under close scrutiny recently as studies of women and gender in the nineteenth century contest both the characterization of the indigenous gender system and the idea that change and progress were products of contact with the West.

The study of the construction of gender in the nineteenth century is now proceeding at two levels. On the one hand, historians are investigating the ways in which certain economic and political developments in the region—the European takeover of major parts of regional trade, the marked increase in commercialized agriculture, the marginalization of at least some indigenous crafts by European manufactured goods, the emergence of both old and new states with reform agendas, and the growth of European political and cultural influences, which in some cases culminated in outright colonial control, patterned life in the long nineteenth century and led, inevitably, to changes and adjustments in gender definition and roles. On the other hand, there is the related project of tracing the encounter of the European gender ideology, a set of notions about gender incubated in the West, with the indigenous views of gender, the products of the specific historical circumstances of the region. Such an encounter, fraught as it was with disparities in power, was bedeviled by problems of domination and the constituent tendency of the European voice effectively to silence the indigenous voice through its representation of the "other" gender system.

It is somewhat dangerous to generalize about the impact of economic and political change on gender; the integration of the region into a global economic system dominated by Europe was very uneven, and indigenous states and European powers were able to exercise their political will in an erratic fashion. Still, we can draw on a small but growing number of specific studies to suggest the nature of change in particular areas.

In rural Egypt, for example, prior to the Muhammad 'Ali period (beginning in 1805), the individual peasant family formed the basic unit of agricultural production. Although the family practiced a division of labor based on age and gender—women did not plow but did work in the fields at harvest and pest-control time and had special responsibility for the care of animals—women were very much part of a productive family unit. Rural women also practiced a number of handicrafts and were particularly active in the spinning of cotton, flax, and wool, which they spun at home, then selling the finished yarn to weavers or middlemen. Not surprisingly, women sometimes owned the family's agricultural implements and animals and, on occasion, asserted rights to agricultural land, as documents in the Islamic court records tell us.[6] Margaret Meriwether has shown how we find similar patterns in the rural areas of northern Syria in the early nineteenth century: Women tended animals, fetched water, gathered wood, and labored in the fields. As in Egypt, women not only worked but enjoyed rights to agricultural implements and to the land.

The emergence of a state in Egypt under Muhammad 'Ali with a novel agenda of military and economic reform and the increase in European demand for cash crops intersected to transform the Egyptian countryside. As agriculture grew more commercialized and land consolidation proceeded, peasant families were drafted for work on agricultural infrastructure and for the cultivation of large estates. Although entire families might be recruited for work on a project, males were more likely than females to be drafted. In addition, Muhammad 'Ali's military reforms, which included peasant conscription, siphoned off more men. Many women were left with a crushing burden of work in the short term, and in the longer term family labor patterns were disrupted. The Muhammad 'Ali period set a new gender pattern that was to persist long after most of the development projects of the time were closed down: Men continued to be recruited for agricultural labor on large estates, while women were relegated to the shrinking family plot. In parts of northern Syria, we find similar patterns emerging in the first half of the nineteenth century. As cotton, grain, pistachio, and gallnut crops were increasingly grown on large estates for export, the labor of both men and women might be utilized, but women were called on less often and were paid lower wages. As in Egypt, we see a heightened gender division of labor with men employed in cash crops and women in household production. In general, in the absence of other information, we can assume that the more commercialized areas throughout the region, such as the Anatolian coast and the Algerian plains, saw similar changes in the early part of the century, while the more remote places, in Iran, Afghanistan, and much of the Gulf area, were little transformed.

In places where land consolidation and population growth quickened in the course of the nineteenth century, many rural women and their families migrated to urban areas. With most craft corporations and the more remunerative trades closed to rural women without special skills, female migrants were likely to gravitate toward the unorganized sector of the economy—peddling and domestic service in particular; in the latter occupation, the outlawing of the slave trade in the region in the late nineteenth century led many wealthy households to replace slave domestics with free servants. For many lower-class women, the developments of the nineteenth century spelled economic marginalization.

Women of the emerging middle and upper classes did not necessarily share the fate of lower-class women. The struggles of reform-minded state administrators in both the Ottoman and Egyptian states to deal with problems of public health and education drew their attention to the need to train and educate women as well as men. In Egypt, as early as the Muhammad 'Ali period, the state opened a school to train women health officers and another palace school to expose women of the *harim* to reading, writing, geography, and drawing. In Istanbul, the Ottoman government opened the first of many girls' secondary schools in 1858, and the subsequent demand for women teachers led to the founding of a women's teacher training school in 1872. Throughout the region, teaching was the first "modern" profession not only open to women but to which women were actively recruited to meet the needs of a sex-segregated educational system. The new educational system seems to have attracted primarily the daughters of upper-middle-class families; the upper class still educated its daughters in the *harim* in the expectation that they would be cultured, not professional, women.

Juan Cole has suggested that the late nineteenth-century embrace of female education by the upper middle class, as reflected in the fervent advocacay of Qasim Amin in Egypt, Semseddin Sami in Istanbul, or Malkum Khan in Iran, was rooted in the changing needs of this class. As an emerging group, linked by education and economic interest to Europe, this new class did not aspire to emulate the lifestyle of the upper class with its elaborate houses and *harims*. It wanted to cut down on the big outlays connected with the *harim* and rationalize domestic affairs; only educated wives could manage a household properly and function, when necessary for the family good, in the public sphere. Although relatively small numbers of women entered the new educational institutions, many were educated so that they might be better household managers rather than professional women; a precedent for educating women was established in the nineteenth century.

The impact of socioeconomic change in the nineteenth century on the indigenous gender system was thus neither necessarily positive nor of a piece. For peasant women, at least in regions where commercialized agriculture came to dominate, the erosion of a family economy and the rise of wage labor could lead to economic marginalization. Some women also lost their means of livelihood as indigenous crafts, particularly connected to the textile industry, faced European competition, although other female-based crafts expanded in the period, and women were recruited into light industry toward the end of the century. The forces of "modernization" did not necessarily integrate poorer women into the economy. Middle- and upper-class women, in contrast, lived through a time when the lifestyle of the old privileged class came under scrutiny; as the world of the *harim* began to decay from within as a result of its perceived incompatibility with contemporary needs. Education and at least the beginnings of female entry into modern professions opened new opportunities.

The changes of the nineteenth century also cast the discourse on gender in new terms. The arrival of European powers in the region, and their rise to economic and political ascendency in almost all parts of the

Islamic world, reverberated through subsequent discussions of gender. The imperial and colonial powers approached the issue of gender in a self-conscious and self-serving fashion. In Egypt and Algeria, for example, colonial authorities claimed the advancement of women as a special concern of their rule, and a justification for it. The degradation of women in "native" society was only to be ameliorated by the policies of enlightened Europeans whose notions about gender were held to be those of a civilized society worthy of emulation. To a certain extent, the historical writing on gender in the nineteenth century adopted this frame of reference, and this tradition has continued until quite recently. The idea that the Europeans arrived with a blueprint for a kind of women's liberation adopted by some forward-looking members of indigenous society (such as minorities and a newly educated middle class) but actively resisted by much of that society for primarily religious reasons informed the standard presentation in most texts. The discussion of this period is now more nuanced and tends to focus on the interplay of the European and indigenous constructions of gender in a context of domination. Actual colonial policy, indigenous discussions of gender in the context of this policy, and the consequent embedding of the gender issue in nationalist discourse are among the topics of most interest.

European colonial policies, despite the rhetorical flourish that invariably accompanied discussion of the native woman, did very little that affected women in any obvious way. In Egypt, for example, the British-controlled government under Lord Cromer paid scant attention to female education on the grounds of fiscal constraint. In the few schools the colonial state did sponsor, European officials imposed a curriculum that mirrored that prevailing in Europe; the primary school examination for girls included testing in cooking, laundering, needlework, hygiene, and "housewifery." Egyptian women, in keeping with dominant European views of gender roles, were educated to take their places as wives and mothers or, if their class background permitted, "native governesses." In French Algeria, where the dominant colonial ideology decried the oppression of native women and heralded French control as the path to liberation, the results were little different. At the end of the nineteenth century, after some seventy years of French rule, 1,984 Algerian girls were enrolled in school in the whole country, including 454 in kindergarten.

Aside from these limited programs in education and some attention to health, the colonial state shied away from reform, such as the legal status of women, usually on the grounds that such tampering would enrage the "traditional" elements in the country. In Egypt and Algeria alike, colonial officials defended inaction in legal reform against critics by invoking the weight of an Islamic tradition. Enlightened European ideas, although they might demonstrate superiority and justify domination, could not be put into practice, the argument went, because they might rock the boat. The

gender arrangements of native society were deeply rooted in religious belief and buttressed a conservative social system that colonial officials might
try to alter only at their peril. Indeed, the very elements that tended to cooperate with colonial rule—conservative large landholders, for example—
were perceived as being most attached to the Islamic social system. Colonial officials, despite their numerous pronouncements on gender, came to
be stalwart supporters of the gendered status quo.

The European discourse on gender was also elaborated in the nineteenth century by European scholars and travelers, the instrumentality of
whose views was less immediate, if not less present. Perhaps most interesting among them were the women travelers, some of whom lived for years in
the Islamic world as wives of European diplomats and officials or residents
in their own right in search of health or adventure. Mary Wortley Montagu (Istanbul), Lucie Duff Gordon (Egypt), and Eliza Rogers (Palestine)
left three of the more detailed accounts of life in the region as European
females. Although they appear to be every bit as imbued with notions of
European superiority and Islamic "otherness" as their male counterparts,
European women had experiences that prompted novel kinds of reflection.
Lady Montagu gave birth in Istanbul and found the process "not half so
mortifying here as in England."[7] Lucie Duff Gordon, who spent the last
years of her life trying to regain her health in Egypt, marveled at the distortions purveyed by previous European accounts of the *harim* world: The
Egyptian *harim*, in her experience, was simply another version of upper-
class society, with all the dullness of a Hampton Court tea party. Eliza
Rogers, easily the least reflective of the three, was still able to appreciate
the novel freedom that life in nineteenth-century Palestine offered to a
hitherto sheltered Englishwoman. All three women dissented, to varying
degrees, from the prevailing European vision of the Islamic gender system; their own experiences of comfort and freedom, and their ability as
women to perceive many similarities in the gender system to that of their
own culture, promoted a more balanced view.

Whatever its details, the European version of a gendered Islam came
to occupy a central place in indigenous discourse as well. Before the nineteenth century, Islamic thinkers did debate among themselves about the
meaning of Islam for gender—we have seen that theologians and jurists
continued to interpret canonical texts and assess the applicability of Islamic
law to specific gender situations they encountered. What is new in the later
nineteenth century, then, is not debate as such about Islam and gender,
but the way in which Islamic thinkers begin to focus on European views
of this question. Islamic intellectuals of the mid-nineteenth century, such
as Rifa 'a al-Tahtawi in Egypt and Ibn Abi Diyaf in Tunisia, still posited
the problem of gender and society as one of shedding new light on the
meaning of the religious law, thus carrying on the tradition of internal

debate and adjustment. In the late nineteenth century, however, Islamic reformers, represented by the Egyptian Muhammad Abduh, adopted the European critique of Islamic society to a far greater extent. Abduh argued that women's current oppression stemmed from the moral disintegration of Muslim society and called for a revitalization that included coming to terms with the inner spirit of Islam and adapting the letter to the needs and demands of modern life. According to Abduh, polygyny, for example, had been allowed in early Islam among righteous believers but had become, in his day, a corrupt practice lacking justice and equity; therefore, in keeping with the spirit and intent of the law, polygyny should be abolished. Women's liberation, for Abduh, was a precondition for the establishment of a "modern" society, a society in which the European model played a definite role.

The thought of the Islamic reform movement intersected in the last part of the nineteenth century with the growing intellectual activities of upper-class and newly educated middle-class women. Ottoman and Egyptian women contributed to women's magazines established in Istanbul and Cairo in the 1890s. Women writers dealt with religious, nationalist, and feminist issues, including discussion about the wearing of the veil and the education of children, especially girls. In many of these discussions, explicit and implicit reference to the European gender system often appears, but a real sense of difference remains. Bahithat al-Badiya, an Egyptian woman, addressed the subject of seclusion in a lecture given in 1909:

> The imprisonment in the home of the Egyptian woman of the past is detrimental while the current freedom of the Europeans is excessive. I cannot find a better model of [sic] today's Turkish woman. She falls between the two extremes and does not violate what Islam prescribes. She is a good example of decorum and modesty.[8]

Historians have disagreed about how to characterize women's writings and activities in this period. Are we, in fact, dealing here with a familiar form of feminism, or do the differences between women's concerns in Europe and in the Islamic world preclude the use of a universalizing concept such as feminism? In general, the former tendency of scholars to assume that women's movements shared similar assumptions about gender inequality and therefore similar aims in the elimination of same have given way to a wariness about generalizing from the European experience. Certainly the development of feminism in Europe was followed with interest by women elsewhere, but it is far from clear that the means and aims of European feminism, to say nothing of its basic assumptions, were adopted wholesale.

Most women writers at the end of the century were clearly at odds, however, with a conservative current of Islamic thought that took the offensive against the Islamic reformers. Tal'at Harb, an Egyptian nationalist and one of the founders of the Bank Misr, embraced the conservative religious argument that men and women were, in fact, unequal and that calls for women's liberation were part of an imperialist plot to weaken Egypt. According to Harb, God created women for domesticity and the pleasure of men, not to "defeat the men nor to give opinions or establish policies."[9] Conservative thinkers made the connection between European domination and any call for women's rights very explicit: The linchpin of the European takeover was the gender system, and indigenous gender practices, defined in a most conservative fashion, must be defended at all costs. While Islamic reformers and many women writers argued that women were meant by Islam to play an active, if not entirely equal, role in society, conservatives underscored the wide distinctions between genders, including disparities in mental, physical, and moral capacities.

In the course of the nineteenth century, then, the "woman question" came to be entwined with issues of Westernization, imperialism, and cultural authenticity. Male reformers, conservatives, and women writers themselves linked gender to religious discourse in the search for the true meaning of Islam. Whatever Islam meant for gender must be defended as part of the national or cultural heritage or both, a bulwark against Western domination. Although there was substantial disagreement about what Islam did indeed signify for gender, the terms of the discussion were thus set in the nineteenth century in the context of a defense of indigenous culture in the face of the European onslaught, a context that has been sustained, in various forms, right up to the present.

The Twentieth Century

Much of the study of gender in the Islamic region in the twentieth century has continued to focus on the themes of gender and economic development, the connections between gender issues and the nationalist movements that have dominated political life, and the ongoing elaboration of a self-consciously Islamic discourse on gender.

Historians and anthropologists who work on gender and economic development have tended to ask, first, what kind of impact did economic development have on the gendered economy? Did the scope or nature of female and male economic contributions change in any significant fashion? And, second, how has the history of sexual segregation influenced change? Have distinct patterns of gendered employment tended to emerge as a result of the preexisting separation between men and women? The old assumption that economic "modernization" gradually brought women into the labor force, ending the practice of seclusion along the way, is being questioned as new research points to the far greater complexity of the process.

In agricultural areas, for example, the growth of the market and the introduction of new technologies might actually emphasize gender inequalities. Mernissi's study of the Gharb in Morocco, for instance, demonstrates how women played an active role in the precolonial subsistence economy and as a result enjoyed recognized rights to the wealth of the community. Although they could not inherit agricultural land, they could expect material support from male relatives. During the French colonial period, however, landholdings were consolidated at the expense of small peasant holdings, and over the course of the twentieth century, peasants increasingly went to work as wage laborers on privately owned or state farms. Only men were hired as permanent employees; women worked as seasonal laborers for lower wages at jobs that spared them for unpaid family labor as well. The cost for women has been great. Jolted out of a subsistence agricultural system in which they worked hard but were guaranteed economic security, rural women now work just as hard but enjoy neither permanent paid jobs nor the benefits of the old family-based system.

State policies could have similar effects as many twentieth-century states formulate plans to speed economic development. Under the Pahlavis in Iran, for example, patterns of national economic development, including industrialization and the modernization of agriculture, transformed the rural economy, rendering peasant-based agriculture unremunerative. A detailed study by Erika Friedl showed how men increasingly joined the wage-labor force, often migrating to large towns at some distance from their homes, while women were relegated to the household. The work women had done in the family-based economy, primarily the care of animals and the processing of their products, no longer existed, and women became totally dependent on the income of male relatives. Deeply ingrained opposition to women working outside the household reduced them to the role of consumers who must try to emulate an urban lifestyle. Women were thus stripped of their economic activities in agriculture but were denied access to new kinds of work. Deniz Kandiyoti has argued that similarly, in Turkey, state policies regarding the dissemination of new agricultural technologies and training have favored men and left rural women outside the modern agricultural sector.

Among urban women, twentieth-century developments had different consequences for middle-class and lower-class women. The expansion of systems of higher education in the region opened professional opportunities to men and women of the upper and middle class. In Egypt, women were admitted to the Egyptian National University in 1928. In Turkey, Ataturk's reforms made education equally accessible, in principle, to males and females. In other areas, in the Arab Gulf for instance, there were virtually no women in higher education until local universities opened to them in the 1970s. Whenever it occurred, however, many women received a professional education and then entered professions in significant numbers. In Egypt, there was a striking feminization of many professions during the 1970s as a result of government policies under Gamal Abdul Nasser and Anwar Sadat guaranteeing jobs for university graduates and the departure of men to military service or employment in other Arab countries. Such feminization occurred not only in the "female" fields of education and medicine but also in the strongly "male" field of engineering. In the Arab Gulf, where women were virtually absent from the professions as of the early 1970s, the change has been rapid. In Kuwait, for example, the number of women in the labor force rose from about a thousand in 1965 to some twenty-five thousand in 1985, most of them employed in the professions.[10]

Although some of these dramatic increases in professional employment may prove temporary because of the downturn in the economies of the region, scholars stress that these patterns of female employment belie the notion that Islamic society raises barriers to the employment of women in public space. On the contrary, at least at the professional level, cultural barriers have proven extremely permeable.

Among lower-class women, many have found cultural inhibitions more pronounced. Whether in a poor quarter of Cairo or in a Moroccan village, the ideal woman has been the woman who remains at home caring for her husband and children; women who have worked for wages outside the household have lost respect. If women have had to work, the most acceptable occupations were those that kept them out of public view and away from unrelated men; clothes washing, spinning and weaving, the raising of small animals, and other home-based activities constituted acceptable forms of female labor in the Moroccan village or Cairo quarter.[11] Other researchers have uncovered contradictory evidence. In the more stable poor quarters of Cairo, women were well integrated into economic life. Many worked as dressmakers and shop assistants, as nurses and government employees, or even as butchers, peddlers of foodstuffs, and coffeehouse keepers. Such women kept the regard of their communities.

In seeking to explain why we might find such different attitudes toward women's work, Judith Gran has focused on the differences in the communities. In the poor quarters of the city populated by rural migrants, the rural pattern of men going into wage labor and women staying in subsistence production was transferred to the city. In the older urban neighborhoods, a vestigial precapitalist economy in which the family functioned as a unit of production was preserved; the boundaries between home and workplace, the private and the public, were blurred; and women's work remained a normal part of the neighborhood scene. The implication of the developments of the twentieth century are clear: The growth of capitalist enterprise and wage labor in urban areas, insofar as it demarcated the home and the workplace in a powerful new way, introduced questions about the propriety of work for lower-class women that were largely absent before.

Economic development in the twentieth century, then, has been found to have had significantly different effects on middle- and lower-class women. While opportunities for professionally educated women expanded, the options available to lower-class women narrowed with their exclusion from the expanding wage-labor market and new skilled occupations. How much this exclusion owed to social constraints, particularly the opposition associated with Islam to women working in jobs that could expose them to public view or association with men, remains a subject of some debate. The relative ease with which women were brought into the wage-labor force—in the 1970s, for example, when male migration to fill jobs created by the oil boom made for job opportunities at all levels—suggests how quickly cultural restraints could be overridden. Overridden is not eliminated, however, and the selective invocation of these constraints continues to appear in discussions of gender in the region.

Many historians have also turned their attention to the role that gender issues have played in the various movements of independence and nationalism so central to the politics of the twentieth century. Most agree that while women participated actively in the political agitation and even violent confrontations surrounding the process of national liberation, nationalism rarely incorporated recognizably feminist goals, and women did not reap rewards in the form of much increased levels of participation in formal politics. Indeed, much of the literature seeks to address the question of how and why women were excluded from political power even after they had been a part of political change.

The twentieth-century nationalist movements of the region—including the Turkish War of Independence (1919–23), the Iranian Constitutional Revolution (1906–11), the Egyptian Revolution of 1919, the Algerian War of Independence (1954–62), and the ongoing Palestinian conflict, to name just a few—all relied on the mobilization of women and men as demonstrators, organizers, speech makers, and even fighters. In Turkey, Halide Edip was a major political figure who spoke and wrote in support of the nationalist cause. In Iran, women participated in demonstrations that proved critical to protecting the new parliament from attack. In Egypt, women of all backgrounds staged street demonstrations protesting the arrest of nationalist leaders by the British in 1919. The Wafdist Women's Central Committee, founded in 1920, played an important role in the nationalist movement, organizing boycotts of British goods, banks, and personnel. In Algeria, women became cadres of the Algerian Front for National Liberation (FLN) and served as messengers, spies, and actual combatants in urban guerrilla warfare. The Palestinian movement has also incorporated women into both civilian and military roles. In the context of such active and visible participation, historians ask why little permanent or revolutionary change in women's position and power has materialized.

The Algerian case has been discussed in the most detail. In 1956, as the guerrilla warfare tactics of the FLN met with ever more sophisticated French counterinsurgency, the FLN came to rely more on its urban cells and involved women in a wide range of activities: Algerian women, wearing Western dress, carried messages, money, and weapons through French checkpoints without arousing suspicion. Some of the most famous combatants of the FLN were women: Jamilah Buhrayd, for example, was only twenty-two years old when she was arrested while operating as a liaison agent, imprisoned, tortured, and condemned to death. *Al-Mujahid*, the organ of the FLN, named her the most famous Algerian woman in 1959. Nor was she alone; other women, such as Jamilah Bupasha, Zohrah Drif, and Djohar Akru, were jailed and tortured during the war of liberation.

The woman fighter was only one gendered role. The FLN, and Algerian society in general, elaborated its view of gender within the context of French colonialism. The Algerian response to the French denigration of the indigenous gender system was to politicize "tradition," to promote women's veiling, for example, as a symbol of the besieged indigenous culture and defiance of the French. Women's participation in the war was heralded as evidence of the freedom and dignity of women under Islam, as validation of the strength and diversity of their "traditional" role as defined by religion and custom. When faced with internal economic and political problems after the war, the new government of Algeria tended to undercut the gains women had made in the revolutionary period, using the theme of cultural continuity. The woman was to be first and foremost a wife and mother, in accordance with "the ethical code deeply held by the people," and the exceptionalism of the revolutionary period was stressed.

The subordination of gender issues to nationalist goals has been a common feature of women's political activity. In general, the women who have been most active in politics—including the Egyptian women who founded and developed the Egyptian Feminist Union in the 1920s and 1930s, the Palestinian women of the Arab Palestinian Women's Union of the same period, and the many Iranian women who worked with various political groups to overthrow the shah—have perceived and constructed their role as auxiliary to the primary national or revolutionary task at hand. As they founded women's associations and unions to advance goals enunciated by a male leadership, however, many women entered the political arena as activists and organizers whose talents and contributions were recognized and applauded. In the process, some of the former constraints on women's freedom of movement and contact with unrelated men were relaxed, and women often took a more active part in these movements than they did or do in establishment politics. The prominence of Hanan Ashrawi, for example, in Palestinian politics can be readily grasped in the context of some sixty years of visible female participation in the various Palestinian nationalist movements. Female visibility and activity did not necessarily lead nationalist or revolutionary movements to confront the issue of women's place and power in society, however; if discussed at all, change in the gender system was assumed to be something that would evolve naturally, after the national or revolutionary struggle was won.

Western feminists, operating in a very different historical setting, have sometimes viewed this historical relationship of feminism and nationalism with a feeling of alarm: Have indigenous women, by putting their energies and time in the service of male-controlled movements, accepted the subordinate status of the gender issue and therefore collaborated with the patriarchal order? Women in the region are quick to point out that their circumstances are indeed different and that they must reach their own conclusions about the ways in which they will order the varying dimensions of gender, nation, and class.

Islam has also remained central to most public discussions about gender. The regulation of gender relations by Islamic law has been of key concern. As secular law codes, largely of Western inspiration, became the law of the land in most Islamic countries, the one area retained under the jurisdiction of the religious law, the *shari'ah* for Muslims, was the area of personal status, that is, the laws governing inheritance, marriage, divorce, child custody, and family relations in general. The Egyptian women's movement fastened on legal reform as crucial; in addition to their struggle for political rights and educational opportunities for women, the Egyptian Feminist Union led by Huda Sha'rawi lobbied for reform of personal-status laws in the 1920s and 1930s. Its members argued within the framework of the Islamic reform movement that they wanted to preserve the intent of the law and remove the accretions that had legalized the oppression of women in the form of child marriage, unbridled polygyny and divorce, and female disadvantage in child custody and inheritance. Although many of their campaigns to open new educational and work opportunities to women met with success, the issue of legal reform proved particularly thorny. Although often faced with similar campaigns, the various states in the region were slow to tackle the *shari'ah*.

The Turkish Republic did dispense altogether with the *shari'ah*, but most other states have retained it, either in pristine form, as in Saudi Arabia, or, more commonly, incorporating some reforms. Any reform that has threatened to change the law significantly, however, has met with resistance. In Iran under Riza Shah, the state fixed a minimum marriage age (absent in Islamic law) and restricted temporary marriage (permitted in the

Shi'i law that predominates in Iran). Under Muhammad Riza Shah, the Family Protection Act of 1967 curtailed a man's unlimited right to divorce his wife and gave the court new powers of discretion in matters of divorce, child custody, and marriage to a second wife. Similar sorts of reforms—the institution of a minimum marriage age, the placing of at least some conditions on the man's right of unilateral repudiation, and the limiting of polygyny—were promulgated in states as diverse as Egypt, Tunisia, Syria, Iraq, India, and the People's Democratic Republic of Yemen in the course of the 1950s, 1960s, and 1970s. The history of reform, however, is not one of steady progress toward a liberalization of the *shari'ah*. As Mervat Hatem has argued, the 1980s was a decade of "re-Islamicization" of the legal structure: In countries like Egypt, Sudan, Algeria, and Pakistan, reaffirmations of the centrality and immutability of the *shari'ah* have eroded the basis of legal reform. Iran has moved the furthest in this direction in the wake of the Islamic Revolution of 1979: Not only was the Family Protection Act revoked, but all divorces obtained under its provisions were declared void.

Outside the realm of the law, the question of what Islam does or does not expect or require of men and women has remained a hotly debated one, as Barbara Stowasser has demonstrated. The Islamic modernist discourse has had its spokespeople, notably Mahmud Shaltut, a rector of al-Azhar University in Cairo in the early 1960s. Shaltut argued that the clearly enshrined women's equality in religious obligations translated into a religious right to be educated. Shaltut also supported women's suffrage on the grounds that women had been among the early supporters of the Prophet Muhammad. Conservative religious thinkers in Egypt and other predominantly Islamic countries have disagreed with the modernist trend and have argued strongly for the veil, in the sense of modest clothing for women that covers all parts of their bodies except their hands and face, as an "Islamic" form of dress. Many conservatives go further to argue that the best veil for the woman is her home. Women should work only out of necessity because work exposes women to unrelated men and disrupts the natural order of the family in which men serve as women's providers. The practice of the early Muslim community is invoked to exclude women from all formal political life, including the holding of office and voting.

The activist–fundamentalist Islamic groups that emerged politically in the 1970s share this conservative view of gender and have given it new life by making it a primary symbol of Islamic authenticity in the face of Western cultural imperialism. They see outside powers as using the gender issue to undermine the Muslim family and thus Muslim society as a whole. Many scholars have focused on the appeal such a position seems to have had for numbers of young women who have joined these movements. Their embrace of a conservative position on gender has been explained on a sociological level by Fadwa El Guind, who has argued that young women of lower-middle-class backgrounds, who were studying or working in urban areas and thereby exposed to all the ambiguities surrounding women in public space, found a refuge in conservative Islam. By adopting the dress and public style of these movements, young women were able to feel more secure and comfortable in public space and justify their schooling and work life more easily. On an ideological level, their behavior has been explained by Arlene Macleod as a women's strategy of sorts, an attempt to retain aspects of traditional social relations that they value and at the same time enter public space, where political struggle and action for change is possible.

Despite the persistence of an explicitly Islamic discourse on gender, the role that Islam plays in the ways Muslim women organize their lives is not clear. Several recent oral history accounts in which women reflect on the ways in which their lives are circumscribed or directed were surprisingly silent on the question of Islam. What women can and cannot do was caught up with their perceptions of local custom and the importance of the good opinion of their family and friends, but rarely was Islam invoked as a guide to gender issues.[12]

We are left, then, with some real questions about the location and resonance of the Islamic discourse on gender. At the level of formal discourse, we find some divided opinions, although the more conservative interpretations have been gaining ground. The extent to which these interpretations actually mold women's behavior or dictate gender patterns in the society remains an open question; many women appear relatively impervious to the guidance offered by established *'ulama* and far more likely to bow to informal opinions on gender not couched in explicitly religious terms. The fact that most public, literate discussion of gender currently takes place with reference to Islam, however, cautions against any facile dismissal of Islam as central to the construction of gender in predominantly Muslim areas.

Conclusion

Much of the research in recent years on gender in Islamic regions has tended to downplay the role of Islam in gender arrangements. Many of the studies of the role played by economic developments and the history of colonialism and nationalism, as well as emphasis on the cultural heterogeneity of the region, have tended to undermine the stereotypes of the *harim* and the bellydance bred of an essentialist Islam. Today's scholars have turned away from defining the study of gender as the study of Islam and tend to look instead to the specific historical context of the time and place they study, a context produced not only, or even primarily, by Islamic culture. The convergence of a variety of cultural patterns, the rise of European domination, economic development of a characteristically Third World kind, and the struggles for national independence are among the elements that have attracted the most attention.

Is Islam, then, simply irrelevant to our discussion of the construction of gender in Islamic regions? Certainly there is little evidence for an Islamic monolith that dictates gender arrangements, that institutes a patriarchal system and imbues it with religious sanctions. The historical record is too rich and varied to support such a vision. But is there, as Deniz Kandiyoti has asked, a way in which Islamic ideology intersects with the preexisting patriarchal systems of Asia, thereby lending new weight and vitality to a patriarchy based on a male-headed extended family and a virtual male monopoly over formal political power? We have but to look at Africa, argues Kandiyoti, where Islam intersected with a very different set of gender arrangements: Islam did not annihilate a system that accorded women more freedom and autonomy because of the absence of the extended and male-dominated family. Instead, the different Islamized African communities made different accommodations to, or "bargains" with, Islamic gender ideology; in general, however, Muslim African women retained significantly more freedom and autonomy than their counterparts in Asia. Islam has been a factor in the construction of gender, but in a complex way that defies easy generalization. Each community has to be studied within its specific context. Certain characteristically "Islamic" gender patterns, including the segregation of men and women, the gendering of public space as male, and the seclusion of women as a cultural ideal, appear to exercise an ideological hold over space and time, but the realization of these patterns, and even the desire to realize them, has varied enormously.

Finally, students of gender have lost much of their former self-confidence about the standards and measures they use. Most specific studies suggest, implicitly or explicitly, that the Western experience of gender does not equip us to come to terms with the construction of gender in a context of racial and national domination. The relationship between nationalist movements and feminism, the problematic nature of uneven development, and the connections between gender and cultural authenticity all pose analytical problems outside the framework of trodden paths in the study of gender in the West. And perhaps most troubling is the idea that even well-intentioned Western scholars could fall into an approach to gender that highlights the exotic differentness of another culture by focusing solely on women as victims of history. This current lack of confidence appears to be having a salutary effect on the field as scholars continually scrutinize their work for cultural bias, for essentialist notions, and for inappropriate generalizations in an attempt to set the study of gender in the Islamic regions on a new course.

NOTES

1. All works referred to in the text are cited in the Bibliography at the end of this essay.

2. Leila Ahmed, "Women and the Advent of Islam," *Signs* 11, no. 1 (Summer 1986): 684.

3. Guity Nashat, "Women in the Middle East, 8000 B.C.–A.D. 1800," in *Restoring Women to History: Teaching Packets for Integrating Women's History into Courses on Africa, Asia, Latin America, the Caribbean, and the Middle East*, ed. Cheryl Johnson-Odim and Margaret Strobel (Bloomington, Ind.: Organization of American Historians, 1988), p. 41.

4. For discussion of extensive women's dealings in urban real estate, see Ronald Jennings, "Women in Early 17th-Century Ottoman Judicial Records—the Shari'a Court of Anatolian Kayseri," *Journal of the Social and Economic History of the Orient* 18, Part 1 (1975): 53–114; Abraham Marcus, *The Middle East on the Eve of Modernity, Aleppo in the Eighteenth Century* (Cambridge, England: Cambridge University Press, 1989), chap. 5; and Judith E. Tucker, *Women in Nineteenth Century Egypt*, Cambridge, England: Cambridge University Press, 1985), chap. 2.

5. Whenever scholars have looked at the records of the actual transactions of the Islamic court system, they have been struck by the high level of female activity in the courts. In Cairo, Jerusalem, and Damascus, for example, poorer women came on their own to settle matters involving disputes and small pieces of property; richer women, for the sake of propriety, commonly sent designated agents to transact their more substantial business.

6. For details of claims often pressed by peasant women, see Tucker, *Women in Nineteenth-Century Egypt*, chap. 1.

7. Mary Wortley Montagu, *Letters from the Levant* (New York, Arno Press, 1971), p. 197.

8. Margot Badran and Miriam Cook, eds., *Opening the Gates: A Century of Arab Feminist Writing* (Bloomington: Indiana University Press, 1990), p. 234.

9. Barbara Stowasser, "Women's Issues in Modern Islamic Thought," in *Women in Arab Society: Old Boundaries, New Frontiers*, ed. J. Tucker (Bloomington: Indiana University Press, 1993).

10. For more information on women in the professions in Egypt and Kuwait, see Kathleen Howard-Merriam, "Women, Education, and the Professions in Egypt," *Comparative Education Review* 23 (1979): 256–70; and Lubna al-Kazi, "The Transitory Role of Kuwaiti Women in the Development Process," paper presented at the Center for Contemporary Arab Studies Annual Symposium, Georgetown University, April 1986. For a general reference on professional women, see Nadia Hijab, *Womanpower* (Cambridge, England: Cambridge University Press, 1988).

11. Both Susan Davis, *Patience and Power: Women's Lives in a Moroccan Village* (Cambridge, Mass.: Schenkman, 1983), and Andrea Rugh, "Women and Work: Strategies and Choices in a Lower-Class Quarter of Cairo," in *Women in the Muslim World*, ed. Lois Beck and Nikki Keddie (Cambridge, Mass.: Harvard University Press, 1978) found such cultural inhibitions.

12. See the collections of oral histories done by Nayra Atiya, *Khul-Khaal: Five Egyptian Women Tell Their Stories* (Syracuse: Syracuse University Press, 1982), and

Fatima Mernissi, *Doing Daily Battle: Interviews with Moroccan Women* (New Brunswick, N.J.: Rutgers University Press, 1989), and Erika Friedl, *Women of Den Koh: Lives in an Iranian Village* (Washington, D.C.: Smithsonian Institution Press, 1989).

BIBLIOGRAPHY

Ahmed, Leila. "Women and the Advent of Islam." *Signs* 11, no. 1 (Summer 1986): 665–91.

———. *Women and Gender in Islam: Historical Roots of a Modern Debate*. New Haven: Yale University Press, 1992.

Atiya, Nayra. *Khul-Khaal: Five Egyptian Women Tell Their Stories*. Syracuse: Syracuse University Press, 1982.

Badran, Margot, and Miriam Cooke, eds. *Opening the Gates. A Century of Arab Feminist Writing*. Bloomington: Indiana University Press, 1990.

Cole, Juan Ricardo. "Feminism, Class, and Islam in Turn-off-the-Century Egypt." *International Journal of Middle Eastern Studies*, 13 (1981): 394–407.

Davis, Fanny. *The Ottoman Lady: A Social History from 1718 to 1918*. Westport, Conn.: Greenwood Press, 1986.

Davis, Susan Schaeffer. *Patience and Power: Women's Lives in a Moroccan Village*. Cambridge, Mass.: Schenkman, 1983.

Eaton, Richard M. *Islamic History as Global History*. Washington, D.C.: American Historical Association, 1990.

al-Faruqi, Lamya'. *Women, Muslim Society, and Islam*. Indianapolis: American Trust Publications, 1988.

Friedl, Erika. *Women of Deh Koh: Lives in an Iranian Village*. Washington, D.C.: Smithsonian Institution Press, 1989.

Goitein, S. D. *A Mediterranean Society*. 3 vols. Berkeley and Los Angeles: University of California Press, 1967–78.

Gordon, Lucie Duff. *Letters from Egypt*. London: Virago, 1983.

Gran, Judith. "Impact of the World Market on Egyptian Women." *MERIP Reports* 58 (1977): 3–7.

El Guindi, Fadwa. "Veiled Activism: Egyptian Women in the Contemporary Islamic Movement." *Mediterranean Peoples* 22/23 (1983): 79–89.

Hatem, Mervat. "Towards the Development of Post-Islamicist and Post-Modernist Feminist Discourses in the Middle East." In *Arab Women: Old Boundaries, New Frontiers*, ed. J. Tucker. Bloomington: Indiana University Press, 1993.

Hijab, Nadia. *Womanpower*. Cambridge, England: Cambridge University Press, 1988.

Howard-Merriam, Kathleen. "Women, Education, and the Professions in Egypt." *Comparative Education Review* 23 (1979): 256–70.

Kandiyoti, Deniz. "Islam and Patriarchy: A Comparative Perspective." In *Women in Middle Eastern History*, ed. Beth Baron and Nikki Keddie, 23–42. New Haven: Yale University Press, 1991.

———. "Sex Roles and Social Change: A Comparative Study of Turkey's Women." *Signs: Journal of Women and Culture in Society* 3, no. 1 (1977): 57–73.

al-Kazi, Lubna Ahmad. "The Transitory Role of Kuwaiti Women in the Development Process." Paper presented at the Center for Contemporary Arab Studies (CCAS) Annual Symposium, Georgetown University, April 1986.

Macleod, Arlene Elowe. *Accommodating Protest. Working Women, the New Veil, and Change in Cairo.* New York: Columbia University Press, 1991.

Marcus, Abraham. *The Middle East on the Eve of Modernity. Aleppo in the Eighteenth Century.* Cambridge, England: Cambridge University Press, 1989.

Meriwether, Margaret. "Women and Work in Nineteenth Century Syria: The Case of Aleppo." In *Arab Women: Old Boundaries, New Frontiers*, ed. J. Tucker. Bloomington: Indiana University Press, 1993.

Mernissi, Fatima. *Beyond the Veil: Male–Female Dynamics in a Modern Muslim Society.* Cambridge, Mass.: Schenkman, 1975.

———. *Doing Daily Battle. Interviews with Moroccan Women.* New Brunswick, N.J.: Rutgers University Press, 1989.

———. "Women and the Impact of Capitalist Development in Morocco. Part II." *Feminist Issues* 3, no. 1 (1983): 61–112.

Montagu, Mary Wortley. *Letters from the Levant during the Embassy to Constantinople, 1716–18.* New York: Arno Press, 1971.

Musallam, Basim. *Sex and Society in Islam.* Cambridge, England: Cambridge University Press, 1983.

Nashat, Guity. "Women in the Middle East, 8000 B.C.–A.D. 1800." In *Restoring Women to History. Teaching Packets for Integrating Women's History into Courses on Africa, Asia, Latin America, the Caribbean, and the Middle East*, ed. Cheryl Johnson-Odim and Margaret Strobel. Bloomington, Ind.: Organization of American Historians, 1988.

Rogers, Mary Eliza. *Domestic Life in Palestine.* London: Kegan Paul International, 1989.

Rugh, Andrea. "Women and Work: Strategies and Choices in a Lower-Class Quarter of Cairo." In *Women and the Family in the Middle East. New Voices of Change*, ed. Elizabeth Warnock Fernea, 273–88. Austin: University of Texas Press. 1985.

Sabbah, Fatna. *Women in the Muslim Unconsciousness.* Trans. Mary Jo Lakeland. New York: Pergamon Press, 1984.

Said, Edward. *Orientalism.* New York: Pantheon Books, 1978.

Sayigh, Rosemary. "Roles and Functions of Arab Women." *Arab Studies Quarterly* 3, no. 3 (1981): 258–74.

Stowasser, Barbara. "Women's Issues in Modern Islamic Thought." In *Arab Women: Old Boundaries, New Frontiers*, ed. J. Tucker. Bloomington: Indiana University Press, 1993.

Tucker, Judith E. *Women in Nineteenth-Century Egypt.* Cambridge, England: Cambridge University Press, 1985.

The World System
in the Thirteenth Century:
Dead-End or Precursor?

JANET LIPPMAN ABU-LUGHOD

Most Western historians writing about the rise of the West have treated that development as if it were independent of the West's relations to other high cultures. At first, thinking about this, I attributed it to ethnocentrism, pure and simple. But then I was struck by something else: Virtually all Western scholars, and especially those who had taken a global perspective on the "modern" world, began their histories in about A. D. 1400— just when both East and West were at their low ebb and when the organizational system that had existed prior to this time had broken down. By selecting this particular point to start their narratives, they could not help but write a similar plot, one in which the West "rose," apparently out of nowhere.

What would happen to the narrative if one started a little earlier?[1] Even more important, what would happen to the theoretical assumption that the peculiar form of Western capitalism, as it developed in sixteenth-century western Europe, was a necessary and (almost) sufficient cause of Western hegemony? What if one looked at the system *before* European hegemony and if one looked at the organization of capital accumulation, "industrial" production, trade and distribution in comparative perspective? If one found wide variation among earlier economic organizations, all of which had yielded economic vitality and dynamism, then it might not be legitimate to attribute Europe's newly gained hegemony to "capitalism" in the unique form it took in Europe. It might be necessary, instead, to test an alternative hypothesis: that Europe's rise was substantially assisted by what it learned from other, more advanced cultures—at least until Europe overtook and subdued them.

A Global History of the Thirteenth Century

It was to explore such questions that I began to study the economic organization of the world in the thirteenth century. At the start, I had no intention of writing a book, but only of satisfying my curiosity over this puzzle. In the course of my five years of research, however, I found no single book, or even several books combined, that gave me a "global" picture of how international trade was organized at that time. Interestingly enough the separate histories I did find all hinted, usually in passing, at the manifold connections each place maintained with trading partners much farther afield. I became preoccupied with reconstructing those connections.[2]

The basic conclusion I reached[3] was that there had existed, prior to the West's rise to preeminence in the sixteenth century, a complex and prosperous predecessor—a system of world trade and even "cultural" exchange that, at its peak toward the end of the thirteenth century, was integrating (if only at high points of an archipelago of towns) a very large number of advanced societies stretching between the extremes of northwestern Europe and China. Indeed, the century between A.D. 1250 and 1350 clearly seemed to constitute a crucial turning point in world history, a moment when the balance between East and West could have tipped in either direction. In terms of space, the Middle East heartland that linked the eastern Mediterranean with the Indian Ocean constituted a geographic fulcrum on which East and West were then roughly balanced.

Thus, at that time, one certainly could not have predicted the outcome of any contest between East and West. There seemed no *historical necessity* that shifted the system in favor of the West, nor was there any historical necessity that would have prevented cultures in the eastern regions from becoming progenitors of a "modern" world system. This thesis seemed at least as compelling to me as its opposite.

True, the "modern" world system that *might* have developed, had the East remained dominant, would probably have had different institutions and organization than the historically specific version that developed under European hegemony. But there is no reason to believe that, had the West not "risen," the world under different leadership would have remained stagnant.

Therefore, it seemed crucial to gain an understanding of the years between A.D. 1250 and 1350.[4] During that period, an international trade economy climaxed in the regions between northwestern Europe and China, yielding prosperity and artistic achievements in many of the places that were newly integrated.

This trading economy involved merchants and producers in an extensive (worldwide) if narrow network of exchange. Primary products, including but not confined to specialty agricultural items, mostly spices, constituted a significant proportion of all items traded, but over shorter distances in particular, manufactured goods were surprisingly central to the system. In fact, trade probably could not have been sustained over long distances without including manufactured goods such as textiles and weapons. The production of primary and manufactured goods was not only sufficient to meet local needs but, beyond that, the needs of export as well.

Moreover, long-distance trade involved a wide variety of merchant communities at various points along the routes, because distances, as measured by time, were calculated in weeks and months at best, and it took years to traverse the entire circuit. The merchants who handled successive transactions did not necessarily speak the same languages, nor were their local currencies the same. Yet goods were transferred, prices set, exchange rates agreed on, contracts entered into, credit extended, partnerships formed, and, obviously, records kept and agreements honored.

The scale of these exchanges was not very large, and the proportion of population and even production involved in international exchange constituted only a very small fraction of the total productivity of the societies. Relatively speaking, however, the scale of the system in the later Middle Ages was not substantially below that in the "early modern age" (i.e., after 1600), nor was the technology of production inferior to that of the later period. No great technological breakthroughs distinguish the late medieval from the early modern period.

The book that resulted from my research, *Before European Hegemony*, describes the system of world trade circa A.D. 1300, demonstrating how and to what extent the world was linked into this common commercial network of production and exchange. Since such production and exchange were relatively unimportant to the subsistence economies of all participating regions, I did not have to defend an unrealistic vision of a tightly entailed international system of interdependence. Clearly, this was not the case. But it was also true in the sixteenth century. Thus, if it is possible to argue that a world system began in that later century, it is equally plausible to acknowledge that it existed three hundred years earlier.

It is important to recognize that *no system* is fully global in the sense that all parts articulate evenly with one another, regardless of whether the role they play is central or peripheral. Even today, the world, more globally integrated than ever before in history, is broken up into important subspheres or subsystems—such as the Middle Eastern and North African system, the North Atlantic system, the Pacific Basin or Rim system, the eastern European bloc (functionally persisting, even though its socialist orientation has crumbled), and China, which is still a system unto itself. And within each of these blocs, certain major cities play key nodal roles, dominating the regions around them and often having more intense interactions with nodal centers in other systems than with their own peripheries.

In the thirteenth century, also, there were subsystems (defined by language, religion and empire, and measurable by relative transactions) dominated by imperial or core cities, as well as mediated by essentially hinterland-less trading enclaves. Their interactions with one another, although hardly as intense as today's, defined the contours of the larger system. Instead of airlines, these cities were bound together by sealanes, rivers, and great overland caravan routes, some of which had been in use since antiquity. Ports and oases served the same functions as do air terminals today, bringing diverse goods and people together from long distances.

Given the primitive technologies of transport that existed during the early period, however, few nodes located at opposite ends of the system could do business directly with one another. Journeys were broken down into much smaller geographic segments, with central places between flanking trading circuits serving as "break-in-bulk" exchanges for goods destined for more distant markets. Nor was the world the "global village" of today, sharing common consumer goals and assembly-line work in a vast international division of labor. The subsystems of the thirteenth century were much more self-sufficient than those of today and therefore less vitally dependent on one another for common survival. Nevertheless, what is remarkable is that, despite the hardships and handicaps that long-distance trade then entailed, so much of it went on.

An analysis of the movements of such trade leads us to distinguish, for analytical purposes, three very large circuits. The first was a western European one that dominated the Atlantic coast and many parts of the Mediterranean. The second was a Middle Eastern one that dominated both the land bridge along the Central Asian steppes and the sea bridge, with a short intervening overland route, between the eastern Mediterranean and the Indian Ocean. And finally, the third was the Far Eastern circuit of trade that connected the Indian subcontinent with Southeast Asia and China beyond. At that time, the strongest centers and circuits were located in the Middle East and Asia. In contrast, the European circuit was an upstart newcomer that for several early centuries was only tangentially and weakly linked to the core of the world system as it had developed between the eighth and eleventh centuries.

These three major circuits were, in turn, organized into some eight interlinked subsystems, within which smaller trading circuits and subcultural and political systems seemed to exist. Map 1 shows a rough delimitation of those eight subsystems. In the section that follows, we take up each of these circuits and subsystems in turn, but our emphasis is on how they connected with one another.

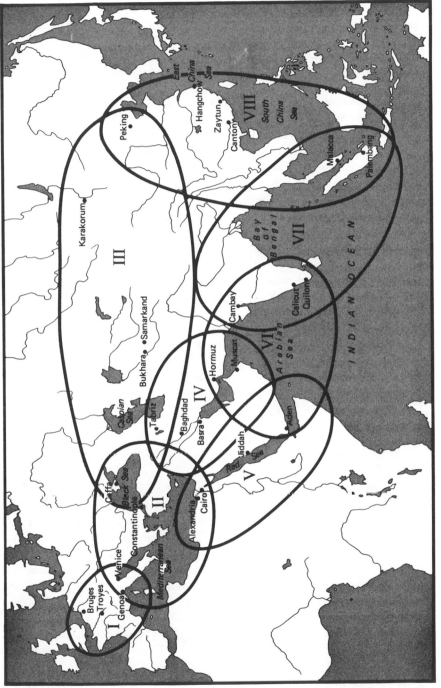

MAP 1.   The eight circuits of the thirteenth-century world system. From Janet Abu-Lughod, *Before European Hegemony: The World System A.D. 1250–1350*. Copyright © 1989 by Oxford University Press, Inc. Reprinted by permission.

THE EUROPEAN CIRCUIT

By the middle of the thirteenth century, three European nodes were forming into a single circuit of exchange. The counties of Champagne and Brie in east-central France hosted the rotating fairs of Champagne, which took place sequentially in four towns: the trading and production centers of Troyes and Provins and the smaller market towns of Bar-sur-Aube and Lagny. A second nodal zone was the textile-producing region of Flanders, where the city of Bruges became the most important commercial and financial capital and nearby Ghent served as the chief industrial town. The third node was in Italy, with the two most international trading ports located on opposite sides of the peninsula: Genoa facing westward and Venice facing east.

The growth of this European circuit was causally linked to the Crusades, which, from the end of the eleventh century, had put western Europe into more intimate contact with the Middle East and which had stimulated the demand for goods available only in the East. Such stimulation in demand, in turn, generated heightened productivity on the European continent—to manufacture goods that could be exchanged for the spices and cotton and silk textiles from the East.

To reconstruct this process, it is important to establish a benchmark for growth. In the second century A.D. the Roman Empire covered a vast territory that included all regions abutting the Mediterranean Sea. The empire extended northward to encompass England and all of western Europe except Germany, eastward to encompass Greece, Anatolia, and the Fertile Crescent, and southward across the entire stretch of littoral North Africa. Rome's southern and eastern peripheral areas were in contact, via overland and sea routes, with sizable portions of the rest of the "Old World" as far away as India and, indirectly, even China. By that time, what might be called the first nascent world system had come into existence, although it did not survive the "fall of Rome."

Internal weakening of the overextended Roman Empire eventually made it possible for Germanic tribes occupying zones north and east of the Italian core—tribes that had formerly been blocked at the frontiers—to break through the Roman lines. The first waves of invasion occurred in the third century, but were soon spent; successive ones were not so easily repelled. Throughout the fifth century a series of more successful incursions culminated in the collapse of unified rule and the fragmentation of the western domains among the Gauls, Vandals, Visigoths, and, later, Lombards.

After the fall of the Roman Empire, much of western Europe underwent significant regression, initiating a period that in Western historiography is referred to as the Dark Ages.[5] Although it is true that much of the subcontinent's economic base retracted to highly localized subsistence activities, it is important to stress that in southern Europe this did not occur. Much of the Iberian Peninsula was under Muslim rule and its economy was thus inherently linked not to Europe's but to that of the thriving Islamic world. And at least parts of Italy, most particularly the port city-state of Venice, continued to prosper because it served as an outpost for the undefeated eastern Roman Empire, Venice's ally in Constantinople.

It is important to remember that the ninth century, when northwestern Europe was just beginning to emerge from its dark ages, was a civilizational highpoint both in the Middle East (under Abbasid rule) and in China (under the Tang Dynasty). These two central powers were establishing trade links with one another via the Persian Gulf–Indian Ocean route, a connection advantageous to both. (This is the time of Sindbad the Sailor).[6] The overthrown Umayyads had relocated to Iberia and were united there with powerful North African dynasties. The tenth and eleventh centuries in both Asia and the Middle East were periods of technological advance[7] and increasingly sophisticated business and credit practices.[8] Most of the "social" inventions that the Italians were to use so effectively, when they later provided the institutional "glue" that integrated the European subsystem, they learned from their Middle Eastern counterparts.

Western Europe was decisively drawn into the preexisting world system through the Crusades, the first of which took place at the end of the eleventh century. It was only after this first incursion that the fairs of Champagne began to expand as the central meeting place for Italian merchants, who imported Eastern goods via the Levant, and Flemish merchants, who marketed the woolen textiles that Europe exchanged for the silks and spices of the Orient.[9] Flemish textile production was greatly stimulated by the Orient's expanding demand for their high-quality cloth. With later Crusades, European colonies were established in the Levant, where merchants handled the import trade on the spot.

The fairs of Champagne had a relatively brief period of prominence as the middleman-exchange center between Flemish textile producers and Italian merchants. By the end of the thirteenth century, Genoese ships were exiting the Strait of Gibraltar and sailing up the Atlantic coast directly to Bruges; this resulted in relocating the "international" market from Champagne to that city. The Venetians were forced to follow suit, although they never became as prominent in Bruges as the Genoese or the Piedmont Italians. This bypassing of France's central massif, combined with the subsumption of the counties of Brie and Champagne under the French monarchy in 1285,[10] spelled the decline of the fairs. Bruges's prominence, however, was short-lived. Gradually, the city's harbors, despite their successive relocation outward, silted up until deep-draft vessels could no longer come directly into port. The Italians then moved their operations, and along with them the associated financial markets, to the better harbor at Antwerp.

During all this time, the Italians were increasing their control over the production and distribution of western European goods because it was their ships that came to control the shipping lanes in the Mediterranean. The Arabs withdrew from that sea, ceding to Pisan, Genoese, and eventually even more to Venetian galleys the task of ferrying goods back and forth between western Europe and the cores of the world system, still focused farther east.[11]

THE MIDDLE EASTERN CIRCUIT

European ships made three landfalls in the Middle East bridge to the Far East. The one on the north passed Constantinople through to the Black Sea. From ports toward the eastern end of the Black Sea, goods were transferred to the overland caravan route to China. The one at midpoint was on the coast of Palestine, from which caravans set out to Baghdad and thence to the head of the Persian Gulf for the long sea journey or joined the southern caravan route across Central Asia. The one on the south was at the Egyptian port of Alexandria, from which connections were then made via Cairo to the Red Sea and, from there, farther eastward through the Arabian Sea and Indian Ocean.

The Genoese and Venetians fought each other for dominance in the Mediterranean sealanes (their only rival, Pisa, was eliminated fairly early) and, by the thirteenth century, had reached some sort of modus vivendi in which Genoa gained hegemony over the northern route while Venice consolidated its virtually monopolistic relations with the Mamluks of Egypt and their Karimi merchants. Both lost out in the Levant when Saladin and later the Mamluk sultan Baybars drove them successively from the Crusader kingdoms Europeans had implanted in Palestine.

These landfalls were the anchors of the three Middle Eastern subsystems that connected the Levant with the Far East. The northern route crossed the Central Asian steppes and deserts that had been newly unified under Genghis Khan and his confederation of Mongol and Tatar tribes. This unification permitted the trading explorations of such notables as Marco Polo and his uncles in the latter part of the thirteenth century and the establishment of small colonies of Genoese and other Italian merchants in Beijing and other Chinese cities (by then under the Yuan, or Mongol, Dynasty). And it was the greater safety and stability of this area that facilitated the marked expansion of overland trade.

The routes through Arab lands were more protected from European incursions. At Palestine, European merchants met the caravans coming from Central Asia or from the Persian Gulf, but seldom followed them eastward on the long sea journey to India, the Malay Peninsula, or China. And at Egypt the European merchants were stopped entirely. They were not permitted to cross from the Nile to the Red Sea and thus had to exchange with local Karimi (wholesale) merchants, under government supervision, all the goods they brought from Europe or other parts of the Mediterranean for the spices, textiles, and other goods they sought to buy from the East. Toward the end of the period in question, the connection between Venice and Egypt strengthened until it virtually monopolized the exchange between the West and India and parts east.

THE ASIAN SYSTEM VIA THE INDIAN OCEAN

The Indian Ocean trade, which long predated Europe's interest and persisted well beyond the European explorers' "discovery" of the New World as an unintended by-product of their search for an alternative route to India, was itself subdivided into three circuits, only one of which overlapped with the southern Middle East subsystems that connected the Red Sea and Persian Gulf with landfalls on the western coast of India. The ports at Gujarat (near current-day Bombay) and on the Malabar or pepper coast to the south contained merchant colonies of Muslims[12] from the Middle East who served as intermediaries and who also spread their religion and business practices wherever they went.

Muslim Arab and Persian merchants were considerably less visible in the second circuit of the Indian Ocean trade, which was anchored on the Coromandel coast on India's eastern side. There, indigenous Indian merchants intermediated much of the sea trade that moved eastward through the Straits of Malacca and Sunda (between the Malay Peninsula and present-day Sumatra and Java) to Chinese ports in the third circuit. Although Persian and Arab ships also participated in this circuit, at that time Europeans had no ships in either the Indian Ocean or the South China Sea. The few Europeans (including missionaries and a small number of traders) who ventured into these regions traveled on Asian ships. It was not until Vasco da Gama's successful circumnavigation of Africa in 1498 that European vessels entered the Indian Ocean arena, and it was not until after the Portuguese men-of-war had destroyed the small Egyptian and Indian fleet defending the Arabian Sea in 1516 that Europeans began to control, although not supplant, the large Asian merchant marine.

In that Asian circuit, the Strait of Malacca (and as a very secondary alternative, the Strait of Sunda between southern Sumatra and Java) was absolutely crucial. All ships traveling between India and China had to pass through the "gullet" of narrow sea that separated Sumatra from the Malay Peninsula. Tomé Pires, the astute Portuguese merchant and author who traveled in the area during the first half of the sixteenth century, acknowledged the undisputed strategic significance of Malacca to world trade, noting that "whoever is lord of Malacca has his hands on the throat of Venice" and that "if Cambay [the port of Gujarat] were cut off from trading with Malacca, it could not live." [13] His phrases were apt. Malacca, the chief entrepôt on the strait after the fall of Srivijaya, [14] served, like the fairs of Champagne, as the place where foreign merchants coming from different directions met to exchange goods, credit, and currencies.

But whereas the Champagne fairs owed their comparative advantage chiefly to political causes, the shifting ports on the strait (of which Singapore is simply the most recent manifestation) owed theirs to the weather. In the days of sailing ships, prevailing winds and monsoon seasons shaped the routes and timing of international trade. Because monsoon winds reversed at the Strait of Malacca, long layovers were required for boats traveling in both directions. Permanent colonies of merchants drawn from points throughout the Asian circuit coexisted in Malacca, giving to this port a cosmopolitan quality far beyond what local resources and institutions could have generated.

If the coasts of India were magnets because on them debouched the products of a rich and partially industrialized [15] subcontinent, and the Strait of Malacca was a magnet because sailors had no other options, China was a magnet par excellence in itself and for all. Through China, the overland subsystem that connected it to the Black Sea and the eastern sea subsystem that connected it to the Strait region and beyond were joined together in an all-important loop.

It is very significant that the entire world system of the thirteenth century functioned smoothly and to the benefit of all players when the connecting link through China operated well. It is perhaps of even greater significance that, as I later argue, the breaking up of the world system in the mid-fourteenth century was in large part due to the wedge driven between China and Central Asia by the Ming Rebellion (but more of this later).

China was by far the most developed civilization in the world and the world's leading technological and naval power until the late fifteenth century. [16] It did not merely sit complacently as (in its view) the "Middle Kingdom" of the universe, but actively conducted both "tribute" and "merchant" trade throughout its own waters and in the Indian Ocean and, periodically, up through the Persian Gulf. China had the world's largest and most seaworthy fleet, [17] capable of withstanding any attack and able to terrorize opponents into submission with flame-throwing weapons and gunpowder-driven missiles that were the equivalent of later European cannons.

Such naval power did not often have to be invoked, however, since over the centuries the trading nations of the Indian Ocean had evolved a remarkably tolerant system of coexistence, unlike the rivalries that plagued the Mediterranean in the post-Roman era. K. N. Chaudhuri has drawn a detailed and graphic image of that coexistence in his seminal books on the Indian Ocean.[18] Although piracy was not unknown in Eastern waters, it did not lead, as in the Mediterranean, to a war of all against all, nor was it suppressed by a single thalassocracy, a naval power capable of eliminating all resistance. Instead, it was contained within the interstices of a larger collaboration in which goods and merchants from many places were intermingled on each other's ships and where unwritten rules of reciprocity assured general compliance. This system was not decisively challenged until the sixteenth century, when Portuguese men-of-war violated all the rules of the game by burning or boarding ships, confiscating cargo, and imposing their system of passes[19] on the numerous indigenous but unarmed merchant fleets of the area.

The Fate of the Thirteenth-Century World System

Now that we have described the complex world system that existed before Europe's rise to hegemony, we are left with two basic puzzles. The first is why the thirteenth-century world system did not simply persist and continue to grow? The second is why the West "rose" when it did? Let us try to answer these questions.

Given the high level of sophistication reached and the widespread character of the contacts among the various participants in the thirteenth-century world system, it is natural to ask why it did not expand even farther and grow increasingly prosperous. After all, one of the laws of motion states that things in motion tend to remain in motion, if only because of the power of inertia, and this principle may also operate in history. (It is not until a trend is reversed that historians feel impelled to explain what happened!)

Yet we know that during the fifteenth century almost all parts of the then-known world experienced a deep recession. By then, the "state of the world" was at a much lower level than it had reached in the early fourteenth century. During the depression of the fifteenth century, the absolute level of intersocietal trade dropped, currencies were universally debased (a sure sign of decreased wealth and overall productivity), and the arts and crafts were degraded. It is natural to look in the fourteenth century for clues to this unexpected reversal of fortune.

Such clues are not hard to find. By the third and fourth decades of the fourteenth century, one finds evidence of problems in Europe: bank failures in Italy and the cessation of port expansions in both Genoa and Venice; scattered crop failures throughout northwestern Europe; labor unrest in Flanders that was not unrelated to the decline in the quality of Flemish cloth, once Spanish wool had to be substituted for the higher-quality English wool hitherto used in production; and local wars and increased costs of protection, as "law and order" began to break down. Signs of weakness were also to be seen at various points in the Middle Eastern and Asian systems.

Whether these were normal fluctuations that historians might have overlooked if the system had regained prosperity sooner, or whether they were symptoms of some larger endemic problems, cannot be determined from this distance in time. But certainly there were already weaknesses when catastrophe struck at midcentury.

Catastrophe came in the form of an epidemic so deadly and widespread that it has been singled out from all the regularly recurring epidemics of premodern times as the Black Death. It is obviously impossible to reconstruct the exact causes and course of this epidemic or even to tell whether plague outbreaks reported in the East had exactly the same medical descriptions as those in the West. But William McNeill, in his *Plagues and People*,[20] has attempted to reason backward from medical information today, and to combine this with known, but far from complete, "facts" from the earlier period.

He concludes that the bubonic plague probably broke out first in the 1320s in a Mongol-patroled area near the Himalayas and that infectious fleas were probably carried in the saddlebags of fast-moving horsemen into south-central China. Certainly, he presents evidence, culled from Chinese yearly chronicles, that from about 1320 on, outbreaks of epidemics were reported in a series of Chinese provinces around the zone of initial infection. From China proper, McNeill contends, infected fleas were diffused to the northern steppes of Central Asia, where they attached themselves to new hosts, the burrowing rats of the plains. Since the populations exposed to the plague had little or no natural immunities to this new disease, mortalities were extremely high, especially, it would seem, among the mobile Mongol soldiers.

From that point on, the story becomes clearer, and we can actually track the spread of the disease along the well-established paths of trade by plotting the dates at which the plague was first reported in various places. Map 2, which superimposes recorded plague dates on the major trade routes of the thirteenth century, does just this. The map demonstrates a supremely ironical twist: The strengths of the system were, indeed, its undoing. Host rats infiltrated the Genoese port of Caffa on the Black Sea, probably from the Mongol forces that were besieging the Italians there. The rats then boarded ships that were returning to the Mediterranean, leaving plague-infected fleas at each of their ports of call. By midcentury, the major centers of trade had all experienced very heavy die-offs, almost proportional to their importance.[21]

Wherever it struck, the plague had long-lasting effects, since outbreaks recurred throughout the rest of the century. But the effects on, and of, depopulation were not at all uniform. The plague stirred the pot of social change, but not in the same way everywhere. First, places that were off the path of international trade suffered lower casualties than those that were central to the trade. England and Scandinavia, for example, had lower proportional mortalities than China, Egypt, or Italy. Second, the mortality rates were higher in cities than in the countryside. These differential mortalities to some extent altered the future "life chances" of various countries and the relative "bargaining power" of peasants versus city folk.

The disturbance to local power structures also permitted political changes that might not have occurred in the absence of the plague, although the effects were not uniform. In Europe, it is acknowledged that the ensuing labor shortage strengthened the hands of workers and yeomen and decisively ended the remnants of serfdom. In contrast, similar die-offs in Egypt had no such effect; there was a change in regimes at the top, but the new set of Mamluk rulers never reduced their pressures on the peasants. In China, however, the political effects were dramatic and had wide-reaching consequences.

The Ming Rebellion, accomplished by 1368, deposed the Yuan Dynasty that had been established after the time of Mongol conquest and replaced it by an indigenous Chinese dynasty. I suspect that the timing was not unrelated to the high plague casualties among the "foreign" military troops that enforced Yuan rule. While the results may have been favorable for Chinese "home rule" and autonomy, they were less advantageous to the world system, since the success of the rebellion once again split off China from Central Asia. Thomas Barfield argues that throughout history there was constant tension along the shifting frontier between the tribal groups of Central Asia and the settled population of China. Only once were the two regions unified politically, and that was in the thirteenth century and first half of the fourteenth century, when China was ruled by the Mongols.[22]

I am tempted to conclude that the thirteenth-century world system had benefited greatly from this union, since it facilitated the free flow of trade in a circuit completed by the Chinese "loop." When this connection broke down, as it did after the Ming Rebellion in the late fourteenth century, its lapse further undermined the viability of the world system as it had previously been organized.

The change in the Chinese regime had one other consequence of great significance: the collapse of the Chinese navy,[23] although that did not occur decisively until more than fifty years later. Chinese attitudes toward trade and the importance of maintaining naval strength were subjects of heated debate in the new dynasty. Some within the palace favored withdrawal from the world system to mend conditions internally. Others

MAP 2. The congruence between trade routes and the spread of the Black Death circa 1350. From Janet Abu-Lughod, *Before European Hegemony: The World System A.D. 1250–1350.* Copyright © by Oxford University Press, Inc. Reprinted by permission.

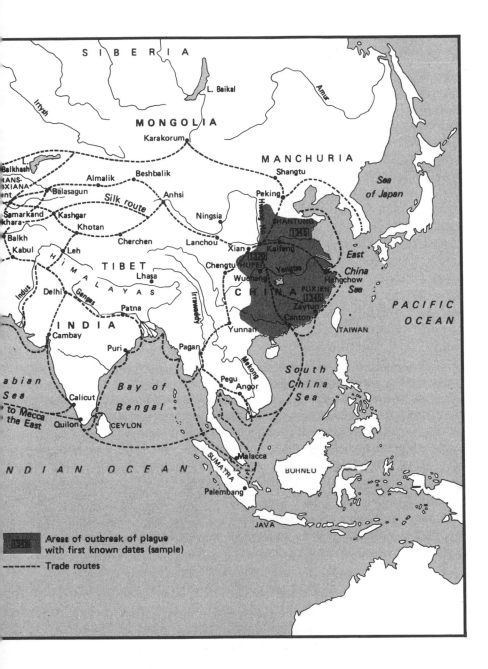

Areas of outbreak of plague
with first known dates (sample)

------ Trade routes

stressed the importance of maintaining an appearance of strength in the outside world. Among the latter was the admiral of the fleet, Cheng Ho, who from the early 1400s headed several expeditions of Chinese "treasure ships" (in convoys containing sixty or more vessels) that paraded through the Indian Ocean, stopping at all important ports.[24]

But these displays were eventually halted in the 1430s. After a few naval skirmishes had been lost, palace policy switched to Cheng Ho's opponents. Although the reasons for this reversal of policy remain shrouded in mystery and enigma, and scholars are far from agreeing on an explanation, the results were clear and disastrous for the prospects of continued Asian independence. The ships were ordered into port and deactivated. Within five years, according to Lo's careful research (cited earlier), the wooden ships had rotted and could not be easily repaired.

The significance of the Chinese withdrawal from the sea cannot be overestimated. The disappearance from the Indian Ocean and South China Sea of the only large and armed Asian navy left that vast expanse defenseless. When the Portuguese men-of-war, following the new pathway opened around the tip of Africa by Vasco da Gama's exploratory journey, finally breached the zone in the early decades of the sixteenth century and violated the "rules of the game" of mutual tolerance that had prevailed in that region for a thousand years, there was no one to stop them.

The rest is, as they say, history. The Portuguese proceeded to impose a harsh system of "passes" to extract protection fees from the unarmed Arab and Indian merchant ships that still carried the trade. Through their military arms, the Portuguese initiated the process of imposing a system of European hegemony over regions that had formerly been wealthy and vital. Successive European naval powers, the Dutch and then the British, followed along paths opened by the Portuguese to subjugate vast portions of the Indian Ocean arena and to establish their own plantations and factories to produce the spices and textiles they had long sought from the East.

It should come as no surprise that Holland and England eventually became the new cores of the "modern" world system. My argument, put simply, is that the "fall of the East" preceded the "rise of the West" and opened up a window of opportunity that would not have existed had matters gone differently.

The second question we must address is whether the later success of western Europe in a newly reorganizing world system was exclusively caused by the particular form of capitalism that developed there, or whether capitalism, under the protection of militarily powerful and more centralized nation-states, was able to take advantage of the windows of opportunity created not only by the collapse of the East but by the chance to exploit the "free resources" available in the New World? There is no way to resolve this controversy, and many historians and social thinkers, beginning with Karl Marx and Max Weber, have expended enormous effort in their attempts to add voices to the ongoing debate.

In what follows I present my own position and indicate in what ways my understanding of the thirteenth-century world system has contributed to that position. I do not believe that the Western invention of a particular variation of capitalism predetermined European hegemony from the sixteenth century on. The fact that a highly sophisticated world system—one that was equally as advanced both in economic and social "technologies"—predated the "modern" one casts doubt on the unique contributions of European capitalism. Because no uniformity prevailed with respect to culture, religion, or economic institutional arrangements in that earlier system, it is very difficult to accept a purely "cultural" explanation for Europe's later dominance. No particular culture seems to have had a monopoly over either technological or social inventiveness. Neither a unique syndrome of psychology nor a special economic form of organizing production and exchange (*pace* Marx) nor any particular set of religious beliefs or values (*pace* Weber) was needed to succeed in the thirteenth century. The fact that the West "won" in the sixteenth century, whereas the earlier system aborted, cannot be used to argue convincingly that *only* the institutions and culture of the West *could have succeeded.*

Indeed, what is noteworthy in the world system of the thirteenth century is that a wide variety of cultural systems coexisted and cooperated and that societies organized very differently from those in the West dominated the system. Christianity, Buddhism, Judaism, Confucianism, Islam, Zoroastrianism, and numerous other sects, often dismissed as pagan, all seem to have permitted and indeed facilitated lively commerce, production, exchange, risk taking, and the like. Similarly, a variety of economic systems coexisted in the thirteenth century—from "near" private capitalism, albeit supported by state power, to "near" state production, albeit assisted by private merchants. Moreover, these variations were not particularly congruent with either geographic region or religious domain. The organization of textile production in southeast India was not dissimilar from that in Flanders, whereas in China and Egypt larger-scale coordination was more typical. The state built boats for trade in both tiny Venice and vast China, whereas elsewhere (and even at different times in Genoa, China and Egypt) private vessels were commandeered when the state needed them.

Nor were the underlying bases for economic activities uniform. Participating in the world system of the thirteenth century were large agrarian societies such as India and China that covered subcontinents, in which industrial production was oriented mainly, although not exclusively, to processing agricultural raw materials. There were also small city-state ports such as Venice, Aden, Palembang, and Malacca, whose functions are best described as compradorial. In places as diverse as South India, Champagne, Samarkand, the Levant, and ports along the Persian Gulf, their importance was enhanced by their strategic location at points where flanking traders met. Other important places contained valued raw materials unavailable elsewhere (fine-quality wool in England, camphor in Sumatra, frankincense and myrrh on the Arabian peninsula, spices in the Indian archipelago, jewels in Ceylon, etc.) These resources did not account for the world system; they were products of it.

The economic vitality of these areas was the result, at least in part, of the system in which they participated. It is to be expected, then, that in the course of *any restructuring* of a world system, such as occurred in the sixteenth century, new places would rise to the fore. We have already suggested that part of that restructuring occurred in Asia and could be partially traced to a complex chain of consequences precipitated (but not "caused") by the Black Death. But, in the long run, the Europeans' ability to sail across the Atlantic must be judged even more important than their circumnavigation of Africa.

As we pass the five-hundredth anniversary of Columbus's voyage, it is important to recall its ultimate significance. It displaced the Mediterranean decisively from a core focus of trade, thus precipitating a long-term marginalization of the Middle East, reduced the relative indispensability of the Indian Ocean arena, and provided the nascent developing nations of western Europe with the gold and silver they needed, both to settle the long-standing balance-of-payments deficits with the East and to serve as the basis for a rapid accumulation of capital. This capital accumulation process, deriving "free resources" from conquered peripheries, eventually became the chief motor of European technological and social change.

While this story lies beyond the period covered in this essay, it is an appropriate point on which to conclude this section. Capitalism, in the form that took shape in Europe in the seventeenth and eighteenth centuries and, even more so, in the nineteenth, might not have "taken off" so dramatically had the shape of the world system not been transformed in the sixteenth century. That is why the study of the world system that preceded it is so important. It helps us to put the truly world-transforming developments of the sixteenth century in perspective and to give a more balanced account of the relationship between capitalism and the "rise of the West."

Historical Perspectives on the World[25]

Only recently have historians begun to take this more global view. Fernand Braudel's magnum opus, *Civilization & Capitalism, 15th–18th Century*, marked a major departure in historical writing. It signaled a shift from what might be called "world" history to a somewhat different approach that I call "global" history. That shift is captured especially aptly in the title of Braudel's third volume, *The Perspective of the World*.[26] Volume 1, *The Structures of Everyday Life*, is devoted primarily to the everyday life of Europeans. Volume 2, *The Wheels of Commerce*, begins to stretch out beyond Europe by recognizing the commercial connections whose profits sustained the European system. But Volume 3, in my opinion, constitutes the true breakthrough, in that its problematic shifts from a focus on disparate places (although not unconnected to other places) to a focus on the *linkages among* places and the systematic nature of those linkages. It is this that I call global, rather than world, history.

The difference between world and global histories is best grasped by contrasting Braudel's third volume with an earlier set of books that perhaps established the benchmark and model for world histories—Arnold Toynbee's ten volumes, collectively entitled *A Study of History*, published between 1947 and 1957.[27] Toynbee took as his unit of analysis an object called "civilizations" and proceeded to explore, in parallel fashion and separate volumes, the rise and fall of specific cultural-geographic entities sufficiently complex and advanced to be called civilizations. True, such civilizational histories were embedded within a comparative time frame (an enterprise most fully realized in the great Wall Chart, a diagram showing parallel chronologies of "history" for various parts of the world) and recognized the influences that "others"—antecedent in time or adjacent in space—had in shaping each individual civilization. But Toynbee's major project was to derive temporal patterns for the origin, growth, maturation, and decline of the various civilizational entities, thus laying bare certain common principles and processes of civilizational change. Such common principles were to be found by studying the parallels in the individual cases, from which might be deduced some intrinsic "laws" of evolution and devolution.[28] Thus, "world history" was constructed by placing into a mosaic of time and space the composite histories of its constituent parts.

To some extent, Philip Curtin's *Cross-Cultural Trade in World History*[29] followed in the Toynbeean tradition. Instead of trying to construct a global history—if only in one civilizational aspect, long-distance trade—Curtin sought commonalities and principles in that recurring phenomenon. But to study long-distance trade immediately required that special attention be paid to the linkages *among* entities; no longer could one focus attention primarily on the coherence and development of each entity in a relative vacuum. In this sense, Curtin stretched *toward* global history, even though the separate chapters in his book addressed different regional "subsystems" of trade and skipped from one historical period to another. He made no attempt, however, to link these systems together along a single chronological line.

Similarly, William McNeill's *Plagues and Peoples* draws selectively on various times and places where cross-cultural contacts have led, inter alia, to the catastrophic spread of infectious disease, as well as to more desired objects of interchange.[30] In this enterprise, McNeill, like Curtin, concentrates, not on the geographic entities over time, but on the effects that linkages among them have had on mortality rates and population fluctuations. In his theory, such fluctuations are the "prime movers" of large-scale societal change. And interestingly enough, the epidemiology of demographic disasters in itself becomes a way for him to trace newly forged geographic linkages. Implicit in McNeill's analysis in *Plagues and Peoples* is the idea of systems and subsystems, which for his purposes he defines as "disease pools."

Two works in which a more global "perspective on the world" begins to be taken are Eric Wolf's *Europe and the People without History*[31] and, of course, Immanuel Wallerstein's path-breaking introductory volume, *The Modern World System*, which, when it first appeared in 1974, placed a very different optic on the study of global history.[32] It may be significant that neither of these authors is, in the strict sense of the term, a historian. Wolf is an anthropologist and Wallerstein is a sociologist. Both are part of a "new breed" of historically oriented macrosocial scientists[33] who seek *patterns* in history—patterns both in human behavior and in social and geographic systems.

Wolf's analytical survey of the "people without history" focuses on societies of the "non-Western" world whose achievements and vital interchanges have remained in shadow and unspoken for (at least in Western-language accounts), as Western historians shaped a highly selective and perspective-specific historical narrative of "world history." He rightly accuses Western scholars of either ignoring or speaking for "the others," whose perspectives have generally been ignored.

Wallerstein also is concerned with the distortions in global history that can arise from a failure to pay attention and give voice to those societies outside the dominant narrative of history constructed by Western scholars. Nevertheless, his account still portrays these other societies primarily from the perspective of western Europe. In his analysis he stresses how the fates of regions located in the semi-periphery and periphery of the evolving modern world system were linked to developments at the European core.[34] Moreover, in order to avoid the error of "blaming the victim," that is, attributing Third World developmental failures to essential flaws in "national character," he sometimes errs in the opposite direction. He tends to argue that the explanations for their different (and generally poor) trajectories in the modern period are to be found, not so much in internal causes, as in the relationships these regions had to the core regions of northwestern Europe which, from the sixteenth century onward, gradually dominated them.

In this, Wallerstein follows the earlier approach of Andre Gunder Frank, first expressed in his "The Development of Underdevelopment,"[35] which emphasized the thesis that Western domination actually *created* underdevelopment. Rather than attribute present-day backwardness to internal causal factors within Third World countries, he blamed the colonial powers for de-developing peripheral regions. Some ten years later, Frank applied his approach to a broader temporal scope in an early attempt to write global history, *World Accumulation, 1492–1789*.[36] He is currently involved in writing a *global* history of what he contends is a single world system that has persisted for some five thousand years.[37] This may well prove to be a much too ambitious project. Although it is certainly true that there are no absolute discontinuities in the history of the world *in real time* (how could there be, when the world itself has continued to exist?), that does not mean that historians should not try to locate logical time brackets for their work. Every discipline, indeed, needs to set cutoff points for attention; otherwise there is no way to handle the material, to distinguish the subject from the big buzzing booming world of potential inclusion. Accepting conventional time brackets does have its costs, however, because *where* one chooses to pick up the threads of the narrative introduces its own biases and blind spots, as the first part of our essay has demonstrated.

An approach similar to that of Wallerstein and Frank can be found in Lefton Stavrianos's impressive *Global Rift*,[38] one of the few books written by a practicing historian, as opposed to a generalist social scientist, which tries to trace the incorporation of other regions of the world into the "modern world system" dominated by the West. Stavrianos acknowledges his indebtedness to Wallerstein, but has set for himself a somewhat different agenda. Despite the fact that Stavrianos follows a rough chronological order, his book is not a global history so much as an episodic account that switches from region to region as each zone shifts its relationship to the core, which is always western Europe during its colonial-imperial development. Therefore, although it takes a sympathetic view of the Third World vis-à-vis the West, the work is no less Eurocentric than studies whose sympathies lie with the victors. To my mind, however, his attempt makes a most useful contribution to the writing of global history, even though specific sections of the more than eight-hundred-page survey can be individually critiqued.[39]

For most Western scholars, the preoccupation, in one way or another, has been determinedly with the West, even when placed in relation to the rest of the world. The chief problematic for these scholars has been to account for the "unchallenged" hegemony of western Europe from the sixteenth century onward. Because their accounts (see, for example, the works of E. L. Jones, Michael Mann, and Robert Brenner)[40] tend to focus on internal developments or emphasize the special "genius" of Western societies, they are less satisfying than those of Wallerstein and Stavrianos, both of whom acknowledge more explicitly the stimuli to growth and development that Europe's imperial reach provided.

Almost all the works mentioned thus far follow, more or less, in the footsteps of William McNeill's *The Rise of the West*,[41] albeit with perhaps different theories and values, in that they concentrate primarily on the time period after 1400. All, therefore, are engaged chiefly in tracking the upward trajectory of Western culture and society from its regressed and abnormally low point in the fifteenth and early sixteenth centuries. The time periods they cover coincide with the era in which early European capitalism was getting under way, in which Western technology was advancing exponentially, and during which western European countries were gradually establishing their hegemony over larger and larger portions of the globe, drawing new and old societies alike into their orbit. It should not surprise us, then, that they should weave all these factors into a causally explanatory narrative in which the rest of the world figures only as background or as passive raw material, to be extracted and shaped according to Western will.

For many years I had been uncomfortable with that narrative. I was familiar enough with non-Western history[42] to know that before Europe's rise to world dominance, there had existed earlier Eastern civilizations whose achievements had far surpassed those of fifteenth- and sixteenth-century Europe. Indeed, even after the "discovery" of the "new world" by Europeans, such places, which included the Middle East, the Indian subcontinent, and China, continued to rival Europe in wealth and culture.

Certainly, Western historians were not ignorant of this, or could easily have dispelled such ignorance if they so chose. On the Middle East they had available the two relevant volumes of Marshall Hodgson's magisterial *The Venture of Islam*,[43] and on other parts of Asia, there were the voluminous Cambridge histories covering the Indian subcontinent. One can also single out the excellent books by K. N. Chaudhuri, which detail the high levels of culture and commerce in the Indian Ocean before the mid-eighteenth century.[44] And for an appreciation of Chinese achievements in science, there were the incredible works of Joseph Needham, and on commerce and trade, those of Mark Elvin and Yoshinobu Shiba.[45] Only by taking such works seriously will it be possible to de-center Western historiography and create truly global history.

The Advantage of Global History

We have tried to demonstrate that taking a global perspective in the writing of history leads to a very different kind of analysis than writing world history as a simple "additive process" that studies the rise and fall of different civilizations as if they were relatively independent of one another.

It is very easy to see the need for global history in today's world, which some have even called a global village. Today we are very much aware of the worldwide repercussions of localized events (e.g., the Iraq-Kuwait border conflict or the rapid, almost instantaneous, effects of fluctuations in the stock markets of New York, London, and Tokyo). It is hard to interpret events in any part of the world today without taking into consideration how such events may have been precipitated by wider forces or without tracing their wider ramifications.[46]

In this essay I have argued that the global village is not an entirely new phenomenon. Historians need a perspective on the world, not only to understand today's events, but those of the past thousand years.

NOTES

1. As every economist knows, in cyclical events it matters very much where one starts the data series and for how long one plots the data entries. Selecting the lowest point of a given "trend" as the initial entry cannot help but show "improvement," whereas on a longer trend this might appear as a small blip on an otherwise long-term downward secular trend. I began to suspect that there had been an unconscious bias that to some extent made the uniqueness of the miracle of the West an artifact, especially with respect to the past, albeit not with reference to the future.

2. In the course of my five years of research, I traveled to almost all the areas that were of central importance to what I came to define as the thirteenth-century world system in order to examine sites and explore local documentation. I also consulted a voluminous body of published primary and secondary sources. While, ideally, such a study should have taken a lifetime of scholarship, I saw my project as creating a synthesis of existing materials, albeit from a different perspective, in the hope that other scholars would not only fill lacunae in our knowledge but reevaluate their own findings in the context of the world system.

3. My conclusions were eventually incorporated into Janet Abu-Lughod, *Before European Hegemony: The World System A.D. 1250–1350* (New York: Oxford University Press, 1989). Several articles appeared somewhat before the book was completed: a preview of the thesis written in 1986, "The Shape of the World System in the Thirteenth Century," *Studies in Comparative International Development* 22 (Winter 1987–88): 1–25; as well as "Did the West Rise or Did the East Fall?" paper presented at the 1988 meetings of the American Sociological Association. The book was followed by "Restructuring the Premodern World-System," *Review* 13 (Spring

1990): 273–86, which critiques a mechanical application of world systems theory and tries to take it a bit further by making it a variable, rather than a constant. Four distinct "cycles" of world-system organization are set forth: a classical period one, between roughly 200 B.C. and A.D. 200; a medieval period, between roughly A.D. 1200 and A.D. 1450; a modern period, between roughly 1500 and 1914; and the "postindustrial" period in which we now find ourselves.

4. The following section of this essay depends heavily on portions of my larger and more detailed text, but it cannot substitute for the complete work. In this brief summary it is not possible to include the complex evidence presented in the complete version, to which the reader is referred.

5. For an excellent study of this period, see Perry Anderson, *Passages from Antiquity to Feudalism* (London: Verso, 1974; reprinted 1978).

6. See, for example, the work of George Hourani, *Arab Seafaring in the Indian Ocean in Ancient and Early Medieval Times* (Princeton: Princeton University Press, 1951).

7. The iron and steel production of the Sung Dynasty in the eleventh century exceeded that of England during the early industrial age. See Robert Hartwell, "A Revolution in the Chinese Iron and Coal Industries during the Northern Sung, 960–1126," *Journal of Asian Studies* 21 (1962): 153–62; and his "Markets, Technology, and the Structure of Enterprise in the Development of the Eleventh-Century Chinese Iron and Steel Industry," *Journal of Economic History* 26 (1966): 29–58.

8. An amazing account of the sophisticated business practices of Arab producers and traders (especially in Baghdad) can be found in Abraham Udovitch, *Partnership and Profit in Medieval Islam* (Princeton: Princeton University Press, 1970). It is clear from this document that many of the innovations in credit, corporate organization, risk equalization, and legal contracts that are usually invoked to compliment western ingenuity and the "genius" of the Italians were actually learned from their Arab trading partners after the Crusades had put the two in closer contact.

9. Europe traditionally ran a trade deficit with the more-developed economies of the Middle East and India, a deficit it met by exporting silver and even gold buillion. The deficit existed because Europe demanded more goods from the East than the Orient wanted from Europe.

10. One of the comparative advantages the fair towns had hitherto had was that they could offer "special" arrangements to traveling merchants; once they came under monarchy control, they lost this right to extend special privileges.

11. The finest study of this period is Frederic C. Lane's wonderful book, *Venice: A Maritime Republic* (Baltimore: Johns Hopkins University Press, 1973). The sources on Genoa are less rich, but see E. H. Byrne, *Genoese Shipping in the Twelfth and Thirteenth Centuries* (Cambridge, Mass.: Mediaeval Academy of America, 1930), for a fine account of Genoese skills in shipbuilding and financing.

12. Jewish trader families from Baghdad and Cairo had early on figured prominently in this trade, but by the thirteenth century, their Muslim compatriots had essentially displaced them. The work of S. N. Goitein is particularly relevant on this point. See, for example, his "From Aden to India: Specimens of the Corre-

spondence of India Traders of the Twelfth Century," *Journal of the Economic and Social History of the Orient* 22 (1980): 43–66; as well as his "Letters and Documents on the India Trade in Medieval Times," *Islamic Culture* 37 (1963): 188–203.

13. Both quotations appear, along with their citations, in Abu-Lughod, *Before European Hegemony*, p. 291. The original source is *The Suma Oriental of Tomé Pires*, ed. A. Cortesão, 2 vols. (London: Hakluyt Society, 1944).

14. Srivijaya was a purported "kingdom" whose exact nature and location (probably on Sumatra) remain surprisingly opaque and mysterious. Without offering a coherent alternative description, most scholars now discount what were earlier considered to be the definitive works by O. W. Wolters. See his *Early Indonesian Commerce: A Study of the Origins of Srivijaya* (Ithaca, N.Y.: Cornell University Press, 1967) and *The Fall of Srivijaya in Malay History* (Ithaca, N.Y.: Cornell University Press, 1970). Before the founding of Malacca in the fourteenth century by a putative "prince" from Palembang, the latter was Srivijaya's capital and presumably the most important port in the strait. Long-standing connections between India and both Srivijaya and Indonesia are obvious from the nomenclatures and are supported by epigraphic and archaeological evidence.

15. India's gossamer cotton textiles had been much sought after in classical Rome and continued to draw customers throughout the Middle Ages. Since, traditionally, others had wanted Indian products more than India had markets for their exported goods, the balance of payments was always in India's favor. Gold from elsewhere, therefore, tended to accumulate in India and remain there. The best sources on this eastward flow of bullion are Artur Attman, *The Bullion Flow between Europe and the East, 1000–1750* (Goteburg: Kungl. Veternskaps-Och Vitterhessamhallet); and the more accessible John F. Richards, ed., *Precious Metals in the Later Medieval and Early Modern Worlds* (Durham, N.C.: Duke University Press, 1983). The rapid inflation in Europe during the early modern period has been attributed to this imbalance of payments in international trade.

16. See, for example, William McNeill, *The Pursuit of Power: Technology, Armed Force and Society since A.D. 1000* (Chicago: University of Chicago Press, 1982), which makes a stunning case for China's preeminence in the premodern world system.

17. The studies by Jung-Pang Lo prove this conclusively. See his "China as a Sea Power, 1127–1368," Ph.D. diss., University of California, Berkeley, 1957, as well as related articles that summarize his thesis: "The Emergence of China as a Sea Power During the Late Sung and Early Yuan Periods," *Far Eastern Quarterly* 14 (1955): 489–503; and "Chinese Shipping and East-West Trade from the Tenth to the Fourteenth Century," in *Sociétés et compagnies de commerce en l'orient et dans l'Océan Indien* (Paris: S.E.V.P.E.N., 1970), pp. 167–74.

18. See K. N. Chaudhuri, *Trade and Civilisation in the Indian Ocean: An Economic History from the Rise of Islam to 1750* (Cambridge, England: Cambridge University Press, 1985), as well as its companion volume, *Asia before Europe: Economy and Civilisation in the Indian Ocean from the Rise of Islam to 1750* (Cambridge, England: Cambridge University Press, 1990), which, alas, appeared too late for me to use in preparing my 1989 book.

19. One can think of "passes" as written proof that protection money had

already been paid to the Portuguese. A "pass" gave a ship presumed immunity from confiscation or destruction *by the Portuguese*, which sounds like extortion to me.

20. William McNeill, *Plagues and People* (Garden City, N.Y.: Anchor Books, 1976).

21. The only area for which I was unable to locate documentation about a particularly virulent epidemic at that time was India. Whether this is because scholars have not yet found the evidence or whether the Indian population already had gained some immunity from prior outbreaks cannot be determined.

22. Thomas Barfield, *The Perilous Frontier* (New York: Basil Blackwell, 1990).

23. See, inter alia, Jung-Pang Lo, "The Decline of the Early Ming Navy," *Extremus* 5 (1958): 149–68, for information on the early decline and eventual precipitous collapse of the Chinese fleet.

24. On Cheng Ho's expeditions, see Paul Pelliot, "Les grands voyages maritimes Chinois au début du XVe siècle," *T'oung Pao* 30 (1933): 235–455, a careful work based on primary sources.

25. While this section surveys some of the literature on world–global history, it makes no pretense to constituting an annotated bibliography, nor is it an exhaustive or even carefully ranked description of the relevant literature. I have omitted many important works and focus on some about which scholars may feel ambivalent. My principle of selection has been simple. I have singled out a few works with which I am most familiar that seem to me to exemplify different logics in approaching more synthetic, wider-ranging, and comparative histories whose object is broadly conceived as "the world," even though none claims to be all inclusive of everything in the world.

26. Fernand Braudel, *Civilization & Capitalism, 15th–18th Century*, trans. Sian Reynolds. 3 vols. (New York: Harper & Row, 1982–84).

27. Arnold Toynbee, *A Study of History*. 10 vols. (New York and London: Oxford University Press, 1947–57).

28. When carried to its logical extreme, this approach leads to a rather mechanical and even a tragically inevitable metaphor of cycles, in which each advance in sophistication plants the seed for its own destruction. The views of Ibn Khaldun, Vico, and much later, Spengler come to mind here.

29. Philip D. Curtin, *Cross-Cultural Trade in World History* (Cambridge, England: Cambridge University Press, 1984). This book selects moments and places when, in the long course of world history, long-distance trade flourished among very different civilizations. Curtin then tries to tease out of these parallel cases some basic processes and principles of organization.

30. William McNeill, *Plagues and Peoples*.

31. Eric R. Wolf, *Europe and the People without History* (Berkeley and Los Angeles: University of California Press, 1982).

32. Three volumes of this still expanding work have appeared thus far. They are *The Modern World System I* (New York: Academic Press, 1974); *The Modern World System II* (New York: Academic Press, 1979); and *The Modern World System III: The Second Era of Great Expansion of the Capitalist World-Economy* (New York: Academic Press, 1989). Only the first volume may be said to have influenced Wolf. It is hard to disentangle the direction of the relationship between *The Modern World*

System and the work of Fernand Braudel because the association of Wallerstein with Braudel was so close. Wallerstein certainly credits the latter as mentor, and the research center at the State University of New York, which Wallerstein founded and continues to direct, is named in honor of, and to acknowledge his indebtedness to, the now-deceased French scholar.

33. Among these, one might list for illustrative, not invidious, purposes, Charles Tilly, Christopher Chase-Dunn, Robert Brenner, Andre Gunder Frank, Daniel Chirot, Michael Mann, Perry Anderson, and myself. Earlier precursors might include such luminaries as Max Weber, Werner Sombart, and Pitrim Sorokin.

34. This Eurocentric perspective probably cannot be overcome entirely. It is inevitable that the "perspective" from which one views the world will shape the questions one asks of history, and that events will be singled out for attention because the writer judges them to have had important consequences for his or her own society. One might make a distinction, however, between this and the type of biased dismissal of the achievements of others that constitutes ethnocentrism, a far greater flaw in historical writing.

35. Andre Gunder Frank, "The Development of Underdevelopment," *Monthly Review* 18 (1966): 17–31.

36. Andre Gunder Frank, *World Accumulation, 1492–1789* (New York: Monthly Review Press, 1978).

37. Much of Andre Gunder Frank's new material is still being circulated in mimeographed form, although some parts have begun to see print. See, for example, his review essay of my book, *Before European Hegemony*, in "A Thirteenth-Century World System: A Review Essay," *Journal of World History* 1 (Fall–Winter 1990): 249–56; his "A Theoretical Introduction to Five Thousand Years of World System History," in *Review* 13; and the most extensive report on his work thus far, which appeared in "A Plea for World System History," *Journal of World History* 2 (Spring 1991): 1–28. I have attempted to evaluate the advantages and disadvantages of periodizing world system history in a paper presented at Harvard University to a Conference on Moghuls, Safavids and Ottomans. See "Discontinuities and Persistence: One World System or a Succession of Systems?"

38. Lefton S. Stavrianos, *Global Rift: The Third World Comes of Age* (New York: Morrow, 1981).

39. It is not quite global, since it tends to ignore the impact on the colonizing states of their conquests. Taken together with the works of Eric Hobsbawm, especially his *The Age of Empire: 1875–1914* (New York: Pantheon Books, 1987), however, a reader can reconstruct the interrelationship between colonizing and colonized states in the nineteenth century.

40. Robert Brenner, "The Origin of Capitalist Development: A Critique of Neo-Smithian Marxism," *New Left Review* 104 (July–August 1977): 25–92; E. L. Jones, *The European Miracle*, 2nd ed. (Cambridge, England: Cambridge University Press, 1987); Michael Mann, *The Sources of Social Power I: A History of Power from the Beginning to* A.D. *1760* (Cambridge, England: Cambridge University Press, 1986), and his *States, War and Capitalism* (Oxford, England: Basil Blackwell, 1988); and even to some extent Charles Tilly, *Coercion, Capital and European States,* A.D. *990–1990* (New York: Basil Blackwell, 1990). All tend to concentrate on intraregional

developments, even though they may also discuss the impact on and implications of such developments for other parts of the globe. Jack Goldstone's comparative study of state breakdowns in Europe and Asia similarly pays closest attention to internal developments within the states he covers and thus his analysis underplays linkages. See his *Revolution and Rebellion in the Early Modern World* (Berkeley and Los Angeles: University of California Press, 1991).

41. William McNeill, *The Rise of the West: A History of the Human Community* (Chicago: University of Chicago Press, 1963).

42. Although my original discipline was not history, I had been drawn into historical research first by my attempt to understand how contemporary Cairo came to have the patterns it did. In the course of writing that history, incorporated into *Cairo: 1001 Years of the City Victorious* (Princeton: Princeton University Press, 1971), I came to recognize the importance of international connections in determining Egypt's fate. These insights were reinforced when I prepared a later book on North African cities, *Rabat: Urban Apartheid in Morocco* (Princeton: Princeton University Press, 1980).

43. Marshall Hodgson, *The Venture of Islam* (Chicago: University of Chicago Press, 1974). This work was unhappily truncated by Hodgson's premature death. Nevertheless, the literature on Islam is far more extensive than this single citation suggests. For a good introduction, see M. Lombard, *The Golden Age of Islam*, trans. Joan Spencer (Amsterdam: North-Holland Publishing, 1975).

44. See Chaudhuri, *Trade and Civilisation in the Indian Ocean*, and his newer *Asia before Europe*.

45. See, for example, Joseph Needham, *Science and Civilisation in China*. 6 vols. (Cambridge, England: Cambridge University Press, 1954–85); *Science in Traditional China: A Comparative Perspective* (Cambridge, Mass.: Harvard University Press, 1985); and *Clerks and Craftsmen in China and the West: Lectures and Addresses on the History of Science and Technology* (Cambridge, England: Cambridge University Press, 1970). On trade and commerce, see among others, Yoshinobu Shiba, *Commerce and Society in Sung China*, trans. Mark Elvin (Ann Arbor: University of Michigan Center for Chinese Studies, 1970); and Mark Elvin, *The Pattern of the Chinese Past* (Stanford, Calif.: Stanford University Press, 1973).

46. For example, the free hand that the United States had in the Gulf War was undoubtedly facilitated by the earlier collapse of the Soviet imperial system.

The Age of
Gunpowder Empires, 1450–1800

WILLIAM H. McNEILL

Any big change in weapons and military organization affects politics and society by helping some people attain their ends more easily than before, while putting new, perhaps insuperable, obstacles in the way of others. The advent of guns was such a change. Appearing as curiosities in the fourteenth century, gunpowder weapons became devastatingly effective in sieges by about the middle of the fifteenth century. This suddenly changed the balance of power between those who owned or occupied fortified strongholds and those who owned or controlled the new artillery, first in western Europe, where these guns were developed, and then in all the other parts of the civilized world.

The spread of big guns inaugurated what may be called the age of gunpowder empires, although, as we shall see, there was no uniformity in the way different peoples exploited the possibilities of the new weapons. Nonetheless, whenever they were able to monopolize the new artillery, central authorities were able to unite large territories into new, or newly consolidated, empires. This occurred in the Near East, in Russia, in India, and, in a considerably modified fashion, in China and Japan. The Spanish empire of the Americas together with the Portuguese empire of the Indian Ocean also relied on artillery, though the most important Spanish and Portuguese guns were on shipboard, not on land.

In western Europe, the original home of these guns, the response was different. No single ruler was ever able to monopolize siege cannon. Within a short time discovery of a different sort of fortification suddenly reduced the effectiveness of the new wall-destroying monsters. Perennial rivalries among neighboring states and rulers therefore put a forced draft under the continued evolution of the art of war, and a long series of improvements in organization, armament, training, and supply gradually raised the effectiveness of European armies above the level other peoples had attained. By 1700 the disproportion between European and other styles of warfare had become pronounced and, in conjunction with parallel improvements in naval management and equipment, allowed Europeans to expand their power literally around the globe in the course of the eighteenth and nineteenth centuries. By 1700, therefore, gunpowder empires of the kind created in the fifteenth and sixteenth centuries had become old-fashioned. One by one they crumbled before the intrusive Europeans in the next century and a half.

This essay therefore deals with an era in which Europeans had begun to exert a limited primacy within the civilized world, but before command of superior military power allowed traders, missionaries, and empire builders from western Europe to trample on other peoples' sensibilities and interests almost at will. Focusing attention on the military and technological underpinning of European power, and on the way other societies borrowed guns and fitted them into their local political, military, and cultural systems, narrows the range of actual civilizational encounters to what mattered most in the eyes of rulers and courts and leaves out intellectual, artistic and religious interactions. This is not quite as silly as it seems because by building a series of vast and impressive imperial states between 1450 and 1650, the rulers of Asia allowed Moslem and Chinese intellectuals to believe they could afford to pay little or no attention to European thought and art. Fatefully, rulers and military administrators, too, did not try to keep up with subsequent European innovations in military and naval matters, leaving them woefully exposed to attack after 1700. The story is therefore an important one, preparing the way for the era of European world dominance that started about 1700 and ended after World War II.

From Catapults to Guns

Gunpowder was invented in China shortly before A.D. 1000 and was first used in war as an incendiary. That, at least, is a plausible interpretation of a text that tells how in A.D. 969 an emperor of the Sung dynasty awarded a prize to officers who had invented a new "fire arrow." The arrow probably carried a charge of gunpowder, since it is hard to imagine what else could be new about such a weapon. Further development of gunpowder weaponry was inhibited by the fact that the Chinese style of warfare under the Sung dynasty (960–1279) was defensive, and since the emperor's troops usually fought from behind walls, they had absolutely no incentive to invent guns that could attack fortifications.

This situation changed, however, when the Mongols conquered China between 1205 and 1279. The horsemen who followed Genghis Khan and his successors were accustomed to attack, but could not hope to capture forts and walled cities from horseback. They therefore welcomed anything that would allow them to break through defensive walls quickly. Catapults had been used for that purpose since Roman times, and the Mongols took to them eagerly. But the explosive force of gunpowder also seemed promising, and Mongol armies routinely used lengths of bamboo filled with gunpowder to attack city gates by blowing them open. In this primitive form, gunpowder weapons reached Europe in 1241, when Mongol armies ravaged Poland and Hungary.

The Chinese pioneered the next improvement in firearms also. If, instead of allowing the powder to shatter its bamboo container, a stronger vessel, open at one end, were constructed to hold the powder, then the exploding gases could be made to launch a missile placed over the vessel's mouth. Chinese texts from 1290 seem to show that this sort of "gun" was in use. By then Genghis Khan's grandson, Kublai, was ruling in Peking. His empire extended across most of the Middle East and included European Russia. Caravans moved across Asia regularly, and ships moved to and fro along the China coast and into the Indian Ocean. Consequently, many thousands of persons, Marco Polo among them, traveled back and forth between the Far East and the Far West and disseminated information more rapidly than ever before.

News of China's new weapons therefore reached Europe quickly. Indeed, the first portrait of the new contrivance, dated 1326, comes from western Europe in the form of a crude manuscript painting preserved at Oxford. It shows a vase-shaped container, lying on its side, with a touch-hole on top and a large arrow affixed to a circular base closing off the mouth. Just six years later, a Chinese drawing shows a very similar vase-shaped receptacle for the powder with an arrow-shaped projectile. The resemblance between the two drawings is so close that a common origin for these vase-shaped weapons seems certain. Chinese priority is hard to doubt, though interpretation of the technical terms in Chinese texts that deal with early gunpowder weapons is beset with uncertainties.

What is clear about the early history of artillery is that Europeans soon outstripped the Chinese and others by building bigger and bigger guns. One reason was that Europeans had access to more metal than other civilized peoples (with the possible exception of the Japanese), thanks to developments in hard-rock mining that dated back to the eleventh century. Methods for cracking bedrock and for ventilating and draining mines allowed Europeans to follow metalliferous lodes deeper into the earth than was done elsewhere. Full and free exploitation of such techniques depended on property law and on political practices that made it safe to invest large amounts of capital in the enterprise. European mining was thus sustained by the general context of Western society and institutions.

Specialized skills centered initially in the Harz Mountains of Germany, but German miners carried them subsequently to other metalliferous regions—the Erzgebirge of Bohemia, the Carpathians of Transylvania (modern Rumania), and elsewhere. Simple transfer of European mining techniques to other societies was difficult or impossible, since the security of property needed to make such an elaborate investment pay off could not be transferred to new ground without far-reaching political change—and this rulers were unwilling to countenance. As a result, Europeans continued to enjoy a persistent advantage over other peoples, all the way from the eleventh to the nineteenth centuries, since cheap and abundant metal was useful both in peace and in war—but especially in war.

A second reason impelling European artificers and rulers to build more powerful guns was a clear idea of how bigger and better guns might make their owners more powerful. To begin with, the idea far outran reality. Early guns were mainly good for scaring horses, and should have scared the men who risked firing them; but they were not efficient weapons. Most of the force of the explosion was wasted because the expanding gases simply rushed around the sides of the projectile, and aiming was extremely inaccurate. Still, the awesome noise and obvious force of exploding gunpowder promised truly superhuman results, if only it could be harnessed effectively. Guns, if powerful enough, might even become capable of destroying an enemy's best-built stone fortifications after just a few shots, thereby abruptly altering the balance between defenders and attackers. Soon after 1400 this vision of the possible took firm hold on the imagination of a few rulers and artisans in western Europe. Substantial resources were therefore lavished on building gigantic "bombards."

These weapons differed from the vase-shaped gun of 1326 in being cylindrical tubes, closed at one end. Instead of firing an arrow, poised at the lip of the gun, they shot spherical stone cannonballs, propelling them the length of the tube before allowing the exploding gases to disperse in thin air. In this way a more accurate aim was assured and a much more effective use of the force of the explosion to accelerate the projectile could be assured. Guns, as we know them, were on their way.

The earliest bombards were made of wrought-iron strips, hammered together. But such guns were liable to burst at the seams. Far stronger guns could be made by casting them as a single block of metal; and it so happened that western European craftsmen were already expert at casting large church bells, using bronze or brass.[1] Preparing a mold, melting ingots to produce the necessary bronze or brass, and pouring the liquid metal into the mold took large resources and considerable skill. But the difference between casting a bell and casting a gun was trivial, so, with the necessary skills already in hand, Europeans pressed rapidly ahead, and soon were making bigger and better guns than anyone else, including the Chinese.

For the first time, western Europeans began to leave other civilizations behind in at least one important respect.

By about 1430, European-made bombards were twelve to fifteen feet long, fired a projectile up to about thirty inches in diameter, and had become truly formidable engines. They weighed so much and were so awkward to move that on some famous occasions artisans actually cast the big guns on the spot, instead of trying to transport them to the site of the siege. Yet such weapons did accomplish their purpose, causing stone fortifications to crumble and allowing a besieging army to storm through the breach after only a brief bombardment.

The capture of Constantinople by Sultan Mohammed the Conqueror in 1453 is the most famous example of how such clumsy weapons could make a decisive difference, allowing a superior field force to overcome otherwise invulnerable defenses. The fact that the sultan hired Christians from Transylvania to build and operate the cannon he needed to overcome the famous and formidable defenses of Constantinople attests the superiority that European metalworkers and gunsmiths had achieved, as well as his eagerness to acquire what he recognized as a clearly superior weapon.

The rapidity with which the Turks reacted to the novelty is striking, for such guns had not existed before about 1430, and the first Western ruler to use them systematically was the king of France, who in 1450 set out to drive the English from the Continent. His new guns made old fortifications quite useless. Consequently, English garrisons surrendered so rapidly that the hitherto interminable Hundred Years War came to an end in 1453—the same fateful year in which Mohammed captured Constantinople. Historians have often used that year to divide medieval from modern history, and not without reason, since the advent of the new weapons system signalized by the twin events for which 1453 is famous did alter the way political and military power was distributed, not just in Europe but around the world.

The Gunpowder Revolution in Western Europe

After defeating the English in 1453, the king of France still faced a formidable rival in the form of an over-mighty subject—the duke of Burgundy, who had accumulated territories stretching from the Low Countries at the mouth of the Rhine to the borders of Switzerland. As it happened, the most skilled gun makers of the age inhabited his territories. Therefore, when the Burgundians decided they must arm against the French, lest the French king do to them what he had done so successfully to the English, they had an ample technical base for improving on the gun design of the 1450s.

The Burgundian–French rivalry promptly precipitated an arms race of the sort so familiar to us in the twentieth century. Metalworkers on both sides aimed at a single goal: to make guns mobile without sacrificing their battering power. Between 1465 and 1477, designers solved their problem brilliantly by resorting to smaller, denser projectiles. They discovered that a comparatively small iron cannonball could strike a more damaging blow than stone projectiles (that fractured on impact) could ever do, no matter how large. This meant that guns could be made smaller but had to be stronger too.

The tradeoff turned out well, for even with thicker walls, the new guns weighed a lot less than the great bombards and became genuinely mobile. Mounted on wheels, a gun six to eight feet long, capable of firing an iron ball of eight to ten inches in diameter, could travel wherever a heavy wagon could go. Simply by unhitching the trail from a forward pair of wheels and planting it on the ground, these guns were ready for action and, having fired, could move on, if need be, to some new vantage point, all in a matter of minutes. Yet such cannon were just as effective as the monster guns of the previous generation when it came to knocking down stone walls.

A gun park with a few such weapons therefore allowed a ruler to threaten his subjects or neighbors with speedy and assured destruction of defenses behind which in earlier times an inferior force could shelter for weeks and months until starved out by besiegers. Keeping a superior force on enemy territory for a long time was always difficult because supplies were hard to deliver in sufficient quantity. With the new guns, that was no longer necessary. A few hours' bombardment now sufficed to bring down the most formidable walls wherever guns could be brought to bear. The balance of power between central and local authorities was thereby transformed, making whoever controlled the new siege cannon into a sovereign and reducing those who could not afford them to a subjection they had not previously experienced.

As it happened, the Burgundians, though they had taken the lead in perfecting mobile siege artillery, were not destined to profit from it. Instead, Charles the Bold, duke of Burgundy, being too impatient to await the arrival of his guns on the battlefield at Nancy, led a cavalry charge against a massed formation of Swiss pikemen, who had dared to oppose him, and met his death on the points of their pikes in 1477. His lands were then swiftly partitioned between the French king, Louis XI, and the Hapsburg heir, Maximilian, who married Charles's daughter and only heir.

Even after Maximilian became Holy Roman Emperor of the German Nation in 1493 he lacked a bureaucracy and army with which to exploit the possibilities of the new artillery. Louis XI and his successor, Charles VIII, were better situated in this respect, and proceeded to consolidate their kingdom as never before. Then, in 1494, Charles VIII, after annexing

Brittany, decided to use his new military power for ventures abroad. He invaded Italy, the richest and most sophisticated part of western Europe, in order to enforce his dynastic claim to the Kingdom of Naples. This required him to march the length of the peninsula. He did so, bringing his big guns with him and using them to threaten anyone who dared oppose his passage. On the rare occasions when he met resistance, his cannon demonstrated their devastating force by reducing famous fortresses to rubble at the word of command.

In 1494, the Renaissance rulers of Italy had long since developed a professionalized art of war, combining cavalry, pikes, and crossbows. They were accustomed to set the pace for all of Christendom in war as well as in peace. To be so suddenly outdistanced by the French was therefore a great shock, which was not diminished by the fact that the French invasion inaugurated a long series of wars (1494–1559) in which foreigners—French and Spanish primarily—fought over Italy. Even the largest Italian states, dwarfed by the newly consolidated kingdoms of France and Spain, proved incapable of defending themselves or of driving the foreigners away.

The reason the Italian wars were so long drawn out was that early in their course military engineers discovered a way to make fortifications safe from the new guns. In 1500 Florence attacked Pisa, using heavy guns to break through the ring wall, only to find that the Pisans had erected a new earthen wall inside, behind the threatened breech. Moreover, to get earth for their emergency wall, the Pisans had scraped out a ditch in front of it that blocked a direct, running assault. But the important thing was that cannonballs fired into the earthen wall buried themselves in the soft soil without doing much damage. As a result, the Florentine attack was foiled, and Pisa retained its independence.

In the light of this experience, Italian military engineers saw quickly how to make fortifications safe again. All they needed to do was to protect brittle stone walls with a sloping layer of earth to absorb cannon fire, while obstructing access to such revetted walls by carving out ditches in front of them, just as the Pisans had done. In a sense, the new design turned ordinary fortification upside down, making empty ditches the principal obstacle an attacker had to traverse, while walls became merely an aid to the defenders in protecting the ditch. The advantage of a ditch, of course, was that it was completely unaffected by cannon fire, and earth-covered walls were nearly as secure. Yet the new style of fortification did not make cannon useless. Rather, guns emplaced on projecting bastions were needed to defend the ditch. Others had to be hidden behind the main ring wall, ready to attack besieging artillery. Careful geometry could assure clear lines of fire for guns of every caliber, making a well-designed and adequately garrisoned city or fortress impregnable to sudden attack.

By 1520 the refinements of building cannon-proof fortifications were well understood, and what came to be called the *trace italienne* made it possible for anyone who could afford the new style of fortification to erect a stronghold that was proof against cannon fire. Sieges therefore again became a feature of European warfare because small garrisons, protected by the new style of fortification, could hold off a superior attacker for months at a time. But there was a difference: The new fortifications were expensive to construct and used even more of the big guns than attackers did. Only states and rulers with access to artillery and with enough money to pay for an ample stock of the new weapons could hope to compete in European war and diplomacy.

As a result, urban wealth and skills became more decisive than before in military matters. Without access to the products of urban workshops, and without money to pay for them, no government and no military captain could expect to succeed. Capitalist enterprise and military enterprise were wedded together more closely than in any earlier age or than anywhere else in the world. Each nourished the other, making European armies, navies, and governments much more powerful than before.

But just because European armies and governments mobilized greater and greater resources for war and defense, no single empire succeeded in uniting western Europe. Big guns were never monopolized, and by 1519, when the Hapsburg heir, Charles I and V, king of Spain and emperor of Germany, had gathered together all the diverse territories he inherited and seemed to have a real chance of defeating the French and establishing hegemony over all of western Europe, it was already too late for the new siege guns to have the sort of effect they had in some other parts of the civilized world. By then the *trace italienne* was already available, so that even when Charles did drive French forces from the field in Italy, he could not press ahead, invade France, and expect to see the French king's fortresses crumble as soon as they were attacked.

In 1450 that could have happened, but not in 1525 or subsequently. Instead, a defeated army could expect to withdraw into prepared defenses and hold off attackers as long as food stocks allowed. Quick and easy conquest had become impossible. The window of opportunity for consolidating western Europe into a single gunpowder empire had closed. One may even speculate that it was the division of the Burgundian lands after the death of Charles the Bold in 1477 that assured this result. To begin with, gun-casting skill was concentrated in the Low Countries near the mouths of the Scheldt and Rhine rivers. If a single ruler had continued to control that region and been able to monopolize the new guns for as long as a generation, he might have been able to use his mobile wall destroyers to achieve hegemony wherever the new siege guns could reach. Instead, the kings of France and the Hapsburgs of Germany divided the Burgundian lands along with Burgundian guns and gun makers between them, assuring a standoff which became permanent, thanks to the improvements in fortification that came into being very swiftly after 1500.

A balance of power therefore persisted, keeping Europe divided among dozens of sovereigns. As far as gunpowder weapons were concerned, after the 1480s military invention shifted away from artillery, concentrating instead on improvements in small arms. Even more decisive were improvements in the training, management, and supply of armies, and in the way officers were chosen and promoted so as to create a reliable chain of command from top to bottom of the armed establishment. Before sketching these developments, however, a brief discussion of the importance of big guns for overseas commerce and naval warfare is called for.

Guns on Shipboard

European shipbuilders had learned how to construct stout, maneuverable, all-weather sailing ships about the beginning of the fourteenth century. Multiple masts and sails, together with a sternpost rudder and a double-planked hull nailed to a rib and keel skeleton, and strengthened by multiple decks, constituted a structure strong enough to withstand both Atlantic storms and the recoil of the new cannon that emerged from the French-Burgundian arms race of the 1460s and 1470s.

Cannon weighed so much that if a ship, specialized for war, were to carry anything like as many guns as it had room for, they had to be mounted near the waterline to avoid top-heaviness. This in turn required cutting gunports in the side of the hull and finding a way of sealing them against stormy seas when fighting was not in prospect. In 1514, a ship built for King Henry VIII of England pioneered a suitable design, allowing the vessel to carry a row of cannon on each side. Innumerable improvements followed, but European warships continued to conform to this general pattern until the 1840s. Such a vessel could shower a broadside of shot against an enemy ship at a range of up to two hundred yards and expect to reduce it to helplessness by damaging masts, sails, rudder, and rigging. To sink a ship completely was difficult because nearly all hits came above the waterline, and stout hulls could take a great many cannon shots without suffering irreparable damage.

Cannon were eminently well suited for the defense of ordinary merchantmen, though of course they did not carry as heavy an armament as specialized warships did. Consequently, from the 1480s, when the cannon first became available, financiers who fitted out ships for long and perilous voyages found it very much worthwhile to install a few of the new weapons on board each ship, because guns improved the chances of a safe return with cargo intact. In many waters, raiding and trading were not clearly distinguished. This was true in the Mediterranean, for example, and wherever else peoples with conflicting loyalties competed for dominion on the seas. When encountering strangers, the decision whether to bargain or to fight all depended on circumstances, and the most important circumstance was the balance of force at the command of the two parties concerned. Guns capable of inflicting damage at a distance were therefore enormous assets for European merchantmen. Indeed, it is scarcely an exaggeration to assert that in the first century of European transoceanic trading, their principal stock-in-trade was the superior force with which they could compel others either to hand over goods as tribute or else to sell at prices the Europeans found advantageous.

European ability to assert superior force in distant regions of the earth reflected the fact that even a few shipboard cannon could render old-fashioned coastal defenses untenable and could completely destroy lightly built ships. In the Mediterranean and in the Indian Ocean, calmer seas made the heavy construction Europeans had developed for Atlantic waters quite unnecessary; but light vessels, fitted for those seas, were unable to use the new cannon. As Newton's laws of motion eventually made clear, the force of a cannon's recoil was exactly equal to the force of the cannonball it launched. Ships less strongly built than those required to withstand the stormy seas of Europe's Atlantic face were therefore liable to be shaken apart by a heavy gun's recoil after just a few firings. They were almost equally vulnerable to shot, for flimsier construction meant that a few smashed boards threatened the integrity of the entire hull.

The result of these facts was to give cannon-carrying European vessels an easy superiority over all other shipping at almost exactly the time when European ships and navigators first discovered how to exploit ocean winds and currents so as to sail at will between home ports and the Americas or Asia. The only shipbuilding tradition that compared in stoutness with the European was Chinese; and Chinese seagoing ships had carried a complement of guns that were smaller than those Europeans favored, but superior to anything they met in the Indian Ocean and South China Sea. But it so happened that the Chinese government, for reasons of its own, prohibited the construction of seagoing ships in 1436. Chinese shipbuilding therefore decayed to the furtive levels that illegal "pirates" could sustain long before the first European ships, with their cannon, showed up on the China coast.

The Moslems, who had played a leading role in Indian Ocean commerce for centuries, and who had successfully rolled back Christian sea power from the eastern Mediterranean after 1453, did not simply acquiesce in the sudden appearance of European ships in seas they had been accustomed to dominate. Ottoman rulers, after all, were acutely aware of the importance of big guns, as the capture of Constantinople showed.

But their naval administrators were unable to imitate Europeans' prodigal use of cannon on shipboard because Mediterranean skills and traditions of naval architecture (not to mention shortages of metal) stood in the way.

Nevertheless, after the news of Vasco da Gama's arrival in southern India in 1498 reached the sultan's court, the Ottoman government dispatched expert gun makers to Sumatra so that the local Moslem ruler might better protect himself from the European threat. In addition, the Ottoman government built a navy in the Red Sea to guard the holy cities of Mecca and Medina from infidel attack and drive the Portuguese from the Indian Ocean, as similar Turkish fleets had driven the Venetians and other Christians from the eastern Mediterranean.

Accordingly, when all was ready, in 1509 the Turkish admiral assembled his fleet and allied Moslem naval forces of the Indian Ocean for a major assault on the Portuguese. Ramming and boarding were the tactics familiar to the Moslem sailors. Crossbows were available to assist their assault, but heavier missiles were difficult or impossible to accommodate on board vessels that depended on rowers for maneuverability in battle and were jammed full of nimble, lightly armed crewmen for the climactic act of boarding hostile vessels. Cannon were worse than useless, since their recoil would have been fatal to the light, fast galleys.

When battle was joined, off the port of Diu in northwestern India, Portuguese cannon proved devastating to the crowded and vulnerable Moslem warships. Despite an enormous discrepancy in numbers, the intruding Europeans easily prevailed because their ships were fast enough and maneuverable enough to prevent the Moslems from coming to close quarters. The battle of Diu (1509) therefore became completely lopsided and established European naval superiority in the Indian Ocean for centuries to come. In 1538 a revised Moslem strategy tried to drive the Portuguese from Diu by land attack, supported by a rebuilt Ottoman fleet, but this also failed ignominiously, whereupon the government in Constantinople gave up the attempt to operate armed forces in the area of the Indian Ocean, leaving the defense of Moslem interests to local rulers and peoples.

Local rulers of the Indian Ocean coastlands did not even attempt to compete with the newcomers by building ships and cannon like those the Europeans brought with them. Perhaps the break with old, established customs and skills was too sharp. More likely, access to the comparatively vast quantity of metal needed to equip a ship with big guns was too expensive to be contemplated, much less carried through. Instead, Indian Ocean sailors persisted in using their accustomed light, cheap vessels and continued to conduct most of the trade up and down the coast simply by undercutting Portuguese charges. The Portuguese tried to assert a trade monopoly, but evading their patrols was easy since the foreign ships were few, and native trading vessels did not have to submit to the police of a regular port, being small enough to beach themselves on any sandy shore where they could do business—and be gone again, leaving no trace.

Further east, European merchant ships met less opposition, partly because at first they came in very small numbers. Thus when Portuguese traders first appeared along the coast of China, beginning in 1520, the Chinese government made no special effort to resist them. That would have required a reversal of the decision whereby the Chinese had prohibited naval construction. In any case, the government had no resources to spare from the defense of the northern land frontier against the nomads, and a few Europeans offered no conceivable threat to the imperial majesty of the Son of Heaven. Instead, the Portuguese were allowed to set up a coastal station at Macao in 1557, where they attended to their own defense and internal governance, thanks to the tacit acquiescence of local Chinese administrators.

In Japan, no central government had practical power over the warrior chieftains who controlled the southern ports where Europeans first arrived in 1543. Local policy depended on local encounters, but for the most part a lively curiosity dominated the earliest Japanese reactions to the European ships and mariners who began to frequent their shores. Intense interest in details of their armament and other novelties was prominent from the start. Even the mysteries of the Christian religion aroused far warmer response in Japan than elsewhere in Asia, as the Spanish Jesuit missionary St. Francis Xavier discovered. Initial curiosity and eagerness to acquire new skills and ideas from the Europeans only gave way to a more suspicious stance at the end of the century. Yet, in 1638 the government eventually imitated the Chinese by prohibiting Japanese subjects from building seagoing ships and limited foreign shipping far more strictly than the Chinese ever tried to do.

From the point of view of the Chinese government, the first Portuguese merchant ships that ventured into Chinese and Japanese waters merged into and became part of a Far Eastern piratical society, based on various offshore islands along the south China coast. The mixed ethnic origins of these pirates allowed the Chinese government to regard them as foreign; but in fact they were heirs of the older Chinese naval tradition, and some of their seagoing junks could carry big guns without suffering undue damage from recoil. The pirates' problem was to get hold of such guns, for neither the craftsmen nor the metal needed for their manufacture was easily accessible to them.

Nevertheless, Portuguese guns and Portuguese manpower did infiltrate the pirate society of the Far East, in much the same way that European sailors and guns infiltrated the world of the Barbary pirates in the Mediterranean in the sixteenth century. Both piratical communities therefore responded to the new European style of naval architecture and warfare in a way the great land-based empires of Asia never did. But pirates lacked the material resources and organization ever to challenge Europeans when it came to long-distance commerce. Instead, each vessel was on its own when sailing through pirate-infested waters, and in such encounters European-manned vessels usually held their own without too much difficulty, having far better access to guns and other equipment than locally based pirates enjoyed.

Oddly enough, despite the Mediterranean Sea's proximity to Atlantic Europe, the superiority of Atlantic-style naval vessels was considerably slower to assert itself there than in the Indian Ocean or the South China Sea. As late as 1571, both Christian and Ottoman fleets used old-fashioned ramming and boarding tactics at the battle of Lepanto. At Lepanto, to be sure, a few Venetian galleasses, equipped with a single bow-mounted cannon, contributed conspicuously to the Christian victory; but that sort of cannonade was a pale imitation of the broadsides Atlantic vessels were by then accustomed to deliver. Ten years later, in 1581, Spain and Turkey signed a truce, thus suspending organized naval war in the Mediterranean. The struggle was never resumed, and although state-supported war galleys continued to sail in Mediterranean waters for several decades thereafter, privately managed cannon-carrying ships of Atlantic design began to dominate both trade and piracy in the Mediterranean from the beginning of the seventeenth century, if not before.

Transformations of European Armies to 1700

Wealth garnered from overseas trade enhanced the Europeans' capacity to pay for land as well as for naval armaments. Cities that could not or did not succeed in protecting themselves from land attack ceased to be seats of large-scale, long-range commerce simply because the men who financed and organized such enterprises wanted security for themselves and their capital and carefully sought out those places where security was best. The fate of Antwerp, sacked by Spanish soldiers in 1576 when it became clear that a bankrupt King Philip II could not pay their back wages, illustrated this fact. Antwerp had been the chief center of northwestern Europe's commerce and finance before 1576; after its sack, capitalists and entrepreneurs fled to Amsterdam, where the merchant oligarchy that ruled that city and the surrounding province of Holland was eminently solicitous of business interests.

Consequently, Amsterdam took over Antwerp's metropolitan role for European big business within an amazingly short time. Unlike the Flemings of Antwerp, the Dutch of Amsterdam took good care to attend to their own defense by hiring soldiers to keep the Hapsburg heir, King Philip II, and his armies at a safe distance. Philip, however, very much wanted to control the wealth of the Low Countries and assumed that the Spanish soldiers who had won so many victories in Italy would be able to bring the rebellious Dutch to heel. As a result, the Dutch wars (1567–1648), which merged into the Thirty Years War in Germany (1618–48) in their final phase, succeeded the wars in Italy (1494–1559) as the principal proving ground for the European art of war.

In Italy, Spanish soldiers had established their reputation as the best fighting force of Europe. The French had relied on native cavalry, Swiss pikemen, and heavy artillery. The Spaniards defeated them by using an infantry army, composed of Spanish pikemen and newfangled arquebusiers, together with extensive resort to field fortifications for protecting their flanks from cavalry attack. The French artillery seldom reached the battlefield, being too slow to keep up with marching men, and cavalry was useless for siege operations, which again came to the fore as the *trace italienne* spread.

Thus, the Spanish army as it emerged from the Italian wars was composed mainly of pikemen, massed in squares and supported in front and on the flanks by what were called sleeves of arquebusiers. Their guns could inflict wounds at a distance of up to one hundred yards, and thus helped to weaken an opposing body of troops for the "push of pike," whereby battles were decided. Sieges were usually terminated by surrender when the garrison faced starvation, although commanders did know how to fill in the ditches and silence the fire from enemy bastions that protected the new style of fortification from direct assault. But such methods were costly in time, effort, and casualties, and it was usually preferable simply to wait for time to do its work.

In the course of the Dutch wars, the Spanish level of military efficiency was left behind by the very miscellaneous body of mercenary troops who served under the command of Maurice of Nassau, prince of Orange, who was captain general of Holland from 1585 until his death in 1625 and commanded the forces maintained by other Dutch provinces for varying periods of time as well. Maurice was university trained and looked to the ancient Romans for models of how to organize, train, and discipline his troops. He was also a Calvinist and, in spite of his noble breeding, shared something of the work ethic with which Calvinists have been credited.

What Prince Maurice did, above all else, was to make sure that the soldiers under his command were kept busy. In siege operations, he imitated the Romans by ordering his soldiers to construct field fortifications for their own protection. Digging became incessant, for Maurice also required his troops to construct elaborate assault trenches so they could close for an attack on the ditch and walls without suffering losses in the approach.

Such tactics turned sieges into victories rather than endurance contests; moreover, it kept the besiegers busy, solving problems of indiscipline and dissipation that had always before corroded besieging armies.

Soldiers, of course, spent most of their time doing garrison duty or just waiting for the next field campaign. Maurice occupied his soldiers' idle hours by insisting on drill—endless, repeated, systematic. He divided his army into battalions, companies, platoons, and squads, with a commander over each unit. A 550-man battalion was the largest unit that could respond to a single human voice; the squad (usually 10 men) was the smallest unit that could act independently—marching, deploying, firing. The chain of command reached symmetrically from Maurice at the top to each and every corporal in command of a squad. In principle, if not always in practice, Maurice could move his troops about on the battlefield as a chess player moves pieces on his board. Flexibility, precision, and predictability in battle increased with such organization and drill, and to make that result even more certain, Maurice established officer-training schools where each rank learned exactly what its role and duties were.

Practice of battlefield maneuvers was only part of Prince Maurice's drill. Soldiers also practiced weapons handling—over and over and over. To make every motion count, Maurice (or someone under him) analyzed the movements needed for the handling of pikes and of matchlock handguns, dividing them into a series of separate, distinct muscular acts. Drillmasters then set out to make the soldiers perform the prescribed movements in unison and at the word of command. The practical effect was to minimize error. If an arquebusier failed to ram a wad down the barrel of his gun so as to keep the powder in place, or to follow that with a bullet, and then another wad, before priming the firing pan and getting his burning match into proper position to ignite the gun, his weapon was sure to misfire. In the excitement and confusion of battle, error and omission of this sort was inevitable, but endlessly repeated practice could reduce its frequency and thereby increase the quantity of lead a given number of soldiers could shoot at the enemy. Time between shots could also be shortened, and the unison of drill produced a concerted volley that demoralized opposing troops more effectively than scattered shooting could do, largely for psychological reasons.

Drill, however, had other and more important psychological consequences. That is because men who live together and confront an obvious risk to life and limb, as mercenary soldiers must do, respond to the experience of moving their muscles in unison by bonding to their fellows in a quite extraordinary way. Such behavior undoubtedly rouses echoes of humanity's most primitive form of sociality. Even before our ancestors were entirely human and had learned to talk, they danced around campfires—celebrating past successes in the hunt and rehearsing what they would do to their quarry next time. Hunting bands that succeeded through such dance rehearsals in perfecting their cooperation and mutual support in the field—each man standing firm when the moment of crisis arose, thrusting home with spear or dagger when the game came within reach, risking wounds, and sharing the triumph of the kill—had an obvious advantage when it came to begetting and feeding their progeny. That progeny eventually peopled the earth, bequeathing aptitudes and sensibilities to their descendants that still affect human behavior profoundly.

Prince Maurice's drill, like that of the ancient Romans and Greeks, was therefore able to call on a very powerful primitive aptitude for cooperation and mutual support, creating a visceral sense of "belonging" to and with one's fellows. Only someone who has undergone long hours of close-order drill in a modern army is likely to appreciate or believe that an activity so mindless (and in our time no longer functional in battle) can have such powerful psychological side effects. But drill sergeants and privates, even in our push-button era, still experience the eerie effect of drill. Young men, subjected to such an experience, are automatically differentiated from civilian society, being united instead by a special bond—an esprit de corps—that soon begins to dominate the consciousness of those who move their muscles rhythmically and in unison. Athletic teams and some religious groups—remember the Shakers and the dancing dervishes—also have tapped this primitive level of human sociality; but its importance for armies, and especially for European armies,[2] far eclipses other manifestations of this peculiar human aptitude.

No one was entirely aware of the full consequences of Maurice's reforms, at the time or subsequently. Commanders got what they were after: greater efficiency in battle. They did not wonder much about how and why their men became so ready to obey and conform. Yet in a longer historical perspective, this was by far the most significant aspect of the Dutch army's transformation. Before the 1590s, infantrymen had been potential revolutionaries within European society, coming, as they did, from the poorer classes. Rulers had often preferred to hire foreigners for that reason, since soldiers who spoke a different language were less likely to sympathize with the lower classes or side with them in case of local riots. But as drill became a normal part of everyday experience for European infantrymen, bonding with fellow soldiers took precedence over every other social sympathy. Esprit de corps took over; pride in themselves and their collective prowess supplanted civilian identities.

As a result, the flotsam and jetsam of city streets and the sons of impoverished peasants became thoroughly reliable instruments of aristocratic and oligarchic rule. European governments could afford to invest in technically proficient infantry armies without fearing that the armed poor would challenge the class hierarchy on which those governments rested. No other civilized society of the age enjoyed the same privilege. No other civilized state could arm the poorest classes of society with impunity. As a result, European armies were cheap as well as effective when compared with the aristocratic, largely cavalry forces that exercised government and maintained the social order in Moslem and Indian lands. In China and Japan, as we will see, the managers of the armed establishments were also inhibited by concern for maintaining the existing social hierarchy. Only in western Europe could rulers afford to pursue efficiency in battle to its logical limits with no concern for the disturbance a predominantly infantry force might offer to existing class relationships.

Instead, in European armies, obedience to the word of command became predictable and almost automatic. Officers as well as men were shaped by their experience of drill. Officers, in addition, were fitted into a bureaucratic hierarchy of rank, so that deference and obedience no longer depended on personal connections and inherited social ties but on bureaucratic appointment and promotion, signified and proclaimed by inconspicuous badges of rank worn as part of a uniform. Indeed, it no longer mattered whose lips framed an order. Soldiers became replaceable parts in a sort of human machine, and so did their officers. A company or platoon obeyed familiar orders that had been practiced endlessly in drill—orders to march, deploy, fire—with about the same accuracy when they came from a competent officer or from a novice. It made scant difference whether the chain of command emanated from a government whose seat was halfway round the earth or whether the sovereign was in the field with his troops, on top of the nearest hill.

Flexible, formidable, and reliable armed establishments of this kind were truly remarkable works of art and ought to count as one of the most extraordinary achievements of the age. The armies of other civilizations fell far short of what western Europeans now began to take for granted. This, with the continued superiority of their cannon-carrying ships, allowed Europeans to continue expansion overseas with less and less concern about whether or not their increased presence aroused hostile reactions from local peoples.

The efficiency of Prince Maurice's Dutch armies in battles and sieges was of course evident to others, and the new pattern of organization and drill spread very rapidly indeed within the European circle of nations. In 1607 the Dutch published a book illustrating each step of their manual of arms, so that even illiterates could learn exactly how it was done. A German edition came out in 1614; a Russian translation followed in 1649, and by then even the Spanish, having been defeated at the battle of Rocroi in 1643 by a French army that had used the new drill, reluctantly went over to their enemy's style of discipline and organization.

Improvements did not halt with Prince Maurice and the Dutch. During the Thirty Years War, Germans and Swedes experimented with battle tactics that involved the coordination of infantry and cavalry with newly designed light field artillery. Later, toward the end of the seventeenth century, arquebuses and matchlocks were superseded by more reliable flintlock muskets as the standard weapon for European infantrymen. As handguns improved, pikes became less important, and when the ring bayonet was invented, about 1690, pikes became entirely unnecessary, since musketeers could now both fire their guns and protect themselves even from cavalry attack simply by fixing bayonets to their guns.

The Peace of Westphalia that ended the Thirty Years War made France the greatest power of Europe, and for a while it looked as though King Louis XIV (reigned 1643–1715) might use his army to extend his kingdom into the Rhinelands and, perhaps, renew a bid for hegemony over the Continent. But a coalition of other states soon formed to check his ambition and thereby maintained the uneasy balance of power that continued to differentiate western Europe from the vast empires that prevailed in other civilized lands.

Nevertheless, the headlong pace of military innovation in Europe slowed perceptibly after about 1700, largely because professional standing armies now dominated the scene, and to profit from the interchangeability of parts and personnel such armies needed uniform equipment. When standing armies numbered more than a hundred thousand, a new design for a handgun, or anything else, cost too much to be accepted lightly. If the proposed weapon required changes in drill routines, it jeopardized any gain the new design offered during an awkward transition period, lasting for years. Minor design improvements therefore ceased. Weapons designs, which had continually evolved by virtue of innumerable small changes ever since gunpowder first came in, therefore stabilized as far as Europe's armies were concerned. (Fine hunting guns for private use did continue to improve, but that had no immediate effect on armies.) As a result, a nearly fixed routine soon set in that made the wars of the eighteenth century less disruptive to European society than those of the sixteenth and seventeenth centuries had been. But stability and modulated warfare at home went along with accelerated expansion overseas, where European military superiority became increasingly evident in comparison with the practices of other peoples and states whose responses to gunpowder weaponry had taken a different path.

Europe's Outliers: Muscovy and the Americas to 1700

The first phase of the gunpowder revolution, focusing on siege cannon, profoundly changed patterns of power in Russia and America. Both regions continued to share in the further elaboration of the European style of warfare, even if they lagged a bit behind the most active centers of innovation. By 1700, consequently, vast regions of the earth, overseas in the Americas and eastward into Asia all the way to the Pacific coast, had been folded into the Europe-centered system of states. By that date, the Russian lands as well as the Americas shared, at least marginally, in a civilization that ought not to be called European any longer, since it had transcended Europe's boundaries.

It is easy to exaggerate the importance of weaponry and of military organization in accounting for this expansion. Disease had more to do with the destruction and displacement of Amerindian populations than did guns, for example; and Russian expansion into the Siberian forests was also accompanied and facilitated by epidemic die-offs among previously isolated and disease-inexperienced peoples. But without guns and the easy military superiority they gave to Europeans in initial encounters with local peoples, the pattern of European expansion would have been very different.

In Russia, the first and quite fundamental consequence of the gunpowder revolution was the consolidation of Muscovy into a vast, single, and autocratic state. Grand Duke Ivan III (reigned 1462–1505) knew what cannon could do. After all, guns had smashed the walls of Constantinople just nine years before he came to power in Moscow. He therefore took great pains to acquire a few of the new wall destroyers, and with their help was able to conquer almost all of the other Russian principalities in a very short time. His consolidation of the Russian lands was exactly like what had happened in France a generation earlier when King Louis XI and his son had consolidated their authority over formerly independent feudal domains.

Having united the Russian lands, Muscovite rulers followed the French example a step further by using their new military capability to attack southward and eastward. But unlike the French, who were eventually driven out of Italy, the Russians stayed in the new lands their armies and cannon allowed them to dominate. Thus, in a series of decisive campaigns between 1552 and 1556, Ivan IV, better known as Ivan the Terrible (reigned 1533–84) conquered the Tartar principalities along the Volga all the way to its mouth. It took another century before Russian power was established securely along the northern shore of the Black Sea, but the dominance of Moscow and of the autocrat who claimed succession to Constantine and the Byzantine emperors of Christendom by taking the title of czar (Caesar) was never successfully challenged again from within the Russian lands. The new Muscovite autocrats relied on the Russian river system, which allowed effective central control over comparatively vast territories. Local resistance to Moscow became impossible when big guns made existing fortresses useless, for the simple reason that cannon could reach them by being hauled up and down the rivers on barges. Portages from one river system to another were more difficult, but sleighs could carry cannon across frozen snowy ground in winter—and the key portages were short with no great elevations to surmount. As a result, all the cities and strongpoints of the Russian lands were easily accessible by water. Simply by controlling the only mobile gun park in those lands, the czar could dominate them all.

Centralization of absolute, unlimited power, which continued to characterize Russian government thereafter, down to our own day, was the result. Absolutism was reinforced and perpetuated by continued difficulty the Russian government faced in coping with overland threats. Danger came partly from the south, where Tartar cavalrymen from the shores of the Black Sea kept on supplying the slave market in Constantinople with captives from Russian villages until late in the seventeenth century. From the west, Swedish and Polish armies, which shared more fully than the Russians in continuing improvements in the European art of war, were able to invade Russian from time to time and even threatened to conquer the whole country during a dynastic interlude—the so-called Time of Troubles (1604–13).

Eastward, beyond the Ural Mountains, Russians had no such problems. Instead, it was they who threatened the various peoples and polities of northern Asia. Small bands of frontiersmen, more or less obedient to Moscow and to fur-trading merchants based in Novgorod and other Russian cities, swiftly learned to portage from one river system to the next until they reached the Pacific in 1637. A vast hinterland thus became tributary to Moscow. Soon afterward, the French in Canada (beginning in 1609) and the British Hudson's Bay Company (beginning in 1670) began to extend exactly analogous fur-trading empires across most of North America, operating from bases at Montreal and Churchill. Russian and British (and, presently, United States) fur traders and empire builders collided on the shores of the Pacific in the last decades of the eighteenth century, closing and completing the geographic range of an extraordinarily far-reaching system of trade. Handguns, together with metal knives and hatchets, were vital to these empires, giving European agents and traders command of instruments of destruction and construction on which the aboriginal hunters and gatherers of those snowy wastes soon came to depend for their livelihood.

In the course of the seventeenth century, the Russians were gradually able to check Tartar slave raiding by building elaborate frontier defenses, stationing garrisons in stockaded forts, and constructing mile upon mile of wooden palisades between adjacent forts. Troops equipped with handguns, when they were able to catch up with the Tartars, could kill mounts and men in such number that the old nomad superiority in the field was undermined. The wooden field fortifications hampered Tartar mobility enough to make it a lot easier to catch raiding parties.

On their western frontier, however, the Russians found themselves at a more persistent disadvantage. Recurrent efforts to catch up by importing the latest forms of European military organization and weaponry sufficed to keep the Russian heartlands immune from conquest, but not from invasion. Thus, in the course of the long Livonian war (1557–82), Swedish armies succeeded in shearing the Baltic coastlands away from Muscovite sovereignty. The Poles, likewise, advanced into the Ukraine in the sixteenth and seventeenth centuries and exercised a powerful attraction on noblemen in the more westerly Russian lands, who resented their subordination to the czar and yearned for aristocratic freedom like that of the Polish Republic.

Under Peter the Great (reigned 1689–1725) a vast effort at military modernization did allow the Russians to catch up, or nearly catch up, with western European levels of organization and equipment. Peter was therefore able to extend his southern borders to the shores of the Black Sea (though initial victories there were almost undone by a subsequent failure in 1711) and even rolled the Swedes back far enough to secure a narrow window to the west along the coast of the Baltic Sea by 1721.

Throughout the eighteenth century, when, as we have seen, European military practices and weapons nearly stabilized, Russian power increased dramatically by comparison with the other states of Europe, thanks to the vast territorial base and growing populations that sustained the czar's armies and brand new navy, all constructed on up-to-date Western models. When an extraordinary industrial and democratic transformation of European polities in the nineteenth century tapped new sources of power, Russian once more fell behind—only to try yet again, in our own century, to catch up and overtake by importing the industrial and military technologies that had raised Western power to new heights.

American development was different. The various colonial societies that arose along the Atlantic face of the Americas after Columbus's discovery were not seriously threatened by overland enemies, but their fate did very much depend on the fluctuating naval power of the competing European states. In imperial warfare, the security of the American colonies depended on guns carried on shipboard, operating in tandem with other guns emplaced in fortresses along the strategic sea routes that were defined by winds and currents as well as by where valued trade goods like furs, silver, and sugar were to be had. Quebec, Halifax, and Havana became the key fortresses for the French, British, and Spanish empires respectively.

Havana and other Spanish strongholds of the Caribbean were defended as much by yellow fever as by guns. Once ashore, soldiers fresh from

Europe became radically vulnerable to a disease to which they had no prior exposure or immunity. No landing force could survive for longer than six weeks before suffering crippling losses from the mosquito-spread virus of yellow fever. Local Spanish garrisons, on the contrary, were already immune, and so could hold on to victory unless supplies ran out. That was why the Spanish empire survived, despite several large-scale British efforts to use their growing naval predominance to conquer the Caribbean. By way of contrast, the French empire in Canada, where disease did not play any critical role, collapsed in 1759 when a British expeditionary force captured Quebec.

Between bouts of imperial, mainly naval, warfare, the various colonies of the Americas had no need of an up-to-date armed establishment of the sort the Russians required for security against their neighbors. Local militiamen were more than enough to cope with sporadic efforts by the Indians to safeguard their hunting grounds and drive intruding whites away. Until after 1700, distance safely separated the land frontiers of the rival colonial systems from each other, although claims conflicted. As a result, a lawless no-man's-land formed between French, English, and Spanish settlements, and in time of war agents of the warring powers supplied Indians with guns to induce them to attack their rivals.

Another lawless zone existed in the Caribbean, where a flourishing pirate world existed very much like the pirate communities of the South China Sea and of the Mediterranean. It was populated by French, English, Dutch, Spanish, Portuguese, and African adventurers together with others of mixed ancestry, sometimes fighting among themselves and sometimes making a common front against legally constituted authorities.

The Russian frontier also supported a fringe of lawless adventurers known as Cossacks. They served as outrunners and pioneers of Russian expansion throughout Siberia and along the empire's southern border. New World frontiersmen of the interior played the same role with respect to European colonial society, most notably in Brazil and trans-Appalachian North America.

Ruthless efficiency as measured by monetary results prevailed in the New World. Military considerations prevailed in Russia. Therein lay a fundamental and enduring difference between the two principal outlying societies arising along the frontiers of Western civilization. Overseas it was the market that mattered most; overland it was armed protection that took precedence over other considerations. That was because, in time of need, high-technology navies and professional soldiers defended European overseas settlements, and for these the colonists did not pay. The Russian lands had no such external resource. They had to pay for their own defense, sporadically importing the latest, most efficient military techniques, whatever the cost.

Where European settlers in the Americas directed the labor of large numbers of black slaves or Indian peasants, the sharp differentiation between rulers and ruled that characterized Russian society was more or less replicated in the Americas, with the difference that economic rather than political–military motives and calculations justified the subordination of the majority to the will of the minority. Where no such ethnic chasm existed, American society became far more egalitarian than was the case elsewhere in the Western world. As a result, the English colonies of North America tended to diverge from the European norm of society in the opposite direction from the way the Russians did. English colonial freedom melting into backwoods anarchy contrasted with Russia's steep social pyramid, which was consciously and deliberately modeled on a military chain of command. Yet the anarchic, egalitarian ideal was not absent from Russian society. It was merely banished to the margins. In remote Siberia and the barren north pioneers lived quite as independently as any American frontiersman. Their freedom constituted an alternative ideal, lurking as a sort of underground in Russian society as a whole. What tipped the balance was the Russians' need for effective, professional, and technically up-to-date military defense—something American colonists did not need to worry about. Contrasts between the United States and the Soviet Union of our own time descend directly and obviously from these differences in the frontier experience of the seventeenth century.

Moslem Responses to the Gunpowder Revolution

As we saw, the Ottoman sultan Mohammed the Conqueror recognized the value of siege guns as early as 1453 and did not hesitate to employ Christian artillerists to cast the weapons he needed to batter down the walls of the city that became his capital thereafter. In addition, the sultan equipped his slave corps of foot soldiers, the famous Janissaries, with handguns from the time that such weapons became effective in the field. Indeed, in the sixteenth century the Janissary corps may have used more handguns than any other armed force in the world, since European infantry were then still mostly pikemen, and in other civilized lands, infantry were not well enough disciplined to be trusted with large numbers of guns.

Until about 1600, therefore, the Ottoman army remained technically and in every other way in the very forefront of military proficiency. Continued territorial conquests attested its superior skill and organization, both against Christians in the Balkans and Hungary and against Moslems in Syria, Egypt, and Arabia. The bulk of the Ottoman army consisted of cavalrymen, equipped according to the steppe tradition with bows and arrows as their principal offensive weapon. But the importance of artillery and of the gun-carrying Janissaries was far greater than mere numbers might suggest.

Artillerymen were few and, often, also foreign, but their field guns helped the Ottoman army to defeat their only serious Moslem rivals, the Safavid shah's cavalry, at the Battle of Chaldiran in 1514. (The Turks carried their comparatively light field guns in wagons and deployed them for battle in the gaps left when the wagons were hitched together to make a laager for protection against cavalry attack.) Portable field guns were not enough to overcome Vienna's walls, however, as the unsuccessful Ottoman siege of that city in 1529 demonstrated. Moreover, the Ottoman army could not remain in the field long enough to starve the city into surrender or even to bring heavy siege guns all the way from Constantinople. Instead, because the season for campaigning was already drawing toward a close, they had to start back for home a few weeks after reaching Vienna's walls.

Thus, it was distance from Constantinople that allowed the Hapsburgs to retain Vienna and its surrounding Austrian provinces as a frontier against the Turks, and it was distance from Constantinople that also permitted the Safavids to establish a rival Moslem Shi'a state in Azerbaijan and Iran. But within the geographical range defined by their need to muster in spring and disband in the fall somewhere close to the capital, the Ottoman field armies remained superior to any they encountered until after the middle of the seventeenth century.

The discipline and numbers that made Ottoman cavalry so formidable depended on the fact that the sultan controlled a private household of armed men that was clearly and obviously capable of nipping provincial rebellion in the bud. Knowing that, landholders reported punctually for service year after year, and became accustomed to obeying the sultan's officers. These officers were selected from the imperial household to serve as provincial governors and field commanders over the cavalrymen of the district they governed.

In addition to such officers, the sultan's household comprised the Janissary corps of foot soldiers, and a corps of privileged cavalrymen as well. All the members of the sultan's military household, from highest field commander to humblest Janissary, were slaves, recruited mainly from Christian peasant villages located in the mountainous wild west of the Balkan peninsula. Recruiters were interested only in boys who were nearly full grown, so the sultan's slaves could well remember their Christian peasant upbringing. But the effect of drill and education on them was as remarkable as the effect of Prince Maurice's regimen on his soldiers. They became obedient, disciplined agents of the sultan's will. For those with unusual natural abilities, the Ottoman slave household offered a career wide open to talent. Even the grand vizier, the chief administrative officer of the entire empire, more often than not had started life as a Balkan peasant boy. The sultan also entrusted all the other major commands of the empire to his slaves.

After the middle of the sixteenth century, this remarkable military and administrative structure began to lose its efficiency. First of all, the sultans ceased to lead their armies in person and gave up annual campaigns. Toward the end of Suleiman the Lawgiver's reign (1520–66) a series of costly campaigns (both by land and by sea) ended only in unsuccessful investment of frontier fortresses, built on the *trace italienne* plan. That made it clear that no further advance into Europe was possible, and, as we saw before, Ottoman efforts in the Indian Ocean met with decisive disaster between 1512 and 1538. North of the Black Sea, potentially rich lands lay within range of the Ottoman army, but the Ukrainian grasslands were almost empty of agricultural settlement in the sixteenth century, and so were hardly worth conquering, since they could not support Ottoman cavalrymen as the Balkan and Asian provinces of the empire did. The Turks did advance into Rumania, but halted there until the 1670s when wars with Poland and Russia for control of the Ukraine revealed the fact that the old Ottoman superiority to Christian armies had begun to decay.

Two factors combined to tip the balance against the Turks in the seventeenth century. First, the internal discipline and morale of the sultan's slave household became unreliable, partly because the sultans ceased to command the army and administration personally, and partly because the pattern of recruitment to the slave household was changed so as to admit persons of urban background and Moslem birth to its ranks. As the sultans became creatures of the harem, mere figureheads for the intriguing courtiers and civil administrators who actually ran the government, ties between civil society and the slave household multiplied. This brought all sorts of special interests to bear on government policy in a way that had been impossible when the empire was governed by slaves who had severed ties with the remote villages of their birth because of geographical removal to Constantinople and by accepting an (often tepid) adherence to Islam.

Urban interests profited and villagers suffered from this transformation of the Ottoman administration. In the absence of annual campaigns, the old discipline and obedience in the provinces weakened. Local magnates and bandits soon began to intercept tax revenues and use them for their own local purposes instead of allowing them to flow freely to the support of the central government and capital city. The result was to undermine the central government quite drastically, and efforts to renew the old traditions, undertaken as part of a convulsive reform movement in 1656, proved only partially successful.

The second factor that weakened the Ottoman military posture vis-à-vis the European frontier states with whom they collided after the middle of the seventeenth century was the unwillingness or inability of the regime to keep up with European technical advances in the art of war. As handguns improved, battle efficiency had come to require infantry armies, but Moslem and nomad traditions valued cavalry too highly to make such a shift acceptable. The social position of Turkish landholders, especially in the Balkans where the peasantry remained Christian, required them to maintain a social distance from the majority, and that was best done from horseback. The government did increase the number of foot soldiers by allowing the Janissary corps to expand. But larger numbers were a strain on the state budget, which was already suffering from a general inflation of prices caused by the influx of American silver. The cure was to permit Janissaries to supplement their pay by working for a living when not on campaign. But this brought on new disorders, for the expanded Janissary corps merged into the Moslem artisan classes of the towns, especially of Constantinople, and ceased to be either obedient to the sultan or willing to submit to the sort of drill that made European troops increasingly effective in battle.

The changing balance of military competence between Ottoman and Christian armies was first demonstrated in the Ukraine, where the Russians succeeded in defeating the Turks in a hard-fought war between 1577 and 1581. When the Turks tried to recover their damaged morale by attacking the Hapsburgs instead, and advanced to besiege Vienna for a second time in 1683, they failed once more. In ensuing years they were driven out of Hungary by the generalship of Prince Eugene, commanding troops that had profited from all the technical and organizational advances which had been so ruthlessly field-tested in Germany during the Thirty Years War. Failure in the Ukraine in 1681, and retreat from Hungary, sealed by the Treaty of Karlowitz in 1699, marked the definitive eclipse of Ottoman military superiority in wars against European troops.

The empire never recovered. Instead, the circumstances that had inhibited the Ottomans from keeping pace with western Europe in the seventeenth century continued to prevail until the violent destruction of the Janissary corps in 1826, and by then it was too late. The Turks could not begin to match the industrialization of war pursued by the leading European powers after the mid-nineteenth century. Repeated defeats and eventual disruption of the empire in 1923 were the result.

In India and Iran two other Moslem empires compared in magnitude and importance with the Ottoman state. Their military history closely resembled Ottoman response to the gunpowder revolution, but lagged behind by a century or more in time, owing to geographical isolation from the European center of technical innovation.

The Mughal empire of India got started in 1526 when a descendant of Tamerlane named Babar crossed the Himalayas and began to conquer northern India. Babar and his followers were heirs of an ancient Persian–Turkish warrior tradition that made them skilled cavalrymen, archers, and gentlemen for whom a delicious Persian love poem was as admirable as heroic single combat. The Mughal invaders met success against rulers already on the ground in India (most of whom also shared in and descended from the same central Asian military tradition) because they had closer connection with the lands to the north whence came the horses and the warriors needed to dominate Indian battlefields. The Indian climate was not good for horses, and they could seldom be successfully bred on Indian soil. Hence, an army had to import mounts from the north just to keep going, and control of the supply of horses became strategically vital, as long as battles were won and lost by cavalry actions.

Babar nonetheless knew about guns and their use in sieges. He even imitated the Ottoman sultan Mohammed the Conqueror by employing artisans to cast siege guns on the spot in order to smash his enemies' fortifications. In that fashion, the superiority of his cavalry in the field could be translated into more lasting victory, since defeated foes could no longer survive by taking refuge in fortified strongholds and expect to live to fight another day.

Nevertheless, Babar's control over northern India was never secure, and a few years after his death in 1530 rivals even drove his son Humayun out of India entirely. But after recruiting fresh followers in the north, Humayun returned to Indian battlefields and won back the hegemony of northern India that his father had gained before him. Stabilization of the Mughal regime was achieved only under Humayun's son, Akbar (reigned 1556–1605), who regularized tax collection, came to a modus vivendi with the indigenous Hindu landowning and military class and acquired an imperial gun park that backed up his superior cavalry by giving him the capacity to destroy even the most formidable fortified refuge of a defeated foe. Akbar's guns, as portrayed in the *Akbarnama*, an illustrated record of his victories, were close replicas of the sort of siege guns that had been invented in Burgundy between 1465 and 1477. Hauling them cross-country to invest strongholds, some of which were perched on top of precipitous heights, was very difficult. For that reason, the Mughal hold on the hilly parts of India was always insecure, and the social gap between Moslem invaders and Hindu subjects made rebellion perennial and very easy to foment.

Nonetheless, the Mughals maintained a quite effective central government at Delhi until after 1707, and were able to extend their jurisdiction southward to embrace almost all of the peninsula. But the Mughal government made no attempt to control the seas, allowing Europeans to establish fortified bases along India's coast to safeguard their trade goods and themselves. Little by little, the importance of these European enclaves increased as more and more Indians began to produce cotton cloth and other goods for sale to the Europeans. Moreover, when English and French trading companies displaced the Portuguese as the principal European traders along the coasts of India, they began to recruit small garrisons of Indian soldiers, known to the English as sepoys, to guard their fortified shore stations. Drilled by European officers in the European fashion, these troops soon became far more efficient than Mughal foot soldiers.

Then, in the course of the eighteenth century, a remarkable power shift took place. The comparatively small numbers of European-trained infantry proved capable of dominating Indian battlefields just as had been the case in Europe since 1477. As a result, it was the British who succeeded the Mughals as rulers of India, thanks to their sepoy troops, and to the Royal Navy that kept the East India Company's shore stations and armies in touch with their home base in London.

But long before the East India Company's troops became engaged in decisive battles, internal disorders and renewed invasions had broken up the unity of Mughal administration. A regime whose military power depended primarily on horses and cavalrymen, originating north of the mountains—both finding the climate of India debilitating—was intrinsically vulnerable. Innumerable earlier conquest regimes in northern India had decayed after only one or two generations for the same reason. What was different between 1556 and 1707 was the added reach that siege guns gave to the central authority, allowing the Mughal government to extend its power over almost the whole of India, as only one of its imperial predecessors had been able to do in earlier centuries. In that limited sense, the Mughal empire, like the Ottoman, was a member of the family of gunpowder empires.

The other great Moslem state of the age, based in Azerbaijan and Iran, was entirely traditional in military matters when Shah Isma'il (reigned 1502–24) declared himself to be the only legitimate successor to the Prophet by claiming descent from Ali, Mohammed's son-in-law. That claim convulsed the Moslem world, much as Luther's claim to reform the church convulsed Christendom fifteen years later. It inspired the Ottoman sultans to embark on a violent repression of the numerous Shi'a sympathizers in Anatolia, who were inclined to accept Isma'il's claim, and, as mentioned above, pitted the Ottoman imperial army against Isma'il's tribal followers at the Battle of Chaldiran in 1514.

Ottoman military discipline and field guns won that battle, and for the rest of the century the Safavid dynasty, founded by Isma'il, relied more on religious incandescence than on technical proficiency to defend itself against its rivals. Then, under Shah Abbas I the Great (reigned 1587–1629), new contacts with the European world allowed the shah to import guns. He thereupon began to create an artillery and an infantry corps at his court, very much on the Ottoman model. The agents who gave Shah Abbas access to the new weaponry were a pair of English merchant adventurers, Anthony and Robert Shirley, who reached Persia by traversing Russia, descending the Volga, and crossing the Caspian Sea. The Russians were willing enough to strengthen the principal Moslem foe of their Ottoman neighbors and rivals, so this circuitous route was not interdicted by political barriers. Instead, the shah was able to build up his personal power vis-à-vis the tribal and territorial chiefs who dominated the Turko-Iranian society he ruled, by counterbalancing their cavalry with his new infantry and artillery just as the Ottoman sultans had done since 1453.

Abbas used his enhanced military strength to attack the Ottomans. He succeeded in capturing disputed borderlands in Iraq and eastern Anatolia, though after his death the Ottomans were able to regain almost all the territory they had lost. These struggles, however, entirely preoccupied the Turks during Russia's Time of Troubles and while western Europe was convulsed by the Thirty Years War.

As far as the Safavid state was concerned, the successors of Abbas found it impossible to maintain the balance between imperial and feudal armed forces that he had created, partly because of difficulties in importing and paying for guns, and partly because vigorous religious and social prejudice against the new-fangled military arrangements at court were very difficult to resist. The commanding personality of Shah Abbas had overcome opposition to military modernization; his successors, weaker men, were unable or unwilling to do so. The Safavid regime therefore disintegrated into warring tribal and territorial fragments by the end of the seventeenth century.

Thus, one must say that guns and the European model of military organization played only a fleeting role in the history of the Safavid state. It ought not, perhaps, to be counted as a gunpowder empire at all—certainly not in its first decades, when its importance in the world of Islam peaked for religious, not military, reasons.

The Far East

Although invented in China, gunpowder and guns played a less revolutionary role there than elsewhere. Indeed, it is not paradoxical to suggest that because gunpowder weapons evolved in China within the context of a very elaborate art of war, Chinese mandarin officials were deliberately able to keep them under close control, allowing only a modest alteration in older patterns of Chinese armament, government, and society.

When gunpowder was first invented (before A.D. 1000) the Sung dynasty's army was very numerous by the standards of other civilized lands, numbering more than a million soldiers. It was composed almost entirely of infantrymen, whose preferred weapon was the crossbow and whose principal role was to guard fortified places along the northern frontier against nomad incursions. Gunpowder was initially of very minor importance— useful only to set nomad tents on fire from a distance, or the like.

As we saw above, when the Mongols invaded and then ruled China (1206–1368), they began to explore the offensive capabilities of gunpowder and developed explosive devices, including the first guns, for breaking into fortified strongholds and attacking in the field. But persistent shortages of gunmetal in China meant that Chinese guns were more expensive than those of Europe, and they tended to remain smaller and less powerful as a result.

Disinterest in the offensive capacity of gunpowder weaponry was re-affirmed under the Ming dynasty (1368–1644), after it came to power by evicting the Mongols from the land of China. Fear of renewed conquest from the steppe dominated Ming military policy. This meant, among other things, that weapons capable of destroying fortifications were of little interest to the Chinese government. Its aim was rather to make fortifications as secure as possible with minimal cost. That required an infantry army, like that of the Sung, to garrison innumerable strongholds along the northwestern frontier, supplemented by a mobile field force, composed mainly of cavalry. Heavy guns, like those Europeans employed so freely, had no place in such a scheme.

Nevertheless, the Chinese continued to know about guns and, indeed, used them to supplement the defense of fortified places. But crossbows, aimed from behind protective walls, were far cheaper and just as effective against nomad cavalry attack, and no one in China advocated a policy of equipping infantry with handguns and then training them so well as to allow them to meet and overcome cavalry in the field. A mobile infantry army, recruited from the bottom of society, would have been difficult for civilian officials to control, and its commanders might refuse to conform to the marginal, quasi-disreputable role that Confucian tradition assigned to soldiers and soldiering.

The Japanese did briefly experiment with gun-carrying infantry, and when they invaded Korea in 1592, detachments of matchlock gunners accompanied the sword-wielding samurai. When the imperial Ming field army intervened, its cavalry, crossbows, and overwhelming numbers helped the Koreans (who had begun to manufacture and use handguns like those the Japanese were employing so effectively) to push the invaders back. In 1598 the Japanese withdrew entirely, taking their handguns with them, and the Chinese never again had to face a well-equipped infantry field force until 1839, when they collided with detachments of British soldiers in the Opium War.

The Ming government also abandoned the navy it had inherited from the Sung and Mongol eras, and in 1436 actually prohibited the construction of seagoing ships in China. Thereafter, supplying cannon for shipboard use ceased to be a drain on imperial resources, making one less reason for trying to keep up with the pace set by European naval armaments.

Traditions of Chinese statecraft, going back to Confucius, deplored resort to military force, viewing fighting as a failure of good government, which ought to depend on the force of example and proper ritual. The task before mandarin officials, shaped by the ideals of the Confucian classics, was to control both the nomads of the steppe and the officers and men of the Chinese army in such a way that neither group would be able to violate the proper order of society by using armed force to ravage the country-side or challenge the mandarins' governance of Chinese society. Careful rationing of supplies delivered to Chinese frontier garrisons, and meticulous fragmentation of military command so that no general could personally control a large field army were the principal methods the civilian administrators used to secure their ultimate control over the soldiery. Subsidies to some chieftains and diplomatic provocation of quarrels among hostile tribes were ways the Chinese sought to keep the nomads from dangerous and concerted attacks.

Obviously, such traditions and methods had no place for heavy offensive weapons, or for troop formations that could dominate battlefields and capture walled cities as European armies were beginning to be able to do. The social structure and Confucian traditions of China made such a development deplorable even to contemplate. Hence, whatever knowledge they had of European military developments remained irrelevant and regrettable to the elite that governed China. Far from being something to emulate, European military organization and techniques looked like yet another deplorable example of the absence of propriety that characterized and defined barbarian behavior.

Yet it turned out that in spite of all the wiles of Chinese diplomacy and military administration, civil wars, arising in the wake of the Korean campaign against the Japanese, paved the way for another barbarian conquest from the north. In the 1640s, cavalrymen from the plains of Manchuria captured the capital, Beijing, and founded a new dynasty, the Qing (1644–1912). The new dynasty established a dual military system, garrisoning key Chinese cities with Manchu detachments but also recruiting Chinese infantrymen for garrisoning frontier posts as before. They entrusted civil administration to Confucian scholars selected in the traditional way by examination, but stationed Manchu observers in most government bureaus to check up on loyalty and efficiency.

As a matter of fact, the Manchu emperors and their immediate entourage had become thoroughly imbued with Chinese cultural traditions and ideals before conquering the Middle Kingdom. Thus, the establishment of a new, barbarian dynasty made less difference to China than had been the case when the Mongols brought with them a central Asian cultural taint that promptly provoked the detestation of Chinese elites. Nonetheless, the new rulers did not overcome the last Ming loyalists until 1683, and even after that date a deep-seated Chinese distaste for those they viewed as barbarians maintained a certain level of distrust between rulers and ruled, even in the most brilliant year of the Qing dynasty.

Being steppe dwellers and cavalry warriors themselves, the Manchus were in a position to deal successfully with China's other barbarian neighbors as soon as the vast resources of the empire came into their hands. As a result, encounters with Mongols and Tibetans (some armed, some merely diplomatic) led to rapid expansion of their imperial influence into the steppe and forest lands of central and east Asia. There the expanding Chinese imperial power fetched up against the expanding Russians, whose pioneers had reached the Pacific coast as early as 1637. Negotiations defined respective spheres of influence and regularized trade, beginning with the Treaty of Nerchinsk in 1689.

The advance of Chinese and Russian administration into the steppe signified the waning of nomad military superiority over settled agricultural populations that had been a fixed feature of Eurasian society since the skill of riding directly on horseback had first spread across the grasslands between 700 and 300 B.C. Infantry handguns from the Russian side, and a complex, ill-understood transformation of both Mongol and Tibetan society that made them more accessible to and dependent on peaceful trade with China, underlay the eclipse of the steppe cavalrymen's military dominance over civilized populations.

This was a profound change in human patterns—perhaps the most fundamental wrought by the gunpowder revolution, since it was ecumenical within Eurasia. Western Europeans, of course, succeeded the steppe nomads as the principal threat to prevailing military, political, and economic balances of Eurasia and the world, but their avenue of approach was by sea. That meant that ports and coastal areas became the critical frontiers for cultural encounter. Time-tested Chinese, Indian, and Middle Eastern modes of coping with invasion and the threat of invasion from the steppe gradually became trivial and archaic. But of course the Chinese were not aware of the fact at the time, nor was the obsolescence of their military system brought home to them until the nineteenth century. Instead, China's old regime flourished throughout the eighteenth century as seldom before. It made the shock of the Opium War (1839–41), in which small British forces overpowered Chinese defenses with ease, all the greater when it came.

Sixteenth-century Japan was the seat of a highly developed military tradition that valued clan loyalty very highly and put a premium on individual valor and skilled swordplay. Japanese ships may have used guns for their protection, as the Chinese did when the imperial navy was in its prime; but as far as land warfare was concerned, guns and gunpowder did not seem to have had any noticeable impact upon Japanese warfare before three Portuguese adventurers arrived in Japan on board a Chinese ship in 1543. Their arquebuses were of immediate interest to the local clan chieftain who received the Portuguese. He purchased the new weapons at once and ordered his swordsmith to make duplicates. Japanese smiths were the most accomplished in the world when it came to making swords, and found little difficulty in turning out handguns in quantity. Matchlocks on the European model therefore began to play a role in increasingly violent battles that broke out among rival clan coalitions as early as the 1560s. In 1575 an army of arquebusiers, ten thousand strong, actually played the decisive role in the battle of Nagashimo. At that time, too, Japanese-made cannon made their first appearance on the field of battle—still relatively small by the standard of European big guns, but able nonetheless to kill at a greater distance than handguns and capable of destroying lightly built fortifications as well.

Rival captains and clan chieftains employed ordinary farmers to serve as matchlockmen, since the necessary skills were elementary compared with the years of training required for wielding bow and sword, as hereditary samurai warriors were accustomed to do. When, in 1584, the mounting intensity of warfare climaxed in decisive victory for an upstart captain named Toyotomi Hideyoshi, Japanese armed establishments were therefore two-tiered, with gun-carrying infantry exercising far more authority on the field of battle than samurai, wedded to their traditional style of single combat with swords, felt to be right. Commanders, of course, were all samurai, and when a further round of war after Hideyoshi's death in 1598 led to the establishment of the Tokugawa shogunate (1600–1868), the new rulers of the country were in a position to act on their dislike of guns, especially when such weapons were in the hands of a social class that might be expected to be restless under the new regime.

The result was a systematic restriction on the manufacture and use of guns, beginning in 1607. By 1625, the government had secured an effective monopoly of gun-making capacity without, however, disarming the country as a whole. Consequently, when Japanese Christians rebelled against the shogun in 1637, handguns again played a key part in the struggle. But it was the last time that these weapons mattered in Japan until Admiral Perry's visits in 1853 and 1854, for after the rebels had been defeated, and Christianity had been systematically harried from the land, guns were allowed to rust and disappear. They were clearly unworthy of a gentleman and warrior. Since wars also ceased, there was no occasion to arm commoners again, and feudal lords had no further reason for maintaining detachments of matchlockmen as part of their armed establishments.

So, uniquely, the Japanese, after first exploiting the potentialities of gunpowder weapons more energetically than any other people—even the Europeans—turned their backs on handguns just as systematically as they had initially espoused them. The self-interest of the samurai, the new peace that the shoguns maintained, and an aesthetic, emotional attachment to swords and single combat all conspired to bring about this extraordinary result.

Nevertheless, guns played a very prominent part in uniting Japan in the first place, and at the same time undermined their future role in society by allowing commoners to kill off large numbers of samurai in bloody and decisive battles. In 1636, distaste for things foreign, mingled with some residual fear that alien contact might upset Japan's hard-won internal peace, persuaded the shogun to seal the country from outside contact. Japanese were no longer legally allowed to sail across the seas. A single Dutch ship was permitted to visit Nagasaki annually, but it was required to anchor near an island in the harbor so that unregulated contacts could not occur.

Japan therefore deliberately preserved its old-fashioned military establishment into the nineteenth century, even though samurai swords had only ritual use, thanks to the unbroken internal peace the shogun's bureaucratic administration secured. In Japan, guns were therefore a flash in the pan—very important for a while, and then no more.

Conclusion

This hasty survey of the variety of responses to gunpowder weapons calls into question the notion of "gunpowder empire" as something common to the civilized world. The new weapons certainly did make a difference— everywhere. But what that difference was depended on social circumstances and public policy. Nothing inherent in the technology of guns dictated the use to which they were actually put by different peoples in different parts of the earth. This should remind us of all the other dimensions of human society—intellectual, artistic, religious, institutional, technological, and ecological—within which gunpowder weapons existed and continue to exist.

Centering attention as much as this essay does on only one variable necessarily creates a partial and imperfect picture of the whole. Historical vision gains in clarity by such a narrow focus, but at the same time loses sight of other aspects of human life that were more or less autonomous and unaffected by changes in armament. Still, it is also true that armed force is important because it constrains and limits other sorts of human behavior; and it seems obvious that some ways of using gunpowder weaponry worked better than others, though here one must distinguish between short- and long-term success.

In China and Japan, for example, ruling elites deliberately and successfully allowed guns to have only marginal importance for more than two centuries—and any policy that works well for that length of time has much to commend it. Yet by the nineteenth century that policy exposed both countries to a real risk of domination by Europeans. On the other hand, the reckless abandon with which western European governments exploited the potentialities of gunpowder weaponry cost innumerable lives and helped to keep European society and politics in turmoil. Yet in the long run it also gave Europeans the means to enrich themselves (with knowledge and skill as well as with material goods) and allowed them to dominate other lands and peoples around the globe. Gains and losses were therefore anything but simple and straightforward—and, of course, practical policy never foresees really long-term results and only occasionally foresees accurately all the important short-range side effects of a particular decision.

Humanity is still caught up in the arms race evolving from Europe's state rivalries, which fanned the gunpowder revolution. As events unfold, we can be sure that the long-term advantages and disadvantages of past actions with respect to gunpowder and other weapons systems will take new shapes. Study and reflection on the record of how different states and peoples coped with gunpowder weaponry in the first centuries of its history will not provide shortcuts to wise policy, but ought at least to prepare us for surprises and unanticipated consequences of whatever decisions we make with respect to the organization and equipment of armed force. That, assuredly, was the fate of our predecesors. As long as human foresight remains imperfect, and our passions continue to induce us to fight one another, managing armed force wisely will remain both difficult and important. It therefore deserves historical study, even though military rivalries are only part of the human condition.

NOTES

1. Iron presented early gun makers with special problems. Its melting point was a good deal higher than that of the copper, tin, and zinc that went into making bronze and brass, but European blast furnaces could cope with that if need be. What could not be solved was the tendency of cast iron to crystallize, producing a hard, brittle substance that was liable to fracture under the pressure of an explosion. Until the 1560s, therefore, big guns were made only of bronze and brass.

Then a bed of iron ore in Sussex, England, was found to be suitable for guns. This was due to trace elements that inhibited crystallization, though ironmasters of the time did not understand why Sussex iron was good for guns when other ores were not. Later still, Swedish beds of iron ore also proved to be a suitable gunmetal. Iron, being abundant in nature, was far cheaper than bronze or brass, and first Elizabethan England, then Sweden, profited greatly from having easy access to cheap iron cannon.

2. The history of drill is obscure. Sumerian bas reliefs show men marching in step behind a shield wall, so some sort of drill must have prevailed in that earliest known civilization. But in ancient and modern times, Europeans alone among civilized peoples seem to have built their armies on infantry drill. (Shaka Zulu did the same in Africa early in the nineteenth century and met with spectacular success.) Greek phalanxes and Roman legions maintained formation in battle only after hours of drill; and the psychological bonds that drill created undergirded classical city-state life as powerfully as it was later to undergird European armies. Moslem, Indian, Chinese, and steppe armies do not seem to have relied on drill to the same extent. Wherever cavalry tactics prevailed, as was the case within the whole range of steppe conquest and infiltration—that is, everywhere in the civilized world except Japan and western Europe—drill had far less scope, since horsemen have to adapt to their horses' motions and cannot establish a muscular unison of their own bodies, even if they can manage a concerted charge.

BIBLIOGRAPHY

This essay, largely based on William H. McNeill, *The Pursuit of Power: Technology, Armed Force, and Society since 1000* A.D. (Chicago: University of Chicago Press, 1983), has been issued by the American Historical Association in pamphlet form. Among the many other books that deal with one or another aspect of the subject, the following are particularly interesting:

Cipolla, Carlo M. *Guns, Sails and Empires: Technological Innovations and the Early Phases of European Expansion, 1400–1700.* New York: Pantheon Books, 1965.

Crone, Patricia. *Slaves on Horses: The Evolution of the Islamic Polity.* New York: Cambridge University Press, 1980.

Duffy, Christopher. *Siege Warfare: The Fortress in the Early Modern World, 1494–1660.* London: Rutledge and Kegan Paul, 1979.

Guilmartin, John F., Jr. *Gunpowder and Galleys: Changing Technology and Mediterranean Warfare at Sea in the Sixteenth Century.* Cambridge, England: Cambridge University Press, 1974.

Hogg, O.F.G. *Artillery: Its Origin, Heyday and Decline.* London: C. Hurst, 1970.

Howard, Michael. *War in European History.* Oxford, England: Oxford University Press, 1976.

Kiernan, Frank A. Jr., and John K. Fairbank, eds. *Chinese Ways in Warfare.* Cambridge, Mass.: Harvard University Press, 1974.

Parker, Geoffrey. *The Army of Flanders and the Spanish Road, 1567–1659.* Cambridge, England: Cambridge University Press, 1972.

Parry, V. J., and M. E. Yap, eds. *War, Technology and Society in the Middle East.* London: Oxford University Press, 1975.

Perrin, Noel. *Giving Up the Gun: Japan's Reversion to the Sword, 1543–1879.* Boulder, Colo.: Shambhala, 1979.

The Columbian Voyages, the Columbian Exchange, and Their Historians

ALFRED W. CROSBY

Historical Interpretations of the Columbian Voyages

For over a year, we have been caught up in the five-hundredth anniversary of the Columbian discovery of America, and with it the obligation to assess existing interpretations of the significance of that voyage and the establishment of permanent links between the Old and New Worlds. The most influential of the several schools of interpretation are, on the one hand, the newest and analytic, and on the other, the classic and bardic. The former is for many recondite and discomforting. The latter, the one most often taught, dramatized, and believed in North America, is for most as comfortable as an old pair of slippers: We learned it in primary school.

THE BARDIC INTERPRETATION

The bardic version of the Columbian voyages and their consequences was the product of narrative historians, most of them nineteenth-century writers, who did their work when the peoples of the republics of the New World looked on the Americas as fresh and "without sin," at least as compared to "decadent" Europe. These historians narrated the American past in ways consonant both with the documentary record then available and with the ethnocentrism of their fellow white citizens of the New World, particularly of the United States. Their readers wanted history books to provide a story of "the steps by which a favoring Providence, calling our institutions into being, has conducted the country to its present happiness and glory,"[1] to quote the innocently arrogant George Bancroft, whose ten-volume *History of the United States* (1834–76) we no longer read but have never forgotten.

The classic narrative that Bancroft and his successors provided can be summarized as follows: At the end of the fifteenth century Christopher Columbus discovered America, adding to the world two continents populated sparsely with "savages" and, in Mexico and Peru, with "barbarians" experimenting with protocivilization. Then the conquistadores, few in number but courageous, conquered the Amerindian civilizations, which, for all their temples and gold, were evidently no more than paper tigers. Lesser conquistadores performed similarly, if less profitably, in other places, most of them also in tropical America, as did their Portuguese counterparts in coastal Brazil. British, French, Dutch, and other European soldiers, merchants, and settlers did much the same thing in those parts of the New World not yet claimed by the Iberians. The history of the New World subsequently became the struggle of European imperialist powers for domination, and Amerindians ceased to be important, except as enemies or allies of whites. African Americans, the other of the two non-European peoples who made major contributions to the development of the modern Americas, were obviously present in large numbers during the colonial period but were almost invisible in American history until the Haitian revolt at the end of the eighteenth century, usually viewed as a nightmarish aberration from the "normal" pattern of colonialization in the Americas. The Columbian era, the period of European exploration and colonization, ended in the decades around 1800 with successful revolutions led by whites, usually of good family and education, against the parent countries. Then came the maturation of independent societies and cultures in the New World, a development paradoxically confirmed and made irreversible by the migration of very large numbers of Europeans to the Americas after the mid-nineteenth century.

This narrative is the version of history that most Americans learned as children. It is also a cautionary tale (or interpretation) for scholars and teachers. The bardic version is as deceptive as it is popular because it is the product of an age that is past, with a characteristically selective view of history. It is as dangerous as it is deceptive because it reinforces European American ethnocentrism and confirms historians and teachers in premises and approaches clearly obsolete at the Columbian quincentennial. On the other hand, this classic interpretation is rational and true to the original sources. That it can be rational as well as deceptive is perhaps a useful lesson for seekers after absolute truth in history.

Rather than make a display of our "superiority" over scholars now dead and buried (thus anticipating the smugness of our own successors), let us praise our forebears. They were skilled practitioners of the historian's craft who did their work well, enabling the present generation of historians to make progress, rather than mere corrections. Men like Spain's Martín Fernández de Navarette and Canada's Henri-Raymond Casgrain drew together the documentary evidence that forms the core of what even revisionists must begin with, and assembled the bare data of who was who and where and when. These scholars performed the laborious work that is preliminary to creative scholarship in any field of history. Among them were creative scholars of the first rank who built a model of the past that reconciled the record as they knew it with the values of their own day and made sense to the literate classes of their time. This is what society pays historians to do.

Two of the best of these bardic historians were New England's William Prescott, historian of the Spanish conquest of Mexico and Peru, and Francis Parkman, the Homer of the struggle of Britain and France for empire in North America. Another was Samuel Eliot Morison, whose 1942 biography of Columbus and two-volume *The European Discovery of America* (1971, 1974) are as close to being definitive works as one can expect in this mutable world. These men all liked to approach history through biography; they chose sides and were transparently loyal to their heroes. For all three men, the stuff of history was almost always documents, preferably letters, diaries, and memoirs, and not statistics. Seldom did they turn for help to economics, archaeology, biology, or any of the sciences, which resulted in some startling omissions. Prescott managed to write magnificent books on the conquests of Mexico and Peru and omit all but the bare mention of the conqueror's best ally, smallpox. The information on smallpox was in the original sources but not within the range of what Prescott was equipped to perceive as important.

The books of the bardic historians were usually neatly organized around great white men, a strategy whose validity seemed to be confirmed by contemporary events. Prescott did not worry his sources like a dog with an old shoe to find the *real* reason for the success of Cortés and Pizarro because he lived in an era when white people seemingly always won their wars with nonwhites. In the Second Opium War, Queen Victoria's plenipotentiary opined that "twenty-four determined [white] men with revolvers and a sufficient number of cartridges might walk through China from one end to the other."[2] Bardic historians thought in terms of biography, and why not? They were children of the nineteenth century, the golden age of rugged individualism and industrial capitalism. It was also an age of rampant nationalism, and when historians thought in terms of large groups of humans, they thought of the nation-state and not of tribes or cultures or language families. It was an age of unembarrassed elitism and racism, and historians tended to ignore plebians in particular and non-Europeans in general. (Prescott and Parkman were in part exceptions, paying a full measure of attention to Amerindians, at least in so far as they influenced European American destinies.) These historians were not much better equipped intellectually to notice those whom Eric R. Wolf called the "people without history"[3] than they were to judge the stability of ecosystems. The social sciences and biology were new; ecology was not born until after Prescott and Parkman died and was still immature when Morison was middle-aged.

THE ANALYTIC INTERPRETATION

America's classic historians did not even try to answer many of the questions that concern us at the end of the twentieth century because neither they nor their audiences were asking such questions. There were a few fresh minds, however, who provided new ways of looking at the world, which led to new ways of sorting data and new kinds of inquiries. Among the greatest of these innovators were Charles Darwin, Karl Marx, and Louis Pasteur, celebrants of paradox who emphasized the importance of instability and the immense power of the humble, even the invisible. Travelers and archaeologists, at a different level intellectually but no less influential, kept exploring and digging, turning up evidence of dense pre-Columbian populations in the Americas, of peoples of undeniably high culture. Who could continue to think of the Maya as savages after John L. Stephen's volumes and Frederick Catherwood's prints? After the works of W.E.B. Du Bois and Melville Herskovits, what excuse remained for a historian to claim that there was nothing to learn about Africans or African Americans?

Above all, after the hell-for-leather advance of the Japanese military in the early 1940s and the swift collapse of Europe's overseas empires in the following two decades (as astonishing, in its way, as the collapse of the Amerindian empires four centuries earlier), there could be no more doubt that a great many of the "people without history" must have at least some history. The effect on the historical profession of the experiences of the last half-century has been like that on astronomers of the discovery that the faint smudges seen between the stars of the Milky Way were really distant galaxies.

The obsolescence of old conceptions persuaded historians to take a fresh look at the origins of European imperialism; perhaps elements less dramatic than gold and God and heroes had been involved. Charles Verlinden led the way by tracing the roots of European imperialism to the Mediterranean in the age of the Crusades, where organizational structures and exploitative techniques that would be imposed on America in the sixteenth century were first tried, and where Europeans first learned to like sugar and to raise it for profitable export to their homelands. Verlinden followed the precursors of conquerors like Cortés and the plantation owners of Brazil from the Levant to the islands of the eastern Atlantic. There, in the triangle of the great western ocean that has Iberia, the Azores, and the Canaries as its boundary stones—an expanse that Pierre Chaunu has shrewdly called the "Mediterranean Atlantic"[4]—the sailors of southern and western Europe studied the patterns of oceanic winds and learned to be blue-water sailors and how to sail to America and Asia. In Madeira white settlers, often led by down-at-the heels Iberian nobility seeking land and wealth to match their titles, discovered how to make a lot of money raising sugar; in the Canaries they learned how swiftly a fierce aboriginal people, the Guanches, could disappear and how easily they could be replaced with imported labor to raise tropical crops for the European market.

While historians of the Middle Ages and Renaissance were disinterring the roots of European imperialism, the students of the Americas and Amerindians were revolutionizing their disciplines. Archaeology thrust the beginnings of American history back at least fifteen thousand years and populated these millennia and both American continents with myriads of clever and mysterious people. Social scientists devised means, often quantitative, to tap into the history of undocumented peoples. The contribution of demographic historians has been of particular value, providing a structure within which other historians can find niches for their own discoveries. Historians opened themselves to (or, fearing obsolescence, rushed to ransack) geology, climatology, biology, epidemiology, and other fields. As a result, the kind of grain that is poured into the historian's mill today would wear out Leopold von Ranke's grindstones. Historians are scientific not only in the care they take with research and attempts to limit bias but also in their exploitation of whatever the sciences provide that is pertinent to the study of the human past.

European historians of the *Annales* school, centered in France, have been the most noted practitioners of this new kind of history, but similar advances in technique have been developed in the New World and applied to the study of the Amerindian past and the impact of the Columbian voyages on American history. The Berkeley school, as it is loosely and sometimes inaccurately called, led by geographer Carl Ortwin Sauer, physiologist Sherburne F. Cook, and historians Woodrow Borah and Lesley Byrd Simpson, began as far back as the 1930s to reassess pre-Columbian and Amerindian history. They used many kinds of nondocumentary data—geological and botanical, among others—and reexamined, and many times examined for the first time, the yellowed sheets of tribute, tax, and population records of the Spanish empire. The Berkeley school has revolutionized American historiography. Not everyone accepts their conclusions, but their questions—rarely asked before except by proponents of *indigenismo* and *indianismo*—plot the course of historical research in the immediate pre- and post-Columbian centuries in America.

There has been a renewal of interest in the whole picture, the world, and therefore in global history. The forces that propelled Columbus and the forces that the European discovery and exploitation of America triggered were supranational and supracontinental. Columbian and post-Columbian exchanges of raw materials, manufactured products, and organisms cannot be described or analyzed to the full extent of their significance within any unit smaller than the world. Scholars of worldly sophistication have accepted the challenge: Fernand Braudel, William McNeill, Immanuel Wallerstein, Eric R. Wolf, and others. Their work leads us to lands, cultures, and questions that the bardic historians of Columbus rarely considered. To cite one example, nearly a hundred years before Columbus and other European mariners crossed the great oceans, the Chinese admiral Cheng Ho launched a succession of huge fleets, manned by thousands, around the Malay Peninsula and across the Indian Ocean as far as East Africa. After this the Chinese ceased their transoceanic voyaging completely. Cheng Ho inspires today's world historians to ask two questions that would never have occurred to Prescott, Parkman, or even Morison: Why did the Chinese stop their voyaging, and, the obvious corollary but not a question asked by Western historians until the present, why did European voyagers start and never stop?

There are vast expanses of time and territory in the new history of the Americas as yet not even roughly surveyed, and the work of detailed description must be left to the next century. There is no body of received wisdom about the New World, but there is a new model of New World history for our consideration and use.

America's classic historians were successful in part because their scope was narrow. They wrote almost exclusively about white heroes in the last five hundred years, while today's analytic historians are concerned with the masses of people of numerous ethnic groups in a much larger time frame. To understand how these peoples fared after they met in 1492, we need to know at least something about the species of plants, animals, and microlife associated with them. To know that, we have to go back further than most of our Victorian ancestors thought there was anything to go back to.

The Old and New Worlds had been separate for millions of years before Columbus, except for periodic reconnections in the far north during Ice Ages. In this immense period the biotas of the Old and New Worlds evolved and diverged. As of 1492, there were many similar species, especially in Eurasia and North America, such as deer and elm, but the differences were impressive. Europe had nothing quite like hummingbirds, rattlesnakes, and hickory and pecan trees. Further south the contrasts between Old and New World biotas were even more amazing. The biggest mammal in Africa was the elephant; in South America, the cow-sized tapir. The native biotas of the Old and New Worlds were decidedly different, and for most of the previous few million years these biotas had not been in competition or even in contact.

The last bout of competition before the arrival of Columbus included the initial migration into America of the Old World's *Homo sapiens* and the spread of that species from the Arctic Sea to Tierra del Fuego, affecting changes as yet only partly understood. After the last Ice Age ended some ten thousand years ago and the continental glaciers melted back, releasing so much water that the land connection between Siberia and Alaska was innundated, the ancestors of the Amerindians were left in complete or nearly complete isolation. They developed autochthonous cultures, domesticated American plants and animals, and adapted to American microlife. In 1492 they were living in equilibrium with each other and with the other tenants of the New World, macro and micro. This homeostasis no doubt wobbled considerably, even violently, in areas with thick settlements of Amerindian farmers, but in all probability it was more stable then than it has been since.

During the same ten-thousand-year period, peoples of the Old World, in adjustment to the biotas of their continents, engendered their cultures and domesticated and bred their crops, beasts, and, unintentionally of course, their own set of pesky and sometimes fatal germs. These humans were also elements in a system that varied constantly but that was, within broad limits, stable. They even had a modus vivendi with the plague, which had reared up in the fourteenth century and killed approximately one-third of the population of western Eurasia and North Africa. By 1500, however, the European population had recovered its pre-Black Death totals and was growing, despite recurrent waves of plague and other deadly diseases.

In 1492 these two systems of homeostasis, one of the Old World and the other of the New World, like tightrope walkers with poles dipping and lifting to maintain balance, collided.

The Old World peoples had some distinct advantages in the biological competition that followed. Although their crop plants were not superior to those of the Amerindians per se—wheat, rice, and yams were "better" than maize, potatoes, and cassava in some ways and inferior in others—the Old World advantage in domesticated animals was great. It was a matter of the Old World's horses, cattle, pigs, goats, sheep, and other domesticated species versus the New World's llamas, guinea pigs, domesticated fowl, and dogs. This advantage was not permanent because Amerindians adopted many of the new livestock, most spectacularly horses in the Great Plains and pampa, where these animals helped the Amerindians to maintain their independence until the last half of the nineteenth century. The greatest influence of Old World plants and animals was probably in making it possible for Old World pastoralists and farmers to live in the American colonies as they had at home or, in most cases, better. Old World livestock, which had evolved in what seemingly had been a rougher league than the New World's, often outfought, outran, or at least out-reproduced American predators. Free of the diseases and pests that had preyed on them at home, the European animals thrived and even went wild, often in amazing numbers, providing mounts, meat, milk, and leather much more cheaply in the New World than in the Old. The most spectacular instances of this were in southern South America. The first Spanish attempt to colonize the pampa failed in the 1530s, and the survivors departed, leaving some livestock behind. When settlers returned in 1580 they found "infinite" herds of horses. In 1587 Hernando Arias left one hundred cattle behind him at Santa Fé de Paraná in Brazil, and when he returned in 1607 he found, according to his testimony, one hundred thousand. These Iberians were speaking colorfully, rather than statistically, but the natural increase in the feral herds of South America was indeed enormous, probably unprecedented in all history. Smaller but comparable explosions in animal populations took place elsewhere in the New World.

The decisive advantage of the human invaders of America was not their plants or animals—and certainly not their muskets and rifles, which Amerindians eventually obtained in quantity—but their diseases. The aboriginal Americans had their own diseases (several of them, like Chargas's disease and Carrion's disease, were as indigenous to the Americas as hummingbirds and tapirs), but the number of these was insignificant compared to the sum of those that came to the New World from the Old after 1492. There is debate about whether certain diseases did or did not exist in America before 1492. Yellow fever, for example, is probably African, but could have been endemic among American monkeys when Europeans first arrived and perhaps attracted no attention until the first epidemic among humans. There is little disagreement on the following list: smallpox, measles, whooping cough, chicken pox, bubonic plague, malaria, diphtheria, amoebic dysentery, and influenza. These were the most lethal of the invaders of the New World in the sixteenth century. Even today the worst immediate threats to the native peoples of remote Amazonia are not the soldiers or road builders per se, but the measles and influenza that they bring with them.

The advantage in bacteriological warfare was (and is) characteristically enjoyed by people from dense and often older areas of settlement moving into sparser and usually newer areas of settlement: the Russians into Siberia, the Chinese into Mongolia, the British into Australia, for example. The diseases that savaged the Amerindians were infections associated with dense populations of humans, which appeared in the Old World long before the New. In addition, it is probable that a number of these diseases were produced by the exchange of microlife between humans and domesticated animals. Such maladies as influenza seem to be renewed in their virulency by exchanges between species and possibly first evolved into human pathogens as the result of such exchanges. Old World peoples domesticated more species of animals than Amerindians and lived in close contact with animals—often literally cheek and jowl, hip and thigh—for much longer. From their animals Old World peoples obtained much more protein, fat, leather, fiber, bone, manure, and muscle power than were available to the Amerindians, and more epidemic and endemic disease as well. Old World peoples adjusted to these infections, socially and immunologically, and were relatively resistant to the diseases. As a result, they practiced bacteriological warfare whenever they went to places remote from the dense populations of the Old World. The Valley of Mexico had fifty devastating epidemics between 1519 and 1810, including smallpox, typhus, measles, mumps, and pneumonia. Even the fragmentary record of Yucatan shows fourteen epidemics. The story of Peru, and of every area for which there are any records, is similar.

"Wherever the European has trod," wrote Darwin after his circumnavigation of the globe on the *Beagle*, "death seems to pursue the aboriginal. We may look to the wide extent of the Americas, Polynesia, the Cape of Good Hope, and Australia, and we find the same result,"[5] which he blamed largely on infectious disease. The Yanomamo of today's Venezuelan–Brazilian borderlands offer a simple explanation for the phenomenon: "White men cause illness; if the whites had never existed, disease would never have existed either."[6]

The most spectacular killer of Amerindians was smallpox, a disease that existed in medieval and Renaissance Europe but did not rise to the first rank of maladies until the sixteenth century. From that time until the spread of vaccination in the nineteenth century, smallpox was one of the Continent's most widespread and deadly diseases, so common that it was considered inevitable among children in areas of dense population. In this period Europe's most important colonies were established in the New World.

Smallpox appeared in the West Indies at the end of 1518 or beginning of 1519 and spread to Mexico on the heels of Cortés, swept through Central America, and preceded Pizarro into the realms of the Incas. Witnesses estimated the losses at one-fourth, one-third, or even one-half of the infected populations. Such estimations may seem extravagantly high, but very high death rates among the unimmunized were not uncommon in more recent, well-documented outbreaks. To cite a few examples of the devastating effects of such epidemics, when smallpox broke out in 1898 among the Moqui Amerindians in Arizona, 632 fell ill. Of the 220 Moqui who refused European-style treatment and, presumably, put their faith in folk therapy (as Aztecs and Incas would have in the early sixteenth century), 163 died; their death rate was over 70 percent. Even twentieth-century therapy could do no more ameliorate the effects of the disease and prevent secondary infections. In 1972 a pilgrim returning from Mecca brought smallpox to Yugoslavia, where it had not been known for over a generation. Before public health measures stopped the spread of the disease, 174 people contracted smallpox and 35 died, a mortality rate of 20 percent. Readers who are still skeptical about the killing potential of new infections should turn to accounts of the Black Death in the Old World or to a consideration of the potentialities of AIDS in the 1980s. Imagine the consequences if AIDS were not a venereal but instead a breath-borne disease like smallpox.

Although European Americans dubbed America the "virgin land," it had not been virgin for many millennia, if the title is used to mean free from human occupation. By the time Old World settlers, following after the explorers, soldiers, and traders, arrived in numbers in most regions— Venezuela, Alberta, Amazonia—Old World pathogens had so reduced the indigenous population that some special name for the ensuing vacancy was required. Francis Jennings, with chilling appropriateness, replaced the phrase the "virgin land" with the "widowed land."[7]

The widowed land was more open to exploitation than any large area to which western Europeans had access, certainly more open to occupation than the nearest alternative, the lands of eastern Europe, bloodied for centuries by the *Drang nach Osten*. The success of the invaders of widowed America, particularly of the British in North America, inspired Adam Smith to issue an unintentional prophesy, appropriately dated 1776: "The colony of a civilized nation which takes possession, either of a waste country, or of one so thinly inhabited, that the natives easily give place to new settlers, advances more rapidly to wealth and greatness than any other human society."[8]

In comparison with Eurasia and Africa, both ineradicably populated with their own peoples, the New World was a tabula rasa. Great fortunes could be made in the Americas by exploiting mineral resources and native biota, such as the beaver with its thick, tough fur. The greatest money-maker in America in the first centuries after Columbus, however, was the plantation, which produced tropical and semitropical crops, most of Old World origin, of an at least quasi-addictive nature for the European market. The foremost crop was sugar, followed by cocoa and tobacco, and then such useful items as cotton. Lands with soils and climates suitable for these crops existed in large parts of the New World, but the establishment and operation of plantations required the incessant labor of a great many people. Entrepreneurs tried using Amerindians as slaves and serfs in the hot, wet lowlands where such crops often grew best, but found not only that the Amerindians were intransigent but, worse, that they wilted and died too fast to be useful as laborers.

The plantation masters turned to their own homelands, using persuasion, propaganda, and even kidnapping to get Europeans across the Atlantic. Even shipments of convicts were acceptable. (An English verb for the transportation of these unfortunates, often Celtic backers of the wrong royal family, was "barbadoing," after the island where tobacco and later sugar promised profit.) But few Europeans could be persuaded or forced to become field workers in the American tropics, especially after the spread of malaria and yellow fever. Most Europeans, even serfs, had some civil rights. They could be dragged off to the hot lands of the New World by the thousands, but not by the millions. Until the end of the eighteenth century most of the people who crossed the Atlantic from the Old to the New World, and the majority of those who took up the ax and machete and hoe to labor on the plantations, were black, about 10 million. The Atlantic slave trade, the greatest such trade in all history and the source of revolutionary changes in all of the four continents facing the Atlantic, was part of the legacy of Columbus.

The Heirs of Columbus

The bardic historians were relatively unconcerned with the geographic, biological, and demographic effects of the Columbian voyages, but these are the themes of current scholarship. The bulk of the research and analysis on these matters remains to be done, especially on the Columbian influence in Africa and Asia, but I can offer an interim report.

THE INTELLECTUAL EFFECTS

"Among the extraordinary though quite natural circumstances of my life," wrote Columbus's countryman, the mathematician and physician Girolamo Cardano, in the 1570s, "the first and most unusual is that I was born in this century in which the whole world became known; whereas the ancients were familiar with but a little more than a third part of it."[9] In 1491 the European conception of the universe was much the same as it had been a thousand years and more before. The earth was believed to be at the center of crystalline spheres carrying the sun, moon, and stars, with the surface of the world above water divided into three parts—Europe, Africa, and Asia. Humans lived in all three land areas, but not in the Torrid Zone, which was dreadfully hot and therefore uninhabitable. The evidence that did not fit this model was still small enough in significance and quantity to be ignored or subdued to conformity by sophistry. But when Columbus returned in 1493 he rendered the old model obsolete in a stroke. Few realized this immediately, but the system was obviously overloaded with new data and bursting by the time Cardano wrote.

Columbus added a fourth part to the world, the Americas, and his successors added the Pacific, an unimagined ocean of unimaginable breadth beyond America. Columbus and his followers also provided eyewitness testimony that torrid America was full of people. (Europeans had somehow been able to ignore earlier reports of Portuguese sailors that tropical

Africa was heavily populated.) In addition, the New World was full of plants and animals about which Aristotle and Pliny had nothing to say— electric eels and camels without humps—and of people who were neither Muslim nor Jew, and certainly not Christian. Carolus Linnaeus papered his rooms and tormented his methodical Scandinavian mind with drawings of exotic American plants, and Alexander Humboldt and Charles Darwin puzzled over their American experiences and based their generalizations in large part thereon. Philosophers and thinkers from Michel de Montaigne to Jean Jacques Rousseau to Henry David Thoreau pondered and wrote on the meaning of Amerindians and their cultures. The Columbian discoveries galvanized anthropology, the product of Europeans trying to understand non-Europeans, into unprecedented acceleration. Protoanthropologists and anthropologists from Pietro Martire d'Anghiera to Lewis Henry Morgan and Claude Lévi-Strauss struggled to fit Amerindians, with all their variety of languages, technologies, religions, and customs, into "rational" explanations of social behavior and founded school after school of thought in the process.

Simply by making a round trip across an ocean, Columbus multiplied humanity's knowledge about its environment and itself many times over, stimulating a multitude of philosophies, literary movements, and sciences. He felt himself a crusader and painted crosses on his sails, but he promoted skepticism. Girolamo Cardano worried that the geographical discoveries of his century would lead in just that direction, and "certainties will be exchanged for uncertainties."[10] He was right, of course, but to humanity's advantage.

The economic effects

Ask an economist about the significance of Columbus, and the economist might look for a connection between the great explorer and Europe's quantum leap in wealth, commerce, and productivity in the centuries following his life. One of the most apparent and immediate of American influences on Europe during the first post-Columbian centuries was crudely financial. The gold and silver of the New World that raised the pulse beat of ambitious hidalgos and landless younger sons all over western Europe had much the same effect on the European economy. There is no doubt that American specie made possible trade with the Far East that would have been slight otherwise. The Chinese were interested in trading their silks and porcelain with Europeans if they brought Mexican silver. Even so, the exact effect of American specie on Europe per se is a matter of controversy. The influx of American bullion was surely an important factor in the inflation of the sixteenth and seventeenth centuries, enriching some and impoverishing others and in general subjecting Europe to more chills and fevers than historians have sorted out yet. If indeed prices, and therefore profits, soared faster than wages and traditional fees and rents, and if the decline of interest rates was due to the influx of precious metals from America, then that influx had a great deal to do with the rise of the commercial classes in power and influence and the decline of the old aristocracy, and possibly with the Industrial Revolution.

One of the most important changes in the generations after Columbus was Europe's creation of a world market, with itself as the entrepôt and bank. Vital to this new phenomenon was the trade between the New World and Europe, the former supplying raw materials and the latter manufactured goods. The American market for manufactured goods became increasingly important as European American populations grew. For instance, English exports to the Americas and Africa (where manufactured goods were exchanged for slaves for the American colonies) increased ten times in the eighteenth century. But for the sake of brevity, let us consider the New World colonies exclusively in what was unambiguously their primary role for a very long time, that of supplier of materials for European consumption and processing.

Siberia, like North America, sent its furs to western Europe but alone could never have satisfied the demand, which over centuries was insatiable. The profits of the fur trade could be astonishingly high: Hudson's Bay Company produced an average of 23 percent profit annually for the first fifty years of its existence, a total profit of 1143 percent on the original investment in a half-century. The islands of the eastern Atlantic, the Indian Ocean, and the East Indian archipelago could and did supply sugar and other tropic products to Europe, but the mass of such goods came from America. In the eighteenth century the most profitable colonies in the world were not African, Asian, or even the burgeoning settlements of North America, but the West Indies, or Sugar Islands, as they were often called. The French colony of Saint-Domingue (Haiti and the Dominican Republic today) employed seven hundred vessels manned by eighty-thousand seamen in its trade in a good year. In 1789 about two-thirds of France's total foreign investments were involved in Saint-Domingue, the greatest of the Sugar Islands. Britain's West Indian colonies provided 20 percent of the homeland's total imports between 1714 and 1773, much of which were re-exported at a profit. A contemporary estimated that an average Englishman driving slaves in the sugar plantations brought twenty times more clear profit to England than he would have had he stayed home.

The American plantations were the reason for the existence of the Atlantic slave trade. The lands of southern Asia supplied their own labor and even had a surplus to export when plantation agriculture spread into Oceania. After the sixteenth century the varying, but in total considerable, profits of the Atlantic trade in black laborers flowed largely to the nations leading the commercial and industrial revolutions: Holland, France, and

Britain. Portugal was also a major recipient of slave-trade profits but could not hold on to them; they slipped away to join the main current of wealth streaming to Portugal's northern neighbors.

The world market, unimagined when Columbus sailed, was a hardy infant by the end of the sixteenth century. A century later, the world market was an important factor in the lives of millions of people in every continent but Australia and Antarctica, drawing coffles of slaves out of Africa every year, herding Amerindians up and down the ladders of the Potosi silver mines, and dispatching Cree braves to trap beaver in the Canadian forests, in addition to what it was dictating to Gujaratis and Filipinos on the other side of the world. For the first time, human labor, raw materials, manufacturing, and transportation systems spanning scores of degrees of longitude and latitude by sail, wheel, and beast of burden were organized on a world scale. The world economy was created by bankers and statesmen, such as the Fuggers and Colbert, but Columbus and his fellow explorers played vital roles, too. These sailors presented entrepreneurs with access to enough land in enough climates, enough bullion, enough visions of potential profit, to spur them from a walk to a gallop. Once in existence, the world market produced a torrent of wealth that swept round and round the globe to and from Ceylon, the Ottoman Empire, Pernambuco, Massachusetts, Java, Muscovy, Quebec, and on every passage Europe took its tithe.

A lot of that capital went to building Brobdingnagian manor houses and to providing fireworks on ducal birthdays, but much was also invested in roads, canals, bridges, warehouses, and the training of naval, clerical, mechanical, and executive talent. The wealth of the New World was not the only cause of the Industrial Revolution, but it is difficult to see how that mysterious and awesome transformation could have happened when and as rapidly as it did without stimulus from the Americas. The Industrial Revolution left Europeans and their descendants overseas richer and with access to more power than men and women of 1492 ever thought possible. Its effects continue today, as other peoples break loose from old moorings and bobble along in the European wake, heading for an age of either material satisfaction or towering disappointment. Columbus's bequest is a sharp sword, and in this case we cannot be sure whether we hold it by the handle or the blade.

THE NUTRITIONAL EFFECTS

"The greatest service which can be rendered any country is to add a useful plant to its culture,"[11] noted Thomas Jefferson. By this standard, Columbus was the greatest benefactor of all time because by bringing the agricultures of the Old and New Worlds into contact, he added many useful plants to each. He enormously increased the number of kinds and quantities of food available to humans by giving them access to all the masterpieces of plant and animal breeders everywhere, and not just those of two or three contiguous continents.

In the last five hundred years food crops and domesticated animals have crossed the Atlantic and Pacific in both directions, enabling people to live in numbers in places where they previously had had only slim means to feed themselves. The Argentine pampa, Kansas, and Saskatchewan, too dry in large areas for Amerindian maize and in the latter case too far north, are now breadbaskets, producing not only enough Eurasian wheat for themselves but much more to export to the world. Eurasia's domesticated animals—cattle, sheep, pigs, goats, and even water buffalo—provide Americans from the Hudson Bay to the Straits of Magellan with the means to do what was only meagerly possible before 1492: to turn grass, which humans cannot eat, into meat and milk. In 1983, according to the Food and Agricultural Organization (FAO) of the United Nations, the New World slaughtered 84 million cattle, 27 million sheep, and 139 million pigs; in 1492 none at all. New World peoples derive all but a fraction of their animal protein, and almost all their wool and leather, from Old World animals.

Conversely, cassava, a root plant of South American origin, provides calories for multitudes of Africans and Asians in areas previously too wet, too dry, or too infertile to support more than sparse populations. Similarly, as the white potato of South America spread across northern Europe, peasants from county Kerry to the Urals found themselves with the means to raise more food in bulk per unit of land than ever before (although ultimately there were dire results in Ireland, where an American pestilence arrived to destroy the American plant in the 1840s). In the Far East the impact of the arrival of the products of Amerindian plant breeders was at least as great as in Europe or Africa. By the late 1930s New World crops amounted to 20 percent of the food produced in China, where approximately one-quarter of the human race lived (and lives now). According to Ping-ti Ho, historian of Chinese demography and agriculture: "During the last two centuries, when rice culture was gradually approaching its limit, and encountering the law of diminishing returns, the various dry land food crops introduced from America have contributed most to the increase in national food production and have made possible a continual growth of population." [12]

In 1983 Amerindian maize accounted for over one-sixth of all the grain produced in the world. Not surprisingly, the United States is the world's largest producer, but, perhaps surprisingly, China is the second greatest producer. China also harvests more sweet potatoes, a native American plant that does marvelously well under conditions that would discourage most other crops, than any other nation; sweet potatoes are an old and dependable famine food for the Chinese. Globally, American root crops, of which the most important are white and sweet potatoes and cassava, exceed in quantity of production all others combined. The world produced 557 million metric tons of root crops in 1983, of which those of Amerindian domestication amounted to 524 million metric tons. The world's leading producer of white potatoes is the former Soviet Union, which forks up ten times more potatoes in weight than South America, the home continent of the tuber. Africa produces over 48 million metric tons of cassava, dwarfing the 28 million of South America, where the plant was first cultivated.

The significance of Amerindian crops in the future will increase because all the most important ones were first domesticated in the tropics, where many of them still grow best. The developing nations of the world, where human populations are expanding fastest, are mostly in the tropics and in hot, wet lands nearby. The maize production of the developed world in 1983 was 187 million metric tons, and that of the developing world about 30 million less, but a great deal of the former tonnage went to feed livestock, while almost all the latter went directly to feed people. The sweet potato production of the developed societies in the same year was 2 million metric tons, and that of the developing societies over 112 million. All of the cassava raised in 1983 about which the FAO has statistics (123 million metric tons) was raised in the developing nations. Compare these figures with those for wheat, the traditional staple since the Neolithic Age in temperate Eurasia: 300 million metric tons were produced by the developed nations, and not quite 200 million by the developing.

Between 1750 and 1986 the population of the world grew from approximately 750 million to 5 billion. The exchange of crops and domesticated animals between the Old and New Worlds cannot be credited with being the sole cause of this awesome increase, any more than the capital produced by Europe's exploitation of America can be said to be the only cause of the Industrial Revolution, but it is hard to see how the colossal effect could have come about without the Columbian exchange.

THE DEMOGRAPHIC EFFECTS

The impact of the Columbian exchange did not always enhance population growth. Columbus triggered population explosion among some peoples and implosion in others. His effect on the Amerindian population, for example, was annihilating.

Fifty years ago Alfred Kroeber, then perhaps the premier anthropologist in the United States, estimated the total Amerindian population of 1492 at 8.5 million. He believed that his figure might possibly be a bit low, but it is unlikely that he thought that scholars would ever conservatively estimate the number of fifteenth-century Amerindians at 30 to 50 million, or that others, at least as well informed, would not hesitate to say 100 million. Extraordinary numbers! At that time Europe from the Atlantic to the Urals had only 80 million people, with Spain's population perhaps 7 million.

The mammoth increase in the estimates of fifteenth-century Amerindian populations during the past few decades quite properly arouses skepticism because the data these figures are based on are, by twentieth-century standards, disconcertingly imprecise. These estimates are the end results of careful examination and meticulous analysis of all the sources available (which are admittedly doubtful, if taken one at a time, but in total impressive). These include the off-the-cuff guesses of the first Europeans to arrive in a given area, the sober judgments and censuses of colonial administrators and churchmen, travelers' accounts, and whatever other scraps of pertinent information that can be found. All are measured against approximations of the carrying capacity of the environment and the size of the Amerindian population suggested by the density of pre-Columbian artifacts and ruins. These figures are matched against each other and then tested by sophisticated demographic techniques, such as careful extrapolation backward from later and more credible data. At the end the demographic historians make their estimates. We can and should argue about these estimates, but we should also note that they do not stand in suspicious uniqueness: The sources about Australia, New Zealand, and the Pacific islands also indicate that their aboriginal populations were much larger when Europeans first arrived than two or three generations later.

Skepticism is imperative in this new field, as it is in the field of the demographic history of medieval Europe, but not stubborn adherence to a half-century-old orthodoxy. After all, the New World had one-fourth of the land surface of the globe and was rich in sources of food; Amerindians had many thousands of years to expand their numbers before Columbus arrived. It seems only sensible to begin with the assumption that there were a lot of Americans in 1492.

The traditional underestimations of Amerindian populations were due not so much to European American ethnocentrism, though this may have played a role, as to the steep plunge of New World populations very soon after Old World peoples entered a given region. The germs sickened and killed thousands, setting off cascades of mortality. For instance, decimation of young adults interrupted farming and hunting, and malnutrition and even starvation followed. As elders died, the old customs went with them to the grave, leaving vacuums and bequeathing despair and anomie to the young. Typically, by the time two or three generations had passed after an initial white settlement, the Amerindian population of the given region was so low that it made the offhanded estimates of the first explorers and conquerors seem extravagant. By the time libraries were founded, colleges were opened, and historians were sharpening their pencils, the local Amerindians were often either extinct or few in number. The crucial first step for demographic historians of the Amerindians is to decide how steep their plunge in numbers was.

The population losses were undisputably considerable and swift. The angle of descent that Sherburne F. Cook and Woodrow Borah offer for central Mexico starts at about 25 million Amerindians at the beginning of the 1520s, falls to 11.2 million in 1532, to 4.7 million in 1548, to 2.2 million in 1568, and to a nadir of 852,000 in 1608. Even if the controversial first estimate is ignored, the drop from 1532 to 1608 is more than 90 percent. The drop from the dependable 1568 number to 1608's equally respectable total is over 60 percent. David Noble Cook, after painstaking research and analysis, puts forward an educated guess of 9 million for the population of Amerindian Peru in 1520, and a solid figure of 600,000 for the region of a century later, again a decline of over 90 percent.

Relatively isolated regions like Yucatan, where the full impact of European invasion was diffused over time, may have suffered smaller declines. But peripheral areas did not necessarily suffer less because of their remoteness or even because of a lower density of population; climate and the amount and kinds of food available must always be taken into consideration. In the cold regions of the far north and south, a crisis, if it struck during the season when vital food resources such as salmon were fleetingly available, could be extremely dangerous. Feverish lowlands, whatever their populations and locations, often lost close to 100 percent of their aboriginal populations. At the beginning of the eighteenth century John Lawson estimated that smallpox and rum had reduced the Amerindians within two hundred miles of Charleston, South Carolina, by five-sixths in only fifty years. A governor of the colony expressed thanks to God for having sent an "Assyrian Angel" among the aborigines with "Smallpox &c. to lessen their numbers: so that the *English*, in Comparison with the *Spaniard*, have but little *Indian* Blood to answer for." [13]

The study of Amerindian demographic history is still at an early stage, and even if enriched with scores of careful local studies (the indispensable next step) will never be a precise science. Conclusions will always be accompanied by caveats that the final figures are *probably* accurate, plus or minus 10 or 20 or 30 percent. But careful studies, fashioned by meticulous and mutually critical scholars, are already producing great advances in the understanding of the American past. After all, in a field where within living memory one expert offered 8.5 million for the 1492 population of the New World and others 100 million, studies producing conclusions dependable within even 50 percent either way are encouraging.

Already we can be sure that in 1492 the populations of the various regions of the New World were comparable in density to similar regions of the Old. Columbus's arrival in America was much more like Marco Polo visiting the Far East, with its advanced empires and primitive tribes, than Robinson Crusoe landing on a desert island. Mexico and Peru obviously had millions of people living in complex societies. Other regions had smaller populations and their societies were not as advanced, but no informed person today would think of endorsing George Bancroft's statement that before whites came to what is now the United States, the area was "an unproductive waste . . . its only inhabitants a few scattered tribes of feeble barbarians, destitute of commerce and of political connection."[14]

Assessing the Columbian Exchange

The effects of establishing permanent links between continents that had been separate, and thereby interweaving divergently evolved biotas and human cultures, were and are too vast to be measured for many centuries and probably millennia, but already the demographic effects of the Columbian exchange are awesome.

Of the three human groups chiefly involved in the linkages between the two worlds—Europeans and European Americans, Africans and African Americans, and Amerindians—the first has benefited most, by the obvious standard, population size. According to the demographer Kingsley Davis, about 50 million Europeans migrated to the New World between 1750 and 1930, and the populations of the lands to which most of them went increased 14 times, while that of the rest of the world increased by 2.5 times. In that same 180 years the number of Caucasians on earth increased 5.4 times, Asians only 2.3 times, and black Africans and African Americans less than 2 times. One may justifiably question the definitions of the terms Caucasian, Asian, African, and African American, but problems of differentiation should not prevent noting that Columbus benefited some kinds of people far more than others.

Columbus's legacy to black Africans and their descendants is mixed. An estimated 10 million Africans crossed the Atlantic to the Americas, where they worked and died as chattel, to the incalculable benefit of their captors and owners. The slave trade transformed West African society, turning its commerce about-face from the Saharan border and the Mediterranean societies to the Atlantic and the New World, enriching some peoples and creating powerful states, and decimating others and destroying them as political and cultural entities. A cold reckoning of the number of black Africans and African Americans suggests that there are now more of them in total than there would be if the slave trade had never existed. Even if the multitudes who died in the Middle Passage and in African wars stimulated by the slave trade were added to the millions of Africans who arrived in the New World, the total of people lost to Africa was probably fewer than were added because of the cultivation of Amerindian crops brought to

Africa by the slavers. The number of African Americans in 1950 was about 47 million, approximately one-fifth of all the blacks on the planet.

Columbus was the advance scout of catastrophe for Amerindians. There were a few happy sequelae—the flowering of equestrian cultures in the American grasslands, for instance—but on balance, the coming of whites and blacks brought disease, followed by intimidation, eviction, alcoholism, decapitation of the ruling classes from the peasant bodies of the advanced Amerindian cultures, and obliteration of many peoples and ways of life. The European invasion of the New World reduced the genetic and cultural pools of the human species, as did, to at least some extent, the advance of Chinese settlers into the Szechuan wilderness and the tropical forests of southeast Asia and the descent of Incan armies down the eastern slopes of the Andes into the jungles. When strangers meet, the degree of difference between their bacterial florae can make more history than the differences between their customs.

The Amerindian population crash in a given area usually lasted no more than one or two hundred years and was followed by a recovery (if there was to be one at all), slow at first and probably not matching the rate of increase of the rest of humanity until the twentieth century. If the nadir populations for Amerindians of the various regions of the New World were added (nadirs were reached in the Caribbean islands by about 1570; in North America not perhaps until 1930), the sum would be about 4.5 million. Although this is no better an informed guess (how was Amerindian defined by the time these populations bottomed out?), in order of magnitude it is acceptable. If this figure is compared to any of the currently and widely respected estimates of Amerindian population in 1492, even to the lowest, 33 million, the conclusion must be that the major initial effect of the Columbian voyages was the transformation of America into a charnal house. The degree to which we have misunderstood our own history is the distance between this undoubted truth, appalling but now solidly established, and the view expressed by the designers of the 1629 seal of the Massachusetts Bay Colony, on which a figure of an Amerindian, longing for a chance to improve himself, calls out, "COME:OVER:AND:HELP:VS." [15] Samuel Eliot Morison repeated this view of the relationship between the Old and New Worlds three centuries later in the peroration to his magnificent *The European Discovery of America*: "To the people of this New World, pagans expecting short and brutish lives, void of hope for any future, had come the Christian vision of a merciful God and a glorious Heaven." [16] We neither ignore nor reconcile ourselves to the sometimes bloody religions of the Amerindians, nor condemn Morison for anything worse than being immured in his own ethnicity, in saying that his was a very selective view of what was surely the greatest tragedy in the history of the human species.

The classic historians of the United States who specialized in the first centuries after the Columbian voyages provided the stories, often deeply researched, accurate, and superbly written, of a small number of white heroes who usually won their battles or who, like Columbus and the Marquis de Montcalm, were noble in defeat. These scholars echoed and amplified a folk version of American history, a hybrid offspring of successful revolution and romantic nationalism, so scanty in disasters and humiliations and so Whiggish in its optimism and blandness that Nathaniel Hawthorne, looking for materials for his novels, complained of his country: "There is no shadow, no antiquity, no mystery, no picturesque and gloomy wrong, nor anything but a common-place prosperity, in broad and simple daylight." [17] The most recent scholarship places beside that plaint a sixteenth- or early seventeenth-century document in the Nahuatl language in which an Aztec matron visits a younger woman in Texcoco to congratulate her on her two sons. The older woman calls the boys "precious jewels and emeralds," as indeed they were at that time, for miscarriages, stillbirths, and deaths of children were common. "Hardly anyone who is born grows up, they just all die off," she says. Her mind strays back to her youth, before the conquest and the new god, when the number of rulers and nobles had been many, the commoners beyond counting, and the slaves as numerous as ants. "But now everywhere our Lord is destroying and reducing the land, and we are coming to an end and disappearing. Why? For what reason?" [18]

American historians, if they will grasp this nettle and accept their responsibility to answer her question, will gain in knowledge of the multiplicity of forces impinging on humanity in all centuries, most of which their liberal arts educations have not prepared them to perceive. They will also gain a sense of tragedy, at present largely missing from at least North American scholarship and essential to mature consideration of the course of our species through time. There is a lot of work to be done. The study of history, said Marc Bloch, "having grown old in embryo as mere narrative, for long encumbered with legend, and for still longer preoccupied with only the most obvious events . . . is still very young as a rational attempt at analysis." [19]

NOTES

1. George Bancroft, *History of the United States, from the Discovery of the American Continent* (Boston: Little, Brown, 1834–73), vol. 1, p. 4.

2. Christopher Hibbert, *The Dragon Awakes: China and the West, 1793–1911* (Harmondsworth, England: Penguin Books, 1984), p. 234.

3. Eric R. Wolf, *Europe and the People without History* (Berkeley: University of California Press, 1982).

4. Pierre Chaunu, *European Expansion in the Later Middle Ages*, trans. Katherine Bertram (Amsterdam: North-Holland Publishing, 1979), p. 106.

5. Charles Darwin, *The Voyage of the Beagle* (Garden City: Doubleday, 1962), pp. 433–34.

6. Donald Joralemon, "New World Depopulation and the Case of Disease," *Journal of Anthropological Research* 38 (Spring 1982): 118.

7. Francis Jennings, *The Invasion of America. Indians, Colonialism and the Cant of Conquest* (Chapel Hill: University of North Carolina Press, 1975), pp. 15–31.

8. Adam Smith, *An Inquiry into the Nature and Causes of the Wealth of Nations* (London: Oxford University Press, 1976), vol. 2, p. 564.

9. Jerome Cardano, *The Book of My Life*, trans. Jean Stoner (London: J. M. Dent, 1931), p. 189.

10. Ibid.

11. John P. Foley, ed., *The Jeffersonian Cyclopedia* (New York: Funk and Wagnalls, 1900), p. 25.

12. Ping-ti Ho, *Studies on the Population of China, 1368–1953* (Cambridge: Harvard University Press, 1959), pp. 191–92.

13. B. R. Carroll, ed., *Historical Collections of South Carolina* (New York: Harper and Brothers, 1836), vol. 2, p. 89.

14. Bancroft, *History of the U.S.*, vol. 1, pp. 3–4.

15. Jennings, *Invasion of America*, p. 229.

16. Samuel Eliot Morison, *The European Discovery of America: The Southern Voyages, 1492–1616* (New York: Oxford University Press, 1974), p. 737.

17. Nathaniel Hawthorne, *The Marble Faun* (Boston: Houghton Mifflin, 1888), p. 15.

18. Frances Karttunen and James Lockhart, *The Art of Nahuatl Speech: The Bancroft Dialogues* (Los Angeles: UCLA Latin American Center Publications, 1987).

19. Marc Bloch, *The Historian's Craft*, trans. Peter Putnam (New York: Knopf, 1961), p. 13.

BIBLIOGRAPHY

Axtell, James. *The Invasion Within: The Contest of Cultures in Colonial North America.* New York: Oxford University Press, 1985.

Chaunu, Pierre. *European Expansion in the Later Middle Ages.* Trans. Katherine Bertram. Amsterdam: North Holland Publishing. 1979.

Ciba Foundation Symposium. *Symposium on Health and Disease in Tribal Societies.* London 1976. N.s. 49. Amsterdam: Elsevier, 1977.

Cook, Noble David. *Demographic Collapse, Indian Peru, 1520–1620.* Cambridge, England: Cambridge University Press, 1981.

Cook, Sherburne F. *The Conflict between the California Indian and White Civilization.* Berkeley: University of California Press, 1976.

———. *The Indian Population of New England in the Seventeenth Century.* University of California Publications in Anthropology, vol. 12. Berkeley: University of California Press, 1976.

Cook, Sherburne F., and Woodrow Borah. *The Aboriginal Population in Central*

Mexico on the Eve of the Spanish Conquest. Berkeley: University of California Press, 1963.

————. *Essays in Population History: Mexico and the Caribbean*, 3 vols. Berkeley: University of California Press, 1971–79.

Crosby, Alfred W. *The Columbian Exchange: Biological and Cultural Consequences of 1492.* Westport, Conn.: Greenwood Press, 1972.

————. *Ecological Imperialism: The Biological Expansion of Europe, 900–1900.* Cambridge, England: Cambridge University Press, 1986.

Curtin, Philip D. *The Atlantic Slave Trade. A Census.* Madison: University of Wisconsin Press, 1969.

Davis, Kingsley. "The Migrations of Human Populations." *Scientific American* 231 (September 1974): 92–107.

Denevan, William M., ed. *The Native Population of the Americas in 1492.* Madison: University of Wisconsin Press, 1976.

Dobyns, Henry F. "An Appraisal of Techniques with a New Hemispheric Estimate." *Current Anthropology* 7 (October 1966): 395–449.

Farriss, Nancy M. *Maya Society under Colonial Rule: The Collective Enterprise of Survival.* Princeton: Princeton University Press, 1984.

Gibson, Charles. *The Aztecs under Spanish Rule: A History of the Indians of the Valley of Mexico, 1519–1810.* Stanford, Calif.: Stanford University Press, 1964.

Hemming, John. *Red Gold: The Conquest of the Brazilian Indians.* Cambridge: Harvard University Press, 1978.

Inikori, J. E., ed. *Forced Migration: The Impact of the Export Slave Trade on African Societies.* London: Hutchinson University Library, 1982.

Jennings, Francis. *The Invasion of America: Indians, Colonialism and the Cant of Conquest.* Chapel Hill: University of North Carolina Press, 1975.

Lovejoy, Paul E. "The Volume of the Atlantic Slave Trade: A Synthesis." *Journal of African History* 23, no. 4: 473–501.

Lovell, W. George. *Conquest and Survival in Colonial Guatemala: A Historical Geography of the Cuchumatan Highlands, 1500–1821.* Kingston: McGill–Queen's University Press, 1985.

Reynolds, Edward. *Stand the Storm: A History of the Atlantic Slave Trade.* London: Alison and Busby, 1985.

Sanchez-Albornoz, Nicolas. *The Population of Latin America. A History.* Trans. W. A. R. Richardson. Berkeley: University of California Press, 1974.

Sauer, Carl Ortwin. *The Early Spanish Main.* Berkeley: University of California Press, 1969.

Stearn, E. Wagner, and Allen E. Stearn. *The Effect of Smallpox on the Destiny of the American Indian.* Boston: Bruce Humphries, 1945.

Trigger, Bruce G. *The Children of Aataentsic. A History of the Huron People to 1660*, 2 vols. Montreal: McGill–Queen's University Press, 1976.

Verlinden, Charles. *The Beginnings of Modern Colonization. Eleven Essays with an Introduction.* Trans. Yvonne Freccero. Ithaca, N.Y.: Cornell University Press, 1970.

Wallerstein, Immanuel. *The Modern World System: Capitalist Agriculture and the Ori-*

gins of the European World-Economy in the Sixteenth Century. New York: Academic Press, 1974.

Webb, Walter Prescott. *The Great Frontier*. Austin: University of Texas Press, 1951.

Wolf, Eric R. *Europe and the People without History*. Berkeley: University of California Press, 1982.

The Tropical Atlantic
in the Age of the Slave Trade

PHILIP D. CURTIN

Characteristics of the Plantation Complex

Over a period of several centuries, Europeans overseas developed an intricate system of plantation agriculture—different from the agricultural institutions they normally used at home. In this essay the term *plantation complex* is used to describe the economic and political order centering on slave plantations in the New World tropics. It reached a peak in the eighteenth century; but its origins can be traced to the medieval Mediterranean, and it lasted through the first two-thirds of the nineteenth century. This political order came to an end only with the abolition of slavery in Brazil and Cuba in the late 1880s, although many aspects lasted well into the twentieth century.

Although the plantation complex centered on the American tropics, its influence was much wider. Political control lay in Europe. Much of the labor force came from Africa, though some came from Amerindian societies on the South American mainland. At its eighteenth-century apogee, many of the trade goods to buy African slaves came from India, while silver to buy these same Indian goods came from mainland South America. Northern North America and Europe were important trading partners, supplying timber and food to the plantations, and consuming the sugar, rum, indigo, coffee, and cotton the plantations produced.

The earliest clear forerunner of the developed plantation complex was the group of plantations that began growing cane sugar in the eastern Mediterranean at the time of the European Crusades. These plantations, unlike the existing Levantine sugar industry, began to grow sugar mainly for a distant market in Europe. They soon became the center of a widespread commercial network bringing in labor and supplies and carrying off the finished product. With the passage of time, the heart of the complex moved westward, by way of the Atlantic islands, to Brazil and the Caribbean. It ultimately stretched from Rio Grande do Sul in southern Brazil to the Mason-Dixon line, and, at its eighteenth-century peak, it had outliers on the Indian Ocean islands of Réunion and Mauritius.[1] In the nineteenth century, a final spurt of growth carried it as far afield as Natal in South Africa, Zanzibar off the East African coast, coastal Peru in South America, Queensland in Australia, and a variety of new "sugar islands" like Fiji and Hawaii. By that time, the plantation form continued, but the labor, though still less than free, was no longer necessarily that of slaves. It was more often supplied by contract workers drawn mainly from India and China.

The plantation complex was therefore much more than an economic order for the tropical Americas alone; it had an important place in world history at large. This essay examines the intercontinental perspective, especially for the commerce across the tropical Atlantic in the eighteenth century.

The plantation complex at its most developed state might be defined by some quantitative measure: either demographic, such as the proportion of slaves to total population, or economic, such as the degree of specialization in production for sale at a distance.[2] Or a historian could pick a particular plantation society as an example. A historian of the United States could take the Cotton Kingdom as it was in the American South from 1830 to 1860. Or a mixed approach could limit the field of choice to preindustrial examples and to societies with the most specialized production and the most intense slave regime. By that standard, the historical model would be Jamaica, Barbados, or Saint Domingue (now Haiti) in the eighteenth century—with Brazil in the seventeenth and Mauritius in the early nineteenth as near competitors.

These and similar places had a number of features that marked them off from other societies, and especially from contemporaneous Europe, their political master. First, most of the productive labor was forced labor; most people were slaves. This was also the case in Russia, since serfs were slaves for all practical purposes, but Russian estates were not nearly as specialized as tropical plantations.[3] Nor did preindustrial non-Western slaveholding societies in the Muslim world or Southeast Asia have such a high proportion of slaves in the labor force.

Second, the population was not self-sustaining. Neither the European managerial staff nor the African workforce produced an excess of births over deaths. Both groups had to be sustained by a constant stream of new people just to maintain their numbers—still larger population inputs if the system were to grow. At the present state of demographic information, it is uncertain how widespread this excess of deaths over births was in the American tropics; but it was undoubted in the key islands and colonies of the plantation complex, and it lasted for a long time—at least a century and a half to two centuries and perhaps more.

Such a long-term demographic imbalance is unusual. Cities are the only common example of non-self-sustaining populations that keep up their numbers through immigration.[4] Many populations have declined—even disappeared altogether—but at the height of the plantation complex large-scale and continuous immigration not only compensated for net natural decrease, it made it possible for these populations to grow as well.

Third, agricultural enterprise was organized in large-scale capitalist plantations. Typically, they might have from fifty to several hundred workers—many more than European farms of the time. The owner of the land and the capital equipment managed all stages of production in person or through his agents. On the plantation itself, his agents gave orders for the conduct of all agricultural operations on a day-to-day and hour-to-hour basis. This again was different from the patterns of work organization and management anywhere in European agriculture.

Fourth, though capitalist, the plantations also had certain features that can be called "feudal." Specifically, the owner not only controlled his workforce during their working hours, he also held, at least de facto, some form of legal jurisdiction. His agents acted informally as police. They punished most minor crimes and settled most disputes without reference to high authority.

Fifth, the plantations were created to supply a distant market with a highly specialized product—at first mainly sugar, but later others like coffee and cotton. The plantation often grew food to feed its own workers, but at times virtually the whole production was exported. This meant that the whole society was dependent on long-distance trade to carry off the crop and to bring in supplies, people, and food. When this happened, more of its total consumption and total production was carried by long-distance traders than in any other part of the world economy of the time. The possible exceptions might be specialized island producers in Asia, like the Maluku Islands that supplied Europe and most of Asia with cloves—just as the slave plantations of Zanzibar were to do in the nineteenth century. Certainly none of the European or African economies was so intensely export-oriented.

Sixth, political control over the system lay on another continent and in another kind of society. Domination from a distance had occurred often enough in history, but rarely from so far away. And political control was fragmented. At various times, Portugal, Spain, Holland, England, France, Brandenburg, Sweden, Denmark, and Kurland (more recently Latvia) were active in either the slave trade or the plantations themselves. This meant that each overseas part of the system in Africa or the Americas was linked to a metropolis in Europe, and all the European metropolises were linked together through the competitive mechanisms of the European state system.

ORIGINS AND MIGRATIONS

Although the plantation complex produced a variety of exotic crops for European consumption, its history has been inextricably intertwined with sugar. Europe's contact with sugarcane began with the Crusades, when new knowledge about the Levant included knowledge of cane sugar. It was an impressive discovery for people whose main source of sugar had been honey. Venetians and Genoese first imported sugar from the Muslim Levant, but other Christians soon began to grow it on territory they acquired in the Crusades—first on the Levantine mainland itself, later on Crete and Cyprus and other east Mediterranean islands. There, an embryonic version of the plantation complex came into existence, with sugar production under capitalist management, using a combination of local labor and slave labor derived mainly from the north shore of the Black Sea.

Sugarcane is a crop with its own physical and economic peculiarities. Production is extremely labor-intensive. Before modern machinery was available, a common rule-of-thumb in agriculture was one worker for each acre cultivated. The weight and bulk of the harvested cane is enormous compared to such grasses as wheat and maize. This meant that it was very costly to haul any distance without first concentrating the sugar by squeezing out the cane juice and boiling it to drive off excess water, producing crystalline sugar and molasses. Every early cane farm, even one with only one hundred to five hundred acres of land, therefore had to have its own sugar factory to concentrate the product for shipment, though cane could be carried farther to a central factory once the cost of road haulage was reduced.

Once concentrated, cane sugar products had a high value-to-bulk ratio. This meant that they could be carried far away, especially by relatively cheap water transport, and still sold at a profit. Economically, therefore, sugar could enter long-distance trade over far greater distances than wheat, rice, or other starchy staples of common use. But sugar also differed nutritionally from these other sources of carbohydrates. Wheat, rice, maize, potatoes, and manioc, among others, normally supplied more than half the total nutritional intake in preindustrial societies. They took a proportionate part of society's agricultural effort, at a time when the vast majority of the population worked the land. Sugar could not serve that kind of nutritional role. It could supplement other foods, but it could not provide most of the calories in a healthy diet. Without export outlets, it could only be a very minor crop for local use. Dates are a similar crop, with very high caloric content and high yields but a limited nutritional role. Both sugar and dates, like spices, have been associated historically with the development of long-distance trade.[5]

From the twelfth century onward, sugar production under European control spread westward to Sicily and on to the southern part of Spain and Portugal, but the Mediterranean with its cool and wet winters was not ideally suited to sugar production. With the European voyages into the Atlantic, colonizers imported plantation managers from the old sugar areas of the Mediterranean to help found plantations on the Atlantic islands of Madeira, the Canaries, and even São Tomé in the Gulf of Guinea. At that point, the need for labor was met by tapping into the nascent maritime slave trade from tropical Africa toward Europe.

In the sixteenth century, with the colonization in the Americas, the process of technology transfer moved the plantations once more from the Canaries to Santo Domingo and other Caribbean islands under Spanish control, and from Portuguese Madeira to Brazil. Two further stages carried the production of slave-grown sugar onward into the French and English Caribbean. The first, beginning in the 1640s, took the sugar and slave complex on into the Lesser Antilles. It was carried by Dutch shippers, who became acquainted with the plantation complex after the Dutch had conquered northeastern Brazil. Finally, at the end of the seventeenth century and the beginning of the eighteenth, this "sugar revolution" moved on to the islands of Jamaica and western Hispaniola, where it would achieve its fullest development.

THE UNITED STATES AND THE PLANTATION COMPLEX

From a North American perspective, the plantation complex might seem to have reached some kind of climax in the American South before the Civil War, but this was not the case. The mainland colonies bought a few slaves in the seventeenth century, usually assimilated to the status of indentured servants. It was only from the early eighteenth century that slave plantations became characteristic of the American South, after the sugar revolution had already moved forward to the Greater Antilles. When plantation slavery did arrive, it was copied from the British West Indies, just as the Lesser Antilles had earlier copied from Brazil.

Even then, the American South was not fully part of the plantation complex. In the typical sugar islands, 75 to 95 percent of the population were slaves, and most of the free people were of African descent. In the American South, generally, most people were not slaves at all, but colonists of European descent. Even where, as in South Carolina, a majority of the working class were slaves, they worked alongside a European American working class that was free.

The American South also differed from the heart of the plantation complex in work organization and plantation size. The typical Caribbean sugar plantation had a force of at least fifty slaves—more often two or even three hundred. In the United States, even in the 1850s when slavery reached its fullest development, fewer than half of all slaves belonged to planters who owned thirty or more. Gang labor, where dozens of men and women worked side by side under constant disciplinary surveillance, was most typical of sugar cultivation. The more diversified plantations of the American South often grew specialized export crops like cotton and tobacco, but they also grew food for themselves and for the rest of society. Raising pigs, cattle, and chickens, as well as field crops, created too great a variety of tasks for continuous supervision.

The demographic history of the American South was also strikingly different from that of the tropical plantation colonies. In the tropics, slave populations experienced an excess of deaths over births from their earliest settlement onward. European populations of the tropical Caribbean also had more deaths than births. Both populations had to be renewed by continuous immigration from Europe and Africa. In North America, in contrast, the slave population soon began to grow from natural increase, and the population of free settlers from Europe grew even more rapidly. Further migration from Europe and Africa simply increased the total. It is not yet possible to account fully for such a striking difference. Part of the explanation must be found in the disease environment of a country with winter frosts to kill off some tropical diseases, though the American South had malaria and occasional yellow fever epidemics. Part of the explanation may be the American achievement of a more even sex ratio in the slave population at an early date, which, in turn, may reflect the greater variety of tasks and the smaller size of the American slave plantation.

In any event, both African American and European American populations of the mainland colonies grew from natural increase, and they increased more rapidly than contemporaneous populations did in Europe. As a result, the United States is thought to have the largest population of partial or total African descent in any American country—about 30 percent of all African Americans in the New World—even though their African ancestors made up only about 6 percent of the total slave trade.

The rest of this essay is concerned with the plantation complex as it was at its peak in the second half of the eighteenth century—not with the workings of the plantations themselves, but with the commercial relations that stretched across the Atlantic to Africa and Europe.

The Slave Trade in the Eighteenth Century

We tend to think of Europe's early trade with Africa as though the slave trade was virtually all of it. In fact, slaves were comparatively unimportant during the first two centuries of maritime contact—roughly from A.D. 1450 to 1650. The Portuguese mariners who made that contact went down the African coast looking for gold, not slaves. The availability of slaves for sale was a fortuitous and unexpected by-product of the gold trade. When the plantation complex crossed the Atlantic to Brazil after 1550, direct slave shipments from Africa to the New World became more important. When the Caribbean sugar colonies joined the plantation complex after about 1650, the Dutch, English, and French (among others) began to be active in the slave trade to the Caribbean, and the numbers of slaves shipped from West Africa to the Caribbean increased. Between about 1650 and 1850, slaves became the main export from tropical Africa to the outside world.

More Americans trace their ancestors to Africa than to any continent other than Europe, and it was the slave trade that brought them. That phase of America's past carries strong emotional overtones—for African Americans and European Americans alike. No one today defends the slave trade as a humane institution, and few indeed defend it on any grounds. It may be well to concede that the era of the slave trade is beyond the effective range of moral condemnation. The more important task is to find out what happened and why, rather than placing blame, however well deserved. The Atlantic slave trade grew to be the largest intercontinental migration up to that time. Whatever else, it operated because the sellers, buyers, and transporters all found it profitable. One place to begin is to see the trade as an economic enterprise.

THE ECONOMICS OF DEMAND

The American demand for slaves arose from two natural conditions. One was the fact that new agricultural enterprises required new sources of labor. In spite of myths to the contrary, the tropical world was not a place where food was readily available for little work. In any region of potential sugar plantations, the people already in place were needed to produce the goods their own society consumed. To set up plantations required new inputs of labor and often new inputs of imported food to keep the workers fed. Sugar was a peculiarly labor-intensive crop; it needed more labor per acre than most food crops, simply to grow the cane. It required even more labor in the sugar factories to process the raw product before shipment. From the early days of sugar planting in the eastern Mediterranean, new labor had most often been supplied through the existing institution for labor mobility—the slave trade—at first in Slavs from north of the Black Sea, but later on in Africans from across the Sahara; even the early settlement of North America from Europe had called on convict labor and less-than-free people to move to America under indenture for a period of years.

The second condition that brought about a strong demand for slaves was the demographic impact of African and European diseases on Native

American populations.[6] Populations out of touch with the African Eurasian intercommunicating zone—as the Americans had been before Columbus—tended to lack immunities to the main diseases of Europe and Africa, including a whole range of formerly common "childhood diseases" like measles, diphtheria, and whooping cough, along with smallpox, falciparum malaria, and yellow fever. With the American voyages that followed Columbus, these diseases were carried to the Americas, where they had a frightening impact. Within a century, most of the population of the tropical lowlands was simply wiped out. Even the highland people of the Andes and Middle America lost as much as 80 percent of their total population within a century after contact with Europe. By the eighteenth century, some of these populations had gained new immunities and began to grow again; but the tropical lowlands of the seventeenth and eighteenth centuries lay underpopulated and ripe for development.

New population might have been drawn from Europe, and it was to some extent. Europeans, however, lacked acquired immunities to the tropical diseases of African origin, like yellow fever or falciparum malaria. Newly arrived settlers from Europe died in such numbers that a European population in the Caribbean could be sustained only with a continuous stream of immigration. That was, of course, true of slave populations on plantations as well, but the slave populations had some immunity to tropical diseases along with a general pattern of immunity to most of the generalized diseases of the African Eurasian land mass. In tropical American conditions of these centuries, therefore, Africans were the most desirable possible immigrants—whether slave or free.[7]

ENVIRONMENTAL FACTORS IN AFRICA

Just as the demand for slaves owed something to the shifting ecology of disease in the Atlantic basin, the supply of slaves from Africa owed something to the African environment. Tropical Africa is a region of notoriously variable rainfall, especially in regions between about 10 and 30 latitude, both north and south. These are regions of recent drought, especially in the Sahel region of West Africa just south of the Sahara, and in equivalent regions of south latitude in Angola. These savanna areas north or south of the equator have a restricted period of rainfall, with the entire year's rainfall occurring in a period of two to four months. When such intense rainfall is badly distributed through the growing season, crop failure and famine can result. Worse still, rain sometimes fails altogether for a whole season—occasionally for two or even three years in succession. When that happens, people have either to flee or die.

Those who fled were easy victims for the slave trade. Some sold themselves or family members in order to survive at all. Others had to take refuge with alien societies, which they entered as kinless people with no

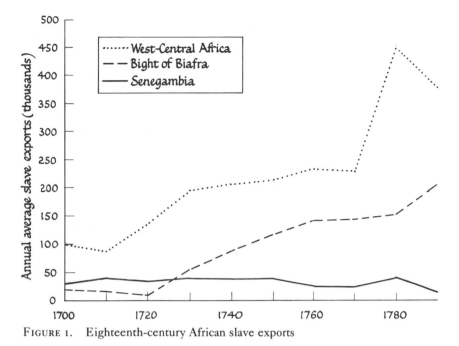

FIGURE 1.   Eighteenth-century African slave exports

rights. As such, they were easily passed on into the slave trade whenever their hosts wished to do so. It is not always possible to distinguish famine victims from other slaves, but a few instances were dramatic enough to come to the attention of Europeans on the coast. Between 1746 and 1754, Senegal experienced a series of bad harvests, which brought measurable increases in slave exports. Even though the general level of the Senegalese slave trade had been falling for decades, French exports from Senegal in 1754 were the highest ever.

The impact of low rainfall is even more striking in Angola, where a severe famine struck in the 1780s, continuing into the 1790s. (See Figure 1.) In the 1780s, slave exports from the west central African region, to which Angola belongs, jumped to twice the level of the 1770s—even though the price rose by only 10 percent from one decade to the next. Where the region had once been a source of supply only for Portuguese slavers, French, British, and Dutch slave traders now began operating on the coast north of the Congo River mouth. These political and climatic disasters were noneconomic in origin, but they had the economic consequence of lowering the price of slaves as they flooded the nearby coastal points and of attracting new groups of maritime slave traders ready to supply the markets of the plantation complex.

THE ECONOMICS OF SUPPLY

Another underlying condition for the development of the slave trade was the low cost of slaves in Africa. The West Indian planters thought that it was cheaper to buy workers from Africa than it was to have them grow up naturally from the fertility of the existing slave populations. Prices changed during the course of the eighteenth century, but the planters may have been correct in this belief at the beginning of that century. If true, this belief implied a puzzle. It implied that African slave dealers could sell slaves for less than it cost to bring up a child to working age. But how could Africans sell people for less than their cost of production?

The local economic situation at the mouth of the Gambia River in the 1680s may illustrate part of this underlying condition. At that time, a young male slave ready for shipment sold for an assortment of goods that cost about £5.50 sterling in Europe. Five pounds sterling would have bought 17 trade muskets or 200 liters of brandy or 349 kilograms of wrought iron. Even at that time of comparatively low prices, these were no mere trinkets, but their value may be clearer translated into local terms. One possibility is to find their equivalent value in staple foods. The most important food cost in any society is that of the local starchy staple, with daily consumption estimated at one kilogram per person. Man does not live by millet alone; nor was anyone likely to eat quite that much millet every day, but the index can serve as a rough guide to the cost of one person's subsistence. For the Gambia of the 1680s, the price of a slave, freight on board, would translate into enough food to support the slave for about six years. It was therefore much less than the probable cost of raising a child to working age. But the selling price on the coast was far more than the value of the slave at the point of enslavement. European slave dealers residing on the coast bought slaves from African dealers for only about £3.40; the difference was their profit and the cost of holding slaves until a ship happened along. The African merchants who brought slaves for sale to the coastal Europeans paid, in turn, less still—prices ranging from about £3 for a slave purchased near the port down to £1 or less for slaves bought in the distant interior. The difference was the cost of tolls and transportation on the way to the coast. At these approximate prices, an original enslaver near the coast received the value of about four-years' support costs, while the enslaver in the far interior received barely a year's support. Such a low price was obviously less than the slave's cost of production, but the first seller was not the producer. The economic model for enslavement is one of burglary, not of production. In economic terms, the value of the slave is not a real cost but an "opportunity cost."

Returning to the hypothetical example from the Gambia of the 1680s, we can imagine a king of Segu on the upper Niger fighting one of his brothers for control of the kingdom. If, in the process, he captured one

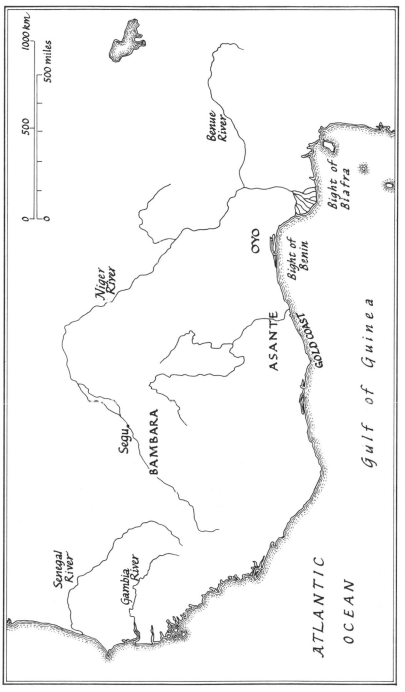

Map 1. West Africa in the era of the slave trade

of his brother's villages, he was entitled by law and custom to enslave the inhabitants. Since he was fighting a war for other objectives, the captives were essentially costless to the king, but the opportunity cost was also low. One possibility was to keep the slaves as an addition to the labor force under his command, but recent enemies of fighting age were dangerous unless they could be kept under constant guard, and few African societies were prepared to run the equivalent of a chain gang. Enforced servitude under guard might have been uneconomic in any case; the cost of food and guards might well exceed the value of labor performed unwillingly. The usual practice was therefore to sell a slave into the trade for transportation to a distant point, whence individual captives had small chance of returning home alone. The new owner could then try to assimilate the captive into a new society.

Political enslavement

Political enslavement occurred when economic motives for enslavement were secondary, though not necessarily absent, as in the example just given. Enslavement of this kind belongs toward one end of a spectrum of motives from the purely political at one end to the purely economic at the other—from enslavement in the pursuit of power to enslavement in the pursuit of wealth. At the extreme political end of the spectrum, captives were not sold at all but killed on the spot. At the economic end, the captors acted solely for material gain.

Large-scale enslavement for mainly political motives arose from civil wars like that of Segu in the 1680s, from international wars of aggression, or from civil disorder following the collapse of a large state. When these disturbances took place, they often caused a major increase in the supply of slaves from that particular region—a change that had little or nothing to do with the price offered on the coast. In the case of the upper Niger, a new, mainly Bambara kingdom based on Segu was formed in the early eighteenth century. From about 1700 to 1730, unusually large numbers of slaves were sold down the trade routes toward the Senegambian coastal ports. Once the dynasty was firmly in control, the price of slaves began its eighteenth-century rise; but the flow of slaves from Segu dropped to a trickle, and the European slavers went elsewhere for their cargoes.

The political expansion of the kingdom of Asante was one of several cases of imperial expansion in eighteenth-century West Africa. The new state was first firmly established in the Gold Coast hinterland in about 1700. It then proceeded to fight a series of wars of aggression, first against neighboring states of the same (Akan) ethnic group, later against its non-Akan neighbors to the north. In later years, the Asante kingdom also fought rebellions in subject states that were unhappy about their subordination to Asante power. With each outbreak, new flows of slaves entered the trade to the coast. The supply of slaves on the Gold Coast rose and fell with these events of Asante military history, not with changes in the price offered.

A third example of political enslavement was the early nineteenth-century collapse of the formerly powerful Oyo empire in southwest Nigeria. Oyo had established a broad region of hegemony over the densely inhabited Yoruba city–states and many of their neighbors. During the height of Oyo's power, comparatively few Yoruba entered the slave trade. When the Oyo empire collapsed, however, a half-century of warfare followed among the successor states, with the result that the Yoruba, who had been rare in the eighteenth-century slave trade, became the largest single ethnic group in the nineteenth-century trade. As a result, New World countries that imported many slaves in the nineteenth century—Brazil and Cuba in particular—received an unusual concentration of Yoruba and an overlay of Yoruba culture that has persisted to the present.

ECONOMIC ENSLAVEMENT

Economic enslavement could take many forms; the most obvious is a war started purely for the sake of booty. European accounts of precolonial Africa feature the "slave-raiding chief" as a stock figure. Whether, or how often, wars were begun for the sole purpose of capturing slaves is hard to establish. Before the eighteenth-century rise in slave prices, the captor's share of the total price was too low to justify any considerable risk to himself—or to his cavalry horses, worth many times the price of a slave. As the coastal price of slaves rose through the eighteenth century, rulers could take these prices into account in decision making—alongside whatever nonmaterial advantage was also present.

The state, however, could recruit slaves in less risky ways. Many African societies sold condemned criminals into the slave trade, which avoided the cost of prisons and brought the state some revenue. Such prisoners also included the king's enemies and other political opponents of the powerful, so that sale into the trade served several ends. Some societies allowed a man to bring judicial action against another man who committed adultery with one of his wives. If convicted, the adulterer could be sold—to the profit of the husband. One form of petty chicanery feeding the slave trade was to use a young and attractive wife to entrap victims.

Some West African societies made a distinction between two kinds of warfare that are similar to the economic and political models of enslavement. In the same Bambara region where the kingdom of Segu emerged early in the eighteenth century, *tegereya*, or banditry, was distinguished from *keleya*, or regular warfare. *Tegereya* tended to emerge whenever the state's power to keep the peace weakened. Young men from a single village or a group of nearby villages would get together on the pretext of going hunting. Once away from home, they would move through the fal-

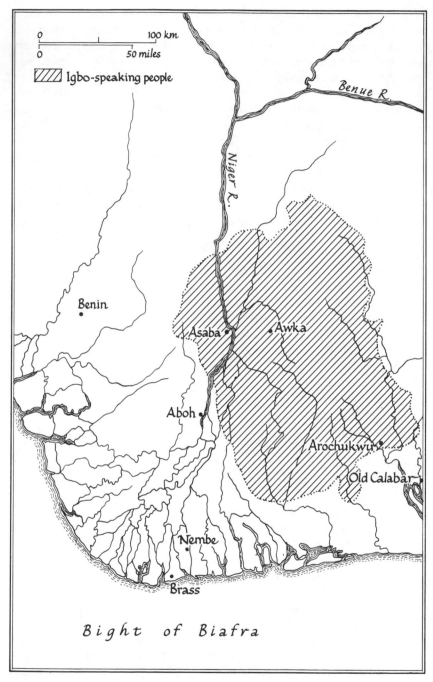

Scale:
0 — 100 km
0 — 50 miles

▨ Igbo-speaking people

Benue R.

Niger R.

Benin

Asaba • Awka

Aboh

Arochukwu

Old Calabar

Nembe

Brass

Bight of Biafra

MAP 2.   The Niger Delta and its hinterland

low savanna country, mainly at night, until they were well away from their own village. They could then begin stealing cattle and kidnapping people, trying to pick up individuals or small groups, like women on the way to the village well or others unlikely to be able to defend themselves. The raiders were often a group of forty to fifty men, who could fight if necessary; but they depended on stealth and speed to make their captures and sell them at a distance before returning home.

Slave taking without warfare predominated in some African regions. The Igbo country of southeastern Nigeria represents a very different set of social and political circumstances from those of Segu. The natural vegetation was high rain forest, though the Igbo people had been densely settled there for centuries, practicing shifting agriculture based on yams and palm oil. It was also a zone of stateless societies, where public order was based on intricate interrelations of kinship groups. The largest permanent political unit was the village group, but political authority was widely diffused through the whole community.

Much of the trade through Igbo country was carried by the Aro, an Igbo subgroup that specialized in commerce. The Aro had settlements widely scattered through the region. Igbo society was not a completely peaceful society, but comparatively few of the slaves exported were taken in war. Violence at a lower level, however, was common. Many people were kidnapped and sold to the Aro, or else sold for crimes, for alleged physical deformity, after inveiglement into adultery, or were contributed as sacrifices to important oracles scattered through Igboland—like the Aro's important oracle at Arochukwu. People "sacrificed" to these oracles were not killed; they were spirited away and sold into the slave trade. This pattern of enslavement made it possible for the Igbo to respond to economic demand from buyers on the coast—rather than to political events or natural disasters. As a result, the eighteenth-century exports from the Bight of Biafra rose steadily along with the rise in slave prices.

RISING DEMAND—RISING EXPORTS

During the eighteenth century, slave prices in West Africa rose by a factor of three to four (see Figure 2), and slave deliveries from most areas rose to match (see Figure 1). In economic terms, the price elasticity of the supply of slaves appears to have been high; rising prices brought about rising deliveries. Unfortunately for historians, this kind of covariance cannot be taken as proof of cause and effect, but it did create a changing climate for economic decision making. An *Asantehene*, or king of Asante, no doubt assessed the pros and cons before engaging in a new war. He would have to take into account the advantages Asante might win balanced against cost and risk. Somewhere in the equation was possible income from the sale of captives. The profit from sales of this kind were probably

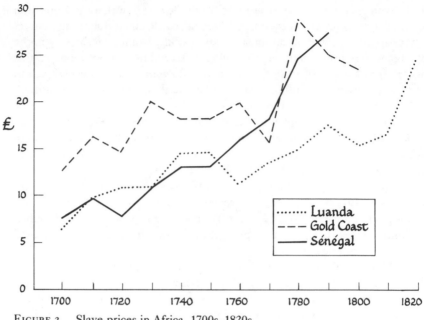

FIGURE 2. Slave prices in Africa, 1700s–1820s

neither a necessary nor a sufficient cause to begin the war; but every rise in the selling price for slaves would increase its weight in the equation, just as every rise in price increased the advantage of taking enemies captive rather than killing them.

But rising slave prices could increase the supply of slaves without necessarily encouraging warfare. When slave prices were low, merchants were limited in the distance they could profitably travel in search of captives. Rising prices meant that they could go farther afield. They could afford to spend more for guards, for food along the way, or for tolls and tariffs paid to the states through which they passed. Such factors seem to account for the fact that, in the course of the eighteenth century, slaves began to be drawn from places farther in the interior. Where most slaves in earlier centuries came from a zone within fifty to one hundred miles from the coast, many by the early nineteenth century came as far as five hundred or even one thousand miles. This suggests the political model of enslavement may still have been important—that high prices merely extended the reach of the trade.

Some of the high price elasticity in the supply of slaves also came from the response of the European slavers. As prices in the Americas rose, they were able to offer higher prices on the African coast, but they were also well informed about conditions in Africa. They could therefore direct their ships to the places where supplies were increasing anyhow in response to famine or anarchy—to the Congo region in the 1790s, for example.

ASSESSING THE DAMAGE

An important debate has begun to emerge from recent research about the slave trade in Africa. It centers on the problem of assessing its damage to African societies. Defenders of the slave trade, while it still existed, used to argue that it was good for Africa, removing excess people, and good for the slaves themselves, bringing them into contact with Western civilization and the Christian religion. Such sentiments sound strange today, but the degree of damage to African societies is still an open question. A few historians would trace "African backwardness" to the influence of the slave trade, and some claim that most of Africa's present problems are traceable to the impact of the trade. Others concede that Africa was isolated from the main intercommunicating zones in world history, but would otherwise deny the accusation of backwardness—an accusation drawn from Western cultural chauvinism and old myths of African racial inferiority.

A satisfactory general assessment may never be possible. But some partial and tentative conclusions are possible. The most obvious is that the slave trade affected different parts of Africa in different ways. Some small societies were completely destroyed; others were barely affected. Some simply refused to participate in the trade for long periods of time; the kingdom of Benin between the Igbo in the east and the Yoruba to the west is one example located on the "slave coast." Other societies devoted much of their common effort to exploiting the slave trade and turning it to their advantage at the expense of their neighbors.

From a high level of generalization, the slave trade appears as a stream of captives leaving Africa in increasing numbers, with only an occasional decline, over a period of two hundred years from the mid-seventeenth century to the mid-nineteenth. That picture is not inaccurate from the perspective of the whole Atlantic economy. Seen from any region within Africa, however, the slave trade rarely lasted so long. Just as slave exports from the Senegambia peaked and then declined, those from other regions were rarely sustained from one decade to the next, perhaps because the human resources for export were no longer adequate. Even when high levels of exports from a particular coastal zone were sustained over long periods, as they were from west central Africa in the eighteenth century, the people for export came from many different and shifting sources in the interior. Slavery within Africa continued at some level through the whole period, but disastrous losses to a particular society from slave exports were rarely sustained for more than a few decades, leaving the possibility of recovery.

The destructiveness of the trade also varied with forms of enslavement. Where the economic model was predominant and led to wars carried out in order to capture slaves, the number of the dead must have been several times the number captured and shipped to the coast or the Sahara. The middle-aged, the old, and the very young were often simply killed because their value to the trade was negligible. Politically inspired warfare was also enormously destructive, even though the slave trade was more a by-product than a cause. Major catastrophes like the collapse of Oyo or the rise of new empires like the Caliphate of Sokoto in the early nineteenth century were especially destructive, but so were similar military and political movements after the mid-nineteenth century—when the Atlantic slave trade had effectively ended so far as West Africa was concerned.

At the other extreme, economically motivated enslavement through the judicial process, petty chicanery, exploitation of wives and adultery laws, "sacrifice" to oracles, even kidnapping, involved comparatively little violence and loss of life. The enslaved were simply removed. That was certainly a serious loss in chronically underpopulated regions, but other damage was limited.

Still, the loss of life was significant. Those who were enslaved as a result of famine died in enormous numbers before they could reach the coast. Others certainly died of disease as they moved out of their home region into new disease environments. In the best of circumstances, deaths in transit to the coast, in confinement awaiting shipment, and at sea on the way to the Americas must have taken 30 to 50 percent of those who began the journey. Most circumstances were less favorable.

Even so, and terrible as it was, if the slave trade is to be interpreted accurately, it has to be seen in the light of other human disasters. Warfare on other continents was also terrible. So was politically motivated destruction like the Nazi holocaust of the 1940s or the Stalinist destruction of the Soviet peasantry in the course of collectivization in the 1920s and 1930s. Climatic disasters like the most serious Sahelian droughts probably killed an even higher proportion of the population over a considerable area, and they still take an enormous toll. So did the epidemiological disasters wrought by European diseases in the Americas in the sixteenth century and the Pacific islands in the nineteenth. The value in making these comparisons is not to apologize for the slave trade, but to help explain how West African societies managed to advance in so many areas of life during the era of the slave trade—and in spite of it.

Atlantic Commerce

By the eighteenth century, the tropical plantation had become a peculiarly specialized economic institution. It produced one or two products, which were sold at a great distance. The factors of production were not merely local land and capital, but capital and managerial labor from Europe, other workers from Africa, and associated products as diverse as Indian textiles to trade for slaves, European cloth for plantation slaves to wear, and New England barrel staves to make hogsheads for shipping sugar. The plantation complex, in short, was supported by oceanic trade over long routes stretching from the Pacific coast of Peru in the west to the Bay of Bengal in the east.

BUREAUCRATS AND PRIVATE TRADERS

European intentions in the outer world had been clear from the earliest expeditions to India and the Antilles. Crown bureaucracies intended to make the overseas ventures profitable for the Crown, producing either revenues for the monarch or power for the state—preferably both. Private traders, in contrast, were among the most self-interested and independent of the early capitalist firms, not always as violent and independent as seventeenth-century buccaneers but equally anxious to evade control over their operations. In the conditions of the time, they were often successful. European governments, even as late as the eighteenth century, had no way to reach or control individual enterprise. If they made general regulations, it was virtually impossible to enforce them. The best they could do was to act through corporate groups like guilds. Some of these were natural corporations, such as the group of people who practiced a particular craft in a particular place. The state could recognize such a group by giving it legal existence as a guild. If a natural group did not already exist, the state could create one, issuing a charter granting particular powers that had previously belonged to the Crown.

European governments had long used corporations of this kind to organize foreign trade, endowing guildlike corporations with the power to regulate the trade carried out by their members, though the profit or loss belonged to the individual member, not the guild. The Merchants of the Staple in the late medieval English wool trade was a regulatory corporation of this sort. Or the government might endow a corporation with power to carry out trade or production on the corporate account. These grants usually included the right to monopolize the trade of a particular area or in a particular commodity. In these cases, the Crown did not need to enforce the monopoly; the self-interest of the corporation would see that it was enforced, if at all possible.

The greatest of the colonial companies had been created in the seventeenth century to control trade and empire in eastern seas—usually defined as everything from the Cape of Good Hope to the western shores of the Americas. The Dutch East India Company, the English East India Company, or the French Compagnie des Indes are the prime examples that survived into the eighteenth century—operating their own armies and navies and fighting wars with each other as well as against the Asians. With such great power, these corporations became virtual branches of European states; and European governments found ways to influence their political moves while leaving their commercial monopolies untouched.

Commercial control in the Atlantic basin was rarely so neat, though each European power worked through a similar combination of institutional forms. Some organized proprietary colonies in the hands of individuals or corporations—like Pennsylvania or Maryland or the early captaincies donatory of Brazil. Other colonies functioned under Crown officials responsible directly to the government in Europe. Among these were bureaucratic structures like the great viceroyalties of New Spain and Peru, as well as such smaller units as Jamaica, Barbados, and Saint Domingue in the Caribbean.

Companies had varied powers. The Dutch East and West India Companies could govern colonies as well as trade. The French Compagnie des Indes held various monopoly rights over the French slave trade, as well as its far greater governmental rights in parts of India. In the late seventeenth and early eighteenth centuries, the Royal African Company briefly held a monopoly over the English slave trade, but later in the eighteenth century the Company of Merchants Trading to Africa was only an infrastructural concern. British merchants trading to Africa had to be members and support its activities, but these activities were limited to the control and management of forts and other trading posts on the African coast.

Each colonial power tended to have one or more agencies with general oversight of its overseas affairs. In Spain it was the Council of the Indies, and an equivalent body existed in Portugal. In France, it was the Ministère de la Marine—and so on, with other bodies, like the Board of Trade and Plantations in Britain or the Casa de Contratación in Seville, especially concerned with economic affairs.

Whatever the institutional forms, the European powers were agreed on the proper goal of commercial regulation. It was to make the state powerful and wealthy; the means were mercantilist economics, spelled out by publicists in the late seventeenth and early eighteenth centuries. One goal was a "favorable balance of trade," meaning an export balance in commodity trade with a consequent inflow of bullion. Colonial trade was to be carried by national shipping. The home country was to supply manufactured goods in return for raw materials.

Ideally, each colonial power ruled over its national sector of the plantation complex and kept it hermetically sealed from contact with any other sector. Such goals, however, were impossible, as even the regulatory bodies came to realize. Even without the additional problem of frequent wars through the eighteenth century, exceptions had to be allowed from the beginning. Spain, having no African trading posts, permitted Portuguese and then other foreign shippers to supply slaves to the Spanish Empire. The Dutch often set themselves the goal of operating as seaborne traders, with few real plantation colonies under their own control. To this end, they worked to break into the sealed system of the others, rather than simultaneously trying to control one of their own. Even aside from legalized exceptions, thousands of individual shippers were willing and able to smuggle goods from one imperial system to another. To enforce a monopoly against such interlopers turned out to be impossible.

The reality of the eighteenth-century plantation trade is hard to discover in detail, simply because so much of it was extralegal. Some trade moved within the legal channels, much (perhaps most) did not. World trade in this period was also marked by some broad flows of money and commodities. Silver from the Spanish Empire and gold from Brazil found their way into the hands of other Europeans—contrary to Spanish and Portuguese intentions. Those other Europeans, in turn, used monetary metals to finance their trade in the Indian Ocean—contrary to their own mercantilist and bullionist goals. In an unofficial and indirect way, then, bullion from the Americas paid for Europe's imports from India.[8] A part of that larger transfer of goods and money passed through the plantation complex in ways far more intricate than some of the old stereotypes of the "triangular trade."

COMMODITIES IN THE AFRICAN TRADE

Textbooks a few decades ago sometimes showed a map of African commerce in the era of the slave trade. The map showed a ship making its outward passage from Europe to West Africa with trinkets, arms, gunpowder, and gin to be exchanged for slaves. The ship then carried the slaves to the West Indies in a middle passage, and finally picked up sugar, indigo, coffee, and other tropical products for the passage home. Ships did, in fact, make similar voyages, but African commerce was far more complex.

For Africa the choice was not slave trade or no trade. Slaves were exported from western Africa over four centuries, but they were the most important single export for only a century and a half, from about 1690 to 1840. Certain regions sold slaves and little else over longer periods. West-Central Africa on either side of the Congo River mouth was one such region; the so-called slave coast along the Bight of Benin (the present-day Republic of Benin and western Nigeria) was another. Other regions sold not just slaves but other commodities as well. For the long coastline between the Gambia and the Gold Coast at the height of the slave trade, about three-quarters of all exports were in slaves; the rest were in pepper, ivory, and timber.

For other regions where we have more solid quantitative information, the picture was not very different. Senegambia, for example, was a heavy exporter of slaves in the early sixteenth century, following the breakup of the Jollof Empire. In the late sixteenth and early seventeenth centuries, however, its most important export to Europe was cowhides. Only in the 1680s did slaves again become more than 50 percent of Senegambian exports by value, fluctuating in the range of 60 to 90 percent of all exports through to the 1780s. By the 1790s, gum senegal or gum arabic, used in Europe for confectionery and printing, had replaced slaves as the main export. By the 1830s, the value of gum exports was already three times the value of slave exports at their peak; by the 1850s, the value of the gum trade had been eclipsed by peanuts.

The Gold Coast (now Ghana) was another region with important trade other than slaves. From 1675 to 1731, the Dutch West India Company, which held a legal monopoly over Dutch trade in West Africa, carried far more gold than slaves, with the annual average of these exports being 8,800 troy ounces or 275 kilograms of pure metal—more than a quarter of a ton.

African trade, in short, was not solely for the support of the plantation complex. These other currents of trade gave African rulers a choice as to whether, or how much, they would be involved in the slave trade. On the import side, the anti-slave-trade publicists in Europe wanted to show that, in return for slaves, the Africans received nothing but trinkets of no real value—or else arms and liquor, which were positively harmful. No one would be injured, therefore, if the trade was abolished. In fact, the trinkets, liquor, and arms were far less important than the stereotype suggests, and other imports were more substantial.

Figures 3 and 4 illustrate the distribution of West African imports at two different periods, one in the late seventeenth century, as the slave trade began to escalate, and a second in the early nineteenth, when the slave trade had virtually ended for Senegambia. If the pies were drawn to scale to represent the actual volume of trade between Europe and Africa, Figure 4 would be vastly larger than Figure 3. Thus the apparent decline in metal and metalware imports was not an actual decline; it was simply that, in the later period, metalware was a smaller proportion of a much larger total. The proportionate distribution of imports was not, otherwise, very different. Textiles made up more than half the total in both periods, with an apparent gain of Indian over European textiles—a little surprising in a period when Europeans were beginning to produce cheap, machine-made cottons. Cowrie shells no longer figured as an important item, but liquor and tobacco now made up nearly a quarter of the total. This increase in luxury imports is largely accounted for by the fact that Africans now had more to spend abroad than they had had in the era of the slave trade. Even

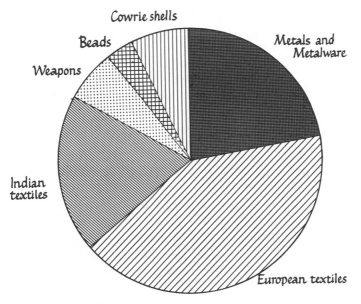

FIGURE 3.   Royal Africa Company exports

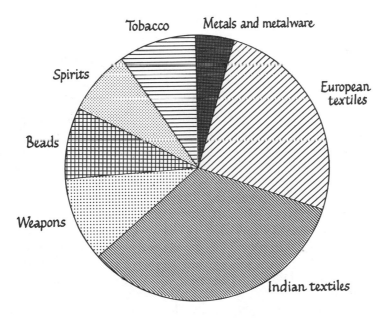

FIGURE 4.   Imports to Scncgambia

in this latter period, only about a third of total imports would fall into the "harmful" category.

THE CONDUCT OF THE AFRICAN TRADE

The trade of the plantation complex was actively cross-cultural at two points—on the Indian coast, where Europeans bought the Indian textiles so important to trade on the African coast. Over the very long run of history, the principal institution for cross-cultural trade had been the trade diaspora. Traders moving out from their home base settled at the important nodes of a trade network; made themselves familiar with the local language, culture, and conditions of trade; and then served traveling merchants as cross-cultural brokers.

Trade diasporas in non-European hands were often made up of peaceful merchants who preferred to pay protection money rather than fight. Not so for the European trade diasporas from the sixteenth century far into the eighteenth; those that operated on the African and Indian coasts were therefore militarized trade diasporas, or "trading-post empires." They wanted only to control strongpoints from which to dominate trade, not to control territorial units in the manner of European empires that followed them.

The Portuguese, for example, dominated West African seaborne trade until the mid-seventeenth century, but they made little effort to rule over African territory. Wherever possible, they based their operations wherever islands lay—the Cape Verde Islands off the Senegalese coast, São Tomé off the Niger delta, and Luanda on the coast of Angola. This trade was regulated by the Casa da India in Lisbon, but it was not assigned to a monopoly company. Cross-cultural brokerage was carried out by individual Portuguese or small Portuguese communities scattered along the coast and living under the rule of African political authorities.

In the middle of the seventeenth century, other European nations began to enter the trade. They quickly took up the alternative of chartered companies with monopoly rights and military as well as commercial authority from their home governments. These companies were especially common from the 1660s and 1670s and on into the eighteenth century. They were expected to build and maintain expensive trade forts on the African coast to protect their onshore officials and their goods awaiting shipment, not to rule over African territory. The hostilities they expected were from other Europeans—not from Africans. These forts served a function when Europeans were at war with one another, which, in the eighteenth century was most of the time. In peacetime, the forts were a heavy financial burden to the companies that ran them, while European private traders, or interlopers, could trade freely on the African coast, having no permanent posts to maintain.

By the middle decades of the eighteenth century, interloper competition had destroyed the profits of the chartered companies so effectively that they were forced to change their function. Instead of selling shipping services, they sold slaves to the interlopers. In effect, they used their shore establishments and knowledge of local conditions to become middlemen and cross-cultural brokers, leaving the shipping business to others.

Even this alternative was a stopgap. Interlopers could enter the brokerage business as easily as they had entered transatlantic shipping. Some of these shore-based interlopers were simply private Europeans who settled on the coast with African permission and began to accumulate slaves and other commodities for sale to European ships. Others were Africans who had learned European languages and enough about European ways to act as cross-cultural brokers on their own. They then began to handle the shoreside business of bulking cargo for shipment, leaving Europeans the shipping business alone. Since the death rates of Europeans sent to the African coast were extremely high, this division of labor could be profitable for both sides.

The European powers were to return in greater strength in the nineteenth century, but, in the eighteenth, Africans took over much of the brokerage function. On the Gambia River, the Africans were especially important in the second half of the century. The Europeans still maintained some fortified posts, like the English trade castle on James Island within the mouth of the river, but the Africans were already managing most of the trade. The French captured and destroyed the fort at James Island in 1779. When peace returned, the English did not bother to rebuild; it was cheaper and easier to leave the cross-cultural brokerage and bulking of exports in African hands.

English and American ships fell into a pattern of trade relations determined by the African rulers and traders. The politics of trade at the Gambia mouth can serve as an example. The kingdom of Nyumi on the north shore of the river controlled all export trade, collecting tolls for anchoring or taking on wood and water. The chief port at the time was a set of four different trade enclaves located within a three-mile radius, each inhabited by a foreign merchant community. Each was allowed, for appropriate fees, to have extraterritorial jurisdiction over its own people, though all four were under the ultimate authority of the king of Nyumi, represented locally by the *tubab mansa* or commander of the foreigners. One of these enclaves was the French post at Albreda; a second was an Afro-Portuguese settlement at Siika. Malinke traders from the interior controlled Jufure, while the British had their own community and fort on James Island until 1779. The fact that the British island was fortified might suggest that it could lord it over a small state like Nyumi, but that was not the case. The Gambia at that point is a tidal estuary, and James Island had no source of fresh water.

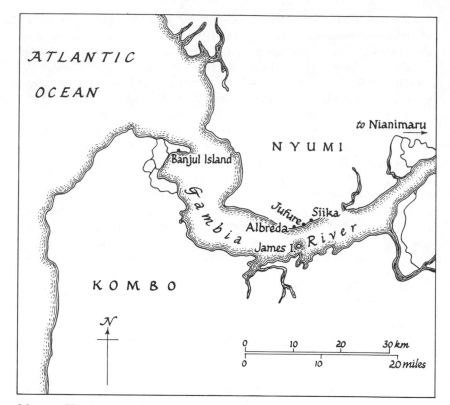

MAP 3.   The Lower Gambia about 1765

The garrison had to send rowing boats ashore to take on water—always dependent on permission from the African authorities.

All transactions in the river were subject to a regular ad valorem duty. If a ship sailed upriver to conduct trade in other kingdoms, Nyumi authorities required it to take along brokers and translators as well as extra crew from Nyumi. This requirement helped to assure good behavior and served to spare the European crew, but the crucial function was brokerage. A "chief linguister" went along in order to act as a broker for the ship's captain or supercargo. At an important point of trade, such as Nianimaru in the kingdom of Niani, the ship paid still more tolls.

The kingdom of Niani also offered trade facilities to caravans from the interior. A caravan leader found himself in much the same position as the European ship's captain. He too had to turn to a local broker, in this case a *jaatigi*, or landlord broker, who could offer lodging for the caravan personnel, including slaves in transit. The actual bargain was struck by the chief linguister and the *jaatigi*, each acting on behalf of his own principal—

in return for appropriate fees. Thus, the foreign Africans and European traders could both do business without necessarily having command of the local language, while the local people shared in their profits.

MERCHANTS AND PLANTERS

At sea, Atlantic commerce followed the norms of Western commercial culture. Commercial rivalry played a large role in European international rivalry, but within any national segment, groups of people with different roles in the plantation complex were rivals of another sort. The most common friction was between merchants on the one hand and planters on the other, and this rivalry took different forms in different national segments of the plantation complex.

In the French segment, the planter grew the cane, manufactured the raw sugar, and carried it to the dock. There his responsibility ended. He sold his product to a local merchant or a local agent of a French commercial house, who took over the responsibility of transporting it to France for sale. The merchant thus acquired the right to any residual profits that might occur. Negotiations between planter and merchant were therefore crucial because they determined the way the final sale price would be divided between production and service sectors—that is, between planters and merchant shippers. Planters often found these negotiations unsatisfactory, partly because the colonies had few sources of credit. For lack of banking facilities, planters were at the mercy of local merchants and ships' masters that happened to be in port.

Many transactions between French planters and merchants were a disguised form of barter. If a French vessel turned up with a cargo of slaves, they were sold for a price expressed in *livres tournois* (the French currency of the time). The captain or supercargo then bargained separately over the price of sugar, indigo, or cotton, also expressed in *livres*. But no physical *livres* were present; they were simply a currency of account, and goods were exchanged for goods, balanced by credit extended from merchant to planter for any shortfall. Planters found themselves chronically in debt, and the debt increased gradually with time. The planter was thus tied to his creditor firm with its home office in Nantes or some other Atlantic port, and his freedom of action was further reduced.

By the 1780s, the web of credit was an acute source of tension between the planters and their French business contacts, even between the planters and the home country as a whole. Planters suspected that the merchants and their friends had influence at court and could manipulate the whole colonial–metropolitan relationship to their own interest. Planters had the theoretical advantage of a protected metropolitan market for their product, but French-produced sugar was the cheapest and most competitive in other markets. Planters gained nothing from tariff protection. They also knew that the things they had to buy—slaves and provisions—were cheaper from non-French sources. The North Americans had the cheapest provisions; British slavers, the cheapest slaves. French planters did, in fact, buy provisions from the North Americans and the Dutch and slaves from the English, but the web of credit fixing them to particular French firms made smuggling more difficult than it might have been otherwise. Like the British North Americans of the 1760s and 1770s, they saw the colonial system of trade controls as one imposed from France and serving French metropolitan interests.

British trade was organized differently, and the economic position of Jamaica was a little different from that of Saint Domingue. Planters had legal access to North American and Irish provisions, and British sugar duties protected Jamaican sugar in the British market. From about 1740 onward, English sugar prices were higher than elsewhere, which meant that British trade controls worked in favor of the British West Indian planters.

Planter resentment of the home country was also moderated by the customary relationship between planters and merchants. Instead of selling in the colony, the British planter shipped his crop to Europe on his own account, where a merchant firm sold it on commission. The planter, not the merchant, was therefore the residual claimant on the final value of the product.

The British sugar merchant also performed a variety of other services. When he sold the crop, he held the balance for the planter; and planters could therefore draw bills on the merchant for a variety of expenses. If a planter needed slaves, he could pay with a bill drawn on the merchant house. If he needed supplies or stores from Britain, he could write to his English agent with a shopping list—again paid for out of sale receipts, with another commission to the merchant house.

It goes without saying that this relationship also involved credit. It was all too easy for the planter to overdraw his account, but that suited both parties well enough. The planter could live like a gentleman, either in England or in the colony. The merchant was glad to loan money on the good security of a sugar estate. The merchants' chief source of profit, indeed, was the interest on these loans. The prevalence of absenteeism among the British planting class meant that both merchants and proprietors of estates were often resident in Britain, so what tensions arose between them did not automatically translate into friction between colony and metropolis. But the very fact that the colonial trade system tended to favor the planters meant that New England traders and others found cause to evade the law.

Caribbean trade

Trade flowed in a variety of channels, often outside the idealized national monopolies and even outside the legal exceptions colonial powers had been forced to allow. Instead of the oversimplified triangular trade, a variety of multilateral trading voyages was possible. A New England ship might sail to Jamaica with a cargo of barrel staves, horses, and salt fish. These could be sold for bullion, derived in turn from smuggling slaves into Spanish America—and Jamaica was the main entrepôt for that trade. In addition, the captain might buy a few slaves for sale on the North American mainland, but his "middle passage" would carry him only to Saint Domingue to complete his cargo with sugar and molasses, bought with bullion. On the way north, he could stop in the Chesapeake Bay to sell the slaves, then back to New England, where he would sell the molasses to be made into rum for the fur trade. The French sugar could then be relabeled "product of the British West Indies" for sale in Britain, where it and any leftover bullion could pay for British manufactures wanted in New England.

Or a French ship might make the outward voyage to Africa, pick up a cargo of slaves, but sell it in Spanish America for bullion. The bullion in turn would find its way to the Compagnie des Indes for shipment to southern India in return for indigo-dyed cloth of a kind much in demand in Senegal. This cloth might be sold in Senegal—not for slaves, but for gum and for Senegalese cloth in demand further down the coast in Dahomey (Benin). The Dahomean slaves would be sold, in turn, in the New World, and variants of the same cycle could be played out again.

The exchanges that might be profitable at any moment changed constantly with markets, prices, war and peace, and a whole range of other conditions. It is, however, possible to make some broad generalizations about the flow of Caribbean trade in reality—as opposed to theory. Some trade did actually flow in legal channels as it was supposed to do, within a single imperial system. Much of it flowed outside those channels. The Dutch and the Danes, with only a small plantation complex of their own, systematically supplied other people's colonies with slaves and took off tropical products out of the proceeds. English slave dealers supplied their own colonies and a good deal more. As a result, they built up balances in foreign colonies that could be used to buy bullion from Spanish America, sugar and molasses from the French islands, and a variety of other products. French sugar supplied the French market and a good deal more. Finally, everyone, including a few Spanish shippers, carried the trade of Spanish America.

To keep this degree of separation between theory and reality imposed certain strains on European governments, strains lubricated in some cases by liberal bribery, tolerated in others with a pretense of ignorance justified as "benign neglect." As time passed, however, some of the strains became more serious. When the time of crisis came, they were exposed and took their place alongside other tensions that ushered in the age of democratic revolution.

Epilogue

The "democratic revolution" is a general term used to cover the broad spectrum of events that began with the American and French revolutions and continued with the Spanish-American wars for independence. In the context of the plantation complex, it would include the American Civil War and even the violence in Cuba and Brazil that led to the final emancipation of New World slaves in Cuba (1886) and Brazil (1888). These revolutions, which ended the slave trade and then slavery, were therefore spread over a "long century" from 1770 to 1890. Indeed, some aspects of the plantation complex, such as using indentured labor, lasted for another two to three decades to the period of World War I; wage-labor plantations that continued the racial domination of European masters over non-European workers lasted even longer.

The plantation complex was far too elaborate to be dismantled suddenly or everywhere at the same time. The American Revolution of 1776–83 broke the unity of the British Empire, with serious repercussions for the British West Indies. It also led in time to the sequential emancipation of the slaves in the northern states, some of them even before the French Revolution began in 1789.

The French Revolution commenced without serious thought that the "rights of man and the citizen" might imply some rights for slaves as well, but in 1794 it led to the formal legal emancipation of slaves within the French Empire. Meanwhile, the slaves in the French colony of Saint Domingue rose in rebellion against their masters in 1791. After more than a decade of anarchy and warfare in the colony, the rebels finally succeeded in getting Saint Domingue recognized as the independent Republic of Haiti in 1804. That date not only marked the first lasting and large-scale emancipation of slaves within the plantation complex; it was also the first achievement of independence for a former European colony free of control by European settlers. Napoleon reinstituted slavery elsewhere in the French Empire, but the first steps to end slavery had nevertheless been taken.

The abolition of the slave trade was a step of even greater importance, since in most places the plantation complex depended on a continuous flow of fresh slaves from Africa to make up for the difference between births and deaths. Denmark and the Netherlands led the way in abolishing their own diminished slave trades in the 1790s, but the first serious blow came with the British and American abolition acts, which took effect in 1808. The abolition of the slave trade to the United States was comparatively unimportant because the American South already had a slave population that could increase by natural growth. As a result, the demand for slaves in the United States was comparatively small compared to developing sugar colonies such as Cuba, British Guiana, and Trinidad.

The British abolition act was far more consequential. The British were the Atlantic's most important slavers at the beginning of the nineteenth century, supplying their own colonies and more. After an intensive campaign before British public opinion, Parliament was persuaded to abolish the trade to British colonies or carried by British ships. Some historians have argued that the West Indian colonies were declining in any event, that abolition was not a sacrifice of British material interests; but the main line of recent interpretation finds that it was indeed an act of "econocide"— the destruction of an otherwise successful economic order in the name of moral principle.[9]

British abolition was far from being the end of the trade, however. France, Spain, Portugal, and Brazil after its independence kept on in the face of growing international pressure. By the 1840s, most European nations had submitted to British pressure for legal abolition, without doing much to enforce their own anti-slave-trade legislation. The total slave trade of the 1840s, however, though mainly illegal, was still nearly three-quarters of the size it had reached in the peak decade of the 1780s, when it was completely legal. Finally, beginning about 1850, Brazil began to enforce the laws, which brought an effective end of slave imports within a few years. After the American Civil War it was harder than ever to keep up the illegal trade to the Spanish Caribbean in the face of a British blockade at sea and occasional enforcement of Cuban and Puerto Rican laws.

The emancipation of Caribbean slaves began even before the slave trade had ended elsewhere. In 1833, the British Parliament, recently reformed to make it more representative of middle-class opinion, passed an Emancipation Act for the British Empire, to take effect in 1834. France followed in 1848, the Dutch colonies a little later, and the United States in 1865. That left only Brazil, Cuba, and Puerto Rico as the main slave states still remaining in those parts of the world controlled by Europe or European colonists. In those countries the 1860s was a crucial decade. The slave trade was now effectively very much reduced, and the number of slaves began to decline through manumission. In the late 1880s, the two final emancipation acts for Brazil and the Spanish Empire represented the end of a declining institution.

NOTES

This essay is largely drawn from *The Rise and Fall of the Plantation Complex: Essays in Atlantic History* (New York: Cambridge University Press, 1989), by permission of Cambridge University Press.

1. In some earlier writing, I used the name "South Atlantic System" for the same set of institutions and interrelations that I now prefer to call the *plantation*

complex. The reasons for the change are two. First, the plantation complex was not really associated with the South Atlantic in the nautical sense of that term—from the equator to Antarctica. It was centered in the tropical world, both north and south of the equator. Second, the intellectual world of the social sciences has been introduced in recent years to a variety of "world systems." The plantation complex was not a "system" or a "world" in the sense of any of those theoretical constructs. I am consciously using a less theory-laden word.

2. See, for example, Lloyd Best, "A Model of a Pure Plantation Economy," *Social and Economic Studies* 17 (1968): 283–326.

3. For a comparison of Russia with the plantation complex, see Peter Kolchin, *Unfree Labor: American Slavery and Russian Serfdom* (Cambridge: Harvard University Press, 1987); and Richard Hellie, *Slavery in Russia, 1450–1725* (Chicago: University of Chicago Press, 1982).

4. William H. McNeill, "Human Migration: A Historical Overview," in *Human Migration: Patterns and Policies*, ed. William H. McNeill and Ruth S. Adams (Bloomington: Indiana University Press, 1978), 3–19, has shown that a similar pattern of high net natural decrease fed by continuous immigration was true of many, if not most, cities until recent times.

5. Philip D. Curtin, *Cross-Cultural Trade in World History* (New York: Cambridge University Press, 1984), 21–24.

6. See Alfred W. Crosby, *The Columbian Voyages, the Columbian Exchange, and Their Historians* (Washington, D.C.: American Historical Association, 1987), 19–21.

7. Philip D. Curtin, "Epidemiology and the Slave Trade," *Political Science Quarterly* 83 (1968): 190–216.

8. Arthur Attman, *American Bullion in the European World Trade 1600–1800* (Gothenburg, Sweden: Gothenburg Universitetsbibliotek, 1986).

9. Seymour Drescher, *Econocide: British Slavery in the Era of Abolition* (Pittsburgh: University of Pittsburgh Press, 1977); David Eltis, *Economic Growth and the Ending of the Transatlantic Slave Trade* (New York: Oxford University Press, 1987).

BIBLIOGRAPHY

Buffon, Alain. *Monnaie et crédit en économie coloniale: contribution à l'histoire économique de la Guadeloupe.* Basseterre, Guadeloupe: Société d'histoire de la Guadeloupe, 1979.

Chaudhuri, K. N. *Trade and Civilisation in the Indian Ocean: An Economic History from the Rise of Islam to 1750.* Cambridge, England: Cambridge University Press, 1985.

Clark, John G. *La Rochelle and the Atlantic Economy during the Eighteenth Century.* Baltimore: Johns Hopkins University Press, 1981.

Curtin, Philip D. *Cross-Cultural Trade in World History.* New York: Cambridge University Press, 1984.

———. *Economic Change in Pre-Colonial Africa: Senegambia in the Era of the Slave Trade.* Madison: University of Wisconsin Press, 1975.

————. *The Rise and Fall of the Plantation Complex*. New York: Cambridge University Press, 1989.

Davis, Ralph. *The Rise of the Atlantic Economies*. Ithaca, N.Y.: Cornell University Press, 1973.

Debien, Gabriel. *Les esclaves aux Antilles françaises (xviiᵉ–xviiiᵉ siècles)*. Basseterre, Guadeloupe, and Fort-de-France, Martinique: Sociétés d'histoire de la Guadeloupe et de la Martinique, 1974.

Dunn, Richard S. *Sugar and Slaves: The Rise of the Planter Class in the English West Indies, 1624–1713*. Chapel Hill: University of North Carolina Press, 1972.

Galloway, J. H. *The Sugar Cane Industry: An Historical Geography from Its Origins to 1914*. Cambridge, England: Cambridge University Press, 1989.

Lovejoy, David E. *Transformations in Slavery: A History of Slavery in Africa*. Cambridge, England: Cambridge University Press, 1983.

Martin, Gaston. *Histoire de l'esclavage dans les colonies françaises*. Paris: Presses universitaire de France, 1949.

Miller, Joseph C. *Way of Death: Merchant Capitalism and the Angola Slave Trade, 1730–1830*. Madison: University of Wisconsin Press, 1988.

Mintz, Sydney W. *Sweetness and Power: The Place of Sugar in Modern History*. New York: Viking, 1985.

Northrup, David. *Trade without Rulers: Pre-Colonial Economic Development in South-Eastern Nigeria*. Oxford, England: Clarendon Press, 1978.

Pares, Richard. *A West India Fortune*. London: Longmans, 1950.

Phillips, William D., Jr. *Slavery from Roman Times to the Early Transatlantic Trade*. Minneapolis: University of Minnesota Press, 1985.

Sheridan, Richard. *Sugar and Slavery: An Economic History of the British West Indies, 1623–1775*. Aylesbury, England: Ginn and Company, 1974.

Solow, Barbara L., and Stanley L. Engerman, eds. *Caribbean Slavery and British Capitalism*. New York: Cambridge University Press, 1988.

Steele, Ian K. *The English Atlantic 1676–1740: An Exploration of Communication and Community*. New York: Oxford University Press, 1986.

Verlinden, Charles. *The Beginnings of Modern Colonization*. Ithaca, N.Y.: Cornell University Press, 1970.

Viliers, Patrick. *Traite des noirs et navires négrier au XVIIIe siècle*. Grenoble, France: Éditions des 4 seigneurs, 1982.

Interpreting the
Industrial Revolution

PETER N. STEARNS

The term *industrial revolution*, referring to a phenomenon inaugurated in late eighteenth-century Britain, has served as a historical label for over a century.[1] As such, it is as familiar as any label outside the strictly political orbit: Most first-year college students have encountered the notion and can attach a bit of meaning to it, while popular publications refer to the industrial revolution either as a benchmark against which to measure contemporary change or as a framework for discussing aspects of nineteenth-century culture.

Yet in history teaching the industrial revolution is not always comfortably used. A few years back, one advanced placement history teacher was cited as regularly advising his students to avoid any essay question in which the term appeared. And the concept has not conveniently stabilized over the past generation, as important new meanings have been added. Despite a presumed familiarity, and precisely because the phenomenon is so central in modern history, the industrial revolution must have its relationship to other historical topics reevaluated and its core definition updated. The two tasks are related because grasping the newer approaches to the industrial revolution may aid strategies to integrate it better in history teaching.

Those who handle the standard topics in modern history—in research, writing, or teaching—are often uncomfortable relating them to the industrial revolution because it requires some shifting of gears. There are three reasons for this. First, and most important, the industrial revolution is a process, a transformation that takes place over a fifty- to one-hundred-year span. This is hard to convey in the style of political history, where the past may be treated as a set of narrative facts. There are dates and events in industrial development comparable to those used in conveying political developments—names and achievements of inventors, installations of first factories and railroads, and changes in business law—but these milestones convey less of what the industrial revolution is about than does a comparable list of major individuals and events in the French or American revolutions. The process aspect of industrialization has received increasing emphasis in historical work over the past two decades, amplifying our understanding of how the industrial revolution altered the framework of life and thought over several decades. This amplification heightens the challenge of relating industrial history to other forms of presentation.

Serious consideration of the industrial revolution brings a second jolt to standard history teaching because it focuses on economic and technological change. It can be disconcerting when a historical survey making politics the essential stuff of the past suddenly detours into a different area, where factors and impulses outside the sphere of government or political theory must be evaluated or given primacy. This is exacerbated when such a survey makes a bow to industrialization and then returns as quickly as possible to the political skein, with scant subsequent reference to what differences industrialization made. The recasting of industrial history in recent work helps broaden our understanding of what the industrial revolution was all about and how both its causes and effects provide a link to other facets of the past. Here teachers can reduce the disjunctures in moving to and from the industrial revolution in a survey course.

Third and finally, the industrial revolution challenges history teaching because of the breadth of its development in different places at different times. While the phenomenon began as part of British history, it did not, of course, remain there. Yet when history teaching is organized into tight geographical and chronological compartments, handling the subsequent manifestations of industrialization may appear awkward. Later industrial revolutions in Europe are not always given due attention, because it is assumed that the British process provides all that need be known on the subject—implicitly, if you've seen one industrial revolution, you've seen them all. Yet the importance of grasping the industrial revolution outside the British or western European orbit has become increasingly clear. Knowledge of which features of the process are similar and which have to be defined and explained separately has steadily improved. The phenomenon of the industrial revolution has entered increasingly into the grasp of modern global history, as it has been amplified beyond one time—the late eighteenth and early nineteenth centuries—and one place—western Europe. The global perspective on industrialization raises exciting possibilities for comparative analysis, but it depends on a solid understanding of what the industrial revolution is as a process, and not as a single narrative chronology where the first occurrence can receive the only full treatment.

The industrial revolution was one of the central transformations of modern history, first in Western society and shortly thereafter globally.

Despite the challenges it poses, its analysis is not only unavoidable but truly beneficial in grasping essential changes in the framework of modern social life—politics included—and in conveying some of the new links and differentiations in the contemporary world.

An understanding of recent additions to the interpretation of industrialization can aid in meeting the teaching challenge. The core definition of the industrial revolution, while by no means altered beyond recognition, has been somewhat modified, particularly through the contributions of new economic historians since the 1960s.[2] Definition established, further exploration moves in several directions. The context from which the initial industrial revolution emerged has been reinterpreted, and the impact and scope of Western industrialization have been recast. These revisions in the standard model of industrialization have expanded the links between the industrial revolution and other major historical topics, as noted earlier. These revisions also provide a somewhat altered standard for comparison to other areas of the world. The global manifestations of the industrial revolution—including full industrialization in areas outside the West, new Western intrusions based on industrial might, and economic "backwardness"—constitute a final area in which a number of recent analyses contribute to general judgments.

The core definition of the industrial revolution remains the transformation of technology based on new sources of power, the revamping of economic and labor organization through the factory system, and the ascendancy of manufacturing in what had been predominantly agricultural economies. This definition is elaborated in the section that follows. We then turn to the revisions in the standard treatment of the context and impact of the industrialization process in Western history, first in the British case but then on the Continent and in the United States. We then treat the global ramifications of the phenomenon. After accomplishing these extensions, we can return to the issues of presentation and integration of one of the fundamental historical processes of the modern era.

Technology and Economy in the Industrial Revolution

Regardless of the time or place where industrial revolution occurs, there are two basic features and several measurable consequences of the phenomenon that historians have long considered essential. The first and most obvious feature in this model is technological, focusing on the substitution of new power sources for a primary reliance on human and animal muscle supplemented occasionally by wind- and waterwheels. New power sources were then applied to various production and transportation systems via new mechanisms of transmission and more automatic processes. In Britain, many of the automatic processes were initially designed to speed manual labor, such as the flying shuttle that semiautomatically crossed threads on a loom and enabled a hand-weaver to increase productivity by 50 percent with no increase in manual power. By about 1770, the British put together the first fully industrial technology by joining a steam engine with transmission equipment and the mechanical spindle, thus permitting the rapid industrialization of cotton thread production. Whatever the precise technology—it can easily include electricity or internal combustion as in industrializations after 1870, or much more sophisticated automatic equipment of the sort available to Russia and Japan by the late nineteenth century—a basic technological component always applies.[3]

An organizational component is also fundamental to a model of industrial revolution. With only a few exceptions, the scale of productive operations increased with industrialization. In scattered instances (as in the American South), where preindustrial agriculture was concentrated on large estates with work systems not fully compatible with industrial needs, early industrialization might involve some reduction of scale in favor of smaller units of tenure. Generally, however, even agriculture participates in the tendency to increase unit size and complexity: as in the famous, if sometimes misinterpreted, case of British enclosure at the outset of the industrial revolution; the rise of commercialized peasant holdings, supplemented by cooperatives, in western Europe from the late nineteenth century on; Russian collectivization; or the growth of larger family farms and ultimately corporate agriculture in the United States.

In other branches of production the expansion of organization began with industrialization and proceeded without major deflection. Manufacturing became increasingly concentrated in factories; even artisanal units such as construction crews tended to grow in size. Banks expanded. In the larger population centers, commerce was conducted in department stores instead of small shops; while in the countryside shops, franchises, and, particularly in the United States, mail-order operations replaced itinerant peddlers.

The growth of large organizations in part followed technology: New modes of transportation increased the volume of goods to be handled and so required new outlets. At the same time, the need to use power from steam engines at close proximity (prior to the development of electricity) and the economies of scale to be found in larger engine sizes, forced workers to cluster in factories. This expansion of organizational size and scale soon took on a dynamic of its own, however, and indeed sometimes preceded significant technical change. Organizational expansion allowed greater division of labor and more centralized discipline and regulation.[4] Among blue-collar workers, and later among clerical and sales personnel,[5] this change encouraged specialization in essentially semiskilled categories. Such expansion also led to the development of management hierarchies and formal methods of planning and control, which brought economic benefits of their own (at least until some twentieth-century distortions). Business historians such as Alfred Chandler have convincingly argued that such a process occurred in the United States.[6]

The organizational thrust should not, of course, be exaggerated. Small shops survived the department store onslaught longer than is sometimes imagined (and better than shopkeepers themselves might claim for political purposes). Likewise, artisanal operations hardly disappeared at the first sign of factory systems.[7] But this is merely a tacit reminder that, as with technology, the industrial revolution must be seen as a process extending over several decades, rather than an overnight or uniform transformation. Efforts to repeal the dynamic of organizational growth, in the name of utopian socialism or radical National Socialism (Nazism) both of which harked to smaller, more personalized production groups, invariably failed. For example, Nazism, once in power, immediately resumed and indeed heightened organizational growth at the expense of more traditional units. The organizational imperative has advanced under all of the political systems that have sponsored the industrialization process, surfacing under communism, fascism, and capitalism alike. The result, among other things, is a tendency to reproduce some similarities in management—worker divisions and attendant social structures in otherwise quite different industrial societies.

The definition of the industrial revolution extends beyond the advent of radically new technologies and the reorganization of economic processes. The relative importance of manufacturing increases automatically when a full industrial revolution is in operation. Substantial changes are effected in the composition of the labor force, away from agriculture and toward manufacturing and urban service occupations. The industrial revolution also stimulates city growth, and in many instances, the rate of urban development can be used as a rough measure of the timing and speed of the industrialization process. Here, however, there is a need for real caution. The industrial revolution in the nineteenth century spurred urban development in some patently nonindustrial areas, where cities grew to facilitate imports of industrial goods and agricultural exports. Bristol, England, and Budapest, Hungary, provide key examples. Bristol grew rapidly in the early nineteenth century without substantial factory industry, while Budapest after 1860 spurted as a political and agricultural–commercial center, reflecting industrialization in Austria and Bohemia. In a different pattern, urbanization has clearly outstripped industrialization in numerous twentieth-century cases, particularly in Latin America and more recently in Africa. Massive city growth, in sum, can proceed independently, even leading to urban dominance in a nonindustrial society; consequently, the industrial revolution must be assessed somewhat separately from urban development.[8]

Sheer rates of economic growth have also been used to measure the industrial revolution, on the valid assumption that technological and organizational change will lead to (and be reflected in) fairly rapid advance. Here is one area where the new economic historians have contributed considerably over the past twenty years, mainly through more imaginative and extensive use of quantitative data.[9] Under the influence of Simon Kuznets, new emphasis has been placed on measurable aggregate variables such as national income growth, rate of capital formation, or the aggregate investment ratio. Some writers, such as Alexander Gerschenkron, prefer to deal with growth rates in the manufacturing sector rather than the entire economy. It was Gerschenkron who extended the effort at detailed historical growth measurement to Russian industrialization both before and after 1917.[10] In general, much of the fundamental work in these categories was done in the 1960s (including work on the stages of industrial development discussed later in this essay), but subsequent research has steadily refined the measurements.

Again, some caution is needed before adding to the definition of industrialization's essential and invariable features. A discernible early industrial revolution may not generate a marked upsurge in overall economic growth, depending on what is happening in those sectors of the economy which are not yet fully enmeshed in industrial change. One of the important findings resulting from improved quantitative analysis is that rapid early industrialization rarely has a major impact on the overall economy because traditional sectors often keep expanding for some time as well. Indeed, by stressing more gradual change, some new economic historians shun the term revolution altogether. Industrialization, stretching over many decades, serves accuracy far better than the term revolution, in their judgment. Regardless of terminology, a reassessment of the revolution's early phases helps explain the fairly uniform insistence on defining industrialization as a long-term process. For instance, Britain's early nineteenth-century growth rates were decidedly modest apart from recurrent fluctuations. Growth rates, in sum, aid in determining when industrialization is taking place, but they are often the result of prior technological and organizational change. In most cases these latter two factors can be charted with reasonable precision, in terms of the average size of units of employment and (though this is somewhat more difficult) the horsepower available per capita. It therefore seems safe to hew to these essentials in launching a broader exploration of the industrial revolution by looking for relationships between the two measures, noting points of rapid change in each, and then charting the resultant economic growth rates over a longer chronological span.

One result of the growth-rate focus warrants additional comment. In the 1960s, considerable attention was devoted to firming up the process of defining the industrial revolution by positing a series of fairly fixed stages that any society undergoing industrialization would experience. Thus, according to the economic historian W. W. Rostow, industrialization begins with a takeoff period, in which the rate of change in certain sectors is very rapid even though the impact on the region's overall economy remains modest.[11] High levels of technological innovation, either through invention or importation of new technology, characterize this phase, which should be distinguished from isolated instances of change, such as a pilot factory or a showpiece railroad line around the capital city. The takeoff phase yields to a more general process of industrial adaptation, in which new technologies spread to a wider array of industries and generate higher overall growth rates. At the end of this process, maturity is reached when a society becomes able to apply industrial techniques to all branches of production (though it may not choose to do so). Obviously, Britain went through all of these phases first, reaching maturity around 1850. The same set of measurements allowed Rostow to conclude that later industrializers, notably Japan and Russia, accelerated the overall process by a decade or two. Thus, while British industrialization took ninety years, Russia and Japan gained maturity by 1950 after only sixty to seventy years of rapid change.

Rostow's measurement effort drew considerable criticism at the time, mainly for imposing Western-based standards on societies that had not managed even to achieve takeoff, thereby implying some criticism for failure. Yet versions of this schema continue to be used, if only because it sets some boundaries on the industrial revolution as a phenomenon—through use of the factors of technology, organization, and growth rates—and so facilitates comparison of various industrial revolutions by phase rather than misleading single chronologies. Indeed, European economic historians had already launched the process of comparing mid-nineteenth-century German industrialization with the British experience of the late eighteenth century, rather than with Britain's own situation around 1850. The latter comparison remains valid, of course, in determining the balance of economic power at the midcentury point, but can seriously impede analysis of the actual framework within which change occurs.

The historical debate about measuring the industrial revolution and defining key phases has largely died down over the past two decades, as a general consensus has emerged over which societies industrialized and roughly when and what criteria were involved. Where active discussion continues, it focuses on measuring economic change and determining the advent of full industrial revolutions in the case of new arrivals or near-arrivals in the later twentieth century. Assumptions about fairly measurable stages have largely quieted earlier arguments about the timing of Russian industrialization, now seen as clearly starting in the later nineteenth century but then massively enhanced under later Bolshevik direction. A similar framework has underwritten recent efforts to remind us that Japan did not leap quickly and easily into industrial maturity, but, like its Western predecessors, developed a full economic revolution only over a period of time and with considerable anguish. The focus of discussion has been on using some standard criteria and phases as part of the core definition of a long-term process, not on raising fundamentally new definitional questions or objections. Only the dispute over whether to replace industrial revolution, as a term, with the less dramatic "industrialization," with its connotations of long-term and gradual change, modifies the substantial consensus over basic criteria.[12]

The most interesting modification of familiar definitions that has emerged within the standard historical vision involves the reassessment of the industrial revolution in France.[13] In many historical studies, French industrialization appeared to lag behind the standards set by Britain, the United States, and Germany. American economic and entrepreneurial historians, in particular, had something of a field day through the 1950s in explaining why the French did so badly. Explanations included France's poor natural resources, clumsy government policies (which were overly interventionist and protectionist), political instability, and a fatal lack of entrepreneurial zest. Now, in part because of France's superior economic performance since World War II but also because of a genuinely new historical vision, the French industrial record of the nineteenth century has been upgraded. Though still laggard in terms of heavy factory industry, the French are now seen as having passed through a real industrial revolution when measured by overall growth rates (compared, for example, to those of Britain) and changes in the technology and organization of artisanal manufacturing. New processes and a standardization of design and work systems in silk, furniture,[14] and similar industries produced significant overall economic change, even as the bellwether steel and mining sectors developed a bit more slowly than elsewhere. Clearly, some improvements in analytical flexibility and an altered comparative vision are involved in this redefinition for France. A precise technological lockstep has given way to greater attention to variations among industries and to organizational changes that can reproduce some of the features of a factory structure in expanded workshops. Industrialization still responds to certain basic measurements, but its diversity within this framework has been enhanced. The idea of a partially artisanal industrial revolution may also have some relevance in assessing more recent varieties of economic change.

Still, the focus of recent historical work on the industrial revolution has primarily involved substantial amplification of what the industrial revolution means as a social phenomenon, rather than issues of basic definition.

Economic measurements have not been jettisoned, but they have been largely accepted and not significantly advanced as attention has turned to restating what the industrial revolution involved in larger human terms.

The Social History Approach

The industrial revolution has constituted one of the central foci in the rise of social history over the past quarter-century. Correspondingly, social historians have considerably reworked the standard statement of what the industrial revolution was all about, not by contradicting the core technological–organizational criteria, but by building on them. Reevaluating the industrial revolution as a transformation of human experience has involved both a restatement of its impact on certain groups and activities and a broadening of the range of groups and activities being considered.

The first tendency appears in the reassessment of the effects of industrialization on women and children.[15] Standard histories of the industrial revolution have long included shocking accounts of the working conditions of women and children in the factories. This image remains, but it no longer provides the central message. For children, the current assessment has been revised in two respects. First, there is an increasing realization of how normal and accepted child labor was at the time. Children assisted in agricultural work, domestic tasks, and menial tasks in artisanal shops, moving toward full-time commitments (including apprenticeships, for artisans) by age twelve or thirteen. Research on preindustrial families has emphasized the work roles of relatively young children and more generally the economic factors that determined parental assessments of children's worth and treatment. While child labor normally took place within a domestic environment, it often occurred outside the biological family unit, as children were shipped to the homes of others where the conditions of life were not necessarily benign. Industrial work for children now appears less of a departure from the norm than once imagined, though it unquestionably brought new problems because of the technology and organizational structure involved.

This revised assessment of children's treatment is not merely a historian's nicety; it also helps explain workers' reactions to early industrial conditions. Many factory workers endeavored to reconstruct a partially familial atmosphere within the factories by hiring their children as assistants. Workers generally became concerned about child labor only when its existence was threatened, or parental control was disputed; they did not initially contest the experience in principle. As Neil Smelser has indicated in an important revisionist presentation,[16] one of the spurs to mounting worker protest in Britain in the 1820s and early 1830s, was precisely the child labor issue—but as workers perceived it, not as we might. English labor had accepted children in the factories for several decades, often in very strenuous conditions, but shifted to protest only when new supervision methods placed their children under the direction of strangers, rather than worker-parents.

The conventional focus on the very real woes of factory children is also altered by a growing recognition that their lot was somewhat atypical. When compared to other nations, conditions of child labor in Britain seem to have been unusually bad. For whatever reason—as the first industrializer, Britain may have had a special need for low-cost labor—France, Germany, and the early industrial United States never replicated the horrors of the children in the British mines. Moreover, early industrialization in Britain probably displaced as many children from work as it recruited into the factories. The decline of manual production, particularly in the countryside, and the reduction in remaining artisanal apprenticeships, posed huge problems for children and their families. Both causes contributed to the migration of the young into the cities and social problems such as urban juvenile crime.

In the long run, the chief impact of the industrial revolution was to dissociate young children from productive labor, even in the families of factory workers. Children's roles were redefined by a growing belief, soon converted to an enforced legal requirement, that the task of childhood was education, not contribution to the family income. While the occurrence of this transformation varied depending on region, social class, and to a certain extent gender, it was obviously industrialization's key contribution to complicating childhood; it required massive adjustments by children, parents, and political institutions in ways that we have yet to probe fully.

The new picture of industrialization's impact on women parallels shifts in the assessment of children. The focus has moved away from the lamentable conditions of female factory workers, though these still have their role to play, particularly when the topic involves industrialization in textiles.[17] One motive for this reassessment follows from changing views of women in contemporary society. It no longer seems intrinsically bad for women to be working outside the home or intrinsically good that factory legislation came along to limit women's factory opportunities.[18] More than this is involved, however. When women are considered in general, and not simply as part of the factory labor force, the limitation the industrial revolution imposed on women's work opportunities is striking, at least in Western society. Most working-class women could not get or did not want factory jobs. A far larger number were recruited as servants into middle-class households during their late teens and early twenties, when they were expected to devote themselves to paid labor.[19] This in itself was a shift from previous lower-class patterns, but rather different from the traditional image of "factory girls."

For women after early adulthood, and for middle-class women generally, the industrial revolution in the West primarily increased the domestic focus, particularly in contrast to men's new work roles in factories and offices.[20] Women were expected to guide families as a counterbalance to the raucous world of industrial labor, not primarily to engage in this labor themselves. While the ideal of family as moral and aesthetic haven, under feminine sponsorship, went furthest in the middle class, the working class also came to rely increasingly on adult women to manage the household and anchor family networks. Industrialization mainly served to initiate over a century of widening differences in gender imagery and experience. While this effect (unlike educational roles for children) has not proved enduring, it reveals a great deal more about women's modern history than did the older assumptions about the burdens of factory work.[21]

Reinterpreting the industrial history of children and women alike involves, first, a firm belief that industrialization's human impact goes well beyond the factories themselves. A necessary focus on the general lives of women and children changes the original factory-confined picture considerably. Second, the consequences of industrialization must be assessed over time. Initial conditions are undeniably important, but long-range results, extending into the late nineteenth century and beyond, are even more significant, as they may differ substantially from the first effects. With regard to women and children, the key result of the industrial revolution was a progressive removal of work from the family setting. This forced a redefinition of family organization and goals to which Western society is, in many ways, still adjusting. This was a shift imposed well beyond the factory working class, though this class was affected particularly vividly and early; and it was a shift that has undergone several restatements over time.

The task of recharting industrialization's larger effects warrants one final illustration, taken from the heart of the process but involving a somewhat different set of factors: What did the industrial revolution do to workers themselves?

Along with bitter impressions of women's and children's labor, treatments of the industrial revolution's human impact a generation ago typically involved some part in a seemingly endless debate over workers' standards of living.[22] Did early industrialization help or hurt British factory workers? Optimists pointed to a lightening of physical tasks due to machinery, the new accessibility of cheap but valuable factory products such as cotton and cloth (more stylish and easily washable), and some possibility of improved real wages. Pessimists disputed the wage contention and emphasized deteriorating housing and health conditions. The two groups argued over evidence about food consumption, particularly meat. Ingenious detail and considerable passion propelled a significant debate: How to interpret and understand trends in material conditions as part of early nineteenth-century history, and the possibility that these trends established more durable reactions and resentments (or accommodations) in key segments of the working class. Whether the debate also shed light on the inherent virtues or flaws of capitalism, as many participants on either side believed, is open to question. Regardless of the passions inflamed by the debate, however, its participants uncovered a great deal of important data, thereby ensuring its enduring historical significance.

The debate has been virtually silent for over a decade, with some of its most distinguished later practitioners, like Eric Hobsbawm, turning to other issues. Historical discussions sometimes languish even when the results remain inconclusive, but three other factors help explain the waning of interest in the debate. First, as with child labor, there is growing realization that some of the dilemmas of early British industrialization are not typical of the general process. Data from Germany, France, and the United States do not yield comparable evidence about deteriorating conditions for most factory workers. Bad conditions certainly existed, and there are signs of deterioration for some other lower-class segments, including rural populations displaced by industrial production. But the real-wage trends for factory labor veer from the British pattern.[23] Second, even in Britain, the problem of deteriorating material conditions occurred within a limited time frame, as all but the most diehard pessimists would grant.[24] By the 1850s, standards of living for British workers were going up in the factory centers, despite important fluctuations and variety. When the long-term impact of industrialization is analyzed, a focus on such narrowly material problems has some inherent limitations.

Finally, a wider vision of workers' lives, particularly the psychological and material effects of industrial work itself, has drawn attention away from analyses of the workers' material standards of living. Studies on the new discipline imposed by time-management and other on-the-job techniques, as well as the subtler workings of the worker–management relationship, have produced a redefinition of industrialization's most unsettling effects. E. P. Thompson's magisterial essay on the new sense of time and work discipline developed during British industrialization has encouraged analogous research on other cases. These new studies point toward the necessity of this broader redefinition of labor industrialization.[25] Similarly, studies on changes in the pace of work reveal another key ingredient, and a recurrent one still at issue in the later nineteenth century. New machines and new shop rules and supervision combined to make workers move faster during their long working day, while traditional respites, such as midday naps, were curtailed. As with the new sense of time, changes in work pace began with the first signs of industrial revolution anywhere and intensified over the long process of industrialization. Research on shifts in management styles and mutual worker–employer expectations add yet another dimension to the focus on work quality. Systems of patronage and decentralized control over assistants changed surprisingly gradually during industrialization's early decades, but yielded sharper alterations after the mid-nineteenth century.

Attention to these changes in the nature of work has also encouraged a deeper understanding of industrial protest, which is now seen less in terms of standard-of-living issues alone and more in terms of conflicts over the control and definition of the labor process. Workers often defended a very different moral vision from that of their employers.[26] Individual acts, such as absenteeism, are also now seen by historians as efforts to regain some traditional balance in a work world perceived as out of "normal" control. Accommodation takes on new dimensions as well when the extent of ultimate reevaluation by workers themselves is understood. Research on the adoption of a more instrumentalist, or market-oriented, approach to labor offers important insights into the dilemmas and adaptations of individual workers and some trade unions, along with the transformation needed to create closer approximations of what economists delight in calling "economic man."[27]

The alterations of work apply to more than factory labor. Again, the industrial revolution's social impact is not as narrow as once emphasized. Artisans found their work redefined, even when they were not forced into factories. Apprenticeship was shortened, which in turn reduced skill levels, while more intense supervision forced higher rates of production and less individualistic, creative products. The redefinition of artisanry was a key ingredient in nineteenth-century France. Clerks and even some rural workers were soon drawn into the pattern of faster pace and more impersonal supervision. Thus, new pace, discipline, and management styles constitute a wider and more durable focus for treating industrialization's impact than the narrow standard-of-living debates.

The new attention to work itself is not without precedent. It builds on important earlier research, such as that of John and Barbara Hammond, and on some of the themes that entered into traditional trade union history. Nor does the new focus close the arena of debate: Much of the research on work reorientation, following the lead of scholars like E. P. Thompson, emphasizes the deterioration of industrial-style work compared to the more traditional moral economy of peasant or craft labor. In contrast, optimists treat the compensations and options that workers developed in response to changes on the job—including a new openness to job mobility. The assessment of industrialization's impact was not wholly altered by the focus on work, but the newer scholarship does provide a more basic and durable—

if somewhat more amorphous—description of human experience than the standard of living debate conveyed.

Social historians have also altered the treatment of industrialization's effects on people's lives beyond reassessments of already established topics. In more recent and encompassing histories of industrialization, where extension of range is the central theme, previously unexplored facets of social activity are now seen as substantially altered by the industrial revolution. Here a few examples must suffice, from a substantial array.

The position and valuation of the elderly were shifted by the industrial revolution, though less obviously by its initial phases than by its ongoing development late in the nineteenth century. Industrialization placed a premium on physical energy and the capacity to learn new techniques. As industrial society took shape in the nineteenth century, cultural and economic spokespersons attributed new value to youth and viewed it as uniquely qualified to respond to societal needs. Old age, correspondingly, tended to shrink in prestige, linked increasingly with images of decrepitude and withdrawal. As industrial society allowed more young people to gain a living apart from inherited property, certain traditional tensions between young and old may also have declined, bringing some compensation for reduced social prestige. For example, older family members won some new functions, by providing child care when mothers and fathers were drawn off to work outside the home. The coresidence of grandparents with younger kin increased in response to initial industrialization, and the grandparental image changed as well. The point, obviously, is not that the industrial revolution starkly worsened or improved the status of the elderly; debate about the balance of gain and loss continues. What it did launch, without question, was a process of substantial change in the lives of older people, which even before 1900 was beginning to produce such unprecedented phenomena as planned retirement.[28]

Just as the number of groups affected by industrialization has grown in recent scholarship, so has the range of activities. The history of leisure under the industrial revolution's spur has become a major topic.[29] It is now recognized that industrialization altered leisure by reducing available time and by so emphasizing work values and obligations that traditional leisure habits were constrained. Zealous middle-class leaders, trumpeting their own work ethic and eager to press the urban labor force into diligence, attacked the tradition of periodic festivals, while the strangeness of the urban industrial environment weakened the community context for these outlets. The result was a significant diminution of leisure during the first decades of industrialization, along with a related tendency to turn to spectator sports and activities and increased reliance on sexual pleasure and drink as a recreational release. The long-run impact of the industrial revolution on leisure, which built from this initial reorientation, included new leisure pursuits organized to a degree along industrial lines. Emerging professional sports like soccer/football were commercially dominated, time- and speed-conscious, rationalized into clearly defined rules and procedures, and dependent on a considerable amount of specialization. Some leisure activities in factories during the second half of the nineteenth century seemed deliberately escapist from the other pressures of disciplined work, but other pursuits converged in some sense with work values.[30] Certainly, in attacking traditional pastimes and then building new leisure forms, the industrial revolution powerfully reshaped the lives and values of people at virtually all social levels. In their debates over the meaning of leisure, including the extent to which new sports and entertainment met the social and simply playful needs of an industrialized populace, historians add this facet to the fundamental redefinition of the scope of activities transformed by the industrial revolution.

This list could be extended: The relationship between the industrial revolution and decisions about sex and children, for example, provides a fundamental framework for the history of nineteenth-century demography.[31] Patterns of crime and policing, indeed the very definition of public order, came to reflect the impact of industrialization.[32] A fledgling field of environmental history obviously relates to the industrialization process.[33] The industrial revolution provides not simply a chapter in nineteenth-century history but a framework for a sweeping redefinition of social institutions and behavior, along with major aspects of personal life. By expanding its overall scope and chronological range, recent scholarship on the social effects of industrialization has produced a substantial shift in the conceptualization of nineteenth- and twentieth-century Western history. This has redefined several specific topics, and, more generally, enlivened the historical utility of an industrial focus.

The Issue of Causation

One final aspect of Western industrialization should be considered before turning to its larger global ramifications: What caused the process in the first place? On the whole, reevaluation in this area has been less focused than treatment of the question of impact, which justifies dealing with causation after result. Nevertheless, there are significant new themes, some of which tie into the reassessments of industrialization's larger meanings. The most important innovation considers the context from which the industrial revolution emerged and relates it to a more sophisticated grasp of the process in global terms.

A narrowly construed list of industrialization's causes in the West has scarcely changed in a generation, which is again to say that some aspects of the industrial revolution appear fairly well figured out. The industrial revolution required capital, a flexible labor supply, and new market demand, as well as inventions that helped put these elements together. It also required access to raw materials and a transportation system that encouraged their combination. Britain was favorably situated in most of these areas and had specific spurs to change, including a shortage of wood for fuel, which encouraged a turn to coal rather than charcoal, and a particularly commercially minded aristocracy. Other parts of western Europe, such as Germany and France, shared some of Britain's advantages. But they had to wait for the additional stimulus of the British example and, in the case of France and its neighbors, for revolutionary changes in the social and legal system (including the abolition of guilds) to remove barriers to industrialization.

Practitioners of the new economic history have contributed to greater detail and precision on some causes of the industrial revolution, including labor force and capital formation, without radically changing the overall list of causal factors.[34] The focus on measurable variables has reduced attention to the fascinating debate over the role of an entrepreneurial spirit. A special business ethic can still be defined and may still have some basis in religious inspirations, particularly (in the English case) minority Protestant sects such as the Quakers. Earlier Weberian interest in the role of Protestantism among French entrepreneurs has declined, however, even as French industrialization under largely Catholic (or agnostic) auspices turns out to be livelier than was once believed. Considerable historical research on the origins of early industrialists, which demonstrates that few were self-made and that many had prior attachments to the middle class and its values, reduces the need to isolate some special belief system.[35] So does the recognition that the outlook of western Europeans in general had been changing for several decades before industrialization's advent. Keith Thomas and others have identified new attitudes toward risk and control and toward family and self in the late seventeenth century, which suggest that entrepreneurial values flowed from a larger redirection in popular culture, even though the values themselves were not universally shared.[36]

If the role of either individual entrepreneurs or some special ethic has receded in a modest rebalancing of causation, the importance of other anonymous forces has increased. The population surge of the eighteenth century, which clearly preceded Western industrialization, was vital in providing new numbers of available workers and, to a degree, a new set of market opportunities. It also had an impact on motivation, spurring individual entrepreneurs to take new risks and to innovate in order to accommodate their own enlarged families.[37]

The role of Europe's colonial expansion and the dominant position the West had gained in worldwide commerce has also moved up the causation ladder, though, like population growth, it has long been on the list. The world systems approach of Immanuel Wallerstein, though challenged from several perspectives, sees western Europe emerging as the core arena of an international commercial economy by the sixteenth century. The West steadily expanded its manufacturing to match new export opportunities, and so the industrial revolution fits into an ongoing pattern of international economic dominance. Western capitalists utilized the funds they had accumulated from earlier commercial ventures (including the slave trade), plus the opportunities they had already developed by selling relatively high-priced processed goods to societies that provided low-cost raw materials. This built an industrial economy that, from an initial global standpoint, was simply a sophisticated and much more powerful restatement of the international economic imbalance developed two centuries before.[38]

Finally, the importance of government has risen on the causal scale. The salience of certain kinds of legal support for industrialization, including appropriate labor law and banking provisions, has long been recognized. A number of explanations of Britain's industrial lead point strongly to the more appropriate laissez-faire political arrangements available in eighteenth-century Britain, in contrast most obviously to the rather heavy-handed regulatory approach of the French state.[39] Political factors also emerge as important in tracing the spread of industrialization in the nineteenth century, where other governments sought to imitate British success. Many analysts, urging that too much attention has been paid to British causal patterns that were by definition atypical, point to the extensive involvement of the Prussian (and later, German) state in industry as more characteristic of government's role. A growing tendency to examine government functions, and not simply issues of constitutional structure (which tended to dominate popular attention in the revolutionary era) leads to an analysis of the state's role in promoting or, in some cases, retarding the industrialization process.

The most important shift in causation discussions, however, goes beyond a realignment of specific factors to a partial restatement of the overall context from which the industrial revolution emerged. The idea of a period of protoindustrialization, in which an increasingly commercialized economy engages in more extensive manufacturing operations well in advance of basic technological or organizational transformation, was put forth several years ago by a number of German historians and has been widely utilized.[40] Partisans of the protoindustrial concept argue that the rapid expansion of domestic manufacturing constituted a substantial change in its own right. Large numbers of rural workers became enmeshed in a market economy, worked for money, and often were employed by capitalist merchants. They learned to deal with strangers; they learned the possibility of altering traditional standards of living and engaged in some early manifestations of consumerism (particularly in the purchase of urban-made, "fashionable" clothing); they also bought food products other than salt for the first time. The growth in popular use of tea, coffee, and sugar marked an important redefinition of interests a century before the industrial revolution began anywhere. Family and sexual values changed with protoindustrialization— one key eighteenth-century symptom was an increasing interest in casual or expressive sex. Social structure also changed in advance of the industrial revolution, dividing societies into propertied peasants and business people (including commercially minded artisan masters) on the one hand and a wage-earning (not necessarily destitute) proletariat on the other.[41] Proto-industrial people differed from traditional peasants and burghers; their values and some of their economic habits and arrangements anticipated the industrial revolution.

The protoindustrial concept has not won uniform acceptance. Some historians judge that it assumes too fundamental a shift by the early eighteenth century, noting also that it amalgamates continental and British experiences more than the more conventional Britain-the-first-industrializer framework suggests. It is also worth noting that, like many of the revisions in recent historiography, this one is not entirely new: It recalls, to a degree, John Nef's earlier argument that Britain had its first industrial revolution in the early modern period.

On the other hand, the protoindustrial concept does contribute to the perception that fundamental shifts occurred in the West several centuries in advance of the industrial revolution. Charles Tilly argues that the two really "big changes" in the whole of modern Western history began in the sixteenth century: growing commercialization with the accompanying advent of the proletariat, and the rise of the nation-state.[42] (Some authorities would prefer to see this second development placed in the later seventeenth century.) In this formulation, the industrial revolution is simply a stage in the larger evolution of commercial and nation-state patterns, capable of redefining some manifestations (such as the specific content and organization of protest), but not of setting basic new trends in motion. Wallerstein's approach also defines the industrial revolution as a new stage in an earlier pattern, but one which was not as revolutionary as the advent of the world system in the sixteenth century. At the same time, the growing interest in tracing a new popular mentality (including new childrearing beliefs and socialization practices) back to the early modern centuries could add the dimension of changing values to this chronological revision.[43]

Whatever the specific formulation of early modern change—Tilly's two "big changes," though attractive, may be too restrictive—the net result is this: The industrial revolution flowed from a much broader reshuffling of traditional structures and beliefs in western Europe than was once realized. The industrial revolution responded to specific causes, to be sure, but larger changes such as protoindustrialization also helped prepare the way.[44]

Whether this diminishes the impact of the industrial revolution is open to question. It calls attention, from yet another angle, to the long process of change involved. Yet it is not surprising that fundamental new developments were essential in setting the groundwork for an even more fundamental departure, particularly in Britain, which experienced the industrial process first, and operated without the spur or guidance of models developed elsewhere. Regardless of where it took place, industrialization was profoundly novel and unsettling.

In a sense, the larger pieces of this analytical puzzle are still being put together, in part because the work of early modern historians and their modern counterparts so seldom overlaps. Some elements of a possible integration are clear, and they can serve as an interim conclusion about the reevaluations of industrialization within the Western context.[45]

Industrialization added a major new ingredient, the technological–organizational revolution, to a society already rapidly changing. If some "big changes" had occurred previously (including the West's ascendancy within the world economy) such that industrialization followed from trends already in motion, it is still possible to see the industrial revolution and its many ramifications in Western society as another substantial transformation. In some cases the industrial revolution amplified other changes already under way. It increased the power and functions of the nation-state, it added to commercialization, and it greatly extended the economic power of the West in the world economy for at least a century.

An understanding of the prior directions of change can also explain key reactions to industrialization. Thus, the tendency to idealize the family, and to rearrange family roles in order to protect that idealization, was not an inevitable product of the industrial revolution, but a Western reaction derived from prior tendencies (dating from the seventeenth century) to emphasize and redefine family functions.[46] The continuities with previous change do not, however, rob the industrial revolution of its power to transform. Thus, using the family example again, Western society had to restructure significantly to accommodate the unanticipated reassessments of the family. The decline of family production, the separation of paternal labor from the household, as well as the recalculation of children's roles and the number of children it was desirable to have, all forced massive changes in family behavior that could not have been predicted by preindustrial trends alone. In an industrial context, new kinds of expertise and government policy began to be directed toward family matters. The preindustrial family should not be compared to some static model of traditional family life (as is still sometimes done, particularly in social science disciplines) as this would ignore important earlier shifts that helped lead to industrial results. Nevertheless, the distinct transforming force of industrial revolution—in this and other areas—should not be downplayed either.

The chronological span in which the industrial revolution is defined and assessed has been extended by attention to industrialization's transforming power. The later nineteenth century is now seen as an integral part of industrial revolution history, even after the pioneering period. As a result, earlier concepts that drew attention to the later nineteenth century, such as a "second industrial revolution" based on new technologies such as the Bessemer and Open Hearth steel-making processes and electric and internal combustion motors, have declined in use. The industrial revolution is now viewed as an extended process of recurrent technological innovation that continued into the twentieth century. Chronological expansion of Western industrialization also reflects an effort to move away from undue fascination with Britain, for in no other case can it be contended that even a basic industrial revolution was completed before the 1890s.

By concentrating on more than the first few decades when factories took hold, an expanded time frame indicates the long-term significance of industrialization in such spheres as leisure and family structure. By evaluating the impact of industrialization over time, and by considering an earlier context from which the industrial revolution flowed, historians have recast the temporal dimension of the whole phenomenon as one segment of transformation in a longer set of historical changes in the West.

The Industrial Revolution as a Global Phenomenon

The fact that industrialization was an international process and not simply a Western development has long been realized. The subject has two facets: First, an examination of the impact of the industrial revolution in enhancing the world power of the industrializers (initially, key Western nations; ultimately, other nations as well); and second, a consideration of the implications of industrialization patterns, which aids an understanding of efforts to industrialize worldwide.

The West's nineteenth-century industrial revolution obviously supported the surge of imperialism. While some explanations of imperialism have focused primarily on a diplomatic dynamic among the European nation-states,[47] most inquiries have included more direct discussion of industrialization's role. Classic debates over the industrially generated need to find new markets, protected sources of raw materials, and opportunities for investment were all built on an understanding of the changes wrought in the Western economies.[48] Economic calculations suggest that imperial acquisitions did not have the effects anticipated. But the perception of growing economic rivalry and a need to use imperial means to compensate for potential restrictions in opportunities were themselves key products of the spread of the industrial revolution throughout most of western Europe and the United States. The further impact of industrialization in discomfiting prominent groups within Western society also played its role in spurring imperialism. In their own ways, many aristocrats, adventurers, and church leaders grew increasingly uncomfortable with their societies for focusing on material acquisition and middle-class ascendancy and sought opportunities in empire largely denied at home.

The technological and organizational core of industrialization unquestionably determined the framework for the new imperialism, as important recent research has emphasized. The West's technological surge provided a new basis for disdaining the rest of the world, which had not grasped the new ways to subdue nature. This was not an entirely novel theme: Earlier travelers' accounts had, for example, criticized Chinese or Ottoman inability to understand the importance of Western technical advances and their apparent preference for settled tradition over innovation. This theme was greatly enhanced when the contrast could be drawn between an industrial world and a world seemingly incapable of following suit— and this contrast continues into judgments of the Third World in the late twentieth century.[49]

More directly, industrial technology also altered the world power balance. Several studies remind us of the advantages that new guns and shipping gave the West. In the first colonial wave, based on initial advantages in ships and ships' gunnery developed by the sixteenth century, the West gained mastery of the sea. New industrial technologies produced a second wave of imperialism and commercial dominance by allowing the West to penetrate inland. Much of the imperialist scramble in Africa can be attributed to industrial–technological advances, once steamships were available to navigate previously impenetrable upstream rivers, and medicines could combat the worst tropical diseases.[50]

Beyond technology, beyond even overt imperialism, the industrial revolution greatly extended the impact of the commercialized world economy. A series of important recent works on Latin American history focus on the late nineteenth century as a time of greatly enlarged commercialization, under the impetus of Western markets and merchants.[51] Far larger portions of arable land and far larger percentages of the workforce were drawn into market-oriented production than ever before. One recent study has even argued that the Latin American labor movement was fundamentally marked by the surge in export sectors,[52] and it is widely agreed that Western industrialization was one of the major new ingredients in Latin American history from the 1870s onward. Research in other areas, focusing on such topics as the rise of Western-directed commercial rug production in the Ottoman Empire,[53] reaches similar conclusions in arguing for a significant penetration of new work forms, organization, and technology as a result of the West's industrialization and attendant changes in international marketing and transport facilities. Before the twentieth century, industrialization had changed the world more fundamentally than the legacy of imperialism alone suggests.

The other aspect of industrialization's global history, drawing on analyses of successes and failures among non-Western industrialization efforts, has invited a variety of comparative or implicitly comparative research projects. The subject obviously relates to the more immediate international impact of industrialization: Most parts of the world, when and if they sought to industrialize, did so with knowledge of the West's lead while grappling with Western economic (and sometimes political) intervention. For example, the West's economic disruption of China from the Opium Wars until at least the 1920s was a clear case where exploitation was not tempered by the responsibilities of outright imperial administration. This has been justly cited as one factor severely retarding China's own economic modernization.[54] Thus, the chance to imitate a successful achievement might spur industrial development, but the disadvantages that stemmed from the West's commercial control and its efforts to perpetuate the production of cheap foodstuffs, raw materials, and a few manufactured items usually outweighed this spur.

There was no single international response to the West's industrial lead. The second global facet of industrial revolution—the international force of the Western industrial model—has been examined by exploring some key cases. Several generalizations have emerged from this research, but the case-by-case approach remains predominant.

The Industrial Revolution in the United States

The case of industrialization in North America is easiest to examine for the simple reason that its industrial patterns, and recent developments in its historical analysis, so closely parallel those of western Europe. United States industrialization operated as part of a common technological pool with western Europe, beginning with the first borrowing of British textile equipment. The pace and timing of the American process coincided with those of the early European industrializers, with only minor variations. Most generalizations about the nature of the industrial revolution based on initial European models fit the United States quite comfortably—which is why Americanists have contributed few novel views of what the process was all about.[55]

This said, there are of course some significant distinctions on specific subtopics. American dependence on European capital for its development through the nineteenth century remains notable. American agriculture, already organized on a basis quite different from European peasant regions, adapted to technological change much more rapidly than its European counterparts. The harshness of the early phases of European industrialization was cushioned in the United States by a considerable labor shortage. Compared to European patterns around 1850 or earlier—and particularly compared to British patterns—American workers had a better bargaining position and thus enjoyed a reasonably high standard of living and considerable voice over working conditions. Work-based protest activities were, again by European standards of the time, surprisingly mild, with only a few important exceptions, such as the 1830s strife among Philadelphia textile workers. Another important difference between industrial revolutions in Europe and America was that male workers in the United States had gained the vote, and an active democratic consciousness, well in advance of the industrial revolution. Political expressions of industrial discontent emerged nonetheless, but on the whole they were, and have remained, more muted than those characteristic of western Europe.[56]

Finally, it is even possible to discern a particularly American genius in the industrialization process: its innovations in organizational structure. Most recent research has emphasized that while the United States produced a few notable inventions during the industrialization period, it remained heavily dependent on Europe for most basic advances.[57] The same does not hold true in the area of business organization. Alfred Chandler has documented the quick surge of American corporate units from the 1870s onward, including their almost immediate establishment of international branches.[58] Thus the two biggest private firms in Russia by 1914 were both American. By this point, American innovation in the manipulation of labor, through scientific management studies and the introduction of the assembly line, also gave an important new twist to the whole theme of organization in the workplace. Emphasis on firm hierarchy in industrial organization contrasted fascinatingly with a democratic political culture. Through its management innovations, capped by such systems as the assembly line and some leadership in developing mass consumption patterns, the United States helped heighten the impact of industrialization in the final phases of an industrially "revolutionary" period in the West.[59]

The common involvement of the United States in a European-style industrial revolution remains the main reason why most American organizational innovations were quickly picked up in western Europe. At the same time, distinctive early features of industrialization in the United States yielded to more standard patterns over time. Thus the full flowering of American industrialization after 1860, based on a large influx of immigrant laborers, reduced the earlier advantages in both living standards and management–worker communications. Herbert Gutman has charted the analogies between labor-force formation at this point in the United States with that characteristic of Britain somewhat earlier.[60] The similarity between these basic patterns appears in available data on social mobility. In the nineteenth century, American industrialization, along with frontier conditions, generated slightly more upward mobility and considerably less downward mobility than was characteristic of western Europe. But the overall patterns were remarkably similar, and the resemblance increased with time. American mobility was vested with a different rhetoric from that of western Europe, having a greater tendency to assume mobility opportunities, welcome and exaggerate examples of change, and criticize those who could not rise; but even this distinction should not be pushed too far.[61]

Furthermore, the U.S. example indicates the wide applicability of research on European industrialization. Examination of protoindustrial features has focused attention on the 1780–1820 period, where a number of recent studies have documented an important increase in commercialization and economic specialization, including preindustrial manufacturing. The United States, like Europe, went through an important way station as it passed from a localized subsistence economy to the beginnings of outright industrialization, though its protoindustrial period may seem slightly truncated by European standards.[62]

At the other end of the process, attention to the larger social ramifications of the industrial revolution in the United States has easily reproduced basic findings yielded in western Europe, from patterns of crowd behavior to family structure to leisure changes. In some instances, as in the area of the family, where some Americanists have been particularly attentive, American patterns have been charted with greater precision than their European analogues. The impact of industrialization in altering fatherhood, by concentrating paternal functions on a fairly remote though often deeply felt set of breadwinning functions, has been sketched more fully for the United States than for western Europe, though there is ample evidence that the basic trends were similar on both sides of the Atlantic.[63]

While having some distinctive features, including an abundance of land and a weak central government, industrialization in the United States fits into a common analytical framework. This aids in the definition of a basic Western industrialization process more than it hurts by requiring a host of qualifiers and caveats. The close fit among Western patterns is all the more interesting in its contrast with the few cases of successful industrialization elsewhere in the world.

Analysis of Latecomers

RUSSIA AND JAPAN

The industrial revolutions of Russia and Japan require somewhat different interpretive frameworks from those applicable to western Europe and the United States, even though the distinctions are not complete. German industrialization, for example, with its concentration in heavy industry and considerable government involvement, obviously bears some resemblance to Russian and Japanese patterns, while differing in these same respects from the British model. Nevertheless, the industrial revolutions in both Russia and Japan began later and with fewer ties to the initial Western process of which the United States as well as Germany were part. Russia and Japan have been analyzed in terms of a "latecomer" model, involving a distinctive set of issues, because they emerged from societies substantially different from the West. Nonetheless, even in these countries, core features of the industrial revolution, and many of its social effects, bear witness to the existence of a common process; but a comparative focus must also discern distinguishing marks.

Russia and Japan were the only two non-Western societies to begin an industrial revolution before 1900 and the only large societies outside the West to complete the process by the late twentieth century. Some special factors must be adduced not only to explain differences from the West but also to account for sets of responses that remain unusual in world history.

While the industrial revolutions in Russia and Japan are usually examined separately, and took quite different courses with quite different social and political consequences, they did flow from some very general common ingredients that were absent from most of the nineteenth-century world. Both societies entered the initial industrial period with relatively strong governments and vigorous, creative intellectual communities, particularly when compared to the declining empires of the Middle East and China or the fledgling nations of Latin America. Questions have been raised, of course, about the effectiveness of both the tsarist and Tokugawa regimes, but both had competent administrative structures that could help guide a reformist drive to maintain national economic independence. Changes in the late Tokugawa period, including rising literacy and the expansion of commercial production of processed foods and textiles, raise some analogies with protoindustrial patterns in the West. Though some researchers continue to see late Tokugawa Japan as a society in outright decline, it seems likely that Japanese industrialization was facilitated by significant—and unusual—change.[64]

Both Russia and Japan also had a tradition of successful imitation of models from abroad. Though the tradition was more immediate in the Russian case, Japan saw its Western contacts grow after 1800, as the "Dutch school" of translation expanded into a program of scientific interest and training. (The "Dutch school" derived from Japanese trained to translate in dealings with Dutch merchants in Nagasaki, the only Western contact allowed between the seventeenth century and 1853.) Unlike western Europe, neither Russia nor Japan was overwhelmed by population pressure in advance of initial industrialization. It was only after mid-nineteenth-century confrontations with the industrialized West demonstrated the dangers of failing to launch a process of economic change (the fleets at Edo Bay, the Crimean War loss) that both societies, after some hesitation, responded with important positive measures. These initiatives began outright industrial revolutions.

As latecomers, Japan and Russia demonstrated some common features in their economic and political initiatives.[65] The importance of the government role is obvious in both countries, particularly the initiatives from economic ministries (which were newly formed, in the case of Meiji Japan, but quickly became the most vibrant units in the state). The role of government in establishing pilot companies and maintaining considerable economic direction built on prior political traditions in both societies (though more obviously in Russia). Government initiatives also helped compensate for early problems of entrepreneurship and capital formation, as well as clear technological lag. The process of borrowing from Western models was inevitably more extensive in latecomer cases, but there was a significant difference between careful Japanese coordination of advice-seeking efforts and the greater direct role that Western capitalists and workers took in the tsarist phase of early Russian industrialization. But the more controlled and limited contacts with Western advisers after the Bolshevik Revolution may be fruitfully compared with the earlier Japanese framework. Finally, as part of the need to amass investment capital quickly and to pay for needed technological imports, both Russia and Japan had to press the lower classes through high taxes and low-wage nonindustrialized export sectors such as Russian grain and Japanese silk production.

The latecomer model remains highly generalized. In spite of many similarities, Russian and Japanese industrializations also differed greatly, as the advent and impact of the Bolshevik Revolution and Japan's great export dynamism clearly attest. Despite a limited entrepreneurial surge,[66] Russian industrialization proceeded from an unusually pervasive peasant base.[67] This context helps explain the strong governmental role, under tsars and Stalinists alike, in providing management and direction. It also necessitates attention to special attributes and problems in the labor force.

Recent work in Russian labor history in the early industrial period has focused on protest.[68] For example, Reginald Zelnik has pointed out how impressive Russian worker unity was by Western standards.[69] Yet social historians, and particularly a new breed dealing with the 1920s and 1930s, are attending to more than the revolutionary tide.[70] They also detail the origins of industrial workers and the role they played in shaping the new production systems. Partly because of communist ideology but partly because of their own vital role in building industrialization from a peasant society, workers maintained a greater voice in Soviet factories and even in the Soviet state (into the late 1930s) than has been commonly imagined. Certainly their ability to articulate goals and grievances in the 1920s was considerable and may in fact have aided their adjustment to an ongoing industrialization process. Also striking, and related to the expression of working-class interest, was the ongoing importance of masses of rural recruits, which created an unusually large (by Western standards) semi-skilled labor force by the time Stalinist planning began. The relationship of this labor force to possibilities of technological change, in a setting genuinely new and genuinely industrial but still backward by current Western standards, also helps explain distinctive features of the ongoing industrialization process in the Stalinist era. Thus, consideration of worker reactions and roles joins the ongoing question of government impetus (both before and after revolution) in defining distinctive features of Russian industrial historiography.

Analysis of Japan's industrial revolution, particularly as it has been informed both by recent research and by recent awe at Japan's surge to Western levels and beyond, has raised two seemingly contradictory questions: First, how could such an isolated society have industrialized at all; but second, was there some Japanese genius that has proved especially congenial to industrial demands, providing a model that latter-day Westerners should try to emulate?

Both questions involve assessment of Japan's preindustrial traditions. The collective consciousness generated by Japanese feudalism, including a pattern of group decision making and an indistinct boundary between political and social institutions, helps explain why the Japanese government was able to rally quickly from the near–civil war generated by initial Western demands for access and to institute reforms that would facilitate economic change. It has been argued that this same consciousness generated a surprisingly smooth transition through the industrial process, and led to the hardworking, community-minded Japanese so envied today. Other Japanese traditions played a part in this transition, to be sure. The Japanese obviously parlayed an unusual awareness of their cultural distinctiveness and long economic isolation into an industrialization pattern that kept the internal economy relatively closed to outsiders and emphasized export expansion above all. This effort at control was enhanced by Japan's unusual resource needs, particularly for fuels, and by the impact of specific events such as the Great Depression, which revealed the vulnerability of a still-backward nation to the oscillations of industrial societies elsewhere. By joining their distinctive needs and experiences with the older traditions, the Japanese produced a capitalist-statist thrust which began to take shape with the great industrial combines of the 1890s, and clearly differed from Western and Soviet patterns alike.[71]

Recent work, however, cautions against unduly facile assumptions about smooth transitions and miraculously suitable traditions. Without denying some possible links between current company paternalism and employment security practices and earlier feudal traditions of mutual obligations, new research challenges the idea of an easy movement from one set of bonds to another. Japanese managers and government officials faced acute labor problems as they launched industrialization. Peasants had to be drawn into low-paying sweatshops, where export goods were produced whose earnings might compensate for Japan's overall industrial backwardness. Workers in heavy industry were recruited from an artisanate with a rich, individualistic history of traveling and job changing. Discipline and stability, as well as suitably low pay, posed serious challenges as managers tried to impose more direct controls over their skilled labor force. Managers articulated an ideology of "beautiful paternalism," but their rhetoric was scorned by workers who valued their independence and were in any event subjected to various degrading treatments. Several periods of labor unrest followed from these conflicting interests, with unions withering under the combined impact of government–employer persecution and, by the 1930s, economic deterioration. Only in the 1950s did something like the current practice of mutually accepted paternalism take shape, after decades of struggle in which worker pressures, not simply tradition or rational management, played a key role.[72]

Further, as critics of contemporary Japan have noted, at all stages in the Japanese industrialization process, now and a century ago, Japan's labor force has been graded into a complex hierarchy. The relationship of skilled male workers to industrialization and to their firms differed markedly from that of largely female part-time workers and men attached to vulnerable subcontracting units. This pattern followed from Japan's tremendous need for low-wage labor and from the interchange that developed with the skilled sector, where concessions were compensated in part by harsher treatment of other sectors. Japan's industrial style was linked to other stresses in modern Japanese development. This included the years of military authoritarianism and an interesting period, around 1900, of unusual family instability—signaled by what was at one point the world's highest divorce rate. The instability of this latter period was intimately linked to the industrialization–urbanization process.

None of this complexity detracts from the focus on Japan's very real industrial achievement or the distinctive organizational forms and spirit it built in the process. It does argue for the importance of historical detail, including internal periodization. Likewise, the distinctive elements of Russian industrialization involve more than revolution and state policy. The study of latecomer industrializations adds to the range of patterns involved in the concept of industrial revolution. It also calls for careful examination of the context from which industrialization springs—a context shaped in part by the West's commanding industrial lead—and the kinds of problems participants in the industrial process had to contend with. Appreciation of the actual historical process of major non-Western industrializations is increasing, raising a number of analytical issues.[73] At the same time, obviously, new uncertainties in the West have opened new understandings of the possibility not only of successful industrialization in other societies but of industrial excellence and innovative leadership.

ADDITIONAL GLOBAL ISSUES

As noted, industrialization provided a stimulus for Western economic and imperial domination, and a few other key societies responded through latecomer industrial revolutions of their own. But these latecomers do not exhaust an understanding of the global impact of the process. Explanations of past industrializations have informed both historical and contemporary inquiry into reasons for continuing economic lag, while models of the past also assist judgments about more recent industrial revolutions.

Historical work on the persistent failure of some societies to industrialize builds on an understanding of the factors present in other more successful cases, while also seeking special factors in particular categories or individual societies. The work is by definition tentative because it seeks to explain what has not yet happened, and (particularly in the past few years) tries not to impose Western expectations on regions with rich modern histories that do not happen to include industrial transformation. Recent literature is enhanced, however, by heightened awareness of the Japanese and Russian cases. Studies on their successful industrialization from a previously backward context are more relevant to analyses of contemporary cases than earlier efforts to impose British or United States causal models.

Immanuel Wallerstein's world systems approach and more specific work on economic dependency in Latin America offer one important approach to the problem of why some areas do not industrialize. Societies that became peripheral or dependent in the capitalist world economy (which began to take shape in the sixteenth century) had little opportunity to develop either the economic or the social–political basis for industrialization. These regions included Latin America, parts of sub-Saharan Africa, the American South (for a time), parts of Southeast Asia, and possibly eastern Europe. These societies were characterized by an economy heavily geared to the export of unprocessed food products and raw materials, handled in Western ships by Western-dominated mercantile companies, and based on cheap (often coerced) labor. Imports focused on more expensive manufactured goods and luxury items, yielding a typically unfavorable balance of trade that discouraged capital formation and by the nineteenth century led to heavy foreign indebtedness. This system produced relatively weak (or outright colonial) governments and an absence of strong entrepreneurial middle classes, which further retarded the kind of industrial breakthroughs that might alter world economic relationships. This sweeping theory has been criticized for, among other reasons, ignoring some important internal manufacturing and trade. It has not been replaced, however, and it certainly explains the barriers many regions faced in attempting to imitate industrial revolutions elsewhere. Revealingly, the only societies outside the West to industrialize fully, at least until quite recently, were never drawn into the full set of dependent relationships (though Russia had veered close, via grain exports and exploitative serfdom, by the mid-nineteenth century).[74]

Historical explanation for industrial backwardness has been applied to China, using a modernization model particularly informed by comparisons to Russia and Japan. (Earlier kinds of comparative analysis, built on a Western model, would stress the place of entrepreneurial spirit, and have therefore been superseded.) The Chinese pattern, obviously significant in itself, is also of interest because China was never fully drawn into a peripheral economic relationship with the West (though, like Russia, it came close). China also had certain moral traditions, such as Confucian secular values, which were similar to the preconditions for Japan's early industrial imitation. Other traditions, however, like bureaucratic conservatism, were less appropriate and differed from Japanese patterns. Further, China's population problem, which began to assume new dimensions from the seventeenth century onward; the kind of Western exploitation that arose by the late nineteenth century, which may have been more damaging than outright colonialism; and the chaos of prolonged revolution and civil war in the twentieth century all fed into China's ongoing economic retardation. History helps explain China's economic position and, more generally, it organizes a great deal of disparate data on modern Chinese trends. The picture is not only more specific than the general economic dependency models but is also more dynamic, in that it takes recent political experience into account.[75]

A global approach to industrialization, brought into the twentieth century, must allow for considerable dynamism and flux. Traditions that were long inhospitable to an industrial revolution may change; even deep-rooted economic dependency may be countered. Measurements of technological innovation and growth rates, taken from recognized instances of industrialization, permit at least tentative identification of several "new" or emerging industrial revolutions since the 1960s. Three instances are particularly noteworthy.

Fringe areas of Europe, such as Spain and Czechoslovakia, where regional industrial revolutions occurred quite early, fall into one general pattern of ongoing industrial change with many of the standard economic, urban, and social consequences.[76] For instance, with other industrial nations as an example and some funding from abroad, genuine industrial revolutions began in certain regions of Spain by the late nineteenth century; in Catalonia for textiles and then around Bilbao in heavy industry. The industrialization process affected the rest of the country more gradually, with rapid growth (under United States and European encouragement) particularly in the past quarter-century.

The Pacific Rim industrializers, notably South Korea, Taiwan, Hong Kong, and Singapore, demonstrate even more striking transformations. Here, too, there may be some fringe effect, in terms of inspiration from established industrial areas, in the wake of Japanese operations and some special contacts with key Western industrial powers. All Pacific Rim industrializations received special stimulus from the United States (or in Singapore's case, Great Britain) after World War II. Some Korean analysts have downplayed a Western role, however, adding their example to that of Japan by noting the importance of a distinctive East Asian cultural base for industrial organization. They cite the importance of Confucian values and some feudal patterns in building an appropriate sense of community discipline that is more fruitful, in terms of industrial potential, than the relevant Western context.[77]

Finally, several Latin American countries, headed by Brazil, may be moving into the new industrial camp, building on a heightened role of the state in planning and development that first emerged in response to the Great Depression. Brazil's vigorous steel industry and its capacity in computer production, where it ranks fourth in the world, are particularly interesting bellwethers of economic change, despite the familiar problems of continued population growth and massive urban impoverishment.[78]

Analysis in all three of these instances involves agreement on suitable criteria for measuring an early industrial revolution and distinguishing it from more isolated pockets of development. Applying historical standards to these cases is vital, but not always easy. It involves a recognition of special features, both in causation and implementation, that flow from particular situations—like the vigorous role assumed by some authoritarian governments in Latin America. A grasp of previous cases of industrial emergence from relative backwardness aids in recognizing the kinds of diversity compatible with genuine industrial change, even though it cannot predict the distinguishing marks of any of the recent examples. The apparent surge of a new group of industrializers invites serious attention to contemporary economic history, too often seen in terms of rather static divisions between the haves and have-nots, or a monochrome Third World incapable (if only because of constraints imposed by earlier industrializers) of breaking through toward genuine change.

A flexible framework for contemporary history, juxtaposed with sensitive use of prior industrial models including the West, yields one other line of inquiry. Some patterns of economic change in the late twentieth century that have not yielded full transformations (at least to date) may bear some comparison with aspects of protoindustrialization experienced in the early modern West and perhaps to some degree in Tokugawa Japan. A focus on identifying revolution should not preclude appreciation of more evolutionary economic change, of the sort visible in India, China, and some parts of the Middle East and Southeast Asia. Forecasting on the basis of this kind of comparison would be risky, and the comparison itself is difficult given the massive changes that successful industrializations have generated in the world economy. Far more technological innovation, for example, may be necessary for a contemporary protoindustrialization than was true in the seventeenth and eighteenth centuries.

The industrial revolution, by its uneven incidence in the nineteenth and twentieth centuries, clearly created huge new imbalances in global relationships, many of which still shape world affairs. It also generated widespread changes even in areas clearly disadvantaged, at least initially, by the surge of the industrial powers. In some cases, additional industrial revolutions have resulted; in some other cases, different kinds of alterations have at least broken through the institutions and habits of the prior agricultural economies. Accounting for such varied impacts sets the framework for a global history of the crucial modern economic upheaval.

Conclusion

The new or modified interpretations of the industrial revolution that have been developed over the past twenty-five years continue to challenge the teaching of modern history—whether global history or the history of particular societies. Since the industrial revolution draws attention to processes of change over a wide range of institutions and behaviors, it fits even less comfortably than before in a predominantly narrative presentation of the past. Yet the broadened understanding of the impact of industrialization, by focusing on the recasting of basic features of social life, applies to politics and war as well as family or business organization. It is possible, in other words, to present industrial history as part of a persistent attention to structures in the past that range from work discipline to essential government functions. Certainly, appreciation of industrialization's complex relationship with earlier history (this applies to Russia or China as well as Britain), plus a grasp of its far-reaching international impact, heightens the need for recurrent attention to the phenomenon in any modern history teaching.

Whether in teaching or research, the history of the industrial revolution, extending over two centuries of the world's history and into its probable future, invites a number of kinds of analysis. The importance of causation is obvious in explaining why industrializations occur and take the shapes they do or why they do not occur. A focus on causes is a key means of tying industrial history to larger and earlier themes in the political, cultural, and economic spheres. The need for comparison among actual industrial patterns is also obvious. New work on cases such as Japan has advanced an understanding of the interplay between core features and distinctive variations in framing comparative work. At the same time, an expanding treatment of industrialization's social impact in the West, which transcends some of the more narrow and immediate effects, raises ongoing challenges to comparative analysis. The interplay between an industrial revolution and a leisure, family, or work outlook—the expansion, in other words, of industrial history from largely economic to an interactive social–economic approach—has not yet generated the sophisticated comparison visible in discussing causation or political contexts. Certain Western reactions to industrialization, such as the development of new spectator sports, quickly took on global dimensions, spreading more rapidly than the industrial revolution itself. Yet more precise relationships and comparisons that will permit discussion of wider social impact are only beginning to emerge. The need to assess the industrial revolution as an international phenomenon, and a recognition of the importance of various kinds of comparison, have both advanced, but important issues remain open.

More generally, both the generation and the impact of industrialization are now seen as more interactive among various levels of participants than was once the case. Western workers reacted to new conditions of labor and shaped not only protest but ongoing organizational efforts. They also actively contributed to the gender environment of the West's industrial revolution. The role of workers, along with managers and the state, in both Russia and Japan have been the focus of much recent research. Industrialization is imposed to some extent, but the most exciting research approaches have gone beyond that, by examining the mutual impacts of industry and society, employers and employed.[79]

Another common interpretive thread continues to involve the tension between the problems and opportunities created by the industrial revolution. This tension has only increased with the new definitions and international amplifications in its historical treatment. On the one hand, it remains accurate to see industrialization as, in Harold Perkin's words, a "revolution in men's access to the means of life, in control of their ecological environment, in their capacity to escape from the tyranny and niggardliness of nature." [80] Obviously, discussion of areas of the world where industrial change lagged picks up implicitly on the advantages of economic transformation: better with it, in the international economy, than without. Yet industrialization also brought strain, even when it flowed from important earlier change in institutions and values. Shifts in the international power balance brought new exploitation to many parts of the world—whether this was theoretically escapable or not. Regions able to imitate Western industrialization did so to the detriment of social and personal stability. The West itself, in its social and family relations, showed at least as much dislocation as progress. This means that the new social analysis must involve assessment of the important distortions in social interactions and personal meaning that the industrial revolution compelled, even when it brought unquestioned new prosperity.

This tension between loss and gain (assessable in early industrial revolutions as well as in later ones, in specific cases as well as internationally) may hold the key to presenting industrialization and its inescapability as one of the dominant frameworks in modern world history. The industrial revolution drew from all sectors of a society, building on prior patterns in politics as well as previous trade or labor systems. It then altered all other sectors as well, making it possible to discuss the impact of industrialization on politics and state just as on leisure or demographic behavior. On this level, the industrial revolution's impact extended to areas economically and politically dominated by the industrial powers, or striving to launch their own industrial process, almost as fully as areas that had already industrialized.

While it remains important to define the core phenomenon of industrialization precisely and to delimit its boundaries in time, the industrial revolution's history remains an ongoing part of world history today. This history must be used to assess the experience and prospects of the newest arrivals to the industrial roster. Differential access to industrialization continues to shape international power politics and economic opportunities. And even in the most established industrial societies, where the industrial revolution ended as much as a century ago and where concerns about lagging progress or deindustrialization often seize center stage, the challenge of adaptation to industrialization's impact remains. Efforts to revise the initial familial response to industrial work systems, for example, by recasting gender roles, attest to the sweeping questions economic upheaval has raised. Conveying the historical roots and reasons for these continuing questions by treating the industrial revolution yields an unusual opportunity to relate past to present.

NOTES

1. Arnold Toynbee, *Lectures on the Industrial Revolution* (Gloucester, Mass.: P. Smith, 1980). Older and/or conventional treatments of the industrial revolution, focusing mainly on Britain and western Europe, are legion, and some still serve as a useful introduction to many basic features. See Paul Mantoux, *The Industrial Revolution in the Eighteenth Century* (New York: Macmillan, 1961; first English ed., 1928); J. H. Clapham, *An Economic History of Modern Britain* (Cambridge, England: Cambridge University Press, 1930–38) and *An Economic History of France and Germany* (Cambridge, England: Cambridge University Press, 1961); T. S. Ashton, *The Industrial Revolution, 1760–1830* (New York: Oxford University Press, 1948); Karl Polanyi, *The Great Transformation* (Boston: Rinehart, 1944); W. O. Henderson, *Britain and Industrial Europe, 1750–1870* (Leicester, England: Leicester University Press, 1965) and *The State and the Industrial Revolution in Prussia* (Liverpool, England: Liverpool University Press, 1958); Arthur Dunham, *The Industrial Revolution in France, 1815–1848* (New York: Columbia University Press, 1955); Rondo Cameron, *France and the Economic Development of Europe* (Princeton: Princeton University Press, 1981); Phyllis Deane, *The First Industrial Revolution* (Cambridge, England: Cambridge University Press, 1969); Eric Pawson, *The Early Industrial Revolution* (New York: Barnes and Noble, 1979); A. E. Musson, *Growth of British Industry* (New York: Holmes and Meier, 1978).

2. For an extremely useful introduction, see Joel Mokyr, ed., *The Economics of the Industrial Revolution* (London: Allen and Unwin, 1985), with a rich bibliography. Substantive contributions include Francois Crouzet, ed., *Capital Formation in the Industrial Revolution* (London: Methuen, 1965)—including Crouzet's own essay, "Capital Formation in Great Britain during the Industrial Revolution," pp. 162–222, originally published in *The Proceedings of the Second International Conference of Economic History* (The Hague, Netherlands, 1965); Phyllis Deane, "New Estimates of Gross National Product for the United Kingdom, 1830–1914," *Review of Income and Wealth* 14 (1968): 104–5, and "The Role of Capital in the Industrial Revolution," *Explorations in Economic History* 10 (1962): 349–64; Phyllis Deane and W. A. Cole, *British Economic Growth, 1688–1959* (Cambridge, England: Cambridge University Press, 1969); J. Mokyr, "Capital, Labour, and the Delay of Industrial Revolution in the Netherlands," *Economic History Yearbook* 38 (1975): 280–99, and *Industrialization in the Low Countries* (New Haven: Yale University Press, 1976).

3. Melvin Kranzberg, "Prerequisites for Industrialization," in *Technology in Western Civilization*, 2 vols., ed. M. Kranzberg and C. W. Pursell, Jr. (New York: Oxford University Press, 1967); David S. Landes, *The Unbound Prometheus: Technological Change and Industrial Development in Western Europe from 1750 to the Present* (Cambridge, England: Cambridge University Press, 1969); Daniel R. Headrick, *The Tentacles of Progress: Technology Transfer in the Age of Imperialism, 1850–1940* (New York: Oxford University Press, 1988), an important recent work on dissemi-

nation; A. E. Musson, ed., *Science, Technology, and Economic Growth in the Eighteenth Century* (London: Methuen, 1972); A. E. Musson and E. Robinson, *Science and Technology in the Industrial Revolution* (Manchester, England: Manchester University Press, 1969); N. Rosenberg, "Technological Change in the Machine Tool Industry, 1840–1910," *Journal of Economic History* 33 (1963): 414–43; "Factors Affecting the Diffusion of Technology," *Economic Journal* 84 (1972): 90–108; and *Perspectives in Technology* (Cambridge, England: Cambridge University Press, 1976); H. J. Habbakuk, *American and British Technology in the Nineteenth Century: The Search for Labor Saving Inventions* (Cambridge, England: Cambridge University Press, 1962).

4. Sidney Pollard, *The Genesis of Modern Management: A Study of the Industrial Revolution in Great Britain* (Cambridge, Mass.: Harvard University Press, 1965); Reinhard Bendix, *Work and Authority in Industry: Ideologies of Management in the Course of Industrialization* (Berkeley: University of California Press, 1974); Peter N. Stearns, *Paths to Authority: The Middle Class and the Industrial Labor Force in France, 1820–1848* (Urbana: University of Illinois Press, 1978).

5. Susan Porter Benson, *Counter Cultures: Saleswomen, Managers, and Customers in American Department Stores, 1890–1940* (Urbana: University of Illinois Press, 1986); Michael Miller, *The Bon Marché: Bourgeois Culture and the Department Store* (Princeton: Princeton University Press, 1981); David Lockwood, *The Black-coated Worker: A Study in Class Consciousness* (London: Allen and Unwin, 1958; rev. ed., 1990); Jurgen Kocka, *Unternehmensverwaltung und Angestelltenschaft am Beispiel Siemens, 1849–1914* (Stuttgart, Germany, 1969), a pioneering empirical study, and his useful synthesis, *White Collar Workers in America, 1890–1940: Social–Political History in International Perspective* (Beverly Hills, Calif.: Sage, 1980); Mario Konig, Hannes Siegrist, and Rudolf Vetterli, *Warten und Aufrucken. Die Angestellten in der Schweiz, 1870–1950* (Zurich, Switzerland: Chronos, 1985).

6. Alfred Chandler, *The Visible Hand: The Managerial Revolution in American Business* (Cambridge, Mass.: Harvard University Press, 1977).

7. A good introduction to artisanal developments is John M. Merriman, ed., *Consciousness and Class Experience in Nineteenth Century Europe* (New York: Holmes and Meier, 1979); William Sewell, *Work and Revolution in France: The Language of Labor from the Old Regime to 1848* (Cambridge, England: Cambridge University Press, 1980); Joan W. Scott, *The Glassworkers of Carmaux* (Cambridge, Mass.: Harvard University Press, 1974); on the other key traditional urban group, Philip G. Nord, *Paris Shopkeepers and the Politics of Resentment* (Princeton: Princeton University Press, 1986).

8. Adna Weber, *The Growth of Cities in the Nineteenth Century* (Ithaca, N.Y.: Cornell University Press, 1963); Paul Hohenberg and Lynn H. Lees, *The Making of Urban Europe* (Cambridge, Mass.: Harvard University Press, 1987); Michael Timberlake, *Urbanization in the World Economy* (Orlando, Fla.: Academic Press, 1985).

9. Robert W. Fogel, *Railroads and American Economic Growth: Essays in Econometric History* (Baltimore: Johns Hopkins University Press, 1970), a classic of the "cliometric" approach; J. G. Williamson, "Regional Inequality and the Process of National Development: A Description of the Patterns," *Economic Development and*

Cultural Change 13 (1964–65): 1–82; E. F. Denison, *Why Growth Rates Differ* (Washington, D.C.: Brookings Institution, 1967); M. W. Flinn, *Origins of the Industrial Revolution* (London: Longman, 1966); R. M. Hartwell, ed., *The Causes of the Industrial Revolution in England* (London: Methuen, 1967) and *The Industrial Revolution and Economic Growth* (London: Methuen, 1971); J.R.T. Hughes, *Industrialization and Economic History* (New York: Oxford University Press, 1970); Crouzet, *Capital Formation*; Mokyr, *Economics*; N.F.R. Crafts, "English Economic Growth in the Eighteenth Century," *Economic History Review* 29 (1976): 226–35.

10. Alexander Gerschenkron, *Economic Backwardness in Historical Perspective: A Book of Essays* (Cambridge, Mass.: Harvard University Press, 1962).

11. W. W. Rostow, *The Stages of Economic Growth* (Cambridge, England: Cambridge University Press, 1960; 2nd ed. 1971); see also his "The Beginnings of Modern Economic Growth in Europe: An Essay in Synthesis," *Journal of Economic History* 33 (1973): 547–80, and *How It All Began* (New York: Oxford University Press, 1975).

12. A useful discussion of whether the industrial revolution is a useful term and whether the discussion is worth attention, with citations of other recent work, is Rondo Cameron, "*La revolution industrielle manquée,*" and R. M. Hartwell, "Was There an Industrial Revolution," *Social Science History* 14 (1990): 559–66 and 567–76.

13. R. Roehl, "French Industrialization: A Reconsideration," *Explorations in Economic History* 12 (1967): 230–81; Flinn, *Origins*; Francois Crouzet, "Western Europe and Great Britain: Catching Up in the First Half of the Nineteenth Century," in *Economic Development in the Long Run*, ed. A. J. Youngson (London: Allen and Unwin, 1972); "England and France in the Eighteenth Century: A Comparative Analysis of Two Economic Growths," in Hartwell, *Causes*; and "Essai de construction d'un indice annuel de la production industrielle française au XIXe siècle," *Annales: Economies, sociétés, civilisatións* (1970): 56–101; see also Charles Kindleberger, *Economic Growth in France and Britain, 1851–1950* (Cambridge, Mass.: Harvard University Press, 1964). For the more traditional disparagement of nineteenth-century French business, see David Landes, "French Entrepreneurship and Industrial Growth in the Nineteenth Century," *Journal of Economic History* 9 (1949): 49–61; some of these arguments also figure in *Unbound Prometheus*.

14. Lee Shai Weissbach, "Artisanal Responses to Artistic Decline: The Cabinetmakers of Paris in the Era of Industrialization," *Journal of Social History* 16 (1982): 67–81.

15. For conventional coverage on children, see Ivy Pinchbeck and Margaret Hewitt, *Children in English Society*, 2 vols. (London: Routledge and Kegan Paul, 1969–73); distinctive approaches include Neil J. Smelser, *Social Change in the Industrial Revolution: An Application of Theory to the British Cotton Industry* (Chicago: University of Chicago Press, 1959); John R. Gillis, *Youth and History: Tradition and Change in European Age Relations, 1770–Present* (New York: Academic Press, 1974); L. Narindelli, "Child Labor and the Factory Acts," *Journal of Economic History* 40 (1980): 739–55; Katherine Lynch, *Family, Class, and Ideology in Early Industrial France: Social Policy and the Working Class Family 1815–1848* (Madison: University

of Wisconsin Press, 1988); Colin Heywood, *Childhood in Nineteenth-Century France: Work, Health, and Education among the "Classes Populaires"* (Cambridge, England: Cambridge University Press, 1988).

16. Smelser, *Social Change in the Industrial Revolution*.

17. Louise Tilly and Joan W. Scott, *Women, Work, and Family* (New York: Holt, Rinehart and Winston, 1978); see also Patricia Branca, "A New Perspective on Women's Work: A Comparative Typology," *Journal of Social History* 9 (1975): 129–53.

18. Mariana Valverde, " 'Giving the Female a Domestic Turn': The Social, Legal, and Moral Regulation of Women's Work in British Cotton Mills, 1820–1850," *Journal of Social History* 21 (1988): 619–34—the article has useful additional references on recent feminist scholarship; Christine Stansell, *City of Women: Sex and Class in New York, 1789–1860* (Urbana: University of Illinois Press, 1982), is a path-breaking study.

19. Daniel Sutherland, *Americans and Their Servants: Domestic Service in the United States from 1800–1920* (Baton Rouge: University of Louisiana Press, 1981); Theresa McBride, *The Domestic Revolution: The Modernization of Household Service in England and France, 1820–1920* (New York: Holmes and Meier, 1976).

20. Mary P. Ryan, *Cradle of the Middle Class: The Family in Oneida County, New York, 1790–1865* (Cambridge, England: Cambridge University Press, 1981); Nancy F. Cott, *The Bonds of Womanhood: "Women's Sphere" in New England 1780–1835* (New Haven: Yale University Press, 1977); Patricia Branca, *Silent Sisterhood, Middle-Class Women in the Victorian Homes* (Pittsburgh: Carnegie Mellon University Press, 1975).

21. Michael Anderson, *Family Structure in Nineteenth-Century Lancashire* (Cambridge, England: Cambridge University Press, 1971); Peter N. Stearns, *Be a Man: Males in Modern Society* (New York: Holmes and Meier, 1979); for a good recent synthesis on family change, Steven Mintz and Susan Kellogg, *Domestic Revolutions: A Social History of American Family Life* (New York: Free Press, 1988), with a useful bibliography.

22. A fine introduction to this debate is A.J.P. Taylor, ed., *The Standard of Living in the Industrial Revolution* (London: Allen and Unwin, 1975)—see particularly the articles by Eric Hobsbawm and R. M. Hartwell; also, Hobsbawm and Hartwell, "The Standard of Living during the Industrial Revolution: A Discussion," *Economic History Review*, 2nd series, 16 (1963–64): 119–46.

23. Theodore S. Hamerow, *Restoration, Revolution, Reaction: Economics and Politics in Germany, 1815–71* (Princeton: Princeton University Press, 1958); David Crew, *Town in the Ruhr: A Social History of Bochum, 1860–1914* (New York: Columbia University Press, 1979); Leonard R. Berlanstein, *The Working People of Paris, 1871–1914* (Baltimore: Johns Hopkins University Press, 1984), is one of the most interesting recent monographs in opening new facets to the history of the working classes and their conditions; see also Peter N. Stearns, *Lives of Labor: Work in a Maturing Industrial Society* (New York: Holmes and Meier, 1975) and Yves Lequin, *Les Ouvriers de la région lyonnaise*, 2 vols. (Lyons, France: Presses Universitaires de Lyon, 1977).

24. Standish Meacham, *A Life Apart: The English Working Class 1890–1914*

(Cambridge, Mass.: Harvard University Press, 1977); Eric Hobsbawm, *The Age of Capital, 1848–1875* (New York: Scribners, 1975).

25. E. P. Thompson, "Time, Work-Discipline, and Industrial Capitalism," *Past and Present* 38 (1967): 56–97; see also his *The Making of the English Working Class* (New York: Vintage Books, 1966; first published 1963).

26. E. P. Thompson, "The Moral Economy of the English Crowd in the Eighteenth Century," *Past and Present* 50 (1971): 76–136; Charles Tilly, *The Contentious French* (Cambridge, Mass.: Harvard University Press, 1986), for his most recent of many studies on patterns of worker protest; see also William M. Reddy, *Money and Liberty in Modern Europe* (Cambridge, England: Cambridge University Press, 1987).

27. Eric Hobsbawm, "Custom, Wages, and Work Load in Nineteenth-Century Industry," in *Laboring Men* (New York: Basic Books, 1965), is a crucial interpretation; see also Stearns, *Lives of Labor*.

28. W. Andrew Achenbaum, *Old Age in the New Land: The American Experience since 1790* (Baltimore: Johns Hopkins University Press, 1978); Brian Gratton, *Urban Elders: Family, Work, and Welfare among Boston's Aged, 1890–1950* (Philadelphia: Temple University Press, 1985); Carole Haber, *Beyond Sixty-Five: The Dilemma of Old Age in America's Past* (Cambridge, England: Cambridge University Press, 1983); Peter N. Stearns, *Old Age in European Society: The Case of France* (New York: Holmes and Meier, 1976); William Graebner, *A History of Retirement: The Meaning and Function of an American Institution, 1885–1978* (New Haven: Yale University Press, 1980).

29. James Walvin, *Leisure and Society, 1830–1950* (New York: Longman, 1978), and Hugh Cunningham, *Leisure in the Industrial Revolution* (London: Croom Helm, 1980), are good introductions, the second with a fine bibliography.

30. Roy Rosenzweig, *Eight Hours for What We Will: Workers and Leisure in an Industrial City, 1870–1920* (Cambridge, England: Cambridge University Press, 1983); William J. Baker, *Sports in the Western World* (Totowa, N.J.: Rowman and Littlefield, 1982); Benjamin G. Rader, *American Sports: From the Age of Folk Games to the Age of Spectators* (Englewood Cliffs, N.J.: Prentice Hall, 1983); Gareth Stedman Jones, *Languages of Class: Studies in English Working Class History* (Cambridge, England: Cambridge University Press, 1983), and "Working-Class Culture and Working-Class Politics in London, 1890–1900: Notes on the Remaking of a Working Class," *Journal of Social History* 7 (1974): 460–508.

31. E. A. Wrigley, *Population and History* (New York: McGraw-Hill, 1969), remains a useful introduction; see also Charles Tilly, ed., *Historical Studies of Changing Fertility* (Princeton: Princeton University Press, 1978); E. A. Wrigley and Roger Schofield, *The Population History of England* (Cambridge, England: Cambridge University Press, 1981); Richard Easterlin, *Population, Labor Force, and Long Swings in Economic Growth: The American Experience* (New York: Columbia University Press, 1968); Maris Vinovskis, "Recent Trends in American Historical Demography," *American Review of Sociology* 47 (1978).

32. Roger Lane, *Violent Death in the City: Suicide, Accident, and Murder in Nineteenth-Century Philadelphia* (Cambridge, Mass.: Harvard University Press, 1979); Howard Zehr, *Crime and the Development of the Modern Society: Patterns of Crimi-*

nality in Nineteenth-Century Germany and France (London: Croom Helm, 1976); J. J. Tobias, *Urban Crime in Victorian England* (New York: Schocken Books, 1972); Eric H. Monkkonen, "A Disorderly People? Urban Order in the Nineteenth and Twentieth Centuries," *Journal of American History* 67 (1981): 539–59.

33. Theodore L. Steinberg, "Dam-Breaking in the Nineteenth-Century Merrimack Valley: Water, Social Conflict, and the Waltham-Lowell Mills," *Journal of Social History* 24 (1990): 25–46.

34. There has been increased attention to certain variables. Some important quantitative work has focused on literacy, in discussing whether measurable advances in literacy and schooling played a causal role in encouraging Western industrialization. There is considerable agreement (as in the case of Germany) that while correlation for initial industrialization is scant, literacy gains salience in advancing the industrial process. A fine recent survey, with good bibliography, is Harvey J. Graff, *The Legacies of Literacy: Continuities and Contradictions in Western Culture and Society* (Bloomington: University of Indiana Press, 1987); Carlo Cipolla, *Literacy and Development in the West* (Harmondsworth, England: Penguin, 1969); Peter Lundgreen offers an interesting case study: *Bildung und Wirtschaftswachstum in Industrialisierungsprozess des 19 Jahrhunderts* (Berlin: Colloquium-Verlag, 1973) and "Industrialization and the Educational Formation of Manpower in Germany," *Journal of Social History* 9 (1975): 64–80.

35. Katrina Honeyman, *Origins of Enterprise: Business Leadership in the Industrial Revolution* (Manchester, England: University of Manchester Press, 1983); François Crouzet, *The First Industrialists: The Problem of Origins* (Cambridge, England: Cambridge University Press, 1985); W. D. Rubinstein, *Men of Property: The Very Wealthy in Britain since the Industrial Revolution* (New Brunswick, N.J.: Rutgers University Press, 1981); Anthony Howe, *The Cotton Masters, 1830–1860* (New York: Columbia University Press, 1984); Hartmut Kaelble, *Social Mobility in the Nineteenth and Twentieth Centuries: Europe and America in Comparative Perspective* (Dover, N.H.: Berg, 1986).

36. Keith Thomas, *Religion and the Decline of Magic* (New York: Scribners, 1986).

37. Michael Drake, ed., *Population in Industrialization* (London: Methuen, 1969), and the much-debated Thomas McKeown, *The Modern Rise of Population* (New York: Academic Press, 1976); Robert Rotberg et al., eds., *Population and Economy* (Cambridge, England: Cambridge University Press, 1986); Ester Boserup, *Population and Technological Change* (Oxford, England: B. Blackwell, 1981).

38. Immanuel Wallerstein, *The Modern World System*, 2 vols. (New York: Academic Press, 1980), and Immanuel Wallerstein and Terence Hopkins, eds., *Processes of the World System* (Beverly Hills, Calif.: Sage Publications, 1980); see also Albert Bergeson, ed., *Studies of the Modern World System* (New York: Academic Press, 1980); and Sidney Mintz, *Sweetness and Power: The Place of Sugar in Modern History* (New York: Viking Books, 1985).

39. Landes, *Unbound Prometheus*.

40. P. Kriedte, H. Medick, and J. Schlumbom, eds., *Industrialization before Industrialization* (Cambridge, England: Cambridge University Press, 1981); see particularly Medick's essay, "The Proto-Industrial Family Economy," and Kriedte,

"Proto-Industrialization between Industrialization and De-Industrialization"; for a critique, see D. C. Coleman, "Proto-Industrialization: A Concept Too Many," *Economic History Review*, 2nd series, 36 (1983): 435–48.

41. A fine recent study using the protoindustrial concept is Gay L. Gullickson, *Spinners and Weavers of Auffray* (Cambridge, England: Cambridge University Press, 1986); see also Carlo Cipolla, *Before the Industrial Revolution: European Society and Economy, 1000–1700* (New York: Norton, 1980); Rudolf Brauns, *Industrielisierung und Volksleben* (Winterthur, Switzerland, 1960); and Dolores Greenberg, "Reassessing the Power Patterns of the Industrial Revolution: An Anglo-American Comparison," *American Historical Review* 87 (1982): 1237–61.

42. Charles Tilly, *Big Structures, Large Processes, Huge Comparisons* (New York: Russell Sage Foundation, 1985).

43. Wallerstein, *Modern World System*; Peter Burke, *Popular Culture in Early Modern Europe* (New York: New York University Press, 1978); Walter J. Ong, *Orality and Literacy: The Technologizing of the World* (London: Methuen, 1982); Lawrence Stone, *The Family, Sex, and Marriage in England, 1500–1800* (New York: Harper & Row, 1977).

44. Peter N. Stearns, *Life and Society in the West: The Modern Centuries* (San Diego: Harcourt Brace Jovanovich, 1988).

45. John R. Gillis, *The Development of European Society, 1770–1870* (Boston: Houghton Mifflin, 1983); Peter N. Stearns and Herrick Chapman, *European Society in Upheaval: A Social History since 1750* (New York: Macmillan, 1991).

46. Edward Shorter, *The Making of the Modern Family* (New York: Basic Books, 1975); Anderson, *Family Structure*; see also Michael Anderson, *Approaches to the History of the Western Family, 1500–1914* (London: Macmillan, 1980); Philip J. Greven, Jr., *The Protestant Temperament: Patterns of Child-Rearing, Religious Experience, and the Self in Early America* (New York: New American Library, 1979).

47. A good introduction is D. K. Fieldhouse, *Economics and Empire, 1830–1914* (Ithaca, N.Y.: Cornell University Press, 1970); see also Tony Smith, *The Pattern of Imperialism* (Cambridge, England: Cambridge University Press, 1981).

48. William L. Langer, *Diplomacy of Imperialism*, 2 vols. (New York: Knopf, 1935); Stewart C. Easton, *The Rise and Fall of Western Colonialism* (New York: 1964). Classic statements are J. A. Hobson, *Imperialism, A Study* (Ann Arbor: University of Michigan Press, 1965); and V. I. Lenin, *Imperialism, The Highest Stage of Capitalism* (New York: International Publishers, 1974; originally published 1917).

49. Michael Adas, *Machines as the Measure of Men: Science, Technology, and Ideologies of Western Dominance* (Ithaca, N.Y.: Cornell University Press, 1989).

50. Daniel R. Headrick, "The Tools of Imperialism: Technology and the Expansion of European Colonial Empire in the Nineteenth Century," *Journal of Modern History* 51 (1979): 231–63, and *The Tools of Empire: Technology and European Imperialism* (New York: Oxford University Press, 1981).

51. Leslie Bethell, ed., *The Cambridge History of Latin America*, vol. 6 (Cambridge, England: Cambridge University Press, 1986), is the most useful general recent survey, particularly essays by William Glade, Rosemary Thorp, and Colin M. Lewis. An old "classic" is Roberto Cortes Conde, *The First Stages of Modernization in Spanish America* (New York: Harper & Row, 1974). There are also a number of

excellent national studies, among them, Warren Dean, *The Industrialization of Sao Paulo, 1880–1945* (Austin: University of Texas Press, 1969); Barbara Weinstein, *The Brazilian Rubber Boom, 1850–1920* (Stanford, Calif.: Stanford University Press, 1983); Thomas F. O'Brien, Jr., *The Nitrate Industry and Chile's Critical Transition, 1870–1891* (New York: New York University Press, 1982); Rosemary Thorp and Geoffrey Bertram, *Peru 1890–1977: Growth and Policy in an Open Economy* (New York: Columbia University Press, 1978); John H. Coatsworth, *Growth against Development: The Economic Impact of Railroads in Porfirian Mexico* (De Kalb: University of Northern Illinois Press, 1982); Marcos Palacios, *Coffee in Colombia 1870–1970: An Economic, Social, and Political History* (Cambridge, England: Cambridge University Press, 1980); Stephen H. Haber, *Industry and Development: The Industrialization of Mexico, 1890–1940* (Stanford, Calif.: Stanford University Press, 1989).

52. Charles Bergquist, *Labor in Latin America: Comparative Essays on Chile, Argentina, Venezuela, and Colombia* (Stanford, Calif.: Stanford University Press, 1986).

53. Charles Issawi, *An Economic History of the Middle East and North Africa* (New York, Columbia University Press, 1982) and, as editor, *The Economic History of Turkey, 1800–1914* (Chicago: University of Chicago Press, 1980); Roger Owen, *The Middle East in the World Economy, 1800–1914* (New York: Columbia University Press, 1981); Donald Quataert, "Machine Breaking and the Changing Carpet Industry of Western Anatolia, 1860–1908," *Journal of Social History* 19 (1986): 473–90.

54. Gilbert Rozman, ed., *The Modernization of China* (New York: Free Press, 1981).

55. Thomas Cochran and William Miller, *The Age of Enterprise: A Social History of Industrial America* (New York: Macmillan, 1962); George R. Taylor, *The Transportation Revolution, 1815–1860* (New York: Rinehart, 1951); Albert W. Niemi, Jr., *United States Economic History* (Washington, D.C.: University Publications, 1987); Douglas North and Terry Anderson, *Growth and Welfare in the American Past* (Englewood Cliffs, N.J.: Prentice Hall, 1983); Jonathan Prude, *The Coming of Industrial Order: Town and Factory Life in Rural Massachusetts, 1810–1860* (Cambridge, Mass.: Harvard University Press, 1983), one of the best recent case studies.

56. David Montgomery, *Workers' Control in America: Studies in the History of Work, Technology, and Labor Struggles* (Cambridge, England: Cambridge University Press, 1979); Sean Wilentz, *Chants Democratic: New York City and the Rise of the American Working Class, 1788–1850* (New York: Oxford University Press, 1984); David Grimsted, "Ante-Bellum Labor: Violence, Strike, and Communal Arbitration," *Journal of Social History* 19 (1985): 5–28.

57. David Hounshell, *From the American System to Mass Production, 1800–1932: The Development of Manufacturing Technology in the United States* (Baltimore: Johns Hopkins University Press, 1985).

58. Chandler, *Visible Hand*; and Alfred Chandler, *Scale and Scope: The Dynamics of Industrial Enterprise: A History—1880–1940s* (Cambridge, Mass.: Harvard University Press, 1989).

59. Loren Baritz, *The Servants of Power* (Middletown, Conn.: Wesleyan University Press, 1960); Daniel Nelson, *Managers and Workers: Origins of the New*

Factory System in the United States, 1880–1920 (Madison: University of Wisconsin Press, 1975).

60. Herbert Gutman, *Work, Culture, and Society in Industrializing America* (New York: Knopf, 1976); Alan Dawley, *Class and Community: The Industrial Revolution in Lynn* (Cambridge, Mass.: Harvard University Press, 1976); Michael H. Frisch and Daniel Walkowitz, eds., *Working Class America* (Urbana: University of Illinois Press, 1983).

61. Kaelble, *Social Mobility*.

62. Clarence Danhof, *Change in Agriculture: The Northern United States* (Cambridge, Mass.: Harvard University Press, 1969); Jonathan Prude, *Coming of Industrial Order*; Steven Hahn and Jonathan Prude, eds., *The Countryside in the Age of Capitalist Transformation* (Chapel Hill: University of North Carolina Press, 1985); Christopher Clark, "Household Economy, Market Exchange, and the Rise of Capitalism in the Connecticut Valley, 1800–1860," in *Expanding the Past: A Reader in Social History*, ed. Peter N. Stearns (New York: New York University Press, 1988), pp. 305–26; James A. Henretta, "Families and Farms: Mentalite in Preindustrial America," *William and Mary Quarterly*, 3rd series., 35 (1978): 3–32.

63. John Demos, *Past, Present, and Personal: The Family and the Life Course in American History* (New York: Oxford University Press, 1986); Tamara K. Hareven, *Family Time and Industrial Time: The Relationship between the Family and Work in a New England Industrial Community* (Cambridge, England: Cambridge University Press, 1982).

64. Herbert P. Bix, *Peasant Protest in Japan, 1590–1884* (New Haven: Yale University Press, 1986).

65. Gerschenkron, *Economic Backwardness*; R. P. Dore, ed., *Aspects of Social Change in Modern Japan* (Princeton: Princeton University Press, 1967); Marius B. Jansen and Gilbert Rozman, *Japan in Transition, from Tokugawa to Meiji* (Princeton: Princeton University Press, 1986).

66. John McKay, *Pioneers for Profit: Foreign Entrepreneurship and Russian Industrialization* (Chicago: University of Chicago Press, 1970); William Blackwell, *The Beginnings of Russian Industrialization, 1800–1860* (Princeton: Princeton University Press, 1968).

67. Stephen Frank, "Cultural Conflict and Criminality in Rural Russia, 1801–1900," Ph.D. diss., Brown University, 1987; Ben Eklof, *Russian Peasant Schools. Officialdom, Village Culture, and Popular Pedagogy, 1864–1914* (Berkeley: University of California Press, 1986); John Bushnell, *Mutiny amid Repression: Russian Soldiers in the Revolution of 1905–1906* (Bloomington: University of Indiana Press, 1985).

68. Rose L. Glickman, *Russian Factory Women: Workplace and Society, 1880–1914* (Berkeley: University of California Press, 1984); Victoria E. Bonnell, *Roots of Rebellion: Workers' Politics and Organizations in St. Petersburg and Moscow, 1900–1914* (Berkeley: University of California Press, 1983); Reginald E. Zelnik, *Labor and Society in Tsarist Russia: The Factory Workers of St. Petersburg, 1855–1870* (Stanford, Calif: Stanford University Press, 1971); Diane Koenker, *Moscow Workers and the 1917 Revolution* (Princeton: Princeton University Press, 1981).

69. Reginald Zelnik, "Passivity and Protest in Germany and Russia," *Journal of Social History* 15 (1982): 484–512.

70. Moshe Lewin, *The Making of the Soviet System: Essays in the Social History of Interwar Russia* (New York: Pantheon, 1985); William J. Chase, *Workers, Society, and the Soviet State: Labor and Life in Moscow, 1918–1929* (Urbana: University of Illinois Press, 1987); Ann D. Rassweiler, "Soviet Labor History of the 1920s and 1930s," *Journal of Social History* 17 (1983): 147–58; Hiroaki Kuromiya, *Stalin's Industrial Revolution: Politics and Workers, 1928–1932* (Cambridge, England: Cambridge University Press, 1988).

71. Kazushi Ohkawa, *The Growth Rate of the Japanese Economy since 1878*, 4th ed. (New York: St. Martin's Press, 1981); G. C. Allen, *A Short Economic History of Modern Japan* (London: Macmillan, 1981); James C. Abegglen, *The Strategy of Japanese Business* (Cambridge, Mass.: Ballinger, 1984); William W. Lockwood, *The Economic Development of Japan: Growth and Structural Change* (Princeton: Princeton University Press, 1954).

72. Andrew Gordon, *The Evolution of Labor Relations in Japan: Heavy Industry* (Cambridge, Mass.: Harvard University Press, 1985); see also Hugh Patrick, ed., *Japanese Industrialization and Its Social Consequences* (Seattle: University of Seattle Press, 1973).

73. Gerschenkron, *Economic Backwardness*, p. 26.

74. Wallerstein, *World Economy*; see also the many articles on the world economy that appear in the journal *Review*.

75. Rozman, *The Modernization of China*; see also Michael Gasster, *China's Struggle to Modernize*, 2nd ed. (New York: Knopf, 1983).

76. I. T. Berend and G. Ranki, *The European Periphery and Industrialization, 1780–1914* (Cambridge, England: Cambridge University Press, 1982); Charles W. Anderson, *The Political Economy of Modern Spain: Policy Making in an Authoritarian System* (Madison: University of Wisconsin Press, 1970); George H. Hildebrand, *Growth and Structure in the Economy of Modern Italy* (Cambridge, Mass.: Harvard University Press, 1965); Jane Horowitz, *Economic Development in Sicily* (New York, 1978); K. J. Allen and G. Stevenson, *Introduction to the Italian Economy* (New Haven: Yale University Press, 1976); Charles Kindelberger, *Europe's Postwar Growth* (New York: Columbia University Press, 1973).

77. Robert L. Downen and Bruce Dickson, *The Emerging Pacific Community: A Regional Perspective* (Boulder, Colo.: Westview Press, 1984); *Pacific Basin Economic Handbook* (New York: Columbia University Press, 1987); Douglas Philips and Steven Levi, *Pacific Rim* (Hillside, N.J.: Enslow Publishers, 1988).

78. See references in note 51; also, Clark W. Raynolds, *The Mexican Economy: Twentieth Century Structure and Growth* (New Haven: Yale University Press, 1970); Laura Randall, *An Economic History of Argentina in the Twentieth Century* (New York: Columbia University Press, 1978); and Peter Evans, *Dependent Development: The Alliance of Multinational, State, and Local Capital in Brazil* (Princeton: Princeton University Press, 1979).

79. Montgomery, *Workers Control*; Patrick Joyce, *Work, Society, and Politics: The Culture of the Factory in Later Victorian England* (New Brunswick, N.J.: Rutgers University Press, 1980).

80. Harold J. Perkin, *The Origins of Modern English Society, 1780–1880* (London: Routledge and Kegan Paul, 1969), pp. 3–5.

Industrialization and Gender Inequality

LOUISE A. TILLY

There is no hardship in women working for a living,
the hardship lies in not getting a living
when they work for it.
—Clara Collet

To what extent did industrialization reduce gender inequality? This blunt and simple question is a basic one in women's history. As Clara Collet suggests, there is no simple answer.[1] Jeffrey Williamson's econometric study of male earnings and income inequality in the British Industrial Revolution finds that during the century from 1760 to 1860, excepting the period of war with revolutionary and Napoleonic France, inequality among men in Britain rose. He sums up: "The income shares at the top rose, the shares at the bottom fell, the relative pay of the unskilled deteriorated, the premium on skills increased, and the earnings distribution widened." In the 1830s and after, however, the real wages of the average (male) worker rose.[2] Williamson's ingenuity in uncovering sources that can be quantified for analysis is matched by that of Claudia Goldin, who has analyzed U.S. wage data for men and women from 1815 to the present, focusing on the ratio of female to male earnings. Although this earnings ratio (for full-time workers) narrowed substantially with the new availability of manufacturing jobs in addition to agricultural ones in the early nineteenth century, and a similar narrowing occurred with the initial opening up of clerical jobs, there has been no sustained improvement for decades.[3] Both Williamson and Goldin produce valuable and interesting comparisons by simplifying the question to the point where relatively reliable evidence over long periods can be found and compared among groups and over time.

For many historians, these econometric analyses leave out too much.[4] Women's historians have excelled in studies of work, gender relations in the household, and politics that draw a less precise, more nuanced, and complex picture. Overall trends in gender inequality are exceedingly difficult to determine not only because any aggregate measure of the phenomenon must combine many dimensions but also because the respective importance of specific forms of gender inequality varies over space and time. In the face of these daunting problems, I have chosen to address the extent to which *forms* of gender inequality have varied with different political and economic conditions, rather than absolute levels or trends. The hypothesis underlying the cross-national comparisons presented here is that over long periods, political economic factors—markets, trade, technology, the organization of production and social reproduction (in particular, the sex division of labor in the workplace and the home), national and local policies—lie behind variations in gender relations. Modifications in these arenas, shaping and interacting with demographic processes and history (including cultural practices, ideologies, and social movements), change opportunities for communities, classes, families, and individuals to make their living, acquire resources, cope with and control their lives.[5] This essay compares recent historical research about these matters (with emphasis on the sex division of labor), puts forward the outlines of a synthesis, and proposes an agenda for continuing historical research.

The Debate on the Industrial Revolution and Women

Writing in the 1920s, Ivy Pinchbeck—the first modern historian who addressed the central question of the effect of the Industrial Revolution on women's lives—was of two minds. Rejecting any preindustrial golden age, she argued that although women workers' conditions in the early factories were bad, they were no worse than those in nonmechanized jobs (dressmaking, for example) done in households, in which they were exploited by greedy middlemen. Factories meant better wages and a higher standard of living. Married women (the majority of whom did not earn wages regularly) were subjected to greater inequality—she admitted—than wives had been when they contributed directly to family income. This was not all bad, Pinchbeck wrote, for the Industrial Revolution "led to the assumption that men's wages should be paid on a family basis, and prepared the way for the more modern conception that in the rearing of children and in homemaking, the married woman makes an adequate economic contribution." Middle-class women, observing women workers' greater social and economic independence, Pinchbeck continued, became conscious of their own rights and demanded education and jobs for themselves.[6]

In the past twenty years or so the histories of women, family, and gender have become flourishing fields, and the relationship of industrial transformation and gender inequality a topic of renewed interest. Contemporary historians, writing in a period when feminists question gender relations in both public and domestic spheres, have not hesitated to historicize the family as well as the workplace. What is the current state of the question?

Not surprisingly, historians are still divided between optimists and pessimists about the effects of industrialization on gender inequality.[7]

Edward Shorter, a representative optimist, concerned primarily with men's and women's relations within the family, argues that a shift toward sex equality occurred about the middle of the eighteenth century. He writes of the "surge of sentiment"—linked with "laissez-faire marketplace organization, capitalist production, and the beginnings of proletarianization" that revolutionized family relations in western Europe. The "First Sexual Revolution," is revealed, he asserts, by increased illegitimacy rates in many parts of Europe. Access to wage-earning jobs, in particular those made newly available by industrialization, made women more conscious of themselves as individuals and ready to seek sexual pleasure.[8]

An exemplary pessimist is Sonya Rose, who addresses the failure of women's wage earning to reduce gender inequality in the workplace or the family. In her studies of the East Midlands hosiery industry, Rose argues for the interdependence of patriarchal and capitalist gender relations: When hosiery making moved to the factory and paid individual wages to men and women who had worked together cooperatively in household production, conflict between workers of the two sexes became more salient. The capitalists' solution was segregated jobs, with lower wages for women, and supervisory posts for some men. Rose concludes that both workers and their employers acted out of the belief that women's proper role was that of wife and mother and in doing so reinforced that ideology.[9]

There are still lacunae in our knowledge of the relationship of industrialization and gender relations. Nevertheless, enough evidence exists to make systematic comparisons, draw some modest conclusions about variation in the forms of inequality, and suggest an agenda for continuing research.

That is the goal of this essay.[10]

A Comparative Framework for Studying Gender Inequality

The task is to compare both patterns of large-scale structural change and social groups at the micro level, seeking regularities in variation of the forms of gender inequality as they are articulated with the process of industrialization.[11] Such comparisons must take history seriously, examining the ways in which what happens at one point in time may constrain what comes after, setting the conditions for developments in a second period.

Gender is defined as the social organization of relations between the sexes. Gender inequality is the structured pattern of gender asymmetries in well-being, as measured by capabilities. Here I adopt the conceptualization of Amartya Sen, who writes that "there is a good case for judging individual well-being, neither in terms of commodities consumed nor in terms of the mental metric of utilities, but in terms of the 'capabilities' of persons. This is the perspective of 'freedom' in the *positive* sense: who can *do* what." [12] The capabilities approach, he argues, can take account of personal characteristics such as sex and age and not simply the resources to which individuals may have access.

Sen has also proposed a dynamic way of conceptualizing the relationship between the sex division of labor in the household and that in the economy. He sees family as a site of cooperative conflict in which bargaining or negotiation is an ongoing process. Family bargaining involves cooperation and conflict because interdependency in the household "makes it fruitful for the different parties to cooperate, but the particular pattern of division of fruits that emerges from such cooperation reflects the 'bargaining powers' of the respective parties." Men's wages earned outside the household undergirded their stronger bargaining power early on; such an advantage could, following Sen, "lead to a correspondingly more favorable cooperative outcome for the men." The advantage gained at one point in time would lead to a stronger position in the next period of bargaining: "Certain 'traditional' arrangements may emerge, e.g., women doing housework and being able to take up outside work *only if* it is additional. These inequalities may solidify over time." [13]

Gender inequality increases when the difference between male and female capabilities increases, and vice versa. (Thus it is critical to distinguish changes that benefit men and women—of a given social group in a specified time and place—equally and those that reduce or increase inequality between them.) I examine capabilities in both domestic and public spheres, in production and reproduction (understood broadly as both physical and social), and in politics. Within arenas, national states, and time periods, I stress variation by class and gender (and where applicable, by race), and seek to show its systematic character. [14]

The English Case: The First Industrial Revolution

The concept of an Industrial Revolution has been challenged by economic and social historians, as Peter Stearns has shown. [15] I continue to use the words *Industrial Revolution* to describe industrialization in England because it was first, and because it was a unique event in its time.

Most of the population in seventeenth-century Britain lived in rural areas and worked in agriculture. Fertility and mortality rates were both high, but population growth was slow because of late marriage, a high degree of nonmarriage (and little reproduction outside marriage), and intermittent peaks of crisis mortality. Rural households produced most of the articles needed in their daily life (food, cloth and clothing, furniture, vessels for cooking and eating) with the help of tools often made by specialists. A sex division of labor existed within these households, but high levels of mortality and the small size of households meant that there were not always individuals of the requisite age and sex to perform a given task; hence there was flexibility in the division of labor.

As the manorial system and its feudal underpinnings broke up, parcels of land were assembled into large farms, rented and directed by farmers employing wage labor. They increased productivity by economies of scale and innovation in crop mix and rotation. Greater specialization in some occupations meant declining flexibility in tasks performed and fewer skills among nonspecialists, including women. Long before the conventional dating of the Industrial Revolution (1760–1860), then, sex and gender had become determinants of who would do a job, not capability. Women's jobs already had familiar characteristics: many fewer types, limited opportunities for advancement or the development of skill, lower pay than male jobs.[16]

Early modern urban economies were more highly differentiated centers of commerce and consumer production, with craft workers usually organized in guilds. Diverse urban populations were linked by the exchange of goods, services, and cash. There too, productive units were small, often households. Construction, food production, and cloth and garment making were all oriented to local demand. Servants (who provided personal service but often participated as well in household production for exchange) were a large proportion of urban workers; there were also wage earners outside the guild system whose numbers increased over the centuries. Although there were some women's guilds, and a woman could inherit her husband's guild mastership, there was a clear sex division of labor in early modern cities, with most women engaged predominantly in petty trading, sewing, domestic, or menial waged labor.[17]

By the end of the seventeenth century, capitalist organization of household production—protoindustry—was spreading outward from the cities, as merchant entrepreneurs sought profits through evading guild control of markets. According to Hans Medick, the sex division of labor in protoindustry was more flexible, task assignment less determined by gender than that in households engaged in large-scale agriculture or urban manufacturing. Capital–labor relations were less oppressive in protoindustry than in later large-scale industry, and households were charged with assigning tasks among themselves; the cooperation implicit in this family economy promoted gender equality, he believes. Others show a residual rigidity in the sex division of labor, however, partly a result of mothers' integral role in physical reproduction, and partly because men do not seem to have contributed to even the limited amount of housework done in the period. Thus it was that women were permitted—and often required by family need—to engage in production for exchange, while men specialized in such work and left physical and social reproduction to their wives. Household-based labor was offered to impoverished rurals; women's family responsibilities were fitted around their wage work. The availability of such work made it easier for rural people to marry young, and population grew more rapidly in many protoindustrial areas than in areas where such opportunities did not exist.[18]

Patterns of employment in British agriculture suggest proportionately increasing, and more regular, employment of males in the south and east in the eighteenth century, with only a postharvest and winter dead season. After 1750, female agricultural unemployment rose in the harvest season and after, as women's wage earning was limited to the spring season (when lower-waged tasks were performed). Gender differentiation had increased in agricultural occupations. In a parallel process, women's agricultural wages fell continuously from 1760 on, while male real wages rose or were steady until about thirty years later. In the west of England, where women were the preferred workers in dairying and pastoral agriculture, a pattern gendered in the opposite sense prevailed, with female real wages rising above male in the early nineteenth century. K.D.M. Snell argues that increased specialization of grain cultivation in the east, changing agricultural technology (the substitution of heavier harvesting tools such as scythes for the sickle), plus social variables like the decreasing age of marriage and higher fertility rates lay behind these changes. By the 1830s, there had been a substantial decline in rural women's earning capabilities. A parallel decline in women's access to apprenticeship occurred in the eighteenth century. There was no "golden age" of women's work: Women were always the minority of apprentices, sometimes a very small one indeed, and they were unlikely ever to be economically independent; " 'male' trades were indeed male dominated."[19]

Changes in rural women's work opportunities sent many women to cities to seek jobs. Domestic service was the chief urban occupation open to girls and women migrating from the countryside. Such jobs were easier for rural women to get than either craft or factory jobs, for which urban connections were important. Service also provided room and board, thus avoiding the problems of finding lodging and its expense. In a Lancashire textile town in the mid-nineteenth century, live-in servants were found primarily in households with no wife or ones with young children. These households were frequently those of retailers, in which servants helped in the shop as well as doing domestic work. The typical servant was a solitary maid-of-all-work. She was likely to be young, as service was a life-cycle occupation, a way for rural women to earn an urban living before marriage. The predominantly rural origin of servants was a consequence as well of urban women's disdain for such jobs, and their alternative opportunities. As the English population urbanized in the course of the nineteenth century, the supply of servants dwindled, and the occupation started to decline proportionately.[20]

To what extent did the industrial revolutionary changes in the organization of production improve or hurt women's position as workers?

Textile manufacturing had long provided work for women. Although the new cotton-spinning machines put women hand spinners out of business, the water frames and jennies continued to provide jobs almost exclusively for women and children. The spinning mule (introduced later) required more physical strength and was more expensive to buy and maintain; it quickly became a male-operated machine, and even when more easily managed models became available, the male mule spinners' union opposed the employment of women and children. (Historians disagree about the mule spinners' motives: To what extent did they seek to exclude women and children totally; or was their opposition a tactic to achieve a shorter workday for all workers in the spinning rooms?) The factory organization of production that developed employed male cotton spinners assisted by women and children piecers, and adult cotton weavers of both sexes, assisted by child tenters. This division of labor entailed a modified family economy with factory textile jobs for persons of both sexes and different ages; in the cotton industry, "family wage" referred to wage pooling. In the late nineteenth and early twentieth centuries, cotton weaving was one of the few specialties in which wage *rates* were equal for men and women in the same occupation, married women worked on a regular basis, and women workers were likely to be union members. Indeed, these three characteristics were integrally connected.[21]

Maxine Berg shows that early technological change in the metal trades neither involved increased scale nor replaced the household workshop. In Birmingham, where small metalwares were the specialty, women and children specialized in button manufacturing; in areas where heavy industry dominated, women were nailers or chain makers, trades already degraded and poorly paid in the eighteenth century. Later, women's jobs were confined to the lighter and unskilled branches. The new technologies did not involve a sharp break, but deepened gender divisions already in place. The worsening wages and working conditions for women in the Birmingham metalware industry in the nineteenth century were consequences of decline in the industry itself and defensive capitalist cost cutting.

The subdivision of labor processes (driven by the search for efficiency) proceeded in other industries as well. Women workers were usually confined, by employers' decisions, to occupations designated as less skilled and were paid lower wages. The reorganization of the clothing industry, for example, writes Angela John, "confirmed rather than disturbed the basis of gender relations."[22]

Courtauld's, one of England's major silk manufacturers, sought to shape its workers' lives in the family as well as the workplace. In the nineteenth century, silk weaving (formerly concentrated in London) migrated to regions such as Essex, where cheap labor could be found because of structural unemployment in the woolen industry and in agriculture. There the company initiated such policies as the gender segregation of jobs, distinctive male and female mobility patterns (the former, involving a minority of workers, provided ladders for vertical mobility; the latter, affecting the majority, permitted only horizontal mobility), and various paternalistic schemes to teach orderly habits, mostly to women. When women's labor-market position improved at the end of the nineteenth century, Judith Lown argues, an alliance of capitalism and patriarchy blocked their efforts to forward their own interests. The "family wage" (one adequate to support a family) granted men workers by Courtauld's at this time tended both to reinforce patriarchy in the household and marginalize women in the workplace.[23]

In the Potteries (the six Staffordshire towns in which most English ceramic manufacturing was concentrated), innovative entrepreneurs had increased productivity organizationally, rather than through labor-saving technology, in the eighteenth century. There were jobs for men, women, and children in the potbanks. From 1861 to 1881, women (37 percent of the workforce), most of them unmarried, specialized in china painting, but some served (along with children) as assistants to skilled male turners and throwers. By 1901, 45.6 percent of ceramics workers were female, with a higher proportion of them married. Pottery couples had high marital fertility (much higher than did textile workers), as retrospectively measured in 1911. Child labor was still important in the twentieth century because of the workers' custom of subcontracting kin as helpers. In the potbanks (as in the cotton industry) the "family wage" referred to wage pooling among family members. Wives both worked for wages when needed and (as was common in all working-class families) were responsible for stretching the family's income. Women's wages were generally lower than men's, but their skill (well remunerated, relative to other women's wages) and their kin and community support networks contributed to two positive features of their lives: their relatively strong household position and high levels of union participation.[24]

The coal mining industry, providing vital fuel to factories, both grew and was transformed. Although earlier, wives and daughters had worked in the mines as members of family economies, helping male family members, by the nineteenth century this type of production had been superseded by larger-scale capitalist enterprise with a male workforce. There were very few women underground workers in the industry, but reformers called for laws to eliminate women from underground work. Abusive conditions were not addressed, nor was women's need for income; restrictive gender ideology drove women's exclusion. Exceptionally, mine owners and workers in Lancashire allied with feminist supporters of women's right to work to except the "pit brow lasses," girls and women who worked at the surface.[25]

Several studies of the effect of industrial transformation on working-class family relations and the domestic arena (which was of course thoroughly interrelated with the world of work) are especially telling in their translation of Sen's notion of family cooperative conflict into flesh and blood.

In the north of England, wives' responsibility for running the household was usually a matter of stretching inadequate wages, not "choosing" how to spend them. Wives were often obliged to pitch in to earn needed cash, through part-time "penny capitalism" (taking in washing, lodgers, or sewing, child minding, and retailing), charring, or full-time paid labor in textile factories. These women lacked developed concepts of their individual interests; their satisfaction came from performing their household tasks well and launching their children into the world of work.[26]

Interviews with Liverpuddlers about life in the 1920s and 1930s, although late for our purposes, provide another perspective on women's responsibility for the household budget. There, "deception and silences between husbands and wives—especially around financial questions—seemed imperative for ensuring household survival and marital stability." Women's labor-intensive efforts to supplement their husbands' wages were often ingenious, but their husbands simply refused to participate in money management, avoiding confrontation over the adequacy of their wage. Violence against wives was often a consequence of their contesting such an arrangement, challenging their husbands as wage earners when their own desperate efforts to stretch resources failed. Most often, the threat of violence was enough to silence wives, for they faced no less insecurity outside marriage.[27]

The emergence of a more rigid division of labor in many households, with husbands as the single wage earner, rendered wives' contribution incommensurate with that of their husbands and opened the way to its devaluation.

Fertility rates remained high among most groups in the English population through most of the nineteenth century. Mortality rates began to decline in the late eighteenth century among children and young people, ending the rough balance between births and deaths that had slowed population growth; the age of marriage fell to a low of twenty-one around 1800, increasing fertility. Earlier marriage has been attributed both to better real wages and to the availability of wages for women and children in protoindustry, booming in the period before 1800. (Since children were welcomed as workers in household production, there was little incentive for protoindustrial families to control fertility.) The 1851 census reported 1.7 million workers employed in factories, the wave of the future. Such industries as ceramics and textiles continued to employ many women and children, at least partly because of the family economy's adaptation to the factory. Protoindustry declined, and heavy industries such as railroad building and operations, metallurgy and engineering, and mining grew as a proportion of the industrial sector in the 1840s and later. Except in urban garment making, in which sweated household-based industry spread in the second half of the century, women's employment fell. Single working-class women continued to do wage work, but married women were more likely to earn in household production or part-time work, or to go in and out of the labor force in patterns shaped by local labor markets.[28]

In Britain as a whole, women's and children's monetary contributions to households declined, the age of marriage edged up, and lifetime non-marriage increased. The new conditions made fertility control a rational decision for working-class families. Couples married in 1861–69 had an average of 6.16 children; those who wed in 1890–99 had 4.13 children; and 1920–24 couples had 2.31 children. By the decade before World War I, average age at marriage was back to twenty-four, its 1700 level. Illegitimate fertility, which had risen along with legitimate fertility in the late eighteenth century, also fell in the last decades of the nineteenth. David Levine links fertility decline to changes in the organization of production and corresponding reorganization of social reproduction in the family.[29]

Another nineteenth-century demographic phenomenon relevant to gender inequality is the high female mortality rate relative to male in age groups from ten to thirty-nine years that became apparent in the late 1830s. In these age groups, rural females had *higher* death rates than urban women, who were in turn better off than urban males. By the 1870s, this age- and sex-specific pattern had begun to erode, and by 1900, it had disappeared. There were similar patterns in continental Europe and the United States. S. Ryan Johansson's explanation is that British rural girls and women were disadvantaged vis-à-vis males because of their reduced access to wage labor and declining economic value. With urbanization and better care in pregnancy and childbirth, female life expectancy improved appreciably: A woman born in 1831 could expect to live into her mid-sixties; a woman born in 1891 would live on average to her late seventies. Male life expectancy increased more slowly and remained lower than female, a pattern still evident today.[30]

In their examination of gender relations in the middle-class family and enterprise from 1780 to 1850, Leonore Davidoff and Catherine Hall argue that middle-class men were "embedded in networks of familial and female support which underpinned their rise to public prominence." Women made contributions to the family enterprise through work, contacts, and inherited capital. Because of civil disabilities, however, married women could not accumulate capital on their own account.

They voted and spoke in dissenting churches, however, and made financial contributions as well. Women's religious activity in the evangelical reform movement brought them into the public sphere at the same time that they were constrained by practices sanctioned by domestic ideologies that evangelical social commentators, many of them women, delineated.

Indeed, middle-class women themselves were committed to an "imperative moral code and the reworking of their domestic world into a proper setting for its practice." Legal, political, and social institutions subordinated women at the same time that they recognized their contribution to the family enterprise. As those businesses became larger scale, women were more and more limited (and limited themselves) to managing their large families (and forwarding their interests in private ways). The social relations that emerged with industrialism defined a middle-class male world of politics and production and a female world of domesticity; middle-class women were denied the citizenship that men earned in the period. Despite ideological and legal impediments, however, some middle-class women earned their living (however inadequate), and many were active in philanthropic causes, thus making an important and acceptable—contribution to society and laying the groundwork for feminist activism.[31]

Increasing electoral participation by men after the Reform Bills expanded suffrage, and collective action by workers promoting their interests did not go unnoticed by women. Middle-class women's aspirations, and need, for jobs of their own often reflected a new feminist consciousness that grew out of their experience as single women and widows, frustrated in their efforts to avoid dependence on men. The diary of a self-supported middle-class woman who found her independence, her income, and her very access to her daughter denied when she separated from her husband echoes other feminists in declaring that respectable jobs, including professions, should be available to "honest independent women."[32]

Starting with Lady Caroline Norton's efforts to gain custody of her children, the first organized English feminist movement focused on married women's property rights (including control of their own earnings and child custody in divorce). Barbara Leigh Smith, one of its activists, published a book on *Women and Work* in 1857, and middle-class women—partly through their own efforts, partly through the creation of new jobs or transformation of old ones—slowly gained access to higher education, to such professionalizing occupations as nursing, social work, and teaching, and to a broad range of service occupations such as office and retail clerking. These were designated women's jobs, for the workforce as a whole remained highly segregated, with all women's jobs more poorly paid than men's with similar qualifications. The growth of service occupations expanded women's capability to support themselves and contribute to their families.[33]

Woman suffrage emerged as an issue with John Stuart Mill's amendment to the Second Reform Bill changing the word "man" to "person." It was defeated. By 1900, when a group of Lancashire women textile workers petitioned Parliament in support of suffrage, middle-class suffragettes were actively promoting working-class women's participation in the movement. They found it among textile workers, who were likely to work for wages over long periods (often throughout their lifetimes) and were active in unions. In their persons, the effects of industrialization on women's rights was much more direct than Pinchbeck realized. After an intensive, broadly based campaign for political rights (suspended in the war years) women over thirty were granted the suffrage in 1918, the vote at twenty-one (like men) in 1928.[34]

In the same period, middle-class women mounted a social movement that forced the repeal in 1886 of the Contagious Diseases Acts, laws that imposed medical examinations and possible arbitrary incarceration on women accused of prostitution in cities with an important military presence. The crusaders objected to the acts as immoral and unconstitutional, for they applied a double standard. Some three thousand women ran for and held local public office from the last decades of the century to World War I. Others founded voluntary associations that set up maternal and child welfare programs and agitated for increased government responsibility in the field. Such influential reformers as Beatrice Webb and Helen Bosanquet were members of the Poor Law Commission of 1909. Women were important actors, along with men, in initiating local welfare policies and contributing to the formulation of national welfare legislation. The welfare programs passed by the Liberal government before World War I included old-age pensions, unemployment insurance, and rudimentary health insurance, all of which were contributory, thus involving wage earners in covered industries. Because many women's jobs were not covered, and because few women spent enough years in the labor force to be covered, they were beneficiaries largely through their husbands' earnings.[35]

The British government sought to reduce women's and children's vulnerability by restricting their access to jobs during the time of rapid industrialization. (Would-be reformers sometimes misidentified the problem, and the "protective" laws they sponsored prevented women and children from earning needed wages while leaving exploitative conditions untouched.) This was the period in which middle-class opinion leaders elaborated an ideology of domesticity that became a general goal—for themselves and for workers and their families. Paternalistic employers and women charity visitors pressed working-class women in particular to conform to these new standards. Neither government nor employers' policies were designed to make it easier for married women to work, whether they had to out of necessity or wished to. (Working mothers had to make private arrangements for child care, buy prepared food, and skimp on housework and cleanliness unless their female kin could help them.) Women workers found it hard to take advantage of support programs for mothers and children (at first private, later incorporated into public welfare) because of demanding rules and impractical office hours in such programs; some also objected to intervention in family affairs. Government programs, then, were not always a positive force in improving women's work and home situations; they forbade women to earn wages under conditions perceived as inappropriate or exploitative, but failed to address real needs.[36]

In sum, over the long run the average standard of living rose substantially in Britain for both women and men. Early immiseration of populations whose way of life was undermined by industrialization, and those who endured the unhealthy housing and working conditions and the cycles of boom and bust of the first factory industries, was attenuated by the middle of the nineteenth century. Mortality rates declined, but suggestions of gender inequality in availability of food and health care persisted in the higher death rates of girls and women and in household budget studies (which continued to show female self-denial). Compulsory primary schooling was available free to boys and girls by the end of the nineteenth century, preparing both for better jobs, and educated women were able to get jobs that challenged their capabilities. Both sexes benefited from the fertility decline, but women doubtless experienced greater gains here, and improved capabilities vis-à-vis men. But the division of labor in the household probably became more rigid in middle- and working-class households in which women did not participate formally in the labor force. Wives whose wage work was vital to family wage pooling, such as those in cotton textiles or pottery making, may have gained (or did not lose) leverage in bargaining with their husbands. These same women suffered double burdens because they had major (or full) responsibility for maintaining the household.

In the workplace, women's occupations were restricted and segregated; crowding in few occupations contributed to lower female wages whether an individual worker was supporting herself, and possibly dependents, or whether she was contributing to a family wage. It became rare for men and women to hold identical jobs, but even when they did (cotton weaving) or when women had jobs with qualifications similar to men's (china painters on the potbanks), women's earnings were lower, and they were highly unlikely to have access to supervisory positions or promotion ladders. (Conditions favorable to women in these industries did, however, bring some women into unions and social movements.) Sex segregation was the rule not only in industrial jobs but in most service and many professional jobs as well. Women professionals were often able to support themselves; these women were less likely to marry, either by choice or by circumstance.

The rigidification of job segregation with the increasing scale of production in industrialization—with "housewife" the most segregated job of all—meant continuing gender inequality in both labor market and family. The specifics of these inequalities were determined quite locally. There were few jobs that women never did anywhere, but there were segregated jobs and occupations everywhere. What was skilled, what was heavy work, what was appropriate for men and women—these were a local matter, sometimes bargained between male workers and employers, sometimes decided wholly on employers' prerogatives. Women and children formed a flexible workforce; they entered labor markets in the interstices, serving as helpers to men, holding jobs that did not require long training or had little authority or that men did not want.[37] The family–wage–work nexus, despite an Industrial Revolution, was one in which inequality was inextricably intertwined.

French and German Comparisons

France and Germany began industrialization with economies and political systems that were quite different from the British; hence industrialization in each of these countries followed distinctive paths. The outcomes shared some characteristics with Britain, but differed in important ways as well.

The French kings' drive for centralization and consolidation in the early modern period failed to impose uniform laws or governing institutions (or an adequate fiscal system) in the process of creating a unified territory. Local law and varying forms of local governance with differently negotiated relationships to the monarchy lingered until the French Revolution of 1789–95.

France's eighteenth-century agricultural economy was organized through noble and ecclesiastical landowners, most of whom left the cultivation of their lands (and often decisions about technique and crop) to peasant households that paid customary rent and labor obligations in return. Peasants' holdings became increasingly insecure, while the customary dues and rents they owed their landlords and their taxes (from most of which the higher orders were exempt) rose in the course of the eighteenth century. French agriculture was not highly productive. Although peasants were usually thoroughly involved in markets (at minimum, in order to raise the cash to pay their rent and taxes), they often had to seek means outside agriculture to piece together a living. Protoindustrial entrepreneurs, as in Britain fleeing urban guilds and high costs, offered poverty-stricken households a way to earn wages. Sending household members to cities or wealthy provincial houses as servants was a common peasant survival strategy as well. Although there was specialization in agriculture directed to urban markets, most households continued to produce their own grain. The proportion of the British and French populations engaged in agriculture was similar in about 1750 (65 and 75 percent respectively); what was different was the organization of agricultural production.[38]

France was less urbanized than England, although Paris, like London, was exceptionally large and economically diverse in comparison to provincial cities. Royal policies to encourage urban industry emphasized luxury consumer products such as tapestry, china, and crystal. Private enterprise, operating within France's restrictive economy, nevertheless had expanded substantially (largely in textile production, where reorganization and increased scale were characteristic). Overall rates of economic growth in the eighteenth century were similar to those in Britain, as was the typical urban economy. The guild system persisted in France, however, despite royal efforts to end it, for the monarchy could not afford to pay off the loans that the guilds had made.[39]

Old regime cities were characterized by a gender division of labor. Girls and women usually worked in food, textile, or clothing production or in domestic service. Servants were not specialists in personal service or housework (except in wealthy households); they often spun, wove, sewed or cooked for their employer's business as well. In Lyon, small-scale production of silk was the chief industry; in Le Puy and several cities of the Nord, domestic lace making occupied many women; and in Normandy and Picardy, some large-scale textile mills grouped hundreds of workers. Women workers were integral to the French economy; in most cities, the female jobs they did were similar to those in Britain, as were the conditions—low wages, long hours, and little opportunity for advancement.[40]

The French Revolution ended many of the economic and political barriers to free internal trade and established principles of constitutional rule with broad-based male citizenship and political rights (women were explicitly excluded from such rights during the most radical period of the revolution). It also led to years of warfare with other European nations, which sought to reverse revolutionary changes. The Napoleonic reforms completed centralization and rationalization of government administration. Overall, both urban and rural manufacturing sectors stagnated from 1789 to 1815, except for the few years of peace under Napoleon.

The peasantry benefited from the sweeping away of elite privilege, including fiscal and labor obligations; some were able to buy land or acquire favorable contracts to farm it. Economic growth resumed after 1815 and the return of peace. A centralized monarchy with limited political participation was restored. France's economy was still primarily agricultural with pockets of protoindustry or small-scale manufacturing and some relatively large-scale manufacturing—of cotton textiles in Normandy, Alsace, and the North, and of metal and machines in Lorraine and the south-central reaches of the Loire Valley.[41]

French demography differed from that of England partly because of diverging economic and political conditions, which were accentuated over the revolutionary period. Earlier, as in England, population had been held in check by late marriage and crisis mortality peaks; but during the eighteenth century, the age of marriage increased steadily in France, unlike in England. During and after the revolutionary and Napoleonic periods, fertility control by the couple spread. Both female age at marriage and rates of celibacy declined over the nineteenth century (again unlike England).

Nineteenth-century sociologists believed that the Napoleonic Civil Code lay behind the fertility decline. Although revolutionary legislation included a more liberal family law, the Napoleonic Code both returned to older patriarchal strictures on women's and children's rights in the family and prescribed a uniform partible inheritance system. Landowning or land-controlling peasants, according to some analysts, faced with the possibility of their newly won landholdings being divided among many children, adopted deliberate limitation of births a full fifty years before English fertility rates declined. So too did the bourgeois class, whose property was equally threatened by partible inheritance. Reviewing the literature on French fertility decline, however, the anthropologist Martine Segalen concludes that inheritance law is not a sufficient explanation for fertility decline; ecological, economic, and cultural factors also contributed to it.[42]

Looking briefly at gender relations in nineteenth-century French peasant households, we find Edward Shorter arguing that these households were characterized by extreme gender inequality and female subordination. Wives served husbands and family unquestioningly; in return, they were treated with indifference or contempt. Martine Segalen argues that, to the contrary, the couple's relations were characterized by complementarity, "not absolute authority of one over the other," that grew out of peasant patterns of work and sociability, often done in same-sex groups rather than married couples. A wife's status was enhanced by the economic contribution she made to the household and her ritual and work relationships with water, fire, and thread. Beyond the household economy and community sociability, however, peasant women had few claims to authority or power, while men enjoyed citizenship and voting rights starting in 1848.[43] Given this important caveat, the centrality of women to peasant households and the reciprocal pressure for cooperation in production and reproduction are consistent with Sen's approach, if one adds his notion of conflict as integral to cooperation.

In the 1840s, transportation and communication improved with the building of railroads and the expansion of local roads to integrate formerly isolated areas. Greater interregional—and international—competition among agricultural producers was a consequence that in turn increased specialization and productivity. French urbanization, which also contributed to greater agricultural efficiency, was rapid, proceeding at a rate only slightly lower than that of the British. Nevertheless, the large peasant agricultural sector, and its distinctive gender patterns, continued to be central in French economic and social organization before 1914.[44]

Industrialization was gradual in France, with few sharp discontinuities. Much nineteenth-century economic growth did not involve major transformations of scale or technology. The spinning jenny, which could be used in the household, and the heavier, more expensive mule jenny and water frame were introduced shortly after they were developed in Britain. By 1840, spinning mills in the Nord and Alsace were relatively large scale. Weaving mechanized more slowly (as in Britain), but after the state encouraged railway building, the French cotton industry became competitive on an international scale. The wool and silk industries also reorganized and expanded in the first half of the century, but transformation there was slower than in cotton.

Handloom weaving continued in the north and west, with impoverished hand weavers being paid so little that their products were competitive with machine-woven cloth. In their households a family economy based on the cooperation necessary for survival continued; inherent in that cooperation, however, were also conflicts between parents and children, husbands and wives. Women in the factory textile industry were clustered in less-skilled and poorly paid jobs; they were favored workers in linen spinning and weaving, but in better-paid wool and cotton spinning or weaving, they were more likely to be preparatory workers or helpers. Patterns of segregation varied from one community to another. In the large-scale cotton spinning mills of Roubaix (in the Nord) women circulated at the bottom of the job hierarchy or did preparatory work. In the smaller-scale spinning mills of nearby Amiens, where there were more men's jobs outside textiles, women were likely to hold a wider range of jobs and were excluded only from the top of the job hierarchy.[45]

Heavy industry—mining, metallurgy, and engineering—was the more dynamic sector after midcentury, and it employed primarily men. At the same time, France's early fertility decline and consequently slower population growth produced chronic labor shortages; as a consequence, women more often held jobs (in the machine industry, for example) that would have been male jobs in Britain.

There were distinct, often local, gendered occupational patterns in France, but compared to Britain, these have been little studied. In Limoges, a center of porcelain production comparable to the Potteries of Staffordshire, for example, there are indications of the substitution of less-skilled women plate decorators for highly skilled males who painted designs by hand, and women workers' substantial representation in unions. There is room here for more industry-specific case studies of gender relations.[46]

As in Britain, there were few female jobs in French coal mining areas. Girls and young women did coal sorting at the surface, but married women were much less likely to do wage work, and there was a sharp division of labor within the household. In many mining towns or villages women ran small shops, sewed, or did laundry for their neighbors; or they sold prepared foods, like the "penny capitalists" reported in English towns. Strikes in mining areas were community affairs, with women and children joining demonstrations and attacking nonstrikers.[47]

The French garment industry was characterized by subdivided organization of production and a gendered discourse. Many of the women who sewed "white goods" (underwear, men's shirts, towels, sheets, and so on) lived in the countryside or in smaller cities, as well as in suburbs or poor neighborhoods in Paris; they received the lowest wages of any branch in the industry. Seamstresses who sewed women's outerwear for individual clients might be better paid, especially if they could copy fashionable styles from magazines. In Paris, more elaborate differentiation was the pattern; skilled, well-paid couturières were permanent employees of large outerwear companies and were assisted by less-skilled women with simple specialties. As elsewhere, men dominated the task of cutting garments. The bane of the garment industry was seasonal unemployment, which made the lives of female garment workers very precarious.[48]

In contrast, France's women tobacco workers were in an exceptionally strong labor-market position. They worked in the twenty government manufactories dispersed throughout France. Women made up 80 to 90 percent of the workers in these plants, and they were highly skilled, having undergone an apprenticeship in which they learned all the women's jobs in the industry, including cigar making; these women often worked in teams and developed a group spirit. The jobs were well paid (although women's wages were never as high as men's in the industry) and stable; women tobacco workers responded to these conditions by making lifelong careers in the tobacco monopoly and becoming activists in their unions and major actors in strikes. The government conceded important benefits to women workers: pensions, maternity leave, nursing breaks, and flexible hours when they had infants—even priority for their daughters in applying for jobs in the monopoly.[49]

The large department store revolutionized French (and world) merchandizing in the second half of the nineteenth century; women became clerks as well as customers. The public sector offered women access to clerical and professional jobs (such as postal clerks and teachers) that had career ladders and were awarded on merit. The latter were both rapidly growing occupations in the nineteenth century. A successful experiment utilizing women postal clerks in 1892 led to rapid feminization of clerical services, opposed by the male union and dismayed moralists, but supported by feminists promoting new opportunities for women. Jobs for women teachers opened up when an act requiring compulsory free public schooling was passed in 1882 because schools were sex segregated. Women were perceived to be the most appropriate teachers for girls and younger children. Normal schools were established for training women teachers, including an elite school for teachers destined for female lycées. Children faced examinations at all levels of schooling, and in government service competitive examinations were the key to entry and advancement. When higher-level jobs, such as school inspectors, were opened to women, they were recruited in the same way as men—by examination. This centralized bureaucratic system was favorable to middle-class women's aspirations for *métiers*.[50]

A comparison of the English and French censuses from 1850 to 1960 shows that French women were consistently a higher proportion of the non-agricultural labor force. There was nevertheless considerable sex typing in jobs, depending on sector and local labor markets.[51]

Relatively little research has been reported about husband–wife relations in French working-class households. Husbands' and wives' motives for controlling births may have differed, but the common methods required cooperation by the couple, whether they were peasant or bourgeois. Some working-class groups, such as miners and handloom weavers, and some peasants, were slower to reduce fertility because wage-earning children continued to be critical to families into the twentieth century.[52]

Married women usually had full responsibility for the household budget. Accounts from textile cities report that nonworking wives expected their husbands' full wage packet, out of which they returned spending money. The son of a Parisian working-class couple described his mother's skill in "managing" his father's modest wages. She also moved in and out of the labor force to help make ends meet; his parents were solicitous of their children's needs, but also expected mutual assistance from them. From the Paris suburbs comes a less happy picture: paydays marked by bitter disputes, even blows over how much of a husband's pay was legitimate for his wife to claim. A mother's sense of competence, a contemporary reported, came from her ability to do her job well. A clean, well-fed, and respectably dressed family testified to her managerial skills. In the best situations, the ethic of mutual assistance prevailed; in others, conflict and disagreements were dominant.[53]

In northern France, bourgeois women participated extensively in the management of family businesses during the early development of the textile industry. Many were as a consequence little concerned with the household and child care; they sent their infants to wet nurses and their children to boarding school, instilling in them a strong sense of family loyalty.

Although the bourgeoises of the Nord made critical contributions to the accumulation of physical and human capital, they were excluded by the Napoleonic Civil Code from full participation in business or the public sphere of politics. The increasing scale of industry in the second half of the nineteenth century made it difficult for married women (especially mothers) to operate in both domestic and industrial arenas. Bourgeois women writers defined and prescribed a domestic ideology for women of their class. Through their church-related philanthropic work, careful management of the domestic economy, and practical upbringing of children, these women contributed to the cultural elaboration of their regional middle-class way of life, but much of their visible participation in business disappeared in the Belle Epoque.[54]

The revolutions of 1789 and 1848 saw the emergence of advocates for women's political rights (many of whom had radical or, especially in 1848, socialist connections); they were silenced both times. Moderate feminist groups organized as a new French republic was constructed after 1870. Sensitive to the fragility of national political consensus (and fearing that women's vote might be dictated by Catholic priests), these republican feminists did not demand suffrage and called instead for reform in the civil status of women (through amendment of the Civil Code) and access to education and employment. Those who did call for women's suffrage were rebuffed by secular republicans in power. Women's civil status was somewhat improved by legislation in the years up to 1914 (women were granted control over their own earnings, for example), but the fight for suffrage failed; it was granted only in 1945.

Marital or sexual rights issues, such as eliminating the gender asymmetrical definitions of adultery and earning the right to file paternity suits, were more widely supported, but those calling for divorce or dissemination of information about and devices for birth control split feminists and other women along religious and class lines. Social feminists (here defined as those who promoted women's issues in a broad framework of social reform) cooperated with Catholic charitable organizations that advocated such reforms as the elimination of licensed houses of prostitution, pacifism, and temperance, programs that women moderates could support. The improvement of maternal and infant health was already on the agenda of pronatalists alarmed about "depopulation." Social feminists worked side by side with them for the early state welfare programs: clinics and maternity leaves, as well as public housing and family allowances, seen by the first as encouraging population growth and the second as supporting the poor and vulnerable. Most French social legislation was shaped by concerns about depopulation, but it was supportive of women's childbearing and relatively uncoercive. Nevertheless, the dissemination of birth control information and devices, and abortion, were criminalized. Social programs benefited women as mothers, but they ignored its pronatalist message. There was no comprehensive system of social insurance in France before World War I, as there was in Britain and Germany.[55]

No matter their politics, feminists were nearly all women of means. Women workers often were second-class citizens in the labor movement; tobacco workers and teachers were significant exceptions. Teacher socialist militants were conscious of gender inequality and argued that class-based organizations, such as unions, failed to support women in their everyday family relationships. No feminist and socialist worker alliance emerged because of genuine differences of interest, because most bourgeois feminists were insensitive to the problems of working women, and because most socialist women (despite organizational efforts across class lines) chose to work within unions and socialist groups, rather than with bourgeois feminists.[56]

France's slow industrialization, the continuing importance of its peasant economy, its early fertility decline, chronic labor shortages, and centralized bureaucratic state shaped gender patterns and the timing and content of change in women's capabilities. Thus Frenchwomen were more likely to be independent wage earners or members of household production units than the British, with the disadvantages (low wages, double burden, intense pressures for cooperation, but increased occasions for conflict) and advantages (a wider range of jobs, a material resource—the wage—to bring to household bargaining) that entailed. One result was that the family–productive work nexus seems to have been more benign (despite a similar ideological discourse) in France than in Britain. French middle-class women probably had more opportunities for meaningful jobs, but where their British sisters mounted a successful movement for the vote, the French failed. Differences in religious institutions and political history in the two countries were important factors here. Public policies supported motherhood for pronatalist reasons, but did not interfere with women as workers, so, because of early adoption of family limitation, they were better able to do wage work. French women's legal rights in marriage and suffrage were granted much later than they were in Britain. French economic and political organization mediated the effects of industrialization to produce forms of gender inequality that were different from the British—ones that provided opportunity for women in the economic arena but counted them out of formal politics.

Germany's industrialization was closely linked to its process of political unification, completed in 1871.[57] Indeed, the earlier lack of unity was a major obstacle to German economic development. At the time of the Treaty of Westphalia in 1648, there were about 350 separate political units in Germany; these were combined and simplified only in 1815.

In western Germany, as well as in the east, pressures against peasant landholding were great. Prussian noble landlords (unlike the French) were actively engaged in production of grain for distant markets. Serfdom in Prussia was not a holdover from earlier times but a system tying serfs to the land, instead of subjecting them to lords; a landless proletariat developed in the eighteenth century.

In this period, German urban manufacturing was primarily artisanal, and most states encouraged guild-controlled production of "manufactures," especially luxury goods and weapons; such schemes enjoyed little success. Jean Quataert argues that guilds conflated illegal and "dishonorable" household production and women's domestic work and sought to exclude women from manufacturing for exchange. This history shaped gender ideology and the sex division of labor into the nineteenth century. To the extent that women continued in household-based production for exchange, it was valued less than wage labor outside the household.[58]

Protoindustry nevertheless spread in Germany, producing not the luxury goods that states promoted but cruder textiles and small metalware for popular consumption. These industries contributed to substantial growth in the eighteenth century economy.[59]

French conquest and occupation in the revolutionary and Napoleonic periods united some German states and abolished internal duties. Areas incorporated into the French Empire were encouraged to expand coal and iron production; others stagnated. Napoleon's Continental System, which excluded British products, shielded some areas (the Ruhr Valley, for example) from competition, facilitating growth. In Saxony, large-scale cotton spinning was born. Crushingly defeated by the French in 1806, Prussia instituted economic reforms in order to resist. Serfs were emancipated in 1807 (implemented only after 1810), and limits on individuals' right to choose an occupation were ended in 1808. The Germanic Confederation, established by the peace treaties of 1814 and 1815, was composed of only thirty-nine sovereign states, including Austria. Prussia was awarded West-phalia and parts of the Rhineland, later to become the center of German heavy industry. It took the lead in promoting economic transformation by abolishing internal duties in 1816 and establishing uniform tariffs in all its territories. Railroad building began in 1835 and proceeded so rapidly that by 1875 the German Empire had more railroad mileage than any other con-tinental country. The outcome was a vigorous expansion of markets, and the development of the iron, steel, engineering (railroad locomotives and other machines), textile, and clothing industries.[60]

The German revolutions of 1848 failed to forge a political union with the Austrian lands. In 1866, Prussia provoked a successful war with Austria-Hungary, gaining lands contiguous to its territory. In 1871, after defeating the French, the confederation was transformed into the German Empire, a federation with the king of Prussia as emperor. Universal male suffrage at the level of the imperial Reichstag belied the more limited suffrage in the state legislatures (where fiscal and other important laws were passed) and the authoritarianism of the political system.

During the first two-thirds of the nineteenth century, the rationaliza-tion of agricultural landholding proceeded, making possible greater per capita output. Earlier, the sex division of labor on German farms had been relatively flexible, with women often substituting for men, who migrated to find temporary wage work. Childbearing and nurture apparently did not hinder women's labor on the farm. Peasants increased their claims on family labor in agriculture as rural protoindustrial opportunities declined and the cost of hiring day laborers rose. Women's tasks multiplied along with regional specialization in labor-intensive cultivation (potatoes, sugar beets, and other root crops) and stall feeding of animals for butchering. Farm women's increased workload (and probable undernutrition) may have contributed to higher female mortality in adolescence and the early child-bearing years, and to infant mortality.[61]

Population increased rapidly in nineteenth-century Germany. Over-seas emigration was heavy, especially between the 1840s and 1870, and again in the 1880s. The distances involved in internal migration grew longer as workers moved primarily from the agricultural east to the indus-trializing west and the older textile areas of Saxony. Could this migration have been an alternative in the east to earlier fertility decline? There has been no conclusive answer to this question, but we do know that female-to-male sex ratios in many of the agricultural sending areas were high, suggesting that women were not only taking over new tasks but were doing routine farm labor as well, because men who had done it in the past were working elsewhere. The earliest signs of German fertility decline began regionally in 1879; the process continued—varying in timing and rapidity from west to east and north to south—until the 1930s.[62]

Coal, iron and steel, and engineering were the leading sectors of German industrialization, responding to the demands of railroad building; the iron industry began its rapid rise in the late 1840s and had caught up with France in terms of annual production by 1870. The Ruhr Valley became a highly concentrated center of heavy industry. Textile mechanization occurred slowly, partly at least because so much of that industry worked with linen (which was both technically more difficult to mechanize and produced for local markets). Germany's comparative advantage in textiles was low wages, and the industry remained smaller scale than the British, selling most of its products in home markets.

Despite the rapidity of these changes, a large part of the German economy and its workers were still involved in small-scale, nonmechanized production. Although domestic production overall declined at the end of the century, it was largely male workers, especially hand weavers, who left to get better jobs elsewhere. Women and child workers became proportionately more important in domestic industry. One possible explanation for this was the new employment code, passed in 1891, that regulated working conditions for firms with over ten workers; children under age fourteen were forbidden to work and required to be in school; women's work hours were limited; and a four-week maternity leave was made compulsory. Women workers in industries that complied with the law were dismissed, but there was widespread noncompliance in industries such as textiles, which depended on women workers. In 1908, an amendment limited adult women to ten hours of work on weekdays, eight hours on Saturday. Household production was wholly unregulated until 1911, when a new law established an inspection system but did not regulate wages. The effort to "protect" women workers by granting them special status in practice limited them to the sector in which exploitation was most likely.[63]

Three manufacturing industries (clothing and cleaning, textiles, and tobacco) employed the largest numbers of women at the turn of the century. Service industries, such as domestic service and inn- and bar-keeping, were the other major employers. In all sectors except textiles, women were concentrated in household or small-scale production. Jobs were segregated by sex and women's wages were one-half to one-third lower than those of unskilled male workers.[64]

Evidence about conditions in industrial homework is abundant. Women who manufactured tobacco products in the household were especially disadvantaged, as were urban clothing workers, domestic servants, and women hand weavers. Nineteenth-century German workers' autobiographies suggest greater misery and family discord compared to the French. Reports of gender conflict increased in the early nineteenth-century records of a Wurttemberg village. A dismal postscript to German women domestic workers' situation is that since women hand spinners, sewers, knitters, and laundresses working in their homes were not covered by the industrial code, they also were not eligible for old-age pensions or health insurance.[65]

Clerical jobs expanded at the end of the nineteenth century, providing new opportunities for women in banking, insurance, shops, and government. These jobs were held primarily by young unmarried women, relatively well educated and possessing some skills (e.g., typing and shorthand), yet poorly paid; clerical work had increased in scale, division of labor, and specialization.[66]

Girls and boys did not have equal access to education in early nineteenth-century Germany despite far-reaching reforms in popular schooling. Literacy—a crude measure of schooling, for there was no one-for-one linkage of literacy and schooling—was lower among women than men in the nineteenth century. Girls were less likely to be schooled in most states. Secondary schools that offered technical training were primarily oriented to transmitting male skills. Advanced public schools inten 'ed primarily for middle-class youth were at first closed to females; when they began to admit girls, they were taught domestic skills, not the classic curriculum offered to boys. Women were teachers primarily in the coeducational primary schools. By 1900, eligible children were in schools, male–female differences in attendance had disappeared, and only curricular differences remained.[67]

Women's rights in the family were severely limited up to 1918. Husbands continued to hold full legal guardianship over children, and illegitimate children could not inherit even if their fathers recognized them. Although wives no longer were required to have their husband's permission to do wage work, and they were given control over their own earned income, the property a wife brought into a marriage was fully in the hands of her husband as administrator. Grounds for divorce were strictly limited.

Women's dependency and social inferiority were linked by social commentators and politicians to their biological (thus "natural" and "immutable") characteristics. In the first years of the empire, Prussia and other states had association laws that barred women, apprentices, and schoolboys from membership in political organizations and from attending their meetings. Women found ways to get around these prohibitions, particularly in the Social Democratic party. Only in 1902 did Prussia permit women to attend political meetings if they sat in separate sections—and in 1908 a national law (which superseded state laws) granted women the right of association.

As in France, women's politics, feminist or not, followed the complex fault lines of party politics but, in Germany, the context was an authoritarian state. Following Frederick Engels and August Bebel, the Social Democrats praised the liberating possibilities of participation in social production. Unlike other parties, they hoped to organize and mobilize women as well as men, and unlike middle-class feminists, they supported both female suffrage and protective labor laws to ease the exploitation of women. Based on the assumption that married women belonged in the home, and troubled by the conditions they observed, the Catholic Center party also supported protective laws.

Early middle-class feminist organizations did not make suffrage a primary goal, nor did they think of equality as a natural right. Instead, they conceived of rights as being achieved through women doing their duty, participating in public life (in local institutions), and eventually being granted the rights they had earned. They were more interested in gaining access to jobs and education (not unlike the French) than in abstract rights. By the late 1890s, suffrage became more central, and some feminists argued that women could contribute important feminine qualities to public life, from the courts to the schools to the factories. Modest reforms were proposed, but there was no alliance with socialists because of class differences and incompatible ideologies.

Women socialists developed thriving women's organizations within the bounds of the working class, but they were "reluctant feminists," eschewing women's issues that cut across classes. In 1914 there seemed little prospect of women getting the vote and other political rights in the near future; in 1918, after defeat in war and a revolution, the franchise was granted to women by decree.[68]

In Germany, unlike France, industrialization was rapidly achieved, and its agricultural sector was proletarianized as the peasant household economy was split by male migration to manufacturing or construction jobs in distant regions. German fertility decline followed industrialization with a considerable time lag, as it did in England. Women wage earners were concentrated in nonindustrialized sectors of the economy—household production, domestic service, and agriculture. Women who needed to earn wages were channeled into menial jobs at least partially through legal and ideological barriers. The family–productive work nexus in Germany seems to have been more troubled than the French or the English, with consequences for women's enjoyment of their capabilities.

In the political arena, the presence of a united socialist party with massive working-class support offered some working-class women scope for political participation while preventing them from seeking alliances with feminists, who were either nonpartisan or allied with other parties. Social legislation to relieve workers' insecurity was passed earlier than elsewhere in an unsuccessful effort to coopt workers' support. Redistributive social policies sometimes contributed to gender inequality, as did labor regulation. By 1914, German industrialization had raised the standard of living for German men and women; reform sponsored by feminists and socialists had improved women's legal position in the political arena and in marriage, thus increasing women's capabilities, and fertility decline was under way. New possibilities for clerical employment had opened up, but in 1914 most women's jobs were still clustered in agriculture and manufacturing, especially at the low waged, labor-intensive level. And gender inequality prevailed in the household. Women's capabilities had expanded, but so had men's, and there were few net gains for women.

The United States

European settlers in North America appropriated a relatively sparsely populated but fertile and spacious land from its Native American inhabitants. From the earliest settlement, agricultural development and its accompanying social organization differed regionally. In the North was a combination of independent family farms and greater urbanization; in the South, large-scale plantation and smaller farm cultivation of tobacco with hired or African American slave labor was more typical. In the eighteenth century, the North became more urban and commercial and began to industrialize, while the southern plantation economy spread, switching from tobacco to cotton cultivation. Labor was in short supply everywhere, so wages were better than those in Britain, attracting immigrants seeking a better life; the "coerced migration" of Africans was also substantial, partly because of their high mortality during passage and in the new disease environment.

The American Revolution was a rejection by the British colonists not only of their collective dependent position vis-à-vis Britain but also of the political and social order of European states. In its place was founded a decentralized state, in which authority was concentrated in the central government, but many political institutions and functions were controlled by the states.

The first water-powered mill was opened in 1790 in Rhode Island, but it was the dearth of manufactured imports during the War of 1812 that stimulated American industrialization. As in Britain, the process began in the cotton industry, where factory production first replaced household spinning, then weaving. The Lowell, Massachusetts, textile mills offered jobs in the 1820s and 1830s primarily to adolescent and young adult women from farm families. These workers' earnings were a transitional stage in their lives; they worked to contribute to a brother's education, to save for their own future marriage, or perhaps for some costly personal project, such as further schooling. They were also distinguished by their consciousness of their rights and willingness to strike for them. The textile industry's expansion ended in the depression of the last years of the 1850s.

By the 1840s, and even more in the 1850s, increasing immigration had eliminated labor shortages, and cotton mill owners found immigrant families from Ireland and French Canada both cheaper and more quiescent workers. Later in the nineteenth and in the first decades of the twentieth century, these immigrant men and women and their children would be both constrained and supported by their household and kin relationships. Before the Civil War, rural workers in household production of hand-woven textiles, palm hats, and shoes labored in small towns and the countryside, far from factories.[69] A progression from small-scale to factory production occurred in the boot and shoe industry in and around Lynn, Massachusetts. In the eighteenth century, women had sewed uppers as assistants to skilled male household members; at the end of the century, shoemaking was partially transformed into protoindustry, as girls and women worked longer hours, and more regularly. The industry mechanized and concentrated in the 1850s (over the protest of skilled males losing their monopoly of the trade), and women followed their jobs into factories.[70]

In the antebellum period, only a small proportion of women worked outside their homes, most of them single women, and an even smaller proportion worked in manufacturing—small scale (e.g., bookbinding) or large (e.g., cotton spinning). Domestic service was the most common sector for women's wage work; like the mill workers, servants were increasingly likely to be immigrants from Europe. Free African American women in the North were excluded from work in factories or skilled jobs; they were likely to be laundresses, cooks, or sometimes seamstresses. In the largely plantation-organized agricultural South, slave labor predominated. Rural areas with available water power housed cotton mills, and the various consumer industries—garment making, food preparation, construction, and skilled crafts—were located in cities; garment and food industries were female, and the latter were largely white male domains. Northern urban economies were not so different, except that immigrants took the place of slaves at the bottom of the occupational hierarchy. Male immigrants were also recruited to build canals and then railroads, which improved transportation on the east coast and toward the west. Many Americans continued to seek opportunity in agriculture and moved westward to find land.[71]

The Civil War opened new jobs in white-collar work for women with education or training—as clerks, professional nurses, and teachers. (The expansion of clerical and professional work for women is considered later.) Working-class women, mobilized for war work (sewing uniforms primarily) or filling in for absent male workers in urban industries had a more difficult time because they had little recourse against exploitative conditions. As individual workers, women were in a particularly weak position, for they often desperately needed jobs but had little work experience.

Dissatisfaction continued in the garment industry after the war ended.

Sewing machines had been introduced in the war years, and women worked either in workshops or at home, for extremely low wages. Where seam-stresses had formerly learned varied skills, now the jobs were broken into discrete tasks, and the garment was passed from worker to worker, each with her specialty. Despite such disadvantages, Carole Turbin shows, Troy women collar makers were successful in organizing a union, partly at least because they had support from men—some of them kin—in the town's iron molding industry; collar workers also set up a cooperative laundry when they lost their jobs in a lockout.[72]

The post–Civil War period saw rapid growth in large-scale grain mill-ing, meat slaughtering and packing, metal and machine production, and mining. Replacement of skilled male workers by women or less-skilled immigrants continued. In newspaper printing, employers attempted to undermine the apprenticeship system and strong organization of males by training literate women to do the job more cheaply. Male printers saw their masculinity compromised by women's competition, but accepted the linotype machine. With male workers' support, employers defined it as requiring endurance, hence boys and men were operators.[73]

Metal and machine manufacturing workers, mostly male, such as Troy's skilled iron molders, suffered deskilling with technological change and reorganization of the labor process. A view of such changes from the perspective of gender and family shows that, in the period in which Pittsburgh switched from iron to steel making and the mill labor pro-cess was subdivided, women's unpaid work in household maintenance and childrearing was essential. The sharp household division of labor in such cities promoted fragile gender relations in families. Women's wage work in Pittsburgh—less common than in cities with a more mixed industrial char-acter—was segregated not only by gender but by race and ethnicity and was poorly paid. The ways in which migration and urban economic change affected ethnic women's work and family lives in less specialized urban settings, such as New York, also involved both cooperation and conflict.[74]

Racial segregation and tensions in southern industry reduced the pos-sibility of workers' coalitions in the early twentieth century, undercutting both class and female solidarity in labor organizing and struggle. In the North Carolina tobacco industry, manufacturers of tobacco products con-structed a workforce ingeniously stratified by race and sex as early as the 1880s. White women operated the newly developed cigarette-making ma-chines; white men supervised them and maintained the machines; black men handled the heavy bales of tobacco and the fermentation process; and black women specialized in stemming tobacco leaves. At least temporary cooperation across race and class occurred in the southern textile indus-try as well. Cross-cutting class, gender, and ethnic divisions affected both middle- and working-class women's activism in Florida. A comparison of male and female labor process and work culture in cigar making as the occupation was mechanized and deskilled illustrates the contrary trends of gendered access to skill and displacement of skilled workers.[75]

Women workers' efforts to organize and strike, as well as their sometimes troubled relations with labor unions, have received a good deal of attention. Conventional historical accounts of the important Lawrence, Massachusetts, textile strike of 1912 that emphasize the role of the International Workers of the World (IWW) have been challenged by gender-centered revision. The garment industry strikes that occurred across the country in the same period have also been reexamined: The International Ladies Garment Worker's Union's (ILGWU) women workers and organizers lost a corset strike in Kalamazoo, Michigan, to intransigent employers despite appeals for support across class lines to middle-class women. The Rochester, New York, Chicago, Cleveland, and most famous of all, New York City garment industry uprisings were also characterized by complex relationships of women workers with male trade union leaders and middle-class women who wished to support but also control their struggle. The Women's Trade Union League was central to many of these efforts.[76]

The debate on the family wage that has engaged British women's historians has an American counterpart. The family wage (a male wage adequate to support a family) was originally a working-class cause that united men and women. Only in the twentieth century did it become an exclusively male ideal supported as well by some employers and middle-class reformers.[77]

The efforts of women industrial workers to organize in their interests and strike, even if successful, changed the relationship of their wages to men's only to the extent that occupational segregation declined (men workers dominated in better-paying jobs and better-paying industries, and they were more often organized in unions that could win better conditions). Claudia Goldin's painstakingly assembled wage-ratio series show a modest rise in the manufacturing earnings ratio in women's favor from 1850 to about 1885 when it reached .56; since then, despite cyclical fluctuation, it has "not materially budged." Around 1881 to 1907, when moral concerns about female employment peaked, women were likely to work more continuously than contemporaries believed, but their total job experience was relatively brief, for they exited the workforce promptly upon marriage, and the vast majority never returned. Because of employers' perceptions, women were limited to dead-end jobs and seldom received training; males had much longer total work experience, longer duration in current occupation and with current employer. Goldin concludes that only 20 percent of the wage differences can be laid to strictly defined "wage discrimination."

The gender wage ratio among *all workers* continued to narrow until the 1930s. This improvement primarily reflected the changing sectoral distribution of women's occupations, in particular the rise of clerical jobs, which were more desireable: cleaner, more respectable, and better paid. They also were at first less segregated, and wages at first hire were similar for the two sexes. A 1940 survey with comparable information on characteristics of individual male and female clerical workers again reveals similar initial wages, but, by this time, an extremely segregated workforce, with women limited to occupations with little possibility for advancement. (Men too were limited to specific occupations, but these were on career ladders.) For Goldin, this reflects "statistical discrimination" in personnel policies that treated women as a group having limited commitment and more likely to leave the labor force than men. Deliberate and conscious policies of sex segregation had become the norm sometime early in the twentieth century.[78]

Goldin's analysis is the most comprehensive done so far, but questions linger in her mind about the extent to which women in manufacturing arrived at the workplace with characteristics already shaped by discrimination and social expectations. There are also suggestions that employers simply sought women for low-waged jobs and men for responsible and better-paid ones. She notes an unexplained "bonus" paid only to married men and speculates whether employers had a notion of a "fair" wage for men. Only in her last chapter does she bring up the issue of women's disproportionate responsibility for children and the household.

The earliest movement of women workers from manufacturing to clerical occupations occurred in the Civil War temporary mobilization of women into government service, as Cindy Aron shows. It accelerated with the expansion of office work connected with large-scale industry, and of banking and insurance at the end of the century. The size of commercial enterprises selling consumer products also increased remarkably. Typewriters, telephones, mechanical bookkeeping machines, and cash registers became women's machines after 1890. Native-born, white, young women with a modicum of education poured into the ranks of clerical workers. In both merchandising and office work there was a good deal of subdivision of tasks and specialization in the labor process.[79]

American middle-class women resemble the British most closely in their involvement with class formation primarily through the domestic sphere (and its social extension in philanthropy and improvement of society) and in the elaboration of an ideology of domesticity, as Mary Ryan shows in her study of Oneida County, New York, from 1780 to 1865. Earlier patriarchal gender relations in the family disappeared in a burst of evangelical revivalism starting in 1814, which lasted until 1838. Women were the first converts to evangelicalism and sponsored the early revivals, changing the name of their Female Charitable Society to the Oneida Female Missionary Society. By the mid-1820s, men had assumed a more active role in revivalism and women retreated to the "home," where they raised their children and smoothed the way for male success in the business world. Women continued to be active in churches and in charitable and mutual support groups (the Maternal Association, for example). American fertility decline began early in the nineteenth century among white women, and (as measured by live births per 1,000 white women aged 15–44) had declined by 30 percent in 1850 and another 33 percent by 1900.

Within-class material conditions and ideological dispositions lie behind systematic variation in women's activity in urban benevolent, reform, and radical associations in the same period. A study of Tampa, Florida, at the turn of the twentieth century finds an "astonishing array of voluntary associations" of middle-class women concerned with the social changes associated with industrialization.[80]

The links between these associations and the women's suffrage movement are Suzanne Lebsock's focus in a synthetic essay that draws on recent monographic studies to map women's voluntarism in the public sphere. By 1890, women had a hundred-year record of fighting—most often in single-sex groups—for temperance, abolition of slavery, prison reform, education, better jobs and higher wages, women's rights in marriage, and suffrage. The Women's Christian Temperance Union (WCTU) was the paradigmatic case, mobilizing women under the banner of protecting the home. The Young Women's Christian Association (YWCA) offered social services to urban single women; women's clubs sought to beautify their towns and build hospitals; settlement houses hoped to help the destitute, support women and children, clean up urban politics, and promote social harmony; the birth control movement took up issues not ordinarily discussed and dispensed advice and devices; and the Women's Trade Union League sought to improve women's working conditions. Progressive women were influential in the passage and judicial acceptance of protective legislation that restricted the industries and conditions in which women could work. Later, still others chose to work with men in political parties—Republican, Democratic, Populist, Socialist—or in nonpartisan local reform politics to create welfare programs or fight corrupt politicians. African American middle-class women also participated in single-sex clubs and the Republican party, seeking to improve the social and political position of their people. Women's broad involvement with issues in the public arena contributed to their belief that suffrage was a prerequisite for achievement of their ambitious agenda. Their associational activity provided experiences that stood them in good stead in the suffrage campaign. In 1920, the Nineteenth Amendment granted women the right to vote.[81]

The United States differed from European countries in its seemingly limitless resources, its decentralized and participatory political system, and its opposition to federal government action in economic and social matters (modified only partially in the Progressive era). Temporal change in the ratio of women's to men's wages suggests that industrialization substantially improved that ratio through women's transfer first from agriculture to manufacturing and later from manufacturing to clerical jobs. In both sectors, however, there was an apparent "glass ceiling," as contemporary analysts have come to call it, by which employer policies, hostile male workers' opposition, and majority women's acceptance of social expectations ended further improvement.

By 1914, industrialization had improved the standard of living of the population as a whole, and fertility decline was achieved. Schooling, although it varied in quality and quantity from state to state, had achieved a minimum standard for white boys and girls; both were more likely to have access to secondary school than were Europeans. Working- and middle-class women were ably defending their perceived interests as well as promoting their vision of social good, activities facilitated by government decentralization. American women's high level of activism distinguishes them from continental Europeans and the British as well; many of the capabilities women gained in the period were at least partly the result of women's own efforts, although their activism was broader than the simple promotion of gender interests. They had clearly achieved high levels of capability. Nevertheless, problems remained: the sex division of labor in the household, gender segregation in the workplace, the barrier to further progress toward wage equality, and the unachieved agenda for women in electoral politics.

Japan

Economic and demographic changes in the last century of the preindustrial Tokugawa period (1602–1867) prepared the way for the more far-reaching transformation that began in the 1870s, after the Meiji Restoration of 1868.

The greater part of the Japanese population in the Tokugawa period was engaged in agriculture (estimates run from around 76 to 83 percent). Of the agrarian population, about 75 percent were peasant proprietors, who owed high land dues to their lord; the rest were tenants, who paid rent. The common unit of production was the household, hence holdings were small. Urban population growth promoted the development of markets, increasing productivity, migration (in theory, illegal), and rural handicraft production. Farm size declined with improved methods of cultivation stressing labor intensity, as larger holdings were subdivided and rented to tenants whose families were their labor force. Peasant living standards were very low, but agriculture became highly productive.

Manufacturing was not as dynamic as agriculture; it was divided between urban crafts organized in guilds producing fine textiles, clothing, decorative objects, food, or buildings and rural industry organized on a household basis by urban putters-out to spin and weave cruder fabrics. Larger-scale production of reeled and spun silk, iron, and sake had begun. Commerce was lively, and a road system was well advanced, partly because local lords (who lived in fortified castle cities with military retainers, servants, artisans, and merchants) were expected to spend long periods each year in the capital, Edo (now Tokyo). The castle cities were themselves important markets; they had developed fiscal and administrative specialization that prepared samurai landlord elites for leadership in later government-promoted economic development.[82]

Studies of the demographic and family changes that accompanied the gradual economic change of the Tokugawa period provide insight into the comparative capabilities of men and women in preindustrial Japan. The emergence of couple-headed households as the unit of agricultural production utilizing new technologies first spurred rapid population growth, followed by a static period, as Japanese peasant couples apparently began deliberately limiting fertility early in the nineteenth century.

How were households formed, and how did they pass on headship to the next generation? Stem households were typical; their rules permitted several generations of married couples in one household, but no more than one from any generation; the inheriting child was selected by the parents, but there was flexibility about which one was chosen. If there were no children, a child could be adopted as heir; when there were no male children, a male might be adopted to marry the inheriting daughter; noninheriting children were sometimes established in branch households.

Temporary (in intent, at least) out-migration to jobs in nearby agriculture or household handicraft industries was common and increased in the nineteenth century for both men and women—a kind of life-cycle service. Many women migrants ended their travels with marriage, at a significantly older average age than women who stayed in their parents' household. Work in handicraft production in one village was similarly connected to women's marriage age advancing by almost two years, as well as to a decrease in the differentially high female infant and child mortality rates. Young women benefited from contributing to their natal household's well-being; a higher age at marriage meant fewer years at risk of childbearing. Although divorce was quite common, compared to the mid-twentieth century, its consequences for women were less serious than its male-initiated arbitrary manner would suggest. This was true because divorce usually occurred early in marriage, remarriage was quite likely, and although the children were usually taken from their mother, they were likely to be valued and well cared for in their father's household.[83]

In preindustrial Japan, then, women's economic productive capabilities were valued relatively higher when wage-earning opportunities existed for them. Both men and women in country or city expected to marry, and in agriculture especially, a *couple* was indispensable for a viable household production unit. Anthropologists studying a remote farming village in the 1930s concluded that the peasant household structure and division of labor led to full interdependence of the couple.[84]

In 1867, disaffected samurai overthrew the shogun and restored the Emperor Meiji; their goal was to resist Western encroachment through rapid indigenous industrialization. Relatively efficient production of military weapons had begun in the Tokugawa period, but after the restoration the sector was quickly industrialized with state support. Large-scale textile industrialization was achieved by buying technology and know-how from Europe, again with initial government support. Rapid growth in agricultural land and labor productivity that met increased food demand (based on increasing per capita income) underwrote industrialization. Key improvements included better irrigation and drainage, better strains of food crops, and increased use of fertilizer. The agricultural productive unit continued to be the small farm household paying high taxes or, if tenants, high rents in kind, and expelling "surplus" young people (often females whose labor was less needed in cultivation) in a sometimes coerced migration to earn wages in urban industry.[85]

Japanese industrialization was "self-financed" by agriculture; the largest source of government income before World War I was the Meiji Land Tax of 1873. Political pressure for economic change, in which export-oriented textile production was critically important, not consumer demand, promoted Japanese development.

Henry Rosovsky believed that the textile labor force was recruited and retained through paternalistic policies that promoted worker loyalty. Although he admitted that the ideal was necessarily far removed from actuality, historians who have looked in more detail at women's jobs and working conditions have challenged this conclusion. The economic historian Gary Saxonhouse first called attention to the problems textile employers had in keeping their young female workers, who ran away regularly; high turnover continued into the 1930s, even after workers' situation improved. His analysis shows that entering cotton spinners had *lower* wages than female agricultural workers; hence they themselves were bearing the cost of training. If they left before their contract was up, however, they could easily find work elsewhere, as skills were similar among mills. Employers did not succeed in solving the problem of worker turnover until after World War II.[86]

The large-scale Osaka Cotton-Spinning Mill (opened in 1883) set the model for two practices that became central to Japanese cotton production: fine grading of job categories in which female's piecework wages were never higher than 58 percent of male and usually less; and shift work, with two twelve-hour shifts daily. By the mid-1890s, the supply of female workers within commuting distance from large mills had been tapped, and mill owners began to build dormitories to house country girls who lived farther away.

Recruiters went to the countryside with tempting offers of good wages, pleasant working conditions, and tasty food; impoverished families willingly signed contracts committing their daughters to long terms in the mills in return for advance cash loans. Daughters dutifully reported for work, only to discover filthy, locked dormitories; long workdays (and night shifts); brutal supervisors; and disciplinary fines withheld from their wages so that neither parents or daughters got the promised wages. Men were more often recruited locally and lived at home; they usually became mule spinners or machine menders and were paid higher salaries; women and girls were ring spinners, piecers, and assistants.[87]

By the 1920s, young women were more likely to have completed at least primary schooling, and they often chose to do factory work not only to help their parents but also to achieve their own goals. Fewer went back to rural areas to marry and raise families. Although conditions were still bad, they had improved at least partly because of strikes in major mills; after 1929, middle-class feminists and reformers persuaded the government to implement laws prohibiting child labor and women's late-night work, and the hours in each shift were cut. As women became more likely to stay with a firm longer, they were promoted to better positions.[88]

Silk reeling had been organized in Tokugawa times in both centralized filatures and merchant-organized putting out, using an improved type of reel. At the end of the period, some entrepreneurs separated the process of reeling from the cultivation of silkworms and set up more efficient mills, using French equipment and technicians; samurai landlords' daughters taught the new techniques to other women. As more labor was needed, poorer girls were recruited and housed in dormitories; they became "a class of temporary indentured servants or debtors," according to Gail Bernstein. Limited mechanization in silk reeling contributed to constant pressure on the women to work faster yet produce high-quality yarn. Nevertheless, it is not clear that the conditions of industrial spinners and reelers were worse than those of impoverished rural families or in prostitution (which together employed many more women workers than cotton spinning and silk reeling). The proportion of women workers in Japanese manufacturing continued to be higher than in the West. This reflected the importance of textile production and the continuing availability of rural females for employment in that industry.[89]

Before turning to the state's definition of women's role in the Meiji period and middle-class women's response, a brief look at women in the

Tokugawa merchant class is in order. Local custom in Osaka permitted women to act temporarily as household heads and indeed a certain number of them seized opportunities to run family businesses on this basis or in cooperative but subordinate relationships with male heads (fathers, husbands, or sons). Although only males were permitted to do the actual brewing of sake, several women ran very sucessful family sake businesses. Tatsu'uma Kiyo (1809–1900) was the power behind a sake brewery she managed with the help of an able male brewmaster. Her shrewd business sense was applied as well to family affairs: The marriages of her six children were veritable business alliances.[90]

The chief object of Meiji policymakers was to mobilize all resources, including people, in the pursuit of their twin goals: industrialization and national power. Hereditary restrictions on occupation and residence were quickly abolished so that an industrial workforce could be recruited. The Meiji Constitution of 1889 granted suffrage to males (based on property tax paid) in elections to the lower house of Parliament. Policies about women and the family took shape more slowly. In 1873, the government mandated compulsory public education for both boys and girls; in the same decade, elite women were permitted to play limited public roles similar to those in the West.

The early feminists, associated with liberal reformers, sought to win equal opportunity in education and work, legal rights in marriage, divorce, property holding, and the vote. In 1890, however, a Law on Associations and Meetings forbade women to attend public meetings (amended only in 1922), or join political parties (in force until 1945). Apparently, women's family and home duties, not their incapacity, were the justification for their exclusion. The Meiji Civil Code of 1898 "samurized" family relations, imposing samurai principles on the population at large: Husbands and fathers were granted absolute power as household heads; wives were considered legally without competence. An 1899 law opened secondary schools to girls; they were to be taught to be "good wives and wise mothers." During the Japanese wars around the turn of the century, women were mobilized in support of the war effort to serve as nurses and distribute assistance to widows and orphans. The feminine virtues that the state wished to see cultivated were modesty, courage, frugality, literacy, hard work, and productivity; neither motherhood nor domesticity was central in the period.[91]

As in Western countries, the service sector, which began to expand especially in the second decade of the twentieth century, opened up new jobs for women. Longer schooling qualified girls for jobs as teachers, social workers, nurses, telephone operators, government workers (here postal and railroad clerks were important), and other clerical work. Middle-class women sought these jobs out of need, because of heightened consciousness, or because they were increasingly available. Although some married women were in the labor force, most female workers were single; their wages were substantially lower than men's (sometimes as low as one-third of male wages for comparable skills).[92]

In the 1930s, as Japan again went to war with its neighbors, the contradiction between women's wage work and their demanding reproductive responsibilities became more acute. The slogans "good wife, wise mother," which exalted women's role in preserving the Japanese family system, and "rich country, strong army," which pushed women's contribution to industrialization, proved to be irreconcilable. Women were both urged to bear more children and mobilized into patriotic associations; a mother–child protection law designed to help single mothers raise their young children was passed in 1937. Motherhood was conceptualized in new ways. Some Japanese feminists collaborated with these war policies as a step toward gender equality because they permitted women a *public* role. In the end, the campaign for higher fertility was contradicted by the drive to hire women for what were formerly men's jobs. Although women were only drafted for war work in 1944, the experiences of the 1930s and the war years prepared the way for postwar changes.

In 1948, the patriarchal household family system (*ie*) was legally replaced by a nuclear family system in which husbands and wives had equal standing. Although initially insignificant, married women's wage work has increased in the postwar period, but men's and women's relationship to jobs and careers remains very different. Male labor unions emphasize firm-specific workplace conditions and stability, rather than collective bargaining about wages; women workers are perceived as needing protection. A structural dualism has emerged with a male elite enjoying lifetime employment and "needing" full-time wives to support the work commitment such a system required. The female–male wage ratio, 52, is the lowest among industrialized countries. Japanese women still usually leave their jobs when they marry and thereafter work only part time. State policy continues to be shaped by the principle that women's only proper role is familial; this ideology is accepted by the majority of men and women alike, and by such institutions as firms and labor unions. The Equal Employment Opportunity Law of 1986 has done little to change business policies that implicitly assume such a gender division of labor in the household and workplace.[93]

The distinctive characteristics of Japanese industrialization—the Meiji government's central role in promoting economic development and its translation into law of earlier ideals of the patriarchal household that had until then been only imperfectly reflected in ordinary people's lives—seem to have effectively limited any trend toward gender equality. Women were important contributors to the process of industrialization, as members of agricultural households on which the tax burden of the process fell, and as low-waged workers in its leading sector, cotton textiles. Although women shared the rising standard of living with men of their class, as well as reduced fertility, longer schooling, expanded participation in politics, and marriage and family law that theoretically is more equitable, the inflexibility of the division of labor in the household and lack of opportunity in the workplace continue to prevent full enjoyment of their capabilities.

China

Long before the British Industrial Revolution, Western countries had impinged on the rest of the world through trade, conquest, and colonization; industrialization increased the wealth and strength of the West and produced greater disparities between developed and less-developed regions.[94]

Although China as a whole was never a colony (as were many non-Western countries), in the nineteenth and twentieth centuries its resources and labor were tapped by foreign capitalists who enjoyed economic, political, and legal privileges not very different from those in colonies. At the same time, China maintained its language and culture and continued to produce thinkers and movements that were quite distinctive, shaped by the history and tradition, large size, and ethnic and ecological diversity of the country.[95] Nineteenth-century Chinese governments and private enterprise, like those of Japan, sought to promote industrialization, but Chinese development gathered force only after World War I, especially in the late 1920s and early 1930s, and again after World War II, under socialist auspices. Both China's Nationalist and Communist revolutionary policies were more consciously gender egalitarian in principle that those in earlier industrializing national states, Western or Japanese. China is not typical of late industrializing non-Western states, but it offers an opportunity to look at questions about the effect of factors present in many parts of the contemporary developing world on gender inequality up to the present.

From 1644 to 1911, the Qing dynasty, Manchu conquerors from the north, ruled China. The first century and a half of their rule saw systemization of the bureaucracy, renovation and extension of the canal system providing better transportation of goods and people, the development of new crops and flourishing crafts, increased monetization of the economy, and efficient tax collection. It also made possible population expansion.

John King Fairbank attributes the strongly patriarchal organization of families (with inheritance shared among male offspring, arranged marriages, patrilocal residence of married sons, and extreme subordination—exemplified by foot binding, a cruel custom that in northern China was common even among peasants—of women as daughters and daughters-in-law) to China's high population density, in addition to the more conventional explanation, the Confucian worldview. He emphasizes as well the "remarkable integration of state, society, and culture" and the highly bureaucratic state. By the end of the eighteenth century, population pressure, together with political corruption and social divisions (between men and women, old and young, landlords and tenants), had produced a highly volatile political situation.[96]

The imperial government, weakened by antirent and antitax rebellions, was unable to prevent opportunistic British export of opium from India to China. A British punitive expedition in 1839 against Canton, then against other coastal cities, opened the Opium Wars. The 1842 peace treaty imposed a huge fiscal indemnity on China, guaranteed British extraterritoriality (legal and political rights under English law in designated places in China) and granted missionaries the right to move freely around the country. A civil war—the Taiping Rebellion—gathered force in the 1850s, to be repressed only with Western assistance in 1864. (The Taipings were a millenarian sect professing a heterodox monotheistic religion incorporating elements of fundamentalist Protestantism.)

As in Japan at about the same time, elements within the government promoted a "self-strengthening" industrialization to produce arms and ships for military preparedness. It had few results. "Compradore capital" accumulation was more successful. Chinese merchants worked first with foreign firms, later on their own account, to develop silk filatures, steamship lines, coal mines, and cotton spinning and weaving companies (not subsidized but often supervised by government agencies) in the 1870s to 1890s.[97]

Foreign interventions and wars continued, however. As China faced the threat of partition in 1898, a liberal reform group persuaded the emperor to begin institutional and economic reforms. The effort lasted only a hundred days, ended by a seizure of power by the conservative traditionalist dowager empress. Despite the failure to reform the state and economy, new ideas began to circulate as greater freedom of speech, press, and association permitted debate among intellectuals and students. Again rebellion and foreign intervention interrupted the process, this time the 1900 antiforeign Boxer uprising in Shandong. The United States renewed its call for an "open door" to foreign commerce, and the Germans, British, Russians, and Japanese agreed to end territorial seizures in China. The settlement humiliated the Qing dynasty and revealed its powerlessness.

Discussion and reform groups, among them Sun Yat-sen's Revive China Society, which preached an anti-Qing nationalist, vaguely social democratic program, proliferated. New government reforms included the elimination of the daunting classical civil service examinations, the establishment of practical schools, and greater possibilities for Chinese to study abroad in Japan and later in Europe and the United States. A mutiny in 1911 (supported by the military and secret societies) against the recently ascended boy emperor led to the declaration of a republic. Sun Yat-sen was forced out of the presidency, and a promonarchy dictatorship was established instead (most Nationalists opposed this regime). During World War I, China seized the German and Austrian concessions, and its native industry thrived as Western imports disappeared from domestic markets.

When the Versailles Treaty was publicized, intellectuals and students vigorously objected to its stipulation that Japan would receive German rights and territorial concessions in Shandong Province. Protest on May 4, 1919, forced the government to refuse to sign the treaty and launched a revolutionary movement in which the Nationalist party (the Kuomintang [KMT]) and—after 1921 when it was founded in Shanghai—the Chinese Communist party (CCP) were uneasily allied. (In response to May 4, the young Mao Zedong organized a progressive society in Hunan.) The Soviet Russian-led Communist International advised the CCP to collaborate with the KMT but keep its own identity for later opposition and communist revolution.

Despite the pious declarations of an eight-power international conference in Washington in 1921–22, respecting Chinese sovereignty and agreeing to work for stability in the country, a period of regional warlordism and intergroup struggles ensued. Sun Yat-sen (then head of an independent KMT-governed region whose military aide in his last years was young Chiang Kai-shek) died in 1925. In 1927 the Communists were expelled from the KMT, and civil war became general. In 1928, the Nationalists under Chiang declared a nominally unified nationalist republic, which succeeded over the next eight years or so in promoting economic development and keeping order in many areas. It failed, however, to prevent the Japanese seizure of Manchuria in 1931, followed by further incursions into Chinese territory. In this period, through their experience in controling a territory in the southeast (the Jiangxi Soviet), the Communists developed strategies for mobilizing peasant military and economic support. The Communists were nevertheless forced to retreat to northern China (Shensi Province) in 1934 on the Long March, during which they suffered enormous losses.

In 1936, dissident warlord KMT troops captured Chiang; their Soviet advisers persuaded the Communists to seek his freedom and unite with the KMT to fight the Japanese. The cooperative effort failed. The Nationalists were weakened by their long fight against Japan and by corruption in their army, while the Communists enjoyed strong grass-roots support. Conflict between the two parties resumed. As World War II ended, the Communists held extensive rural bases in northern and central China, and the KMT nominally controlled the south. Starting in 1945 the Communist People's Liberation Army (PLA) conquered mainland China, and on October 1, 1949, declared the People's Republic of China (PRC).[98]

Mao Zedong was the PRC's undisputed leader in 1949, working with an experienced and tested team. Fairbank divides the period from 1949 to the present into economic and political consolidation to 1958, two great popular mobilizations supported by nongovernmental groups outside the party leadership—the Great Leap Forward (GLF, 1958–60) and the Great Proletarian Cultural Revolution (GPCR, 1966–69)—with the intervening and succeeding periods more focused on economic development.

In the postrevolutionary period, rural land redistribution virtually eliminated the landlord class, and in urban areas Communist cadres achieved first consolidation and then "socialist transformation" (1955–57). The 100 Flowers Campaign in 1956–57 encouraged criticism of the party, but those who took advantage of the more open discussion soon found themselves labeled rightists. The GLF program (starting in 1958) sought to increase productivity through increased socialist organization of the rural economy, that is, rural people's communes and producers' cooperatives. Agricultural production increased in the first year of the GLF, but in 1959–60 crop failure and a devastating famine that killed millions haunted the program. The attempt to decentralize industrial production also failed. Under fire, Mao began a rectification campaign to educate the peasants through struggle sessions with intellectuals and bureaucrats; it failed to reduce the importance of elites. He then went outside the party for help in rectifying their errors.

In the GPCR, Red Guards attacked cultural figures and party officials in what Mao conceived as a revitalization of revolutionary values. The campaign included ultraleftist bullying that disrupted production and social relations; by mid-1968, Mao was forced to demobilize the Red Guards and call on the army to restore order. Antinatalist fertility-control policies were begun in urban areas in the period; they were extended to the whole country in 1970. From then until Mao's death in 1976, the military backed attempts by his old companions in arms, like Zhou Enlai, to rebuild the party and government. Those of Mao's associates who tried to prolong the Cultural Revolution were attacked after his death as the Gang of Four.

The slogan of the Four Modernizations has since become the watchword; rural to urban migration was closed off; rural collectivization was scaled back and replaced by the "household responsibility system," which provides incentives for agrarian families to produce; China was opened to foreign trade, technology, and investment; industrial policy was changed from self-sufficiency based on heavy industry to export-oriented light industry; banking has been decentralized; and the one-child family has been proclaimed as the norm in an effort to level off population growth.[99]

How does gender, women's work, and the sex division of labor fit into this panoramic sweep of rebellion, war, reaction, idealistic goals, and the mixed record of Communist revolution?

The first modern histories of Chinese women focused on the extremes of inequality to which they were subjected in traditional China—the material miseries of female peasants and workers and the social and psychological denial of identity to upper-class women; women heroes of rebellion and revolution; and the oppositional ideas of cultural figures, reformers and revolutionaries, whether men or women, about women's role.

Some examples: The Taipings forbade foot binding and welcomed women members, establishing single-sex communities in which women were freed from family control and did useful work for the cause; they, as did the Boxers later, organized women into fighting groups, but these were brutally repressed. Reforms proposed in the 1890s included formal education for women and the abolition of foot binding, while utopian theorists proposed new ways of raising children and forms of egalitarian social relations. The Japanese schools for Chinese girls raised the revolutionary consciousness of future activists and gave them the skills to act politically. Thus Ch'iu Chin became a teacher in a Chinese women's school and plotted revolution with secret society members in the first decade of this century; the plan failed, and she was executed in 1907. There were reports of women in military units in the 1911 revolution, and women's suffrage groups emerged in the period of constitutional discussions in 1911–12. Several suffrage groups published in 1912 a parliamentary program calling for equal rights for men and women, education for women, improvement of their position in the family, monogamy, free choice of marriage partner, a ban on divorce without justification, an end to concubines and the sale of women, and reform of the licensed prostitution system. The attempt to work within the parliamentary system failed.

The discussion of women's rights was not hushed, however. The May 4 protest again brought women into popular politics and gender questions into the press. From Hunan, Mao Zedong wrote several articles on female suicide in 1919 that condemned the conditions (often a forced marriage) that drove women to suicide and urged them to struggle against the system instead of killing themselves in protest. Women students and teachers joined street crowds, read the new journals, and agitated in their own interests; they perceived women's rights as basic to a democratic society. In Hunan, a provincial constitution in 1922 granted women the suffrage in provincial and local elections. There the movement stopped, as warlordism and civil war engulfed the country.

Some of its members, however, went on to activism in the Communist party. One of them was Sister Shi, a Shanghai textile worker who joined a strike in 1922 and was recruited to the CCP; fired from her job, she ran a workers' school and was active in communist underground organizations. Xiang Jingyu, a Hunanese teacher, joined other young people in her province to sponsor a study group for workers; she was able to go to France to work and study communist ideas. She later was trained in Moscow as well, and organized women textile workers in China; the KMT executed her in 1928, during a wave of anticommunist repression. In rural Kwangtung, in areas where the economy had two bases—mulberry and silkworm cultivation, silk reeling and spinning, in which female workers predominated, and fishing, which employed primarily men—customs unknown in the rest of China occurred: Newlywed wives did not live with their husbands immediately, and young women refused to marry, organizing independent sisterhoods for social support.[100]

A second phase of research on Chinese women's history, done after the PRC permitted social scientists to interview people in villages and historians to explore archives, brought new studies closer to those done on other geographical areas. An example is Emily Honig's study of women in the Shanghai cotton mills from 1919 to 1949, which parallels those for Japan. Conditions were often similar to the Japanese (unscrupulous recruiters, crowded dormitory housing, poor wages and working conditions), but the Shanghai contract-labor system was not copied from the Japanese; instead, it was shaped by traditional Chinese labor recruitment practices. Women's experience as workers in Shanghai mills sometimes brought them into political struggles, as with Sister Shi and many other less-well-known women whose collective personal lives, wage-work patterns, and strikes are explored by Honig.[101]

An analysis of Japanese demographic records on Taiwan looks at gender relations, marriage, and childbearing, focusing on women in unconventional but socially accepted marriages. The marriages of adopted daughters raised as children with their future husbands were characterized both by much lower fertility and more frequent divorce. (These characteristics did not necessarily indicate better lives for these women, since both outcomes were highly stigmatized in the period.)[102] Gender relations in marriage and family are one of the most frequently addressed subjects of recent studies of China. Questions about the workings of the Confucian patriarchal system, the process by which it was reformed by law, the relationship between law (or tradition) and behavior, the extent to which socialist policy, with its commitment to gender equality and its belief that participation in social production is the driving force behind it, has succeeded, and the unintended or unanticipated consequences of other policies on gender and family relations have been widely discussed.

These historical studies explore new sources shedding light on gender and marriage in the past. A study of ritual guides, advice books, and commentary on marriage customs available to brides and their families in the late Qing period suggests that the possibilities for class-endogamous marriage were being undermined; one result was an intensified discourse about women as moral guardians of the family. The contractual differences in the price of, and expectations of services from, wives, concubines, and maids in the Hong Kong region in the early twentieth century trace a continuum rather than distinct breaks in status. An exploration of prostitution in Shanghai shows how women's bodies were commodified and made more accessible to men of all classes (previously concubinage was common primarily among elites). But even among prostitutes there were status differences, and perhaps more important, differences in what pay they might receive, what their conditions of work were, and what possibilities they had to leave the profession.

In 1907, in the waning years of the Qing, a revision of the Civil Code ended the right of the husband's family to control its daughters-in-law and introduced the notion of marriage as a contract between individuals. This was reinforced in the KMT 1930 Civil Code that prescribed freedom of marriage and facilitated divorce, but assumed that husbands had greater rights in marriage. Males continued to enjoy full authority over children, more grounds for divorce, and first claim to child custody. Any and all legal and institutional changes in these years were unevenly applied between rural and urban areas and among areas controlled by individual warlords or parties.[103]

During the Jiangxi Soviet, communists granted women new rights and sought their cooperation in replacing men as agricultural workers and as auxiliaries to the Red Army. The land law, for example, specified that landless laborers and peasants were to have equal rights to land portions regardless of sex. This law, which sought primarily to equalize property holding, not to emancipate women, gave class precedence over sex; hence landlords' wives shared their mates' class identity and were excluded from land redistribution. The two marriage laws (1931, 1934) promulgated in the Jiangxi Soviet followed USSR family law precedents. Marriage was defined as "free association between a man and a woman to be entered into without interference from other parties and to be ended by mutual agreement or upon the insistence of either husband or wife"; both marriage and divorce required official registration. There is little information about the implementation of these marriage laws, but some indication that the communists were uneasy about provoking male–female animosity.[104]

The marriage law of the PRC was drafted in 1949, before the civil war ended, and promulgated in 1950. Its principles echoed those of the 1931 law: free choice of partners, monogamy, equal rights of partners. The old customs—bigamy, concubinage, child betrothal, bride price, rejection of widow remarriage—were explicitly forbidden. Husbands and wives were declared equal in choice of occupation and activities, household status, the management of the household and its possessions, and their duty to work for the family's welfare. This marriage law was publicized, and efforts to enforce it started immediately, with uneven results; both private and official evasion continued in rural areas even as urban women flocked into wage work. Despite new legislation granting equal inheritance to males and females, the practice has not yet been accepted by rural families, who continue to disinherit daughters who marry out. The Women's Federation was created by the government to deal with some of these issues and promote women's interests. It accepted the party line that women should seek emancipation through social production and political activity, but also organized housewives.[105]

By the early 1980s, sociologists and anthropologists had more evidence about the effects of the marriage law, and their evaluation of it (reflecting the development of feminist theory) was less favorable. Judith Stacey argues that the revolution drew on patriarchy and compromised with it, producing a "new democratic patriarchy." The return to household-based agriculture and the one-child system suggested problems ahead. Margery Wolf's interviews (arranged by the government, as she emphasizes) in factories, schools, and neighborhood brigades put flesh and blood on the ideological–institutional sketch presented by Stacey. Wolf doubts any conscious intent of the revolutionaries to preserve patriarchy. Kay Johnson concludes, however, that "government policies have directly and indirectly supported the living dynamic of traditional values, behavior and family structure." [106]

Like France, the PRC has had long-standing demographic policies, but antinatalist rather than pronatalist ones. Chinese were told to marry late (women at eighteen or older), wait longer between births, and have fewer children. In the 1970s, even higher age minimums were aggressively pursued in administrative practice, and the 1979 one-child prescription was more forceful yet. The results: At the age-specific fertility rate prevailing in 1963 (an exceptionally prolific year), women would bear more than seven children in their lifetime on average; at 1985 rates, only slightly above two. This rapid achievement must be tempered, however, by the slowdown of rate of decline since 1980, and its partial reversal. The marriage law of that year raised the permissible age of marriage for women from eighteen to twenty, but administrative enforcement of higher age limits has been abandoned. The result has been increasingly young brides, at risk for childbearing for more years. Further, although rates of second and third births have declined, the relaxation of the one-child policy in rural areas has caused overall fertility to rise again there. It appears that marriage and childbearing policy, confronted by the return to household responsibility in agriculture (which might spur higher fertility in farm families seeking to ensure an adequate future workforce) has recently been undercut by lower ages at marriage.[107]

Feminist scholars have also been concerned by the effect on girl babies of the one-child policy; would agrarian parents who "needed" sons as family workers kill or neglect their daughters? There have been reports of such outcomes, but so far it has been hard to separate new effects from long-present trends. There is strong statistical evidence for Chinese female infanticide in the past, sometimes, but not always, linked to famine and crisis.[108]

China is one of the contemporary countries with a highly masculine sex ratio (1.074, compared to India's 1.066 or Pakistan's 1.105), attributed to higher female mortality rates at most ages from one to fifty or sixty. This phenomenon has received coverage in the popular press, but it, like its temporary historical parallel in European mortality statistics, is not fully understood.[109]

A recent review of Chinese women's position in the 1980s argues that the turbulent revolutionary years, despite their destruction and violence, gave young women a chance to escape from family control and develop new capabilities. The end of the GPCR narrowed such opportunities but did not silence debate about women's issues. New evidence from urban areas provides a unique and valuable summation of contemporary urban gender relations. Family structure in the cities changed rapidly after 1949; patrilocality withered away, and women's wage earning (and greater say in family spending and other decisions) became the norm. In the 1980s, divorce became more common, but as in the West, it is difficult for women to divorce because their wages are much lower than men's, and divorced women are stigmatized. The division of labor in the economy in the past decade appears to have sharpened sex segregation in jobs, with women in lower-paid and subordinate positions; this change is attributed to discrimination in work groups, which now are responsible for hiring. No government policy has been proposed to alleviate these outcomes. They, the continuing vulnerability of women to male violence, and increasing attention to beauty, dress, and adornment are officially condemned as feudal hangovers, the chaos of the GPCR, and Western influence. Both officials and ordinary people claim that the working out of socialist revolution will with time solve such problems, thus no special attention to them is needed. This seems unlikely, given the continuing resistance and government reluctance to enforce the laws. The Women's Federation has not taken an independent collective stand on most issues.

Under these conditions, Emily Honig and Gail Hershatter conclude that "women's subordination seem[s] certain to continue, if not by machination then by default."[110] This conclusion would be even more pessimistic if rural conditions are taken into account. Nevertheless, the continuing debate about women's status offers a glimmer of hope for the resumption of progress toward gender equality.

Conclusions and Agenda for Comparative Research

The comparisons made in this study confirm several generalizations: In most cases, early urbanization and industrialization probably decreased women's contribution to production overall, but the growth of the service sector made possible greater female contribution to the economy once more (the Chinese decision to promote export-oriented consumer industries may keep women in industry, however); government policy has been important not only to the organization of production, sectoral distribution, and division of labor in the economy as a whole but also to the division of labor and gender relations in the household; German and Japanese authoritarian government policies hindered gender realignment (the Chinese legislated gender equality and wavered on enforcement); among demographic factors, declining fertility and, in the West and Japan, reduced sex differentials in mortality among some female age groups made it possible for women to develop their capabilities through education and work; differences in forms of gender inequality both within states during the process of industrialization and between and among states at a given point in time were shaped by patterns of economic change, political stability, and government policies; variability in women's recourse to rights-based gender politics (especially social movements) was mediated by differences in political systems and power relations in regimes. Economic and political change in Britain first, then Western Europe and the United States, both offered a model for the rest of the world to emulate and had at least an indirect—and often a deleterious—impact on economic and political opportunities for non-Western men and women.

The improvements for men and women that followed industrialization, as well as variability in the forms of gender inequality among national states and within them across time and among social groups, have been summarized in each section. Here I would emphasize typical intergroup differences best documented for the West. For example, women in urban (excluding household production) and service industries (excluding domestic service) were better off economically than male day laborers in agriculture, and the wage gap between them and men in declining sectors such as household manufacturing and certain handicrafts was probably narrow as well. Middle-class women in social movements such as temperance, abolition, and suffrage were enjoying their capabilities more than most rural, immigrant, or racial-minority men were likely to. And rural, racial-minority, immigrant, and working-class women were less likely to benefit from urban and service-sector jobs (except those in domestic service) than their middle-class sisters. In the periods considered, women's capabilities compared to men's have varied with political and economic conditions, but despite positive increases in such capabilities as lower fertility, access to education and jobs, and political rights, gender inequality lingered. Continuing inequality in the household limited women's political and economic capabilities, preventing their full development.

Future research on the following questions would contribute to our understanding of the remaining problems. Did the discontinuities in wage inequality (improved female–male ratio in the move from agriculture to manufacturing, and from manufacturing to clerical work) that Claudia Goldin found in the United States occur in other countries? And do the same limits on improvements appear? (Here the role of large public-sector employment and the comparative impact of policies promoting or hindering wage equality seem critical.) To what extent would extending the period covered for Western countries to the welfare state and its greater intervention in women's access to jobs, social support policies, wages, education, and (to a lesser degree) household gender relations modify the picture of continuity within change? To what extent and through what mechanisms have public policies reduced gender inequality in households? To what extent can we historicize the concept of patriarchy, or are more-grounded concepts the prerequisite to systematic comparison seeking historical variation across political–economic systems? Under what conditions, and by what means, did men workers gain leverage to combine with employers at the expense of women workers? To what extent can we explain differences within specific feminist movements in their emphasis on workplace or family issues?

New research has greatly increased our knowledge about economic change and gender relations—in particular, the household and broader social divisions of labor by sex. This impressive record should encourage us to pursue the continuing agenda with optimism and energy.

NOTES

This essay was written while I was a fellow at the Center for Advanced Study in the Behavioral Sciences, Stanford, California. I am grateful for financial support provided by National Endowment for the Humanities #RA-20037-88, the Andrew W. Mellon Foundation, and the John Simon Guggenheim Memorial Foundation. Thanks also to Charles Tilly and Martin Whyte for reading the manuscript and making valuable suggestions for reorganization or revision.

1. Clara Collet, quoted in *Unequal Opportunities: Women's Employment in England 1800–1918*, ed. Angela John (Oxford, England: Basil Blackwell, 1986), p. 31.

2. Jeffrey G. Williamson, *Did British Capitalism Breed Inequality?* (Boston: Allen and Unwin, 1985), p. 200.

3. Claudia Goldin, *Understanding the Gender Gap: An Economic History of American Women* (New York: Oxford University Press, 1990).

4. For fuller discussion of Goldin's findings, see pp. 272–73.

5. Karen Oppenheim Mason, "The Status of Women: Conceptual and Methodological Issues in Demographic Studies," *Sociological Forum* 1 (Spring 1986): 284–300; and Sherry Ortner, "Gender Hegemonies," *Cultural Critique*, Winter 1989–90, pp. 35–81, both discuss the multidimensionality of women's prestige or status, male dominance, and the relative power of each sex and suggest alternative formulations to that adopted here.

6. Ivy Pinchbeck, *Women Workers and the Industrial Revolution, 1750–1850* (London: Virago, 1969; originally published 1930), p. 313.

7. Janet Thomas, "Women and Capitalism: Oppression or Emancipation? A Review Article," *Comparative Studies in Society and History* 30 (July 1988): 534–49, makes this point.

8. Edward Shorter, *The Making of the Modern Family* (New York: Basic Books, 1975), quote on p. 258.

9. Sonya O. Rose, "'Gender at Work': Sex, Class and Industrial Capitalism," *History Workshop Journal* 21 (Spring 1986): 113–31; "Gender Segregation in the Transition to the Factory: The English Hosiery Industry, 1850–1910," *Feminist Studies* 13 (Spring 1987): 163–84; and "Gender Antagonism and Class Conflict: Exclusionary Strategies of Male Trade Unionists in Nineteenth-Century Britain," *Social History* 13 (May 1988): 191–230. See also Sonya Rose, *Limited Livelihoods: Gender and Class in Nineteenth-Century England* (Berkeley: University of California Press, 1992).

10. This essay is primarily written in a comparative history mode rather than with a global perspective; ideally it would be desirable to explore the global systemic connections among and between the cases considered.

11. In the introduction to their edited volume, *Women's Work and the Family Economy in Historical Perspective* (Manchester, England: Manchester University Press, 1991), Pat Hudson and W. R. Lee argue that women's experience in industrialization can best be approached through local or sectoral studies.

12. Amartya Sen, "Economics and the Family," *Asian Development Review* 1 (1983): 19. See also Jocelyn Kynch and Amartya Sen, "Indian Women: Well-Being and Survival," *Cambridge Journal of Economics* 7 (1983): 363–80. On p. 365 Sen develops his argument against utilitarian conceptions of pleasure and pain, John Rawls's position that individuals' advantage is based on their possession of widely desired goods like rights, liberties, opportunities, and wealth, and Ronald Dworkin's case for opportunities as the key to advantage. In "What Did you Learn in the World Today?" *American Behavioral Scientist* 34 (May–June 1991): 530–48,

Sen argues that equity (fairness in the distribution of "good things") should be given more weight in evaluating policy than efficiency (referring in part to having more "good things") and calls for disaggregated internal comparisons as well as cross-national aggregated ones in analyses of inequality.

13. Amartya Sen, "Gender and Cooperative Conflicts," in *Persistent Inequalities: Women and World Development*, ed. Irene Tinker, pp. 123–49 (New York: Oxford University Press, 1990), quote on p. 131; idem, "Economics and the Family," *Asian Development Review* 1 (1983), quote on p. 18.

14. The arenas in which capabilities are examined are not intended to suggest hierarchies of importance. These may vary from case to case, in different times or places. In the eighteenth and nineteenth centuries in the West, access to food and health care may have varied by gender; today it is effectively equal. In some parts of Asia and Africa today, however, such capabilities are still unequally distributed. See Kynch and Sen, "Indian Women," and Tim Dyson and Mick Moore, "On Kinship Structure, Female Autonomy, and Demographic Behavior in India," *Population and Development Review* 9 (March 1983): 35–60. Ray Langsten, "Determinants of High Female Mortality in South Asia: Are the Data Consistent with Theory?" has challenged the differential feeding hypothesis; his manuscript is discussed by Lillian Li, "Life and Death in a Chinese Famine: Infanticide as a Demographic Consequence of the 1935 Yellow River Flood," *Comparative Studies in Society and History* 33 (July 1991): 501.

15. Peter N. Stearns, *Interpreting the Industrial Revolution* (Washington, D.C.: American Historical Association, 1991). Revisions include C. K. Harley, "British Industrialization before 1841: Evidence of Slower Growth during the Industrial Revolution," *Journal of Economic History* 42 (1982): 267–89; Donald M. McCloskey, "The Industrial Revolution, 1780–1860," in *The Economic History of Britain since 1700*, ed. Roderick Floud and Donald M. McCloskey (Cambridge, England: Cambridge University Press, 1981); Rondo Cameron, "The Industrial Revolution: A Misnomer," *History Teacher* 15 (1982): 377–84, and "La revolution industrielle manquée," *Social Science History* 14 (1990): 559–65; see also the vigorous dissent by R. M. Hartwell, "Was There an Industrial Revolution?" *Social Science History* 14 (1990): 567–76; John Komlos, "Thinking about the Industrial Revolution," *Journal of European Economic History* 18 (1989): 191–206; Charles Sabel and Jonathan Zeitlin, "Historical Alternatives to Mass Production: Politics, Markets and Technology in Nineteenth-Century Industrialization," *Past and Present* 108 (August 1985): 132–76.

16. Chris Middleton, "Women's Labour and the Transition to Pre-Industrial Capitalism," in *Women and Work in Pre-Industrial England*, ed. Lindsey Charles and Lorna Duffin, pp. 181–206 (London: Croom Helm, 1985). See also the other case studies in this volume.

17. See the essays in Barbara A. Hanawalt, ed., *Women and Work in Preindustrial Europe* (Bloomington: Indiana University Press, 1986); and Susan Amussen, *An Ordered Society: Family and Village in England, 1560–1725* (Oxford, England: Basil Blackwell, 1988). The classic study is Alice Clark, *The Working Life of Women in the Seventeenth Century* (New York: Routledge, 1982).

18. For an early statement of the "protoindustrial thesis," see Franklin F.

Mendels, "Proto-industrialization: The First Phase in the Industrialization Process," *Journal of Economic History* 32 (1972): 241–61; Hans Medick, "The Proto-Industrial Family Economy: The Structural Function of Household and Family during the Transition from Peasant Society to Industrial Capitalism," *Social History* 3 (1976): 291–315. See also David Levine, *Family Formation in an Age of Nascent Capitalism* (New York: Academic Press, 1977); and idem, "Industrialization and the Proletarian Family in England," *Past and Present* 107 (1985): 168–203. Both Middleton, "Women's Labour," and Maxine Berg, "Women's Work, Mechanization and the Early Phases of Industrialization in England," *On Work: Historical, Comparative, and Theoretical Approaches*, ed. R. E. Pahl, pp. 61–94 (New York and Oxford, England: Basil Blackwell, 1988) see protoindustrialization as more oppressive than do Medick and Levine. The latter's position on the demographic correlates of protoindustrialization is also challenged by Richard M. Smith, "Putting the Child Before the Marriage: Reply to Birdsall," *Population and Development Review* 9 (1983), 124–36; and, for France, by Pierre Jeannin, "La protoindustrialisation: developpement ou impasse?" *Annales: Economies, Sociétés, Civilisations* 35 (1980): 52–65. In their *Population History of England, 1541–1871* (Cambridge, Mass.: Harvard University Press, 1981), E. A. Wrigley and Roger Schofield show that women's childbearing and household responsibilities increased in the period of protoindustrialization, although they attribute higher fertility to better real wages, not the spread of the new organization of production. David Gaunt has labeled this increased fertility the "demographic background to woman as the beast of burden in the Industrial Revolution." See Gaunt's contribution to "The Population History of England 1541–1871: A Review Symposium," *Social History* 8 (1983): 139–68. For critiques of the protoindustrialization literature that emphasize the proletarianization of urban crafts, see Maxine Berg, Pat Hudson, and Michael Sonenscher, *Manufacture in Town and Country before the Factory* (Cambridge, England: Cambridge University Press, 1983).

19. K.D.M. Snell, *Annals of the Labouring Poor: Social Change in Agrarian England, 1660–1900* (Cambridge, England: Cambridge University Press, 1985), quote on p. 311.

20. Edward Higgs, "Domestic Service and Household Production," in John, *Unequal Opportunities*, pp. 125–50. For an overview (based on census aggregates) of patterns of servant employment in English middle-class households, see Patricia Branca, *Silent Sisterhood: Middle-Class Women in the Victorian Home* (London: Croom Helm, 1975).

21. Berg, "Women's Work, Mechanization." The heavy employment of children in the factory-organized cotton industry attracted the attention of reformers. Although child labor was declining, laws were passed in the nineteenth century to protect child workers. The first effective Factory Act (1833) extended the age of protected workers to eighteen, provided for inspectors, and required factory owners to establish schools for their workers under age thirteen. Women were added to the protected groups in an 1844 amendment. Cotton textile workers opposed the elimination of half-timers (children who both attended school and worked in the factories) well into the twentieth century, resisting both Trades Union Congress policy and the notion of a primary male breadwinner in the interests of their family

economies. Per Bolin-Hort, *Work, Family and the State: Child Labour and the Organization of Production in the British Cotton Industry, 1780–1920* (Lund, Sweden: Lund University Press, 1989). See also Margaret Hewitt, *Wives and Mothers in Victorian Industry* (Westport, Conn.: Greenwood Press, 1975; originally published 1958).

"Family wage" referred also to a wage adequate to support a family, a concept the implementation of which male craftsmen and some unionists urged through laws limiting women's access to jobs and prohibiting married women's wage work. See Sheila Lewenhak, *Women and Trade Unions* (New York: St. Martin's Press, 1977); and Barbara Drake, *Women in Trade Unions* (London: Virago, 1984). In "The Working Class Family, Women's Liberation and Class Struggle: The Case of Nineteenth Century British History," *Review of Radical Political Economics* 9 (Fall 1977): 25–41 and "Class Struggle and the Persistence of the Working Class Family," *Cambridge Journal of Economics* 1 (1977): 241–58, Jane Humphries argues that the family wage was a tactic to preserve the working-class family and support its reproductive capacities by improving its standard of living through class struggle. See also Harold Benenson, "The 'Family Wage' and Working Women's Consciousness in Britain, 1880–1914," *Politics and Society* 19 (March 1991): 71–108, who shows that many women cotton textile workers opposed any "marriage bar" or protective legislation that limited their access to jobs; and Mariana Valverde, " 'Giving the Female a Domestic Turn': The Social, Legal and Moral Regulation of Women's Work in British Cotton Mills, 1820–1850," *Journal of Social History* 21 (1988): 619–34, who shows that male workers' opinions on this issue changed over time, and they eventually settled not for exclusion but the marginalization of women in factories. The proportion of women working did not decline despite the discourse of domesticity.

22. Angela John, discussing Jenny Morris, "The Characteristics of Sweating: The Late Nineteenth-Century London and Leeds Tailoring Trade," in John, *Unequal Opportunities*, p. 11. John's volume was published at the same time as Jane Lewis, ed., *Labor and Love: Women's Experience of Home and Family, 1850–1940* (New York and Oxford, England: Basil Blackwell, 1986); the two collections were conceptualized to cover two aspects of gender relations: those in the workplace (John) and those in the home (Lewis).

23. Judith Lown, *Women and Industrialization: Gender at Work in Nineteenth-Century England* (Minneapolis: University of Minnesota Press, 1990).

24. Marguerite Dupree, "The Community Perspective in Family History: The Potteries during the Nineteenth Century," in *The First Modern Society: Essays in English History in Honour of Lawrence Stone*, ed. A. L. Beier, David Canadine, and James M. Rosenheim, pp. 549–73 (Cambridge, England: Cambridge University Press, 1989). Dupree's focus on Stoke-upon-Trent provides the opportunity to compare two labor markets—those of ceramics workers and coal miners—and their social context in one setting. Richard Whipp, "Kinship, Labour and Enterprise: The Staffordshire Pottery Industry, 1890–1920," in Hudson and Lee, *Women's Work*, pp. 184–203.

25. Angela V. John, *By the Sweat of Their Brow: Women Workers at Victorian Coal Mines* (Boston: Routledge and Kegan Paul, 1984).

26. Elizabeth A. M. Roberts, "Women's Strategies, 1890–1940," in Lewis, *Labor and Love*, pp. 223–47; and *Women's Work 1840–1940* (London: Macmillan

Education, 1988). See also John Benson, *The Penny Capitalists: A Study of Nineteenth-Century Working-Class Entrepreneurs* (New Brunswick, N.J.: Rutgers University Press, 1983), which gives most attention to male enterprises; and Diana Gittins, "Marital Status, Work and Kinship, 1850–1930," and L. Jamieson, "Limited Resources and Limiting Conventions," both in Lewis, *Labor and Love*; Carl Chinn, *They Worked All Their Lives: Women of the Urban Poor in England, 1880–1939* (New York: Manchester University Press, 1988).

27. Pat Ayers and Jan Lambertz, "Marriage Relations, Money, and Domestic Violence in Working-Class Liverpool, 1919–1939," in Lewis, *Labour and Love*, pp. 195–219. A strict division of household responsibility was also reported in mining families; see Norman Dennis, Fernando Henriques and Clifford Slaughter, *Coal Is Our Life: An Analysis of a Yorkshire Mining Community* (London: Eyre & Spottiswoode, 1956). On working-class wives' health and diets, see Jane Lewis, *The Politics of Motherhood: Child and Maternal Welfare in England, 1900–1939* (London: Croom Helm, 1980); and John Komlos, "Anthropometric History: What Is It?" *Journal of Social and Biological Structures* 14 (1991): 353–56, which cites several gender-specific studies that connect height differences by gender to women's malnutrition. For studies of working-class married life in London, see Ellen Ross, " 'Fierce Questions and Taunts': Married Life in Working Class London," *Feminist Studies* 8 (1982): 575–602, and "Survival Networks: Women's Neighborhood Sharing in London before World War One," *History Workshop Journal* 15 (1983): 4–27. See also Wally Seccombe, "Patriarchy Stabilized: The Construction of the Male Breadwinner Wage Norm in Nineteenth-Century Britain," *Social History* 11 (January 1986): 53–76; and Wally Seccombe, *A Millenium of Family Change: Feudalism to Capitalism in Northwestern Europe* (London: Verso, 1992).

28. Michael Anderson, "The Emergence of the Modern Life Cycle in Britain," *Social History* 10 (January 1985): 69–87; Ellen Jordan, "The Exclusion of Women from Industry in Nineteenth-Century Britain," *Comparative Studies in Society and History* 31 (April 1989): 273–96; Wrigley and Schofield, *Population History of England*.

29. Levine, "Industrialization and the Proletarian Family." To those who would associate declining fertility with the spread of education, Levine points out that the "introduction of mass education *followed* the working-class family's recomposition; it did not precede it" (p. 195).

30. S. Ryan Johansson, "Welfare, Mortality and Gender: Continuity and Change in the Explanation of Male/Female Mortality Differences over Three Centuries," *Continuity and Change* 6 (1991): 135–77. See also Roger Schofield, "Did the Mothers Really Die? Three Centuries of Maternal Mortality in the World We Have Lost," in *The World We Have Gained: Histories of Population and Social Structure*, ed. Lloyd Bonfield, Richard M. Smith, and Keith Wrightson, pp. 231–60 (New York: Oxford University Press, 1986).

31. Leonore Davidoff and Catherine Hall, *Family Fortunes: Men and Women of the English Middle Class, 1780–1850* (Chicago: University of Chicago Press, 1987), quotes on pp. 12, 25; Anne Summers, "A Home from Home—Women's Philanthropic Work in the Nineteenth Century," in *Fit Work for Women*, ed. Sandra Burman, pp. 32–63 (New York: St. Martin's Press, 1979).

32. Catherine Hall, "Strains in the 'Firm of Wife, Children and Friends'? Middle Class Women and Employment in Early Nineteenth-Century England," in Hudson and Lee, *Women's Work*, pp. 106–31.

33. Lee Holcombe, *Victorian Ladies at Work: Middle-Class Working Women in England and Wales, 1850–1914* (New York: Archon Books, 1973), and *Wives and Property: Reform of Married Women's Property Law in Nineteenth-Century England* (Toronto: University of Toronto Press, 1983); Mary Lyndon Shanley, *Feminism, Marriage, and the Law in Victorian England, 1850–1895* (Princeton: Princeton University Press, 1989); Samuel Cohn, *The Process of Occupational Sex-Typing: The Feminization of Clerical Labor in Great Britain* (Philadelphia: Temple University Press, 1989); Meta Zimmeck, "Clerical Work for Women, 1850–1914," in John, *Unequal Opportunities*, pp. 153–77. See also Dina M. Copelman, "'A New Comradeship between Men and Women': Family, Marriage and London's Women Teachers, 1870–1914," in Lewis, *Labour and Love*, pp. 175–93, for discussion of the continued participation of wives in small business and commerce and of the willingness of more prosperous working-class and lower-middle-class families to forego daughters' financial contribution to prepare them for better jobs, such as school teaching.

34. Jane Rendall, ed., *Equal or Different: Women's Politics, 1800–1914* (Oxford, England: Basil Blackwell, 1987), and *The Origins of Modern Feminism: Women in Britain, France and the United States, 1780–1860* (Chicago: Lyceum, 1985); Jill Liddington and Jill Norris, *One Hand Tied Behind Us: The Rise of the Women's Suffrage Movement* (London: Virago, 1978).

35. Judith R. Walkowitz, *Prostitution and Victorian Society: Women, Class, and the State* (Cambridge, England: Cambridge University Press, 1980); Patricia Hollis, *Ladies Elect: Women in English Local Government, 1865–1914* (Oxford, England: Clarendon Press, 1987); Rendall, *Equal or Different* and *The Origins*; Seth Koven and Sonya Michel, "Womanly Duties: Maternalist Politics and the Origins of Welfare States in France, Germany, Great Britain, and the United States, 1880–1920," *American Historical Review* 95 (October 1990): 1076–1108.

36. Jane Jenson argues in "Gender and Reproduction: Or, Babies and the State," *Studies in Political Economy* 20 (Summer 1986): 9–46, that the British politics of motherhood restricted women's access to jobs while the French offered ways to balance wage work and domestic roles. Ellen Mappen, *Helping Women at Work: The Women's Industrial Council, 1889–1914* (London: Hutchinson, 1985) shows that some social feminists were conscious of this problem and despite sometimes contradictory ideology and practice initiated local projects to support women workers who were mothers.

37. See Barbara F. Reskin and Patricia A. Roos, *Job Queues, Gender Queues: Explaining Women's Inroads into Male Occupations* (Philadelphia: Temple University Press, 1990), for discussion of similar processes in the contemporary United States.

38. See Alan S. Milward and S. B. Saul, *The Economic Development of Continental Europe, 1780–1870* (Totawa, N.J.: Rowan and Littlefield, 1973), for a description of the French economy in European perspective.

39. François Crouzet, "Angleterre et France au XVIIIe siècle: Essai d'analyse comparée de deux croissances économiques," *Annales: Economies, Sociétés, Civilisations* 21 (March–April 1966): 254–91.

40. Olwen Hufton, *The Poor of Eighteenth-Century France* (Oxford, England: Clarendon Press, 1974), and "Women and the Family Economy in Eighteenth-Century France," *French Historical Studies* 9 (1975): 7–22; Jeffrey Kaplow, *Elbeuf during the Revolutionary Period* (Baltimore: Johns Hopkins University Press, 1964), and *The Names of Kings: The Parisian Laboring Poor in the Eighteenth Century* (New York: Basic Books, 1972).

41. Gay Gullickson's study of protoindustry in the Pays de Caux (Normandy) in the eighteenth and nineteenth centuries challenges some of the original generalizations about protoindustrialization as explicated by Franklin Mendels, Hans Medick, and David Levine (see note 17). She shows that protoindustry in the Caux involved a gender division of labor (with men in commercial agriculture and women weaving) rather than a family economy with all members in a single industry. Gullickson, *Spinners and Weavers of Auffay: Rural Industry and the Sexual Division of Labor in a French Village, 1750–1850* (Cambridge, England: Cambridge University Press, 1986). See also Tessie Liu, *The Weavers' Knot: The Contradictions of Class Struggle and Family Solidarity in Western France, 1750–1914* (Ithaca, N.Y.: Cornell University Press, 1994).

42. Martine Segalen, "Exploring a Case of Late French Fertility Decline: Two Contrasted Breton Examples," in *The European Experience of Declining Fertility: A Quiet Revolution, 1850–1970*, ed. John Gillis, Louise A. Tilly, and David Levine (Oxford, England: Basil Blackwell, 1992); Etienne van de Walle, *The Female Population of France in the Nineteenth Century: A Reconstruction of 82 Departments* (Princeton: Princeton University Press, 1974), and "Motivations and Technology in the Decline of French Fertility," in *Family and Sexuality in French History*, ed. Tamara Hareven and Robert Wheaton, pp. 135–78 (Philadelphia: University of Pennsylvania Press, 1980).

43. Martine Segalen, *Love and Power in the Peasant Family: Rural France in the Nineteenth Century* (Chicago: University of Chicago Press, 1983), quote on p. 9.

44. Gender relations in Languedocian vineyards and winegrowing are discussed in Laura Frader, "Grapes of Wrath: Vineyard Workers, Labor Unions, and Strike Activity in the Aude, 1860–1913," in *Class Conflict and Collective Action*, ed. Louise A. Tilly and Charles Tilly, pp. 185–206 (Beverly Hills: Sage, 1981). According to Paul Bairoch, "Niveaux de developpement économique de 1810 à 1910," *Annales: Economies, Sociétés, Civilisations* 20 (November–December 1965): 1096, the relatively small scale of French agriculture meant that in 1910, according to an index comparing levels of agricultural development (in terms of productivity) across nations, France came in well behind the United States, Britain, and Germany but well ahead of Russia, the Mediterranean countries, and Japan. Adna Ferrin Weber, *The Growth of Cities in the Nineteenth Century* (Ithaca, N.Y.: Cornell University Press, 1967), shows that while 79 percent of the French population lived outside cities of over 20,000 in 1891, only 41 percent of the English population did (p. 144).

45. Louise A. Tilly, "Individual Lives and Family Strategies in the French Proletariat," *Journal of Family History* 4 (Summer 1979): 137–52; idem, "The Family Wage Economy of a French Textile City: Roubaix, 1872–1906," *Journal of Family History* 4 (Winter 1979): 381–94; idem, "Linen Was Their Life: Family Strategies and Parent–Child Relations in Nineteenth-Century France," in *Interest and Emo-*

tion: Essays on the Study of Family and Kinship, ed. Hans Medick and David Warren Sabean, pp. 300–316 (Cambridge, England: Cambridge University Press, 1984); and idem, "Worker Families and Occupation in Industrial France," *Tocqueville Review* 5 (Fall–Winter, 1983): 317–36.

46. John M. Merriman, *The Red City: Limoges and the French Nineteenth Century* (New York: Oxford University Press, 1985).

47. Michelle Perrot, *Les Ouvriers en Grève: France, 1871–1890* (Paris and The Hague: Mouton, 1974). See also Louise A. Tilly, "Paths of Proletarianization: The Sex Division of Labor and Women's Collective Action in Nineteenth-Century France," *Signs: Journal of Women in Culture and Society* 7 (Winter 1981): 400–417, and "Coping with Company Paternalism: Family Strategies of Coal Miners in Nineteenth-Century France," *Theory and Society* 14 (July 1985): 403–17.

48. Joan Wallach Scott, "Men and Women in the Parisian Garment Trades: Discussions of Family and Work in the 1830s and 1840s," in *The Power of the Past: Essays for Eric Hobsbawm*, ed. Pat Thane, Geoff Crossick, and Roderick Floud, pp. 69–73 (Cambridge, England: Cambridge University Press, 1984); Marilyn J. Boxer, "Women in Industrial Home Work: The Flowermakers of Paris in the Belle Epoque," *French Historical Studies* 22 (1982): 401–23, and "Protective Legislation and Home Industry: The Marginalization of Women Workers in Late Nineteenth-Early Twentieth-Century France," *Journal of Social History* 20 (1986): 45–65; Judith Coffin, "Social Science Meets Sweated Labor: Reinterpreting Women's Work in Late Nineteenth-Century France," *Journal of Modern History* 63 (June 1991): 230–70.

49. Marie-Helène Zylberberg-Hocquard, "Les ouvrières de l'État (Tabacs et Alumettes) dans les dernières années du XIXe siècle," *Le Mouvement social* 105 (October–December, 1978): 87–108.

50. Theresa M. McBride, "A Woman's World: Department Stores and the Evolution of Women's Employment, 1870–1920," *French Historical Studies* 20 (Fall 1978): 664–83; Susan Bachrach, *Dames Employées: The Feminization of Postal Work in Nineteenth-Century France* (New York: Institute for Research in History/Haworth, 1984); Frances I. Clark, *The Position of Women in Contemporary France* (Westport, Conn.: Hyperion Press, 1981; originally published 1937); see also Michelle Perrot's introduction (which opens with the words "Women have always worked. They have not always had métiers") and the other articles in *Le Mouvement social* cited in note 49. See also Jo Burr Margadant, *Madame Le Professeur: Women Educators in the Third Republic* (Princeton: Princeton University Press, 1990).

51. For further comparisons of France and England, see Louise A. Tilly and Joan W. Scott, *Women, Work and Family*, 2nd ed. (New York: Methuen, 1987).

52. Louise A. Tilly, "Occupational Structure, Women's Work and Demographic Change in Two French Industrial Cities, Anzin and Roubaix, 1872–1906," in *Time, Space and Man*, ed. Jan Sundin and Erik Söderlund (Atlantic Highlands, N.J.: Humanities Press, 1979), and "Individual Lives and Family Strategies in the French Proletariat," *Journal of Family History* 4 (Summer 1979): 137–52.

53. See Jacques Caroux-Destray, *Une Famille ouvrière traditionnelle* (Paris: Anthropos, 1974); Henry Leyret, *En Plein faubourg: moeurs ouvrières* (Paris: Charpentier, 1895), esp. pp. 49–50, 122.

54. Bonnie G. Smith, *Ladies of the Leisure Class: The Bourgeoises of Northern France in the Nineteenth Century* (Princeton: Princeton University Press, 1981).

55. For the 1789–95 revolutionary period, see Harriet Applewhite and Darlene Levy, eds., *Women and Politics in the Age of the Democratic Revolution* (Ann Arbor: University of Michigan Press, 1990); Louise A. Tilly, "Women's Collective Action and Feminism in France, 1870–1914," in *Class Conflict and Collective Action*, ed. Louise A. Tilly and Charles Tilly, pp. 207–31 (Beverly Hills: Sage, 1981); Karen O. Offen, "The 'Woman Question' as a Social Issue in Nineteenth-Century France," *Third Republic/Troisième République* 3–4 (1977): 238–99, "Depopulation, Nationalism and Feminism in Fin-de-siècle France," *American Historical Review* 89 (June 1984): 648–76, and "Defining Feminism: A Comparative Historical Approach," *Signs: Journal of Women in Culture and Society* 14 (Autumn 1988): 119–57; Steven C. Hause and Anne R. Kenney, *Women's Suffrage and Social Politics in the French Third Republic* (Princeton: Princeton University Press, 1984); Miriam Cohen and Michael Hanagan, "The Politics of Gender and the Making of the Welfare State, 1900–1940: A Comparative Perspective," *Journal of Social History* 24 (1991): 469–84; Jenson, "Gender and Reproduction"; Peter Flora and Arnold J. Heidenheimer, *The Development of Welfare States in Europe and America* (New Brunswick, N.J.: Rutgers University Press, 1987); Mary Lynn Stewart, *Women, Work, and the French State* (Montreal: McGill–Queens University Press, 1989).

56. Patricia Hilden, *Working Women and Socialist Politics in France, 1880–1914: A Regional Study* (Oxford, England: Clarendon Press, 1986); Marilyn J. Boxer and Jean H. Quataert, eds., *Socialist Women: European Socialist Feminism in the Nineteenth and Early Twentieth Centuries* (New York: Elsevier, 1978); Charles Sowerwine, *Sisters or Citizens? Women and Socialism in France Since 1876* (Cambridge, England: Cambridge University Press, 1982); Maité Albistur and Daniel Armogathe, *Histoire du feminisme français du moyen âge à nos jours* (Paris: Editions des femmes, 1977).

57. Its territory then encompassed regions now in France, Belgium, Poland, Lithuania, Czechoslovakia, and Denmark. Before that, it was an amalgam of smaller states; when I speak of them collectively, I use the word Germany, but when I speak of a specific area, I either identify it geographically or use the name of the state then in control. Milward and Saul, *Economic Development*, is the source for the economic history that follows.

58. Jean H. Quataert, "The Shaping of Women's Work in Manufacturing: Guilds, Households, and the State in Central Europe, 1648–1870," *American Historical Review* 90 (December 1985): 1122–48.

59. Peter Kriedte, Hans Medick, and Jürgen Schlumbohm, *Industrialization before Industrialization: Rural Industry in the Genesis of Capitalism* (Cambridge, England: Cambridge University Press, 1981).

60. Milward and Saul, *Economic Development*, pp. 304, 371, 383–84.

61. W. R. Lee, "Women's Work and the Family: Some Demographic Implications of Gender-Specific Rural Work Patterns in Nineteenth-Century Germany," in Hudson and Lee, *Working Women*, pp. 50–75; and Arthur E. Imhof, "Women, Family and Death: Excess Mortality of Women in Childbearing Age in Four Communities in Nineteenth-Century Germany," in *The German Family in Nineteenth- and Twentieth-Century Germany*, ed. Richard Evans and W. R. Lee, pp. 148–74 (London:

Croom Helm, 1981). See also David Sabean's study of a Württemberg community, *Property, Production and Family in Neckarhausen, 1700–1870* (Cambridge, England: Cambridge University Press, 1990), for discussion of women's heavy labor in stall feeding and the increased family conflict, nonmarriage, and illegitimacy that occurred in this period in Neckarhausen. Note that the German evidence about the intensification of women's agricultural labor offers a distinct contrast to Snell's findings (*Annals of Labor*) in southeastern England and to Johansson's use of Snell's conclusion to explain nineteenth-century elevated death rates among English adolescents and young women.

62. John Knodel, *The Decline of Fertility in Germany, 1871–1939* (Princeton: Princeton University Press, 1974); Milward and Saul, *Economic Development*, pp. 131–32.

63. Barbara Franzoi, *At the Very Least She Pays the Rent: Women and German Industrialization, 1871–1914* (Westport, Conn.: Greenwood Press, 1985).

64. Kathleen Canning, "Gender and The Politics of Class Formation: Rethinking German Labor History," *American Historical Review* 97 (1992): 736–68, offers a sensitive picture of women textile workers. Case studies of workers in German cities dominated by heavy industry reveal the near nonexistence of jobs for women workers and their almost total absence from workers' organizations or socialist politics. See David F. Crew, *Town in the Ruhr: A Social History of Bochum, 1860–1914* (New York: Columbia University Press, 1979); and Mary Nolan, *Social Democracy and Society: Working-class Radicalism in Dusseldorf* (Cambridge, England: Cambridge University Press, 1981).

65. Robyn Dasey, "Women's Work and the Family: Women Garment Workers in Berlin and Hamburg Before the First World War," in Evans and Lee, *The German Family*, pp. 221–55; Katharina Schlegal, "Mistress and Servant in Nineteenth Century Hamburg: Employer/Employee Relationships in Domestic Service, 1880–1914," *History Workshop Journal* 15 (Spring 1983): 60–77; Mary Jo Maynes, "The Contours of Childhood: Demography, Strategy, and Mythology of Childhood in French and German Lower-Class Autobiographies," in *The European Experience of Declining Fertility, 1850–1970: The Quiet Revolution*, ed. John R. Gillis, Louise A. Tilly, and David Levine, pp. 101–24 (Cambridge, Mass.: Blackwell, 1992); Jean H. Quataert, "Social Insurance and the Family Work of Oberlausitz Home Weavers in the Late Nineteenth Century," in *German Women in the Nineteenth Century: A Social History*, ed. John C. Fout, pp. 270–94 (New York: Holmes and Meier, 1984), uses evidence from government investigations and appeals in pension cases to show that women weavers were often denied pensions—despite the 1894 law extending them to hand weavers—because they were considered to be assistants to their husbands (this even though their husbands by this period were likely to be only part-time weavers, with construction or other seasonal jobs elsewhere). Quataert argues that families were complicit in this misrepresentation because they were unable or unwilling to pay the required contribution to the pension plan for two members of the household.

66. Carole J. Adams, *Women Clerks in Wilhelmine Germany: Issues of Class and Gender* (Cambridge, England: Cambridge University Press, 1989).

67. Mary Jo Maynes, *Schooling for the People: Comparative Local Studies on*

Schooling History in France and Germany, 1750–1850 (New York: Holmes and Meier, 1985), and *Schooling in Western Europe: A Social History* (Albany: SUNY Press, 1985).

68. Frederick Engels, *The Origin of the Family, Private Property and the State* (New York: International Publishers, 1942; originally published 1884); Jean Quataert, *Reluctant Feminists in German Social Democracy, 1885–1917* (Princeton: Princeton University Press, 1979); Amy Hackett, "The German Women's Movement and Suffrage, 1890–1914: A Study of National Feminism," in Robert J. Bezucha, *Modern European Social History*, pp. 354–79 (Lexington, Mass.: D.C. Heath, 1972); see also Richard J. Evans, *The Feminist Movement in Germany, 1894–1933* (London: Croom Helm, 1976).

69. Thomas Dublin, *Women at Work: The Transformation of Work and Community in Lowell, Massachusetts (1826–1860)* (New York: Columbia University Press, 1981), and *Farm and Factory: The Mill Experience and Women's Lives in New England, 1830–1860* (New York: Columbia University Press, 1981). Evidence collected by Claudia Goldin and Kenneth Sokoloff, "Women, Children, and Industrialization in the Early Republic: Evidence from the Manufacturing Censuses," *Journal of Economic History* 42 (December 1982): 741–74, shows that the ratio of female to male full-time wages was higher in manufacturing. See also Lucy Simler, "The Landless Worker: An Index of Economic and Social Change in Chester County, Pa., 1750–1820," *Pennsylvania Magazine of History and Biography* 114 (April 1990): esp. 185–87, for evidence of equal wages paid to men and women agricultural workers; Goldin, *Understanding the Gender Gap*, pp. 59–68; and Alice Kessler-Harris, *Out to Work: A History of Wage-Earning Women in the United States* (New York: Oxford University Press, 1982). See also Thomas Dublin, "Women's Work and the Family Economy: Textiles and Palm Leaf Hatmaking in New England, 1830–1850," *Tocqueville Review* 5 (Fall–Winter 1983): 297–316, and "Rural Putting-Out Work in Early Nineteenth-Century New England: Women and the Transition to Capitalism in the Countryside," *New England Quarterly* (1991): 531–73. Jeanne Boydston, *Home and Work: Housework, Wages and the Ideology of Labor in the Early Republic* (New York: Oxford University Press, 1990), examines the conditions under which housework lost both visibility and value with the rise of market relations; she argues that the process became the prototype for the "restructuring of the social relations of labor under . . . early industrialization" (p. xx). Tamara Hareven, *Family Time and Industrial Time* (Cambridge, England: Cambridge University Press, 1982), carries the story of the cotton industry, its immigrant workers, and their families into the twentieth century with a study of the world's largest textile mill. The Amoskeag Company in Manchester, Massachusetts, failed in the 1920s as the industry pursued a new low-wage strategy—moving to the job-hungry South. Jacqueline Dowd Hall et al., *Like a Family* (New York: Norton, 1989), partially based on oral history, as is Hareven's study, examines the conditions of textile work and family in North Carolina in the first decades of this century; race as well as gender and class are factors in this history.

70. Mary H. Blewett, *Men, Women, and Work: Class, Gender, and Protest in the New England Shoe Industry, 1780–1910* (Urbana: University of Illinois Press, 1987).

71. Christine Stansell, *City of Women: Sex and Class in New York, 1789–1860* (New York: Knopf, 1986), offers a complex and nuanced picture of gender relations

in the metropolis; James Oliver Horton, "Freedom's Yoke: Gender Conventions among Antebellum Free Blacks," *Feminist Studies* 22 (Spring 1986): 51–76; and Suzanne Lebsock, *The Free Women of Petersburg: Status and Culture in a Southern Town, 1784–1860* (New York: Norton, 1984), look at free African American women in the North and South.

72. Carole Turbin, "And We Are Nothing but Women: Irish Working Women in Troy," in *Women in America: A History*, ed. Carol R. Berkin and Mary Beth Norton (New York: Houghton Mifflin, 1979), and "Beyond Conventional Wisdom: Women's Wage Work, Household Economic Contribution, and Labor Activism in a Mid-Nineteenth-Century Working-Class Community," in *"To Toil the Livelong Day": America's Women at Work, 1780–1980*, ed. Carol Groneman and Mary Beth Norton, pp. 47–83 (Ithaca, N.Y.: Cornell University Press, 1987).

73. Ava Baron, "Contested Terrain Revisited: Technology and Gender Definitions of Work in the Printing Industry, 1850–1920," in *Women, Work, and Technology: Transformations*, ed. Barbara Wright (Ann Arbor: University of Michigan Press, 1987); Ava Baron, "Questions of Gender: Deskilling and Demasculinization in the U.S. Printing Industry, 1830–1915," *Gender and History* 1 (Summer 1989): 178–99; and Ava Baron, "An 'Other' Side of Gender Antagonism at Work: Men, Boys, and the Remasculinization of Printers' Work, 1830–1920," in *Work Engendered: Toward a New History of American Labor*, ed. Ava Baron (Ithaca, N.Y.: Cornell University Press, 1991).

74. Daniel J. Walkowitz, *Worker City, Company Town: Iron and Cotton Worker Protest in Troy and Cohoes, New York, 1855–1884* (Urbana: University of Illinois Press, 1978); S. J. Kleinberg, *The Shadow of the Mills: Working-Class Families in Pittsburgh, 1870–1907* (Pittsburgh: University of Pittsburgh Press, 1989). On Pittsburgh, see also John Bodnar, *Workers' World: Kinship, Community, and Protest in an Industrial Society, 1900–1940* (Baltimore: Johns Hopkins University Press, 1982); and John Bodnar, Roger Simon, and Michael P. Weber, *Lives of Their Own: Blacks, Italians, and Poles in Pittsburgh, 1900–1960* (Urbana: University of Illinois Press, 1982). On New York, see Donna Gabaccia, *From Sicily to Elizabeth Street: Housing and Social Change Among Italian Immigrants, 1880–1930* (Albany: SUNY Press, 1984); and Miriam Cohen, *From Workshop to Office: Employment, School and Family in the Lives of New York Italian Women, 1900–1950* (Ithaca, N.Y.: Cornell University Press, 1993). Elizabeth Pleck, "A Mother's Wages: A Comparison of Income-Earning among Married Black and Italian Women, 1896–1911," in *A Heritage of Her Own: Toward a New Social History of American Women*, ed. Nancy F. Cott and Elizabeth Pleck, pp. 367–92 (New York: Simon and Schuster, 1979), compares African American and Italian women in several cities.

75. Dolores Janiewski, "Seeking 'a New Day and a New Way': Black Women and Unions in the Southern Tobacco Industry," in Groneman and Norton, '*To Toil the Livelong Day*,' pp. 161–78; and Dolores E. Janiewski, *Sisterhood Denied: Race, Gender and Class in a New South Community* (Philadelphia: Temple University Press, 1985); Jacqueline Jones, "The Political Implications of Black and White Women's Work in the South, 1890–1965," and Nancy Hewitt, "Varieties of Voluntarism: Class, Ethnicity, and Women's Activism in Tampa," both in *Women, Politics, and Change*, ed. Louise A. Tilly and Patricia Gurin, pp. 108–29, 63–86 (New York:

Russell Sage Foundation, 1990); Jacqueline Jones, *Labor of Love, Labor of Sorrow, Black Women, Work and the Family from Slavery to the Present* (New York: Basic Books, 1985); and Patricia A. Cooper, *Once a Cigar Maker: Men, Women, and Work Culture in American Cigar Factories, 1900–1919* (Urbana: University of Illinois Press, 1987). See also the case studies in Baron, *Work Engendered*, for specific industries and localities.

76. Ardis Cameron, "Bread and Roses Revisited: Women's Culture and Working-Class Activism in the Lawrence Strike of 1912," in *Women, Work and Protest: A Century of U.S. Women's Labor History*, ed. Ruth Milkman, pp. 42–61 (Boston: Routledge and Kegan Paul, 1985); Karen M. Mason, "Feeling the Pinch: The Kalamazoo Corsetmakers' Strike of 1912," in Groneman and Norton, *"To Toil the Livelong Day,"* pp. 141–60; Joan M. Jensen and Sue Davidson, eds., *A Needle, A Bobbin, A Strike: Women Needleworkers in America* (Philadelphia: Temple University Press, 1984): chapters by Joan M. Jensen, "The Great Uprising in Rochester," pp. 94–113; N. Sue Weiler, "The Uprising in Chicago: The Men's Garment Workers Strike, 1910–1911," pp. 114–39; Lois Scharf, "The Great Uprising in Cleveland: When Sisterhood Failed," pp. 146–66; Ann Schofield, "The Uprising of the 20,000: The Making of a Labor Legend," pp. 167–82. See also Meredith Tax, *The Rising of the Women: Feminist Solidarity and Class Conflict, 1880–1917* (New York: Monthly Review Press, 1980); Robin Miller Jacoby, "The Women's Trade Union League and American Feminism," *Feminist Studies* 3 (Fall 1975): 126–40; Nancy Schrom Dye, *As Sisters and as Equals: Feminism, Unionism and the Women's Trade Union League of New York* (Columbia: University of Missouri Press, 1980); and Sarah Eisenstein, *Give Us Bread but Give Us Roses: Working Women's Consciousness in the United States, 1890 to the First World War* (London: Routledge and Kegan Paul, 1983). Three articles by Alice Kessler-Harris lay out many of the issues later pursued in this field: "Where are the Organized Women Workers?" *Feminist Studies* 3 (Fall 1975): 92–110; "Organizing the Unorganizable: Three Jewish Women and Their Union," *Labor History* 17 (Winter 1976): 5–23; and "Stratifying by Sex: Understanding the History of Working Women," in *Labor Market Segmentation*, ed. Richard C. Edwards, Michael Reich, and David M. Gordon, pp. 217–42 (Lexington, Mass.: D.C. Heath, 1975).

77. Martha May, "The Historical Problem of the Family Wage: The Ford Motor Company and the Five Dollar Day," *Feminist Studies* 8 (Summer 1982): 399–424, and "Bread before Roses: American Workingmen, Labor Unions and the Family Wage," in Milkman, *Women, Work, and Protest*, pp. 1–21; Alice Kessler-Harris, *A Woman's Wage: Symbolic Meanings and Social Consequences* (Lexington: University Press of Kentucky, 1990).

78. Goldin,⁻ *Understanding the Gender Gap*, quote on p. 66. See also Ileen DeVault, " 'Give the Boys a Trade': Gender and Job Choice in the 1890s," in Baron, *Work Engendered*, pp. 191–215, who shows that in the first decades of this century, men's clerical jobs in Pittsburgh were characterized more by respectability and stability than by exceptional possibilities for advancement; and Joanne Meyerowitz, *Women Adrift: Independent Wage Earners in Chicago, 1880–1930* (Chicago: University of Chicago Press, 1988), who discusses the individual and collective strategies by which working women made their own independence viable.

79. Cindy Sondik Aron, *Ladies and Gentlemen of the Civil Service: Middle-Class Workers in Victorian America* (New York: Oxford University Press, 1987); Margery W. Davies, "Women's Place Is at the Typewriter: The Feminization of the Clerical Labor Force," in Edwards, Reich, and Gordon, *Labor Market Segmentation*; and Margery W. Davies, *Women's Place Is at the Typewriter: Office Work and Office Workers, 1870–1930* (Philadelphia: Temple University Press, 1982); Cohen, *From Workshop to Office*; Susan Porter Benson, *Counter Cultures: Saleswomen, Managers, and Customers in American Department Stores, 1890–1940* (Urbana: University of Illinois Press, 1986). Kleinberg's Pittsburgh study shows that these jobs increased even in a primarily heavy industrial city.

80. Nancy F. Cott, *The Bonds of Womanhood: 'Woman's Sphere' in New England, 1780–1835* (New Haven: Yale University Press, 1977); Mary P. Ryan, *Cradle of the Middle Class: The Family in Oneida County, New York, 1780–1865* (Cambridge, England: Cambridge University Press, 1981); Nancy A. Hewitt, *Women's Activism and Social Change: Rochester, N.Y., 1822–1872* (Ithaca, N.Y.: Cornell University Press, 1984); and Hewitt, "Varieties of Voluntarism." See also Lori D. Ginzberg, *Women and the Work of Benevolence: Morality and Politics in the Northeastern United States, 1820–1855* (New Haven: Yale University Press, 1990).

81. Steven M. Buechler, *The Transformation of the Woman Suffrage Movement: The Case of Illinois, 1850–1920* (New Brunswick, N.J.: Rutgers University Press, 1986); Suzanne Lebsock, "Women and American Politics, 1880–1920," in Tilly and Gurin, *Women, Politics, and Change*, pp. 35–62. In the same volume, see the following: Jacqueline Jones, "The Political Implications of Black and White Women's Work in the South, 1890–1965," pp. 108–29; Nancy F. Cott, "Across the Great Divide: Women in Politics Before and After 1920," pp. 153–76; Evelyn Brooks Higginbotham, "In Politics to Stay: Black Women Leaders and Party Politics in the 1920s," pp. 199–220. On women's political mobilization via their role as managers of household budgets, see Dana Frank, "Housewives, Socialists and the Politics of Food: The New York Cost of Living Protests," *Feminist Studies* 11 (1985): 255–85.

82. See Henry Rosovsky, *Capital Formation in Japan, 1868–1940* (New York: Free Press of Glencoe, 1961); Thomas C. Smith, *The Agrarian Origins of Modern Japan* (Stanford, Calif.: Stanford University Press, 1959); John W. Hall, "The Castle Town and Japan's Modern Urbanization," *Far Eastern Quarterly* 15 (November 1955).

83. Laurel Cornell, "Hajnal and the Household in Asia: A Comparativist History of the Family in Preindustrial Japan, 1600–1870," *Journal of Family History* 12 (1987): 143–62, and "Peasant Women and Divorce in Preindustrial Japan," *Signs: Journal of Women in Culture and Society* 15 (1990): 710–32. See also Laurel Cornell, "The Deaths of Old Women. Folklore and Differential Mortality in Nineteenth-Century Japan," in *Recreating Japanese Women, 1600–1945*, ed. Gail Lee Bernstein, pp. 71–87 (Berkeley: University of California Press, 1991), which shows that there is little evidence of gerentocide but abundant suggestion of differential mortality among women; the important variables positively related to female early death were widowhood, being an outsider marrying in, or being without a family. G. William Skinner of the Anthropology Department, University of California, Davis, has looked at infanticide, reproductive strategies, and gender and power within couples

as part of his comparative study of several cities and their regions in late Tokugawa Japan. See also Kathleen S. Uno, "Women and Changes in the Household Division of Labor," in Bernstein, *Recreating Japanese Women*, pp. 17–41, who describes considerable flexibility in the household division of labor in the Tokugawa period (varying by class, with the samurai class least flexible, peasants and merchants more so), which disappeared with the spatial separation of work and family in industrialization and the Meiji redefinition of women's place.

84. Laurel Cornell, "Why Are There No Spinsters in Japan?" *Journal of Family History* 9 (1984): 326–39; Robert J. Smith and Ella Lury Wiswell, *The Women of Suye Mura* (Chicago: University of Chicago Press, 1982). Gail Lee Bernstein, *Haruko's World: A Japanese Farm Woman and Her Community* (Stanford, Calif.: Stanford University Press, 1983), shows similar practices persisted in the 1940s and 1950s. For insights into the experience of women in wealthy peasant families, see Anne Walthall, "The Life Cycle of Farm Women in Tokugawa Japan," in Bernstein, *Recreating Japanese Women*, pp. 42–70. An earlier collection of useful essays on Japanese women is Joyce Lebra, Joy Paulson, and Elizabeth Powers, eds., *Women in Changing Japan* (Stanford, Calif.: Stanford University Press, 1976).

85. Gary Saxonhouse and Gavin Wright, "Two Forms of Cheap Labor in Textile History," in *Technique, Spirit and Form in the Making of the Modern Economies: Essays in Honor of William N. Parker*, ed. Gary Saxonhouse and Gavin Wright, pp. 3–31, *Research in Economic History*, Supplement 3 (Greenwich, Conn.: JAI Press, 1984).

86. Gary Saxonhouse, "Country Girls and Communication among Competitors in the Japanese Cotton-Spinning Industry," pp. 97–125 in *Japanese Industrialization and Its Social Consequences*, ed. Hugh Patrick, pp. 97–125 (Berkeley: University of California Press, 1976).

87. Patricia Tsurumi, "Female Textile Workers and the Failure of Early Trade Unionism in Japan," *History Workshop Journal* 18 (Autumn 1984): 3–27, and *Factory Girls: Women in the Thread Mills of Meiji Japan* (Princeton: Princeton University Press, 1990).

88. Barbara Molony, "Activism among Women in the Taisho Cotton Textile Industry," in Bernstein, *Recreating Japanese Women*, pp. 217–38. See also Saxonhouse and Wright, "Two Forms of Cheap Labor."

89. Gail Lee Bernstein, "Women in the Silk-reeling Industry in Nineteenth-Century Japan," in *Japan and the World: Essays on Japanese History and Politics in Honour of Ishida Takeshi*, ed. Gail Lee Bernstein and Haruhiro Fukui, pp. 54–87 (New York: St. Martin's Press, 1988).

90. Joyce Chapman Lebra, "Women in an All-Male Industry: The Case of Sake Brewer Tatsu'uma Kiyo," in Bernstein, *Recreating Japanese Women*, pp. 131–48.

91. Sharon L. Sievers, "Feminist Criticism in Japanese Politics in the 1880s: The Experience of Kishida Toshiko," *Signs: Journal of Women in Culture and Society* 6 (1981): 602–16, and *Flowers in Salt: The Beginnings of Feminist Consciousness in Modern Japan* (Stanford, Calif.: Stanford University Press, 1983); Sharon N. Nolte and Sally Ann Hastings, "The Meiji State's Policy Toward Women, 1890–1910," in Bernstein, *Recreating Japanese Women*, pp. 151–74.

92. Margit Nagy, "Middle-Class Working Women during the Interwar Years," in Bernstein, *Recreating Japanese Women*, pp. 199–216. See also Miriam Silverberg, "The Modern Girl as Militant," ibid., pp. 239–66.

93. Yoshiko Miyake, "Doubling Expectations: Motherhood and Women's Factory Work under State Management in Japan in the 1930s and 1940s," in Bernstein, *Recreating Japanese Women*, pp. 267–95; and Larry S. Carney and Charlotte G. O'Kelly, "Women's Work and Women's Place in the Japanese Economic Miracle," in *Women Workers in Global Restructuring*, ed. Kathryn Ward, pp. 113–45 (Ithaca, N.Y.: ILR Press, Cornell University, 1990).

94. The topic of women in economic development in the contemporary world is one that logically should close this study. Since the early 1970s, much research has been done in this area, following up and going beyond the early analyses of Ester Boserup, *Woman's Role in Economic Development* (London: Allen and Unwin, 1970). Balanced coverage of this experience proved impossible within the length limitations with which I was working. Studies that look comparatively at women in late-industrializing and nonindustrial Asia, the Middle East, Africa, and Latin America, past and present, include Janet Z. Giele and Audrey Smock, eds., *Women and Society in International and Comparative Perspective* (New York: Wiley, 1977); Lois Beck and Nikki Keddie, eds., *Women in the Muslim World* (Cambridge, Mass.: Harvard University Press, 1978); Barbara Rogers, *The Domestication of Women: Discrimination in Developing Societies* (New York: St. Martin's Press, 1979); Lourdes Beneria and Gita Sen, "Accumulation, Reproduction, and Women's Role in Economic Development: Boserup Revisited," *Signs: Journal of Women in Culture and Society* 7 (1981): 279–98; Naomi Black and Ann Baker Cottrell, *Women and World Change: Equity Issues in Development* (Beverly Hills: Sage, 1981); Kate Young, Carol Wolkowitz, and Roslyn McCullagh, eds., *Of Marriage and the Market: Women's Subordination in International Perspective* (London: CSE Books, 1981); Richard Anker, Mayra Buvinic and Nadia H. Youssef, eds., *Women's Roles and Population Trends in the Third World* (London: Croom Helm, 1982); June Nash and Maria Patricia Fernandez-Kelly, eds., *Women, Men and the International Division of Labor* (Albany: SUNY Press, 1984); Daisy Dwyer and Judith Bruce, eds., *A Home Divided: Women and Income in the Third World* (Stanford, Calif.: Stanford University Press, 1988); Susan Tiano, "Gender, Work, and World Capitalism: Third World Women's Role in Development," in *Analyzing Gender*, ed. Beth Hess and Myra Marx Ferree (Beverly Hills: Sage, 1987); Valentine M. Moghadam, *Gender, Development, and Policy: Toward Equity and Empowerment* (Helsinki: World Institute for Development Economics Research [WIDER], 1990); Irene Tinker, ed., *Persistent Inequalities: Women and World Development* (New York: Oxford University Press, 1990); Nikki Keddie and Beth Baron, eds., *Shifting Boundaries: Women and Gender in Middle Eastern History and Theory* (New Haven: Yale University Press, 1991); Nancy Folbre, Bina Agarwal, Maria Floro, and Barbara Bergman, eds., *Women and Work in the World Economy* (London: Macmillan, 1991); and Hilda Kahne and Janet Giele, ed., *Women's Work and Women's Lives: The Continuing Struggle Worldwide* (Boulder, Colo.: Westview Press, 1992). This list includes only comparative studies; there are also many that are country specific.

95. John K. Fairbank, *The Great Chinese Revolution: 1800–1985* (New York:

Harper & Row, 1986), a survey for general readers based on vols. 10 to 15 of the *The Cambridge History of China*, which he helped edit, is the source of the following overview of Chinese political history.

96. Foot binding was much less common in southern China, where women were important workers in household-based rice production, and the Manchus eschewed it altogether. For a firsthand description of the painful process, see Ida Pruitt, *A Daughter of Han: The Autobiography of a Chinese Working Woman* (Stanford, Calif.: Stanford University Press, 1967; originally published 1945), p. 22.

97. Albert Feuerwerker, *China's Early Industrialization: Sheng Hsuan-Huai (1844–1916) and Mandarin Enterprise* (Cambridge, Mass.: Harvard University Press, 1958), quote on p. 16.

98. Thomas G. Rawski, *Economic Growth in Prewar China* (Berkeley: University of California Press, 1989). See also Albert Feuerwerker, *Economic Trends in the Republic of China, 1912–1949*, #31 of Michigan Papers in Chinese Studies (Ann Arbor: Center for Chinese Studies, University of Michigan, 1977). Looking back at economic developments from 1912 to 1949, Rawski argues that despite much disorder, the Chinese economy overall grew at a respectable rate from the end of the World War I to 1937, permitting the population to increase consumption modestly as well as to reproduce itself. Both manufacturing and transportation sectors made substantial gains. There was neither economic collapse nor industrial transformation. Republican governments did not tax agriculture for industrial investment, as did Japan, but the absence of rural reform (of inequal landholding, absentee landlordism, usurious rents, and an inequitable tax system) laid the groundwork for peasant support of the Communist party and its revolution. Both urban and rural economies had collapsed completely by mid-1948.

99. See Dorothy J. Solinger, *From Lathes to Looms: China's Industrial Policy in Comparative Perspective, 1979–1982* (Stanford, Calif.: Stanford University Press, 1991).

100. Most of these examples appear in Ono Kazuko, *Chinese Women in a Century of Revolution: 1850–1950*, ed. Joshua A. Fogel and trans. from Japanese by him and others (Stanford, Calif.: Stanford University Press, 1989; originally published 1978). Yazuko is a Japanese historian of Ming and Qing China who became interested in the modern period and in women's history in the late 1960s, taught courses and gave lectures, and finally wrote this book. Articles published by American scholars that touch the same subjects include Roxane Witke, "Mao Tse-tung, Women and Suicide," and "Woman as Politician in China of the 1920s" (includes Xiang Jingyu); and Suzette Leith, "Chinese Women in the Early Communist Movement" (also discusses Xiang Jingyu), all in *Women in China*, ed. Marilyn B. Young, #15 of Michigan Papers in Chinese Studies (Ann Arbor: Chinese Studies Center, University of Michigan, 1973); and Mary Backus Rankin, "The Emergence of Women at the End of the Ch'ing: The Case of Ch'iu Chin," Marjorie Topley, "Marriage Resistance in Rural Kwangtung," Margery Wolf, "Women and Suicide in China," Yi-Tsi Feuerwerker, "Women as Writers in the 1920's and 1930's," all in *Women in Chinese Society*, ed. Margery Wolf and Roxane Witke (Stanford, Calif.: Stanford University Press, 1975). Janice Stockard, *Daughters of the Canton Delta: Marriage Patterns and Economic Strategies in South China* (Stanford, Calif.:

Stanford University Press, 1989), is the most recent discussion of the "bridedaughters" of Kwangtung and their silk-reeling wage work.

101. Emily Honig, *Sisters and Strangers: Women in the Shanghai Cotton Mills, 1919–1949* (Stanford, Calif.: Stanford University Press, 1986). Another example: Christina Gilmartin, "Gender, Politics, and Patriarchy in China: The Experiences of Early Women Communists, 1920–27," in *Promissory Notes: Women in the Transition to Socialism*, ed. Sonia Kruks, Rayna Rapp, and Marilyn Young, pp. 82–105 (New York: Monthly Review Press, 1989).

102. Arthur P. Wolf, "The Women of Hai-shan: A Demographic Portrait," in Wolf and Witke, *Women in Chinese Society*.

103. Susan Mann, "Grooming a Daughter for Marriage: Brides and Wives in the Mid-Ch'ing Period," pp. 204–30; Rubie S. Watson, "Wives, Concubines, and Maids: Servitude and Kinship in the Hong Kong Region, 1900–1940," pp. 231–55; and Gail Hershatter, "Prostitution and the Market in Women in Early Twentieth-Century Shanghai," pp. 256–85—all in *Marriage and Inequality in Chinese Society*, ed. Rubie S. Watson and Patricia Buckley Ebrey (Berkeley: University of California Press, 1991). In the same volume, see also Patricia Buckley Ebrey, "Introduction," pp. 1–24, and Rubie S. Watson, "Afterword: Marriage and Gender Inequality," pp. 347–68, both of which put the volume's empirical studies into theoretical and comparative frameworks. See also Delia Davin, *Woman-Work: Women and the Party in Revolutionary China* (Oxford, England: Clarendon Press, 1976), which examines marriage and the family in the context of women in the Jiangxi Soviet and liberated areas (i.e., places where Communists were able to institute policies before the declaration of the PRC in 1949).

104. Davin, *Woman-Work*, pp. 26–30, quote on p. 28.

105. Compare, for example, Aleen Holly and Christine Towne Bransfield, "The Marriage Law: Basis of Change for China's Women," in Lynne B. Iglitzin and Ruth Ross, *Women in the World: A Comparative Study*, pp. 363–73 (Santa Barbara: Clio Books, 1976); with Davin, *Woman-Work*, and Jane Barrett, "Women Hold up Half the Sky," in Young, *Women in China*, pp. 193–200.

106. Judith Stacey, *Patriarchy and Socialist Revolution in China* (Berkeley: University of California Press, 1983); Margery Wolf, *Revolution Postponed: Women in Contemporary China* (Stanford, Calif.: Stanford University Press, 1985); Kay Johnson, *Women, the Family and Peasant Revolution in China* (Chicago: University of Chicago Press, 1983), quote on p. 216. An analysis of interviews with emigrés from mainland China and available statistics done by William L. Parish and Martin F. Whyte, *Village and Family in Contemporary China* (Chicago: University of Chicago Press, 1978), had come to similar conclusions earlier. For more recent evaluation, see Jonathan Ocko, "Women, Property, and Law in the People's Republic of China," in Watson and Ebrey, *Marriage and Inequality*, pp. 213–346, which discusses the retreat from free divorce in the marriage law of 1980 and asks whether "changes in enacted law influence changes in practice or merely reflect changes in social and economic organization" (p. 358). On the possibility that village collectivism may again be encouraging patrilocal marriage, see William Lavely, "Marriage and Mobility under Rural Collectivism," in Watson and Ebrey, *Marriage and Inequality in Chinese Society*, pp. 286–312. And for the current views of early commentators,

see Marilyn B. Young, "Chicken Little in China: Women after the Cultural Revolution," pp. 233–47, and Delia Davin, "Of Dogma, Dicta and Washing Machines: Women in the People's Republic of China," pp. 354–58, both in Kruks, Rapp, and Young, *Promisory Notes*.

107. Ansley J. Coale, Wang Feng, Nancy E. Riley, and Lin Fu De, "Recent Trends in Fertility and Nuptiality in China," *Science* 251 (January 26, 1991): 389–93. The 1963 peak was caused by a mini baby boom after the country's recovery from the famine of the GLF and the lingering malnutrition of the following years. In the years from 1940 through 1958, the total fertility rate had ranged from 5 to 6.5 only. See Janet Banister, *China's Changing Population* (Stanford, Calif.: Stanford University Press, 1987), p. 230, table 8.2.

108. Lillian Li, "Life and Death in a Chinese Famine," and James Lee, Cameron Campbell, and Guofu Tan, "Infanticide and Family Planning in Late Imperial China: Price and Population History in Rural Fengtian, 1772–1873," in *Chinese History in Economic Perspective*, ed. Thomas G. Rawski and Lillian M. Li (Berkeley: University of California Press, 1992).

109. Amartya Sen, "More than 100 Million Women Are Missing," *New York Review of Books* 37 (December 20, 1991): 61–66, and unsigned article in the *New York Times* (West Coast ed.), Tuesday, November 5, 1991, pp. B5, B9. See also Ansley Coale, "Excess Female Mortality and the Balance of the Sexes in the Population: An Estimate of the Number of 'Missing Females'" *Population and Development Review* 17 (September 1991): 517–23.

110. Emily Honig and Gail Hershatter, *Personal Voices: Chinese Women in the 1980s* (Stanford, Calif.: Stanford University Press, 1988), acknowledge the urban bias of their sources (magazines addressed to women, advice books for the young, letters to newspapers); only around 30 percent of China's population is urban. Quote is on p. 340.

"High" Imperialism and the "New" History

MICHAEL ADAS

Between roughly 1870 and the outbreak of World War I in 1914, global history took on a new meaning as contacts and exchanges between the world's cultural areas and diverse environments multiplied and intensified dramatically. The final burst of centuries of European overseas expansion, which had begun as far back as the late Middle Ages, culminated in the extension of European formal colonization—at the annual rate of territories equal to the size of metropolitan France—or of informal control to virtually all of the globe. This imposition of global hegemony was accompanied by the completion of a Europe-centered global communications network and the migration of tens of millions of Europeans to overseas settlement colonies from New Zealand to Argentina. The needs of Europe's industrializing economies and the continent's concomitant political and social instability also led to the inexorable spread of the capitalist market system to areas hitherto as isolated from outside contacts as the interior of Africa and the islands of the South Pacific. By August 1914, European colonial bureaucracies had laid the basis for the widespread reproduction of the uniquely European form of political organization, the nation–state. Colonial schools and workshops had become relay stations for the global diffusion of European languages, institutions, and ideas, as well as the material culture spawned by the scientific and industrial revolutions. Thus the five decades before World War I formed a period of unprecedented closure for the human community and consequently all of the life and lands of the earth.

Scarcely four decades ago, most of what had been written and was being written about this watershed era in world history dealt with the motives, decisions, and activities of Europeans, usually Europeans from the privileged classes. The history of imperialism consisted largely of nar-

311

rative accounts of the machinations of European politicans and diplomats, descriptions of colonial policy formulation and administrative systems, and romanticized sagas of intrepid explorers and self-sacrificing missionaries. The most lively debates centered—as they had since the nineteenth century—on the fears and calculations of European leaders that had been responsible for the imperialist "scramble" for territory in the last decades of the nineteenth century. The most apt metaphor for this overwhelmingly Eurocentric historiography was the figure of Charles George "Chinese" Gordon, reproduced in innumerable paintings and lithographs from the 1880s onward. Resplendent in white uniform and pith helmet, Gordon fearlessly strides across the veranda of his headquarters in Khartoum to confront single-handedly the barbaric hordes of the Mahdist rising that threatened Anglo-Egyptian control of the Sudan.

Today, the great majority of scholars of the history of European colonialism concentrate their efforts on the impact of imperialism on the colonized peoples. They seek to reconstruct the colonial experience by building from the everyday lives of once-neglected social groups, such as the peasantry, urban workers, women, and increasingly those on the margins— indigenous prostitutes, bandits, vagabonds, and outcasts from the colonizer community. From this new perspective, the colonizers are drawn into expansion by local conditions and ad hoc decisions by commanders on the spot, rather than considerations of grand strategy. European conquest and rule become dependent on indigenous collaborators. The impact of imperialism is reckoned through the study of its effects on colonized groups and ecologies, rather than on the basis of balance sheets of the debits and credits of European capitalists and great powers. From this perspective, Gordon is reduced to a sweat-drenched, defeated commander on a mission conceived in arrogance, desperately striving to ward off the forces of Muhammad Ahmad, the Mahdist liberator of the Sudan. Instead of the climax of the dramatic confrontation on the veranda, his death results from a chance shot that finds him as he peers over the battlements at Khartoum.[1]

As the radical transformations in the historiography of imperialism sketched here suggest, there is perhaps no better barometer of the sweeping changes that have revolutionized Western approaches to the writing of history in the decades since the end of World War II. By the 1970s, the first wave of the "new history" had produced a shift away from the elitist, political and military emphasis of much of the earlier literature on imperialism to a focus on social history and questions of political economy, largely relating to the European societies whose overseas expansion accounted for the global hegemony of the West. Concurrent with the exploration of the social and economic origins of the great burst of European overseas conquest in the last decades of the nineteenth century was the increasing attention given to the impact of imperialism on African and

Asian societies that the Europeans ruled directly, as well as those in Latin America and parts of Asia, particularly the Middle East and China, that they sought to control informally. This move away from a Eurocentric perspective was given great impetus by the failed attempts of the Western powers, led by the postwar U.S. colossus, to control events in the (at least formally) decolonizing Third World. Foreign policy setbacks in China, Latin America, and elsewhere, which culminated in the French–American debacle in Indochina, brought a concomitant shift away from an elite focus to a proliferation of scholarship on the African, Asian, and Latin American peasantry; urban poor; and other social groups that had hitherto constituted the "people without history."[2] Added impetus for this shift was given by the increasingly influential writings of African and Asian scholars, whose works mirrored the fundamental challenges that political decolonization had posed for Western global hegemony.

The application of the cliometric techniques that were in vogue in the 1970s in American and European social history and in the history of slavery played a surprisingly minor role in the transformation of the historiography of imperialism. But additional permutations in the "new history" of the postwar decades were readily apparent in further reorientations in approaches to the history of colonized societies. The burgeoning of area studies programs, which had become a dominant factor in research and scholarship on non-Western peoples in virtually all the social science disciplines by the 1960s, enhanced the nonelitist, non-Eurocentric approaches of the social historians. In fact, at their most extreme, non-Western area specialists sought to fashion "autonomous" histories of colonized societies that pushed the colonial officials, missionaries, and explorers, who had once held center stage, into the wings, if not offstage altogether.[3]

Area studies programs also facilitated interdisciplinary approaches to the history of the age of European global hegemony that privileged social issues and, increasingly from the late 1970s, largely as a result of the influence of anthropological research and theory, culture. In African historiography in particular, great emphasis was placed on the collection and interpretation of oral evidence from royal genealogies to folktales and indigenous curing practices. Oral history techniques pioneered in African research were increasingly applied to reconstruct the history of nonliterate, nonelite groups throughout Asia and Latin America, as field research at the village and local levels was taken up by historians with extensive anthropological training.[4] New approaches were also devised for the interpretation of more traditional textual materials that incorporated techniques of literary analysis pioneered by such French deconstructionists as Jacques Derrida and the theoretical insights of such anthropologists as Pierre Bourdieu and of social historians, especially Michel Foucault.[5] The increasing emphasis on the use of nontraditional sources and innovative theoretical frameworks in the writing of the history of nonelite social groups resulted in a somewhat belated, but often quite sophisticated, attention to gender issues as they converged in the colonial context with questions of racial division and foreign domination.

Social History and the Origins of Imperialism Controversy

In part, the historiography of imperialism best underscores the radical nature of broader postwar transformations in our approaches to history because writing on colonialism had traditionally been so resolutely Eurocentric and elite centered, so overwhelmingly focused on issues of policy formation and diplomacy, and so wedded to the narrative style rather than analysis or the testing of theory. Ironically, the first stirring of the revolution that was to occur in the writing of the history of imperialism began with the renewal of a half-century-old debate that had been centered on the motivations of politicians and diplomats and the forces of political and economic change within Europe itself. The protracted controversy concerning the origins of the late nineteenth-century burst of European imperial expansion in Africa, Southeast Asia, and the Pacific Islands had begun with works that were in large part focused on social and economic, rather than diplomatic, issues. From very different perspectives, J. A. Hobson, a journalist and Liberal critic of British colonial involvement in South Africa, and V. I. Lenin and other Marxist writers who wrote in the years on either side of World War I, argued that the acceleration of European overseas conquest after roughly 1870 could be traced to flaws (in Hobson's view) or the fundamentally dysfunctional nature (in Lenin's interpretation) of the industrial, capitalist economies of western Europe.[6] In the interwar years and especially in the two decades after World War II, the economic origins thesis in its various guises was assailed by scholars as diverse in approach as William Langer, J. A. Schumpeter, and Raymond Aron.[7] By the 1960s, arguments both for and against the political economy views of the origins of imperialism had been marshaled repeatedly, and very often redundantly, in both synthetic works and collections of essays on the question.[8]

Neither Hobson nor Lenin had provided convincing empirical data on or an in-depth analysis of the workings of Europe's industrial economies in the era of expansion. In fact, until the early 1960s those engaged in the origins of imperialism debate added very little to our understanding of the social origins of the prewar acceleration of colonization.[9] The protracted debate had bogged down in quarrels over the motivations of European policymakers and the meaning of various diplomatic initiatives in the areas undergoing colonization. By the late 1950s, those arguing that the outburst of expansion was rooted primarily, if not exclusively, in calculations of political and diplomatic advantage were clearly in the ascendancy. Accordingly, writing on imperialism was overwhelmingly focused on straight narrative accounts of the maneuvers and policy decisions of European politicians and diplomats.

Interestingly, an important impetus to innovation in the writing of the history of imperialism came from a revolution that was occurring in a related, but until then clearly distinct, field of historical controversy. In works such as William Langer's *European Alliances and Alignments* and (some have argued[10]) even in Lenin's *Imperialism*, the forces that had led to European overseas colonization were (at least implicitly) linked to those that brought on World War I. The publication in Germany of Fritz Fischer's *Griff nach der Weltmacht* in 1961[11] not only linked European imperialist ambitions to the coming of the war but rooted both in the skewed economic and social history of Wilhelmine Germany. Fischer's writings and the heated debate they generated among German historians[12] were centered on his thesis that Germany's leaders deliberately used the assassination of Archduke Ferdinand at Sarajevo to provoke a *European* war in 1914, and that before and during the war German policy was shaped in accordance with a series of expansionist war plans and aims. But Fischer's argument that the decision for war and the plans to pursue it arose from the determination to remedy domestic economic problems and social tensions through war and imperial expansion gave great impetus to attempts to revive the economic interpretation of the origins of European imperialism.

What amounted in Fischer's works to overviews of Wilhelmine domestic dislocations were analyzed in great detail and in turn linked to late nineteenth-century German overseas expansion in Hans-Ulrich Wehler's seminal study of *Bismarck und der Imperialismus*.[13] Wehler's work and subsequent writings extensively reworked economic arguments regarding the origins of imperialism, shifting the focus away from the problem of surplus capital to a broader analysis of the effects of the series of agrarian and industrial depressions that struck the industrial powers of Europe and North America between the 1870s and the early 1890s. Wehler's emphasis on the responses of Bismarck and other German leaders to the domestic tensions generated by recurring economic downturns was complemented by a number of revisionist studies that focused on the external manifestations of the prolonged crisis. The most pathbreaking of these was D.C.M. Platt's monograph on *Finance, Trade and Politics in British Foreign Policy, 1814–1914*.[14] On the basis of a meticulous examination of Foreign and Colonial Office documents, Platt explored in depth the nature of the interaction between British mercantile and industrial interests and the British political and diplomatic elite that reluctantly expanded the empire in the last decades of the nineteenth century. Platt concluded that the British policymakers who favored expansion acted to shore up a free-trade–based domestic economy and an imperial network that were increasingly threatened by tariff barriers, both in other industrial nations and in their colonial dependencies; rising competition for markets on the part of industrial rivals; and the British perception that diplomats and government officials of competing industrial nations were intervening unfairly to secure markets and investment outlets for their citizens. In Platt's view, rather than abandon free trade in the face of the tariff barriers and interventionist policies of rival industrial powers, the British chose to carve out colonial preserves where their own merchants and entrepreneurs would be guaranteed equal (if not favored) access to market and investment opportunities.

Revisionist approaches to the economic interpretation of the origins of European imperialism radically altered the terms of the long-standing debate by exposing the ex post facto fallacy that had informed most of the critiques of the Hobson–Lenin theses. To argue that investment did not flow to the new colonies, or that markets did not materialize or European emigrants settle there, ignored the actual fears and calculations that shaped the decisions of the European leaders who were responsible for overseas annexations. Such arguments anachronistically read back outcomes that lay years, often decades, in the future. In the face of unstable industrial economies and growing competition for overseas markets and resources, expansion-minded European leaders acted to allay the *Torschlusspanik*, or "fear of the closing door," that threatened to foreclose on future potential for industrial growth. They were very likely to overestimate that potential with regard to African or Asian areas that became targets of their colonizing drives. Colonial markets and raw materials were hailed as ways of leveling off the boom-and-bust cycles that gripped the industrial economies of Europe and North America in the late nineteenth century. Advocates of expansion, such as Cecil Rhodes and Jules Ferry, argued that this stabilization would exorcise the Marxist specter of social revolution and shore up the deteriorating hegemony of the aristocracy and the middle classes. Recent scholarship has also revealed the extent to which these advocates packaged the imperial mission for popular consumption in the European metropoles both before and after World War I.[15]

Revisionist approaches, which at their best melded socioeconomic forces with diplomatic moves and political initiatives, also underscored the shortcomings of the tendency of those on all sides of the origins of imperialism debate to compartmentalize political, economic, and humanitarian motives. Revisionist works demonstrated that there was no need to demonstrate the direct influence of financiers and industrialists that Hobson and Marxist writers argued had determined the decisions of politicians. Political leaders could and did act in what they perceived to be the economic interest of their nations as a whole. Decisions to extend colonial possessions could be motivated by strategic and economic interests at the same time. The British intervention in Malaya, for example, was prompted by both a concern to secure the vital sealanes that passed through the Malacca Straits and to put an end to the recurring wars in the interior of the peninsula that threatened the flow of tin and other export commodities. The defense of India that Ronald Robinson and John Gallagher argued underlay British decisions to "go ashore" in Africa in the late nineteenth century,[16] was ultimately grounded in economic considerations. India provided a major field for British investment and critical outlets for the sale of its manufactures, from cotton textiles to railway locomotives. The subcontinent also supplied a steady flow of cheap labor for the rest of the empire and armies that had repeatedly been used to force open markets and access to resources from China to the Persian Gulf. Even missionary motivations included an important economic dimension, for "native" converts were sure to make better laborers and buy more machine-produced textiles than "lazy, half-naked heathens."

Another form of compartmentalization that revisionist approaches to imperialism challenged was the tendency to exclude from the discourse on colonialism consideration of dominance that fell short of outright conquest and annexation. The revisionist works of the 1960s and 1970s did much to advance our understanding of the forces within the industrializing nations of Europe that accounted for the shift from a preference for gunboat diplomacy and informal control before roughly 1870 to an orgy of conquest and direct annexation in the decades leading up to World War I.[17] The importance of informal imperialism, particularly as it related to the rise of the American empire,[18] in the overall process of Western global hegemony was increasingly realized. In addition, the fate of areas such as China, Persia, and Siam, which were not formally incorporated into the empires of any of the industrialized great powers, was scrutinized with reference to the legacy of imperialist dominance.

In the 1970s and 1980s, the social history and political economy approaches that had radically transformed the origins of imperialism debate with regard to the expanding industrial powers were extended to the colonized areas. Increasing attention was given to the ways in which the spread of the European-controlled world-market system had destabilized Asian and African economies and social systems and thus precipitated severe economic crises. These crises had in turn led to political instability that prodded European colonizers, ever fearful of industrial rivals, to intervene in and ultimately colonize much of the rest of the globe. From Egypt and West Africa to Malaya and the Indonesian archipelago, the forces that had destabilized states that had formerly been able to check European expansion were explored in depth. Increasing stress was placed on the ways in which the expansion-minded Western leaders used indigenous fiscal and political crises to justify wars of conquest and long-term annexations of additional territories.[19] Thus the social history and political economy perspectives that had made possible the transformation of the debate on the origins of late nineteenth-century imperialism also fueled the shift from what had been overwhelmingly Eurocentric approaches to the history of imperialism to a growing emphasis on the roles and fate of the colonized at a variety of social levels.

The reassessment of imperialist expansion that focuses on the relationship between instability on the "periphery" and European interventionism can also be linked to issues raised by Fritz Fischer and his school regarding the outbreak of World War I. These connections suggest new ways of looking at the crises in North Africa and the Balkans that set the stage for the 1914–18 conflict and ultimately precipitated the war. Though these links have thus far been dealt with only from a rather traditional diplomatic perspective,[20] a good deal of evidence points to the importance of internal dislocations and turmoil in both Morocco and the Balkans that proved critical in the series of confrontations that led up to the war. From this perspective, the Balkan states can be seen as informally colonized areas, clearly dominated economically, and to varying degrees politically, by one or the other of the great powers. The ethnonationalist sentiments of the Balkan peoples were perhaps more pronounced than those of most other colonized groups at this time. But the influence exerted by the great powers and their squabbles over and designs on the Balkan states very much resembled the scramble to partition Africa, Southeast Asia, and other parts of the globe that have routinely been covered by historians of imperialism.

The End of the White Hero in the Tropics: Rethinking Colonial Conquest and Rule

The growing attention given to conditions in the areas colonized in efforts to understand the late nineteenth-century spurt of imperialist expansion was part of a larger reassessment of the patterns of conquest and empire building in this era. Early writings on the partitions of Africa, Southeast Asia, and the South Pacific had stressed the overwhelming advantages that the scientific and industrial revolutions had given Europeans in waging wars of conquest. Works on the expansion of European empires were predominately narratives of key battles, and in some cases protracted military campaigns, that stressed the good use to which redoubtable European commanders, such as Sir Garnet Wolseley and Charles Mangin, had put the breech-loading rifles and field artillery bequeathed by rapid advances in metallurgy and ballistics in industrialized nations. Emulating the boys' adventure tales that enjoyed such great popularity in the age of "high" imperialism, historical accounts endlessly chronicled the stunning victories of small bands of well-disciplined, stalwart European soldiers over motley (but often "fierce," as appropriate for barbarians or savages) "hordes" of ill-disciplined "native warriors." The massacre of the Mahdist cavalry at Omdurman in 1898, the brave stand of a tiny force of British soldiers against a vastly larger force of Zulus at Rourkes Drift in 1879, the rout of the Boxer "rebels" by the defenders of the international legations in Beijing in 1900, all contributed to the elaboration of the myth of heroic white conquerors, sweeping aside the "native" defenders of degenerate and despotic African and Asian rulers and imposing the honest and efficient rule of the European colonizers. In all instances, the coming of European rule was seen as a watershed event in the history of the peoples thus subjugated; the beginning of an era of political stability, economic growth, and progressive social reform.

The remarkable staying power of the myth of the white hero in the tropics is amply evidenced by the presumed links between colonialism and educational, technological, and social advances embedded in much of the modernization literature that was in vogue among American social scientists in particular in the 1960s and early 1970s.[21] But the work of African and Asian area specialists over the past three decades or so has revealed a very different, and vastly more complex, understanding of the dynamics of European conquest and colonial rule. Though organizational advantages of European-led military forces were apparent in Java and India by the late eighteenth century, European land weaponry was not markedly superior to that of many of the indigenous forces that contended for control of these areas. On the sea, the Europeans had attained supremacy in most areas of the globe centuries earlier, and access to reinforcements and supplies via naval linkages often proved a critical factor in the outcome of wars between the Dutch and English and Asian kingdoms.

On land the (often narrow) margin of victory that the Dutch and British enjoyed resulted mainly from divisions among rival kingdoms and within indigenous ruling groups; the Europeans' ability to buy allies and recruit soldiers from the peoples of the Indonesia archipelago and South Asia; and even (as the research done in the past two decades has made clear[22]) the financial backing of indigenous trading groups disgruntled by the exactions and constraints imposed by indigenous rulers. The critical victories that the English East India Company won over indigenous lords in Bengal in the 1750s and 1760s, for example, had less to do with the generalship of Robert Clive, which traditional accounts stressed, than the cooptation of key indigenous social groups. Local commercial magnates, especially the Jagat Seths, helped finance the troops and pay the spies working for the East India Company. Critical allies of Siraj-ud-Duala, who led the coalition opposing the British, had been bought out with money or promises of political gain or a combination of the two. Thus, pivotal East India Company victories, such as that at Plassey in 1757, were won more through subterfuge and sowing division among the Indian princes than as a result of Clive's skills as a commander on the battlefield (which nonetheless were considerable) or the superior courage of the troops in the pay of the future colonizers of the Indian subcontinent.[23]

Most of these earlier patterns continued throughout the nineteenth century and into the decades of high imperialism after 1870. With the spread of industrialization in Europe and North America, the technological advantages of the colonizers improved dramatically and at an accelerating pace. Advances in communications, land transportation, and in the firepower and accuracy of hand weapons and artillery were most critical.[24] But long-standing rivalries among the indigenous peoples and kingdoms of Africa and Asia remained key factors in most conquest situations, and troops recruited from among the colonized remained the mainstay of European colonial armies and expeditionary forces.[25]

From the mid-nineteenth century a new pattern of collaboration and conquest in the military sphere emerged as areas colonized earlier provided the armies for further European conquests. Most notably, the Indian army became Great Britain's "barrack in the Oriental seas."[26] This reservoir of armed manpower played a critical role in the extension of the empire into Burma and elsewhere in Southeast Asia, East Africa, and the Middle East and provided the bulk of the punitive forces sent against China, Afghani kingdoms, and other states that dared to resist British designs in the late nineteenth century. The financial support of indigenous mercantile groups for the European colonial advance declined or disappeared in the late nineteenth century, but increasingly European expeditionary forces, and in many cases their European commanders, were paid for by revenues drawn from areas colonized earlier. Just as Bengali commercial profits and agrarian taxes had proven vital to British efforts to establish paramountcy over the Indian subcontinent as a whole, revenues from the Indian Empire were used to finance the great expansion of the British Empire across the Indian Ocean zone in the last half of the nineteenth century.

The growing realization of the importance of indigenous peoples to the building of European overseas empires in the age of "high" imperialism has led in turn to a fundamental recasting of our understanding of the process of conquest and the consolidation of colonial rule. To begin with, the gradual nature of this process has been increasingly emphasized, as historians have realized that what had been seen as "decisive" battles and formal seizures of power often had minimal effects on the great majority of the peoples colonized as a result. What earlier historians had characterized as watersheds in fact distorted by obscuring the continuities that were the dominant theme in formally colonized societies. In addition, heightened attention to the responses of the colonized soon made clear the impressive extent to which African and Asian peoples had been able to resist European domination, despite internal divisions and the superior firepower of the colonizing armies. From the decades of frustration felt by French commanders attempting to subdue Muslim leaders like Samory Turé and Ahmadou Sekou in the western Sudan to the sustained guerrilla resistance of local Vietnamese notables and their peasant followers in Indochina, the efforts of indigenous peoples to forestall European conquest and rule were widespread and persistent.[27] In the past decade or so, a growing number of studies have also emphasized the extent to which African and Asian peoples undermined European efforts to exert effective control over their lives by employing time-honored techniques of collusion, concealment, and feigned ineptitude, as well as avoidance protest tactics, which have included flight, banditry, and sectarian withdrawal from the agents of the European colonial order.[28]

Increasing emphasis on the African and Asian side of European colonial expansion has inevitably led to radically different approaches to European administration and rule. Early studies on the history of imperialism concentrated on the personalities and policies of French, British, or Dutch proconsuls and elaborate descriptions—often bordering on the equivalent of bureaucratic handbooks—of the administrative structure of the colonial empires, both in Europe and overseas. Research over the past two or three decades has shifted the emphasis in the analysis of European colonial rule to groups among the colonized that collaborated with the Europeans in ways that were essential to their capacity to govern overseas dependencies. This shift has resulted in a very different view of the composition of empires in the era of European global hegemony.

Whatever the intentions and policy decisions of the European overlords, recent research has revealed that the actual impact of colonial rule depended far more on the responses and actions of indigenous allies, particularly those at the level of the regional gentry and the local community. In this view, ultimate authority rested with the handfuls of civilian officials and military commanders who perched precariously atop jerry-built colonial administrative edifices. But for day-to-day administration or special operations, such as the taking of censuses and the vital collection of revenues, Indian or African subaltern officials, clerks, accountants, surveyors, and local notables were largely in control. At the top of the imperial administrative pyramid, colonial officials were dependent on indigenous clerks and recordkeepers, surrounded by guards recruited from the colonized population, and dependent in their decisions on the reports and advice proffered by indigenous administrators, captive princes, and men of influence in the localities or at the all-colony level.

As one moved down the bureaucratic hierarchy, the ranks of European personnel thinned rapidly as layer after layer of Asian or African intermediaries, "native" soldiers and policemen, and finally city and village notables took over the actual running of the empire. Very often these indigenous allies of the colonizers exercised the effective power (and in doing so reaped a good portion of the status and pecuniary rewards) that the Europeans regarded as their entitlement in view of their victories on the battlefield. Furthermore, many of these subordinate administrators and functionaries were carryovers from precolonial states. The colonizers were often content to leave the "traditional" administrative apparatus and bureaucratic hierarchy of conquered areas pretty much intact, given the costs and potential social upheavals involved in extensive restructuring and reform.[29]

This new vision of the dynamics of colonial rule points to the conclusion that the European overlords knew a good deal less about colonized peoples and administered them far less effectively than they or we had long assumed. The pivotal roles played by indigenous intermediaries in colonial governance also meant that they could use the colonial overlords to enhance their own wealth and social standing; that many of the colonizers' allies gained markedly as a result of European conquest. But their gains inevitably came at the expense of European colonizers in the form of revenues they were able to siphon off for their own uses, of their ability to frustrate European initiatives for political and social reforms, and of the influence they continued to wield over their subordinates and the colonized population that fell under their jurisdiction.[30] The devices with which indigenous intermediaries were able to check the actual power exerted by European officials very often resulted mainly in the personal aggrandizement or enrichment of the African or Asian officials or functionaries in question. But embezzlement, collusion, underreporting, and pilfering were also seen by the colonized as ways of buffering the revenues and forced-labor demands of colonial regimes. Though the benefits were invariably unequally distributed, whole communities and patron–client networks that extended to numerous households could conspire in these schemes to frustrate the demands of the alien European overlords.

Although Margaret Strobel explores in detail gender issues relating to imperialism in another essay in this volume, one facet of the roles that European women played in the empire has important bearing on the dynamics of colonial governance. Following Percival Spear and a number of pre–World War II writers,[31] historians of imperialism long accepted the thesis that the growing presence of European women in the colonies was a critical factor in the decline of the symbiotic interdependence between European colonizers and indigenous elites and administrative subordinants on which the early consolidation of European colonial rule had been anchored. In this view, increasing numbers of European women in the colonies led to growing disapprobation of and strictures against the sexual liaisons between European administrators, merchants, and soldiers and indigenous women that had been widespread in the early stages of European empire building in Asia and Africa.

Whether the conduits were the local brothels, longer-term relationships with indigenous mistresses, or—in a surprising number of cases—marriages, these links to females from the colonized population were deemed vital channels through which European officials built enduring links to key groups and, more generally, kept abreast of developments in the societies they ruled. The European wives and prospective spouses of colonial officials and military commanders understandably, in Spear's rendering, objected to sexual liaisons of any sort between European men and indigenous women. Thus, the jealousy and pronounced racism of growing numbers of European women—buttressed by the pronouncements of multiplying numbers of Christian missionaries—increasingly cut the colonizers off from indigenous society and ways of learning about the attitudes and culture of indigenous peoples. Stung by the growing exclusivism and racism of the colonizers, indigenous elite groups and subordinates grew hostile and eventually determined to overthrow European imperialist dominance.

Helen Callaway has countered the vision of the *memsahib* as the catalyst for the demise of the imperial symbiosis between European conquerors and indigenous allies with the argument that rather than destroy the empires through their racist exclusivism, the "feminization" of colonial administration provided the qualities—"sympathetic understanding, egalitarian rather than authoritarian relations, diplomacy and flexibility"—that in fact extended the life of the European imperium and made for a relatively nonviolent process of decolonization.[32] But as a number of other authors have pointed out,[33] the notion of the destructive *memsahib* distorts the actual forces at work in the colonial setting. Male administrators in the colonies, not their wives, designed the settlement patterns that set colonizer communities physically apart from the populations they ruled, and males formulated the laws that forbade miscegenation and even significant social contacts between European women and African or Asian males. Fears of sexual assault and broader racist sentiments among European males were no less, and perhaps often more, pronounced than among females coming out to the colonies, as evidenced in contemporary literature, such as E. M. Forster's *A Passage to India*, by the contrast between the attitudes of Ronny Heaslop and the views of his newly arrived fiancée, Adela Quested, and Heaslop's mother, Mrs. Moore.

Ironically, the growing social divide between colonizer and colonized was felt most keenly by those groups among the latter that had allied themselves to the Europeans and served in their courts, district offices, and counting houses. Those who worked with the colonizers on a day-to-day basis and who had adopted European culture the most extensively were the most humiliated by the growing arrogance of the Europeans and the most affected by the racist attitudes and legal ordinances that increasingly constricted the social contacts and career prospects of even the most able and best educated of the colonized. As a number of recent studies have shown,[34] though the rise of European global hegemony and social relations within the colonies had much to do with the hardening of racial boundaries, scientific and technological transformations within Europe itself played a pivotal role. The ideology of imperialism in the age of European global hegemony was grounded in the demonstrated material superiority of the Europeans; a superiority evinced by the mastery of nature they had gained through their scientific discoveries and the power that their technological advancement gave them to wage war, conquer time and space, and tap hitherto unknown or scarcely used resources of the earth. Presumed scientific and technological superiority informed most variants of the civilizing mission ideology by which the European colonizers sought to justify the casualties caused by wars of conquest, the revenues and labor demanded from subjugated peoples, and the reform initiatives introduced by well-intended administrators and missionaries to uplift backward and benighted peoples.

The historiographical shift in perspectives on empire from the European metropolis to the complex variations of administrative structures and power alignments in diverse colonial locales has prompted some historians to question whether the empires were in any meaningful sense unified entities in the age of European global hegemony.[35] Within the British Empire alone, these writers argue, one finds several clearly distinct types of colonial dominance. At a minimum, these would include the so-called White Dominions (Canada, Australia, and New Zealand); settler colony–tropical dependency mixes like Kenya and Southern Rhodesia; protectorates like Egypt and Kuwait; vestigial plantation colonies like Fiji and those remaining in the West Indies; and a bewildering range of tropical dependencies from the massive conglomeration of cultures and civilizations that made up the Indian Empire to what the colonizers perceived as the wild backwaters of Borneo and the islands of the South Pacific. Even in the metropolis, these diverse dependencies were administered or affected by policies formulated in separate government departments and bureaucracies—in London, for example, the Colonial Office, the India Office, the Foreign Office, the Admiralty—that jealously guarded their own prerogatives and often worked at cross-purposes to members of other agencies whom they perceived as rivals, sometimes on a par with the French or Germans.

Those who contend that visions of unified European empires, such as that exemplified by the notion of the Pax Britannica, were more myth than reality point out that there was little of substance to bind together geographically divided and quite distinctive colonial locales. Colonial policies were highly variable and often contradictory across the empire, and contacts between officials in different dependencies were sparse and often surprisingly antagonistic. Particularly before the age of the telegraph and steam transportation, administrators in each colonial territory tailored their approaches to governance to local conditions and to accommodations dictated by the persisting power of indigenous elites much more than in response to directives emanating from London. Even in the age of rapid communications, officials in London or Paris were often reluctant to countermand the orders of colonial administrators or to intervene extensively in local imbroglios when they were largely ignorant of local conditions.

There is much of value in this questioning of the unity of the European empires forged in the nineteenth century. It is in fact an inevitable outcome of the shift in focus in studies of colonialism from ministries in European capitals to the dynamics of power sharing among European officials in the colonies and complex configurations of indigenous allies and subordinate officials. But there is a danger that important linkages within each of the European colonial empires may be obscured; that the very real connections that gave continuity and coherence will be written out of history and then have to be rediscovered. As a number of recent studies have shown,[36] the European empires were linked in numerous ways. These included the circulation of colonial officials, who took with them to their new posts attitudes, ideas about administration, and even personnel encountered in earlier service in other areas. The impact of Lord Cromer's tenure in India on the policies he pursued for decades as the de facto ruler of Egypt is well known, as is the impact of Lord Lugard's experiences in the princely states of India and in the kingdom of Baganda on his formulation of the influential administrative strategy of indirect rule.[37] The formulation and application of policy in the French and German empires was a good deal more uniform and consistent than in their ramshackle British counterpart,[38] though again there were important variations between settler colonies and tropical dependencies and between African and Asian possessions. Precedents established in one colony in matters as vital as land tenure, military recruitment, and famine relief shaped policymaking in other dependencies, both within each of the European empires and often between them.

Within the largest and most diverse of the empires, the British, India served as a unifying core for all but the White Dominions. It provided Britain with its major source of military manpower outside the British Isles and was the main colonial outlet for manufactured goods and investment capital. In addition, South Asian merchants and moneylenders played vital roles at the middle levels of economies from Malaya to East Africa, and

Indian indentured laborers proved essential to the viability of plantation economies from Fiji in the Pacific and Natal in South Africa to the West Indies. Just how interconnected the European empires were, despite their great diversity, was perhaps best demonstrated by the crisis of World War I, throughout which both the British and French relied heavily on the soldiers, laborers, voluntary contributions, and raw materials drawn from their colonial dependencies to survive the global challenge of the German colossus and its allies.[39] At other levels, the European (and American) empires were bound together by common ideological currents, most notably racist doctrines and the tenets of the civilizing mission. They also shared a determination to extend the capitalist market economy to all corners of the globe. And they all enjoyed the daunting advantages that their science and technology gave them over preindustrial African and Asian states in waging war and controlling the populations of areas that were colonized as a result. Thus research that has demonstrated the diversity of the parts that made up the colonial empires in the age of European hegemony ought not to preclude recognition of the links that bound them together and the underlying processes and preoccupations that gave coherence to the overall European and North American pursuit of global dominance.

The World That the Empires Have Shaped: Reassessing the Impact of Imperialism

As recent reassessments of the pattern of European overseas conquest and colonial rule suggest, the shift from a Eurocentric to a global perspective in the writing of the history of imperialism has been dramatic and thoroughgoing. Perhaps the most striking manifestation of this shift can be seen in the fact that in the past three decades the overwhelming preponderance of historical research and writing on imperialism has focused on the responses of the colonized and the short- and long-term effects of European rule. If the final wave of European global expansion drew virtually all the peoples of the world into a European-dominated global order, that process also set the conditions under which the majority of humankind—often clumped together under the rubric of the Third World—would struggle to build viable polities and social systems and fashion vibrant cultures in the postcolonial era. To understand these struggles and ongoing transformations in much of Africa and Asia, it has been essential to explore both precolonial legacies and the impact of colonialism on the diverse peoples and cultures whose history has been profoundly shaped by Western domination.

In terms of approaches to the assessment of the impact of imperialism, the most striking trend in the past couple of decades has been the move away from grand attempts to draw up balance sheets of imperialism. Though some serious efforts in this direction are still attempted,[40] the growing sense of the variations and complexities of the symbiotic interaction among manifold agents of the colonizers and indigenous social groups in different colonial settings has rendered the task of determining overall winners and losers an exercise in oversimplification and ultimately futility. Insights can be gleaned from the great debates that once raged over the issue of whether on balance European colonial rule was beneficial or harmful to those on whom it was imposed.[41] But scholarly enterprise has increasingly concentrated on unraveling the complex, and often countervailing, effects of imperialism on the different social groups drawn into the colonial nexus in specific locales at varying points in time.[42]

Approaching the impact of imperialism in this manner has made it abundantly clear that it is difficult to arrive at overall conclusions about the profits or losses of *whole* nations engaged in overseas expansion. Meaningful assessments of which Europeans profited from European colonization can best be made when the focus is specific mercantile or manufacturing groups, European firms, or investors and speculators, and when their fortunes are traced over appropriate time spans.[43] This sort of approach is equally applicable to efforts to gauge the impact of imperialism on the colonized. Rather than balance sheets for whole colonies or social groups, scholars of imperialism have concentrated on in-depth studies that seek to sort out those who profited—collaborating officials and landlord groups, merchants and moneylenders, "yeoman" peasants—under the new administrative arrangements and the expanding market networks of the colonial order from those who experienced declining working conditions and living standards, diminished influence in their local communities, and cultural impoverishment. A large and growing corpus of historical works devoted to these issues over the past three or four decades has revealed significant variations between colonies and between regions (and even districts) within colonies, as well as important diachronic shifts in the fortunes of different social groups.[44]

Another attempt at grand theory that has been rendered problematic by the proliferation of local studies on the impact of imperialism is the world systems approach to the interaction between Europe and what are seen as its economic dependencies. Built on the presuppositions of dependency theorists, such as Andre Gunder Frank and Fernando Cardoso, and achieving its fullest and most influential exposition in the works of Immanuel Wallerstein and his school,[45] world systems analysis seeks to provide structuralist explanations for the rise of Europe, and later North America, as the dominant core of the global capitalist economic order and the related underdevelopment of much of the rest of the world. Though the world systems perspective has underscored important connections between political and economic transformations in the nation-states of Europe and patterns of extraction and skewed development in their (informal as well as formal) colonial dependencies, it has frequently been dismissed by African and Asian specialists working on the impact of imperialism as Eurocentric (or North American centered) reductionist, and too rigidly determinist to fit the complexities of their areas of expertise.

The division of the world into a western European core, a middle zone labeled the semiperiphery, and the colonized periphery, for example, belies the fact that Europe itself remained on the periphery of alternative "world" systems, principally that of the Indian Ocean, until well into the eighteenth century and played only a marginal role in many areas of the world until well into the nineteenth century.[46] Wallerstein's recognition of these discrepancies is implicitly suggested by his neglect of the Indian Ocean zone and Africa in volumes 1 and 2 of *The Modern World System* and his explicit acknowledgment that the former lay outside the world system oriented to the western European core that emerged from the fifteenth century onward. In an earlier work and her contribution to this volume, Janet Abu-Lughod stresses the importance of seeing Europe's original position as one segment of a larger system, anchored on the Middle East and the Indian Ocean network. This perspective is critical to understanding the profound shift that occurred in the eighteenth and especially the nineteenth century as industrialized Europe and North America extended their political, economic, and ultimately cultural hegemony to most of the rest of the globe.

From the vantage point of area specialists working on colonized areas, even more fundamental shortcomings of the world systems approach arise from the fact that Europe and its settler colony outliers become the engines that drive the hierarchical global political economy that the world systems approach privileges as the central force in all human history from the first stages of European overseas expansion onward.[47] In this vision, Europe is expansive, active, dynamic; the cultures and civilizations of much of the rest of the world in retreat, passive victims, reactive. Thus the peoples and cultures of the colonized world are deprived of agency. Vital historical forces that arise from the internal workings and indigenous imperatives of ancient African and Asian civilizations are obscured or distorted by the structuralist reduction of the last five centuries of modern history to the process by which Europeans extended market capitalism to the often reluctant, and invariably exploited, peoples of the rest of the world.

Resistance to this process is seen as ultimately futile and is thus neglected; alternative or countersystems are given short shrift or are ignored entirely. The core–periphery framework that undergirds the world systems approach also leads to overgeneralization and a false homogenization of the bewildering diversity of patterns of interaction between the agents of an expansive Europe and the peoples of colonized areas. Though these are the

sorts of problems that plague all who attempt to propound grand theory—
and Wallerstein has tried to correct for them in the later volumes of *The
Modern World System*—they go far to explain the rather marginal role that
the world systems approach has played thus far in the ongoing assessment
of the impact of imperialism in the age of European hegemony.

Many of the drawbacks encountered in trying to analyze the experience of colonized peoples through the reified lens of the world systems
approach apply equally to the modernization paradigm that informed much
of the work done on the history of imperialism in the 1950s and 1960s.[48] As
obviously linked to Cold War ideological agendas as dependency theory
and world systems analysis, the modernization paradigm was perhaps even
more Western-centric. In fact, in many ways modernization theory was an
extension of the civilizing mission ideology of the European colonizers,
with racial barriers to the global diffusion of Western institutions, ways
of thinking, and social organization removed. Those who adopted this
approach divided the world into essentialized, binary opposites: the "traditional" and the "modern." They viewed the era of European colonization
as an inevitable, if at times painful, stage in global history in which processes that had culminated in the industrial development of Europe and
North America were extended to stagnant and backward societies throughout the rest of the globe. In many studies the colonized, at least at the elite
level, were given agency, and indigenous factors weighed more heavily in
assessments of the impact of imperialism than in works built around a world
systems approach. But the colonized were judged mainly in terms of the
extent to which they resisted or advanced the inexorable process of modernization, and indigenous cultural phenomena were treated as "barriers"
or "obstacles" to the drive for modernity.

As has been evidenced by writings on industrialized societies, major
recent challenges to the modernizers' progressivist assumption of the inevitable global diffusion of the Western path to development have come
from historians concerned with the ecological consequences of European
colonial domination. Alfred Crosby has traced the often disastrous effects
that the diffusion of plants, animals, and diseases from Europe have had on
the indigenous flora and fauna or settler colony areas, such as those in the
Americas and New Zealand, which he labels neo-Europes.[49] In the tropical dependencies of Africa and Asia, which fall outside the range of case
studies that Crosby considers, the immediate ecological effects of European intrusion were a good deal less dramatic in the short term than in the
neo-Europes. Millennia of contacts and interchange between the civilized
centers of the Old World ecumene meant that much of Africa and Asia
already shared or was resistant to the diseases, plants, and animals carried
overseas by the expansive Europeans. In fact, in the tropical regions in
particular, the Europeans encountered diseases, such as yellow fever and

new strains of malaria, to which they had little or no immunity, and animal species much better able to thrive in local environments than those the Europeans sought to import.[50]

Although they were spared the ecological shocks experienced by long-isolated peoples, plants, and animals of the Americas or Australia, the deleterious impact of the European demand for raw materials and the spread of market production at the expense of subsistence agriculture have taken a heavy toll on most of the regions of Africa and Asia that came under European control. At times ecological destruction was directly linked to the dictates of the commanders of invading imperialist armies, as when swaths of forest and high grasses were systematically destroyed to deny cover and refuge to those resisting the British conquest of India. Military needs also prompted the clear cutting of forests to provide timber for fortresses and settlements as well as wood, such as the invaluable teak of western India, for European warships. In other colonized areas, colonial officials actively promoted peasant settlement of what were termed "wastelands"—usually scrub zones but often heavily forested areas—in order to render these regions "productive" and, of course, increase revenues.

As population increases in many tropical dependencies put increasing pressure on the available arable land, the pace of deforestation grew exponentially, and in many instances the displacement of forest-dwelling peoples, flooding, and soil erosion resulted. The demands of hard-pressed peasants for firewood and other forest staples also led to the degradation and contraction of forest reserves. Grandiose, but often ecologically inappropriate, colonial irrigation schemes, aimed at promoting the production of export crops, had unexpected side effects, such as salination of the soil, which led to long-term environmental degradation.[51] Over much of Africa, forest clearing and the introduction of the European heavy plow has resulted in the depletion and erosion of the thin and fragile layer of humus with devastating consequences for the viability of agriculture. In marginal farming areas, such as the Sahel, where the intrusion of Western implements and techniques and the substitution of market monocrop production for finely balanced mixes of an array of subsistence crop cultivation and pastoralism has occurred, the long-term colonial legacy has been massive soil erosion and consequent desertification, the decimation of animal herds and wildlife, recurrent famines, and chronic poverty.[52]

Despite the difficulties that the findings of area specialists have made for those who aspire to propound grand theories of global development, colonial case evidence has proven critical to the middle-range theorizing and the comparative study of a number of themes that have held a prominent place in the historiography of the post–World War II era. Work on colonial history has, for example, vastly increased our knowledge of peasant societies and our understanding of the workings of peasant culture.[53]

It has revealed the power of patron–client networks that were a critical dimension of rural social relations before, during, and after the imposition of colonial rule. Recent works on peasants under colonialism have documented the importance of factionalism in most rural settings; the complexities of rural social hierarchies that defy earlier, pat divisions into landed or landlord and landless cultivators; and the highly variable effects of the imposition of colonial rule and the spread of the capitalist market on different groups in different colonial settings. Historians working from colonial case evidence have also called into question theories relating to peasant outlooks and behavior arising from field work done in Europe, most notably the once widely discussed "image of the limited good" and the concept of "amoral familism." In addition, a wide range of new theoretical insights and concepts, such as Clifford Geertz's "agricultural involution" and the Scott–Popkin exchanges regarding the "rational" versus "moral" basis of peasant economies have generated fruitful debates and informed work in European and even American agrarian history.[54]

Studies of the changes in peasant societies under colonial rule have also contributed in important ways to the study of protest and revolution, which, along with slavery, has been the area of inquiry where the comparative technique has thus far been employed most productively. In part because of the post–World War II revolutionary transformations in China and Vietnam as well as the prolonged Vietnamese peasants' war against the French colonizers and then the Americans, case studies involving revolts on the part of peasants responding to the effects of both direct and informal imperialist domination have been central to most of the works that have set the agenda for the study of revolution over the past two or three decades. Though his work as an area specialist had been focused on modern Europe, Barrington Moore, Jr., devoted well over half of his pioneering *Social Origins of Dictatorship and Democracy* (1966) to Asian examples of elite–peasant interaction, while Eric Wolf's remarkably durable *Peasant Wars of the Twentieth Century* (1965) contains five cases of peasant revolution in colonial situations, with the sixth, Russia, arguably a semicolonial setting. Jeffrey Paige's *Agrarian Revolution* (1975) is overwhelmingly devoted to colonial and postcolonial instances of peasant mobilization. Despite her intention to avoid the complications that colonialism brings to revolutionary situations, in one of the three major examples that Theda Skocpol employs in *States and Social Revolution* (1979), China, the impact of imperialism played a major role; in another, Russia, economic imperialism and related pressures that drew the tsarist regime into World War I were not insignificant factors. As we have seen, the "moral" versus "rational" economy debate has been waged largely with reference to evidence drawn from the history of colonized peasants.

In the past decade or so, scholars interested in the impact of European colonization on the African and Asian peasantry have altered the terms of the discourse on social protest more generally by questioning the almost exclusive attention to rebellion and revolution that had been characteristic of earlier studies. They have argued that this emphasis on incidents of violent and confrontational protest, in which peasant participation was relatively rare, obscures the everyday forms of resistance—slander, pilfering, feigned incompetence—and modes of avoidance protest—concealment, shifting patrons, flight, banditry, sectarian withdrawal—that most peasant groups relied on most of the time to buffer the demands of indigenous lords and European colonizers.[55] Attention to these less dramatic but more enduring and preferred tactics of peasant defense and resistance caution against acceptance of the romanticized view of the peasant as an incipient revolutionary and of a rebellion-centered approach to peasant history. Advocates of this approach have stressed the need to center the study of agrarian protest on the broader context in which peasants have lived their day-to-day lives, rather than see it as the background to past revolutions or those yet to come.

This quotidian focus has given a new kind of agency to peasant groups and new meaning to their resistance to colonial dominance. Rather than search the archives for references to periodic and usually short-lived riots or rebellions, such as those featured in the writings of the "subaltern" school of South Asian historians,[56] emphasis has been placed on the peasants' persisting defenses against and ongoing evasions of the colonizers' demands. This perspective has broadened significantly the meaning of resistance and compelled historians to turn their attention to causes and social groups that had been largely ignored in earlier work on anticolonial protest. Three of the most important areas of research that have been opened up as a result have been the study of women's roles in anticolonial resistance, protest movements that have centered on environmental issues, and the struggles of hill-dwelling shifting cultivators and "tribal" peoples to defend their sparsely populated homelands from *both* the colonizers and indigenous migrant groups.

Mainly in the past two decades, there has been a proliferation of studies dealing with changes in gender roles in African and Asian societies in the colonial period. Much of this literature has focused on the ways in which development initiatives in the colonial and postcolonial eras have favored men in terms of employment and educational opportunities, technology, and skill transfer and increased cash earnings. These initiatives have also often resulted in a decline in the relative importance of subsistence-crop production, in which women had traditionally played pivotal roles, and the contraction of localized marketing systems, which had often been dominated by women peddlers, in the face of the extension of the global capitalist market. The combined effect of these processes has been the marginalization of women in the international capitalist sectors of many Third World economies[57] and a devaluing of the contributions of women to production—contributions that were often considerable in the precolonial era. This marginalization has in turn led to a diminution of women's leverage and status within local communities and the household, and in many societies, particularly sub-Saharan Africa, has increased emphasis on their reproductive functions.[58]

These trends have meant that women's struggles in the colonial and postcolonial era have often focused on everyday tactics aimed at shoring up their position within the household or finding viable means of escape when conditions in the home became unbearable.[59] But recent research has shown that women often mounted protest movements of their own, such as the much-studied antitax riots led by the market women in Igboland in 1929, or have played much more active roles in nationalist organization and protest, including violent revolts, than historians had hitherto imagined.[60] As Judith Tucker has noted in her essay, the defense of what were seen to be the "traditional" roles and position of women in the face of European disapprobation and reformist campaigns also provided the basis for anticolonial agitation.[61]

Particularly in South and Southeast Asia, research on resistance movements mounted by hill- and forest-dwelling "tribals" has usually been grounded in explorations of broader questions regarding the ecological impact of European imperialism. European conquest often brought unchecked forest cutting in its wake in areas such as the Himalayas, central India, and the Salween Valley of Burma. By the late nineteenth century, colonial officials, anxious to conserve dwindling hardwood supplies and mindful of the advances in "scientific" forestry pioneered by the Germans in Europe, sought to set off forest reserves in once heavily logged forest areas. The policies of the newly created forestry departments brought on direct, often violent, confrontations with the hill peoples whose livelihood was dependent on the foods, medicinal plants, firewood, and building materials that they obtained from local woodlands. From the tribal risings that raged in India through much of the nineteenth century to the Chipko ("tree hugging") movement of recent decades, the agriculturalists of South and Southeast Asia have struggled to preserve their forest environments and customary ways of life.[62] In recent years, the important gender issues involved in this protest have been emphasized by Vadana Shiva, Rajni Kothari, and others,[63] who stress the ways in which women, low-caste groups, and tribal peoples have been displaced or marginalized by colonial forestry policies and postcolonial multinational projects geared to the global export market.

Consolidating the Revolution in the Historiography of Imperialism

The vastly increased emphasis on the responses of colonized peoples and the effects of colonialism on their societies and cultures has compelled more than shifts in perspective in the writing of the history of imperialism. It has necessitated the employment of nontraditional sources, extensive interdisciplinary interchange, and the development of new techniques for cross-cultural analysis. Practitioners of the new history of imperialism have done much to advance the study of oral traditions, which have proven essential to the analysis of the colonial experience in much of sub-Saharan Africa, upland South and Southeast Asia, the nomadic zones of the Middle East, and the island cultures of the Pacific.[64] Pioneered by anthropologists, these techniques reflect the long-standing interchange between historians and anthropologists that has been central in recent decades to the study of colonialism. The influence of anthropological work has also been increasingly felt in decisions regarding the topical focus of historical research, from that focused on groups, such as women, the urban poor, and shifting cultivators that traditionally fell outside the historian's purview to issues such as factionalism, clientage, and the semiotics of rituals and elements of material culture. Anthropological research has provided information on and understandings about peasant and pastoral cultures that have proved essential to deciphering vital, but often poorly documented, aspects of the colonial encounter, such as religious resistance to European authority or shifts in gender roles and perceptions engendered by the impact of imperialism.

Perhaps the most important contributions that anthropologists have made to the writing of the new history of colonialism can be found in the concepts and analytical techniques that have allowed less theoretically inclined historians to interpret patterns and relationships that might otherwise have been obscured by the complexity and volume of their empirical data. In no area have these contributions been more influential than in the identification and interpretation of symbol systems, ritual forms, and patterns of social interchange. In these endeavors, Clifford Geertz's semiotic concept of culture—both as a prescription for analytical practice and as a foil for alternative interpretations—has been particularly influential.[65] But the writings of anthropologists such as Victor Turner, Louis Dumont, Pierre Bourdieu, and Jean Comaroff,[66] who have been more inclined than Geertz to mix the material and the ideological, have done much in recent years to set research agendas and shape the analysis of the multifaceted interactions between colonizer and colonized in the age of European hegemony.

In no aspect of the historiography of imperialism has the analysis of symbol systems had a greater impact than on recent work focusing on the ways in which the European colonizers sought to restore, recast, or create outright the "traditions" of the African and Asian peoples they came to dominate politically, economically, and culturally. Some of this "invention of tradition" was unintended, the by-product of European attempts to "rationalize" the governance of the colonized peoples; to substitute what the colonizers viewed as honest and efficient administrative and legal codes and systems for the corrupt and arbitrary rule of the indigenous princes and elites they had supplanted. But as recent research has shown, these reforms had the effect of rigidifying social divisions and institutions that colonial bureaucrats, and often the African and Asian nationalists who later vied for their jobs, came to see as the embodiment of the "traditional" cultures of the colonized. Thus the fluid and overlapping identities of African peoples in the precolonial era became fixed and bounded by their division into "tribes," the concept itself a creation of colonial ethnologists and administrators. In India, caste stratification was likewise codified and ossified by the legal reforms and especially the successive censuses conducted under the auspices of the British overlords. In both Africa and India, invented traditions, often mirroring those then being constructed in Great Britain or France, were employed in a wide range of ceremonies, from those for the installation of indigenous princes and "chiefs" to those designed to cement the loyalty of soldiers recruited from colonized peoples whom the European overlords regarded as martial "races." [67]

Invented traditions were just one side of the colonizers' attempts to forge symbolic links to African and Asian elite and subaltern classes. As European colonial dominance was increasingly challenged by indigenous nationalist movements, the colonizers turned to systematic and conscious efforts to reconstruct what they believed to be the traditional political and social systems of the African and Asian peoples they ruled. The invention of tradition continued. But much of what colonial administrators and ethnologists thought they were doing from the 1890s onward was recovering and restoring indigenous institutions, customs, and symbols that had been allowed to fall into disuse or had been degraded by the rationalizing campaigns of reform-minded European administrators and missionaries or the impact of commercializing capitalism. To shore up the legitimacy of collaborating elites and indigenous bureaucrats and soldiers, on which the survival of the colonial order depended, colonial officials and administrator-ethnologists devoted ever greater energies and ingenuity to the reconstruction of what they believed to be the authentic, indigenous institutions, customs, and rituals that had been displaced or discredited by the advance of European imperialist hegemony. [68] Enshrined in policies of "indirect rule" and "association," this project of reconstruction proved the most persistent and creative, if ultimately futile, response of the colonizers to the rising tide of nationalism in their tropical dependencies.

In the past decade or so, the fecund blending of history and anthropology in the study of colonialism has merged with a further strain of scholarly endeavor: literary criticism. Textual analysis, whether based on the techniques of Derrida or Bakhtin, has produced some important insights and has allowed us to identify critical precautions that need to be taken in interpreting the mass of documents and ethnological field evidence that are one of the main legacies of the era of European imperialist hegemony.[69] The writings of Edward Said[70] have also underscored problems that have hounded those attempting cross-cultural observation and discourse throughout the centuries of European global expansion—and by implication those in earlier times and between the representatives of all civilizations. Said's strictures raise challenges that students of colonialism cannot ignore, and they have exposed the essentialist assumptions that have informed much, at times even the best, of historical scholarship on the colonial experience.

Despite important contributions by some advocates of close textual analysis, much of the recent work in this vein threatens to divert historians of imperialism from essential tasks that would allow us to bring the revolutionary changes that have occurred in the last half-century to full fruition; to consolidate the gains in terms of the recovery and interpretation of evidence and in terms of the range and sophistication of objects of inquiry and analytical techniques that so dramatically set this period off from all that has gone before.[71] The decontextualized exercises in jargon-ridden solipsism that constitute so many of the forays into the constricted realm of the written or oral text are no substitute for the massive amounts of lonely and less glamorous, but essential, field work and archival research that still needs to be done just to fill in the vast stretches of the colonial landscape that remain poorly mapped or altogether uncharted. Esoteric quibbles over textual meanings distract us from critical ongoing debates and from following up on the conceptual and methodological breakthroughs that have been made in recent decades by social scientists working on colonial issues from a number of disciplinary perspectives.[72] These divertissements are a luxury we cannot afford. The questions at stake in the historiography of imperialism have too much relevance for the present and future world situation to be sidetracked by intellectual games. Understandings derived from historical research on the colonial experience have the potential to affect exchanges in the coming decades between the industrialized and "developing" nations vitally, and to enhance the opportunities available to a majority of the world's peoples for social justice, decent living standards, and viable environments.

NOTES

I would like to thank Scott Cook, David Engerman, Malia Formes, and Ram Guha for their careful readings and helpful comments on an early draft of this essay. The references cited in relation to the different themes discussed are intended to be suggestive rather than comprehensive; guideposts to illustrative or exemplary further readings, rather than a cumulative bibliography.

1. For an able demythologizing of the iconography of Gordon's demise, see D. H. Johnson, "The Death of Gordon: A Victorian Myth," *Journal of Imperial and Commonwealth History* 10, no. 3 (1982): 285–310.

2. To borrow Eric Wolf's apt characterization of the marginalization of the great majority of humankind. See *Europe and the People without History* (Berkeley: University of California Press, 1982).

3. For early and cogent statements of this approach, see John R.W. Smail, "On the Possibility of an Autonomous History of Modern Southeast Asia," *Journal of Southeast Asian History* 2, no. 2 (1961): 80–120; and J. D. Legge, *Indonesia* (Englewood Cliffs, N.J.: Prentice Hall, 1964).

4. Some of the more thoughtful essays on the implications of the fusion of literary analysis and innovative approaches to oral research on anthropological and historical field research can be found in James Clifford and George E. Marcus, eds., *Writing Culture: The Poetics and Politics of Ethnography* (Berkeley: University of California Press, 1986).

5. For a recent monograph that creatively applies each of these elements to colonial history, see Timothy Mitchell, *Colonizing Egypt* (Cambridge, England: Cambridge University Press, 1988).

6. J. A. Hobson, *Imperialism: A Study* (Ann Arbor: University of Michigan Press, 1971); and V. I. Lenin, *Imperialism: The Highest Stage of Capitalism* (New York: International Publishers, 1939).

7. Respectively, "A Critique of Imperialism," *Foreign Affairs* 24 (1935): 102–19; J. A. Schumpeter, *Imperialism and Social Classes* (New York: Kelley, 1961); and Raymond Aron, "The Leninist Myth of Imperialism," *Partisan Review* 18 (1951): 646–62. The most elaborate critique of the economic interpretation of imperialism came in Henri Brunschwig, *Mythes et réalités de l'impérialisme colonial français, 1871–1914* (Paris: Colin, 1960), translated into English as *French Colonialism, 1871–1914: Myths and Realities* (New York: Praeger, 1966). For a rather different and much more nuanced view of these connections, see Jacques Marseille, *Empire colonial et capitalisme français* (Paris: Michel, 1984).

8. Best summaries in Tom Kemp, *Theories of Imperialism* (London: Dobson Books, 1967) and Winfried Baumgart, *Imperialism* (Oxford, England: Oxford University Press, 1982). See also the rather original analysis in M. Doyle, *Empires* (Ithaca, N.Y.: Cornell University Press, 1986).

9. Excepting a number of important works that explored the flow of European overseas investment in the 1870–1914 era. See, for examples, Herbert Feis, *Europe: The World's Banker* (New Haven: Yale University Press, 1930); S. B. Saul, *Studies in British Overseas Trade, 1870–1914* (Liverpool, England: Liverpool University Press, 1960); and Matthew Simon, "The Pattern of New British Portfolio

Foreign Investment, 1865–1914," in *Capital Movements and Economic Development*, ed. J. H. Adler (London: Macmillan, 1967).

10. Eric Stokes, "Late Nineteenth-Century Colonial Expansion and the Attack on the Theory of Economic Imperialism: A Case of Mistaken Identity?" *Historical Journal* 12, no. 2 (1969): 285–301.

11. First published in English in 1967 under the title *Germany's Aims in the First World War* (London: Chatto & Windus; New York: Norton).

12. For samples of the arguments on each side, see H. W. Koch, ed., *The Origins of the First World War* (London: Macmillan, 1972); Gerald D. Feldman, *German Imperialism, 1914–1918* (New York: Wiley, 1972); and Fritz Fischer, *World Power or Decline* (New York: Norton, 1974).

13. Cologne: Kiepenheuer & Witsch, 1969. Wehler's findings were supported by those of Harmut Pogge von Strandmann who stressed political divisions on the domestic side of things. See, for example, "Domestic Origins of Germany's Colonial Expansion under Bismarck," *Past and Present* 42 (1969): 140–59.

14. D.C.M. Platt, *Finance, Trade and Politics in British Foreign Policy, 1814–1914* (Oxford, England: Oxford University Press, 1968). For a superb analysis of the workings of these forces in the French colonial context, see Jean Stengers, "L'impérialisme colonial de la fin du XIXe siècle: mythe ou réalité?" *Journal of African History* 3 (1962): 469–91.

15. See, for examples, John M. MacKenzie, ed., *Imperialism and Popular Culture* (Manchester, England: Manchester University Press, 1986), and *Propaganda and Empire: The Manipulation of British Public Opinion, 1880–1960* (Manchester, England: Manchester University Press, 1984).

16. Ronald Robinson and John Gallagher (with Alice Denny), *Africa and the Victorians* (London: Macmillan, 1961).

17. Which John Gallagher and Ronald Robinson had argued in their seminal article on "The Imperialism of Free Trade" *Economic History Review* 6, no. 1 (1953): 1–15, was the defining difference between the two periods in terms of imperialist expansion.

18. The now standard overview is William Appelman Williams, *The Roots of the Modern American Empire* (New York: Random House, 1969).

19. Here again the work of Gallagher and Robinson was pivotal. See, for examples, "Non-European Foundations of European Imperialism: Sketch for a Theory of Collaboration," in *Studies in the Theory of Imperialism*, ed. Roger Owen and Bob Sutcliffe (London: Longman, 1972); and the contributions to *Imperialism: The Gallagher and Robinson Controversy*, ed. W. R. Louis (New York: Macmillan, 1976). Roger Owen, *The Middle East In the World Economy, 1800–1914* (London: Metheun, 1981), provides one of the most detailed case-study examinations of these patterns over a broad area and extended time period.

20. Most notably in a slim but important volume by L.C.F. Turner, *Origins of the First World War* (New York: Norton, 1970).

21. For classic examples of these assumptions, see the contributions to *The Politics of the Developing Areas*, ed. Gabriel A. Almond and James S. Coleman (Princeton: Princeton University Press, 1960); L. H. Gann and Peter Duignan,

Burden of Empire (New York: Praeger, 1967); and William Woodruff, *Impact of Western Man* (New York: St. Martin's Press, 1967).

22. The work of C. A. Bayly in particular has highlighted the importance of the linkages between European trading companies and indigenous banking and mercantile networks. See, for example, *The New Cambridge History of India II/1: Indian Society and the Making of the British Empire* (Cambridge, England: Cambridge University Press, 1988), esp. chaps. 2 and 3.

23. The most detailed account of the East India Company's machinations can be found in Michael Edwards, *The Battle of Plassey* (New York: Macmillan, 1963). The most up-to-date analysis of the role of indigenous forces in the East India Company victory and the conquest of Bengal more generally is provided by P. J. Marshall in *The New Cambridge History of India II/2: Bengal The British Beachhead 1740–1828* (Cambridge, England: Cambridge University Press, 1987). M. C. Ricklefs, *Jogjakarta under Sultan Mangkubumi, 1749–1792* (London: Oxford University Press, 1974), contains the best account of these patterns in Java.

24. These factors are emphasized, perhaps too exclusively, in Daniel Headrick, *The Tools of Empire* (New York: Oxford University Press, 1981).

25. By far the most comprehensive and insightful account of these patterns has been provided by Philip Mason, *A Matter of Honour: An Account of the Indian Army, Its Officers and Men* (London: Jonathan Cape, 1974). For parallels and contrasts in the French Empire, see Charles Balesi, *From Adversaries to Comrades-in-Arms: West Africans and the French Military 1885–1918* (Waltham, Mass.: Crossroads Press, 1978).

26. Quoted in Gallagher and Robertson, *Africa and the Victorians*, p. 12.

27. Bayly provides a good overview in his volume of *The New Cambridge History of India*, and a sense of the extensive literature on the African side of these issues can be gained from the contributions to Michael Crowder, ed., *West African Resistance* (London: Hutchinson, 1971), and Robert Rotberg and Ali Mazrui, eds., *Protest and Power in Black Africa* (New York: Oxford University Press, 1970). For a superb case example from Southeast Asia, see James Siegel, *The Rope of God* (Berkeley: University of California Press, 1969).

28. See the essays on the colonial period in James Scott and Benedict Kerkvliet, eds., *Everyday Forms of Peasant Resistance in South-east Asia* (London: Frank Cass, 1986), and in Donald Crummey, ed., *Banditry, Rebellion and Social Protest in Africa* (London: Heineman, 1986). For revealing case studies, see Allen Isaacman, *Mozambique: From Colonialism to Revolution* (Boulder, Colo.: Westview Press, 1983), and Hue-Tam Ho Tai, *Millenarianism and Peasant Politics in Vietnam* (Cambridge, Mass.: Harvard University Press, 1983).

29. These patterns have perhaps been the most thoroughly explored by practitioners of the so-called Cambridge School of South Asian history. For an overview of the approach of these writers and a survey of some of the key works, see Howard Spodek, "Pluralist Politics in British India: The Cambridge Cluster of Historians of Modern India," *American Historical Review* 84, no. 3 (1979): 688–707. For exemplary African and Southeast Asian explorations of these themes, see respectively A. I. Asiwaju, *Western Yorubaland under European Rule 1889–1945* (London: Long-

man, 1976), and L. H. Palmier, *Social Status and Power in Java* (London: University of London, 1960).

30. A pioneering exploration of these themes, which some scholars have seen as too extreme in its depiction of European empires dominated by subaltern officials, can be found in Robert Frykenberg, *Guntur District 1788–1848* (Oxford, England: Clarendon Press, 1965). See also, Clive Dewey, "*Patwari* and *Chaukidar*: Subordinate Officials and the Reliability of India's Agricultural Statistics," in *The Imperial Impact in Africa and South Asia*, ed. Clive Dewey and A. G. Hopkins (London: Institute of Commonwealth Studies, 1979).

31. Percival Spear, *The Nabobs: A Study of the Social Life of the English in Eighteenth Century India* (London: Oxford University Press, 1932), esp. chap. 8.

32. In Helen Callaway, *Gender, Culture, and Empire: European Women in Colonial Nigeria* (Urbana: University of Illinois Press, 1987), quoted portions on p. 244.

33. Margaret Strobel in this volume and in *European Women and the Second British Empire* (Bloomington: Indiana University Press, 1991), esp. chap. 1; and Ann Stoler, "Rethinking Colonial Categories: European Communities and the Boundaries of Rule," *Comparative Studies in Society and History* 31, no. 1 (1989): 134–61. My thinking on these issues owes a good deal to the essays of Malia Formes, who is currently at work on a comparison of the gender roles and attitudes exhibited by different British social groups in colonial India.

34. Philip Curtin's *Image of Africa* (Madison: University of Wisconsin Press, 1965) was the first work to stress these factors. For more recent treatment of these themes, see William B. Cohen, *The French Encounter with Africans: White Response to Blacks, 1530–1880* (Bloomington: University of Indiana Press, 1980); and Michael Adas, *Machines as the Measure of Men: Science, Technology and Ideologies of Western Dominance* (Ithaca, N.Y.: Cornell University Press, 1989).

35. D. K. Fieldhouse, "Can Humpty-Dumpty Be Put Together Again? Imperial History in the 1980s," *Journal of Imperial and Commonwealth History* 12, no. 2 (1984): 9–23; or Ged Martin, "Was There a British Empire?" *Historical Journal* 15, no. 3 (1972): 562–79.

36. One of the most detailed explorations of these linkages between two seemingly very different parts of the British Empire is featured in Scott Cook's, "The Example of Ireland: Political and Administrative Aspects of the Imperial Relationship with British India, 1855–1922," Ph.D. diss., Rutgers University, 1987.

37. Afaf Lutfi al-Sayyid, *Egypt and Cromer* (London: John Murray, 1968); and Margery Perham, *Lugard: The Years of Adventure, 1858–1898* (London: Collins, 1956).

38. Raymond Betts, *Association and Assimilation in French Colonial Theory 1890–1914* (New York: Columbia University Press, 1961); Hubert Deschamps, *Les methodes et les doctrines coloniales de la France du XVIe siècle à nos jours* (Paris: Armand Colin, 1953); and Woodruff D. Smith, *The German Colonial Empire* (Chapel Hill: University of North Carolina Press, 1978).

39. For the fullest study of this ironic dependence of the European powers on their "dependencies," see Marc Michel, *L'appel à L'Afrique: Contributions et réactions à l'effort de guerre en A. O. F. 1914–1919* (Paris: Sorbonne, 1982).

40. Perhaps the most notable being the recent work by Lance B. Davis and Robert A. Huttenback, *Mammon and the Pursuit of Empire* (New York: Cambridge University Press, 1986), and the essays in the special issue on "Money, Finance, and Empire 1790–1960," *Journal of Imperial and Commonwealth History* 13, no. 3 (1985).

41. See, for example, the contrasting assessments set forth in Walter Rodney, *How Europe Underdeveloped Africa* (London: Bogle-L'Ouverture, 1972); and Gann and Duignan, *Burden of Empire*.

42. Two exemplary studies that take this approach are A. G. Hopkins, *An Economic History of West Africa* (New York: Columbia University Press, 1973); and A. K. Bagchi, *Private Investment in India 1900–1939* (Cambridge, England: Cambridge University Press, 1972).

43. See, for example, D. K. Fieldhouse's study of *Unilever Overseas: The Anatomy of a Multi-National 1895–1965* (London, Croom Helm, 1978); and covering a wider range of investment outcomes, Marseille, *Empire et capitalisme français*.

44. For sample case studies, see the contributions to *Land Control and Social Structure in Indian History*, ed. R. E. Frykenberg (Madison: University of Wisconsin Press, 1969); Imran Ali, *The Punjab under Imperialism, 1885–1947* (Princeton: Princeton University Press, 1988); Anand A. Yang, *The Limited Raj: Agrarian Relations in Colonial India* (Berkeley: University of California Press, 1989); Sara Berry, *Cocoa, Custom and Socio-Economic Change in Rural Western Nigeria* (London: Oxford University Press, 1975); and for a comparative analysis of these patterns in different colonial settings, see Michael Adas, *Prophets of Rebellion: Millenarian Protest Movements against the European Colonial Order* (Cambridge, England: Cambridge University Press: 1987).

45. See especially the successive volumes of Wallerstein's *The Modern World System* (New York: Academic Press, 1974, 1980, 1988), and the contributions to *Review*, the journal devoted to works with a world systems perspective.

46. For a detailed exploration of these relationships, see K. N. Chaudhuri, *Asia before Europe: Economy and Civilisation of the Indian Ocean from the Rise of Islam to 1750* (Cambridge, England: Cambridge University Press, 1990).

47. Perhaps the most provocative and in-depth treatment of some of the issues surveyed here can be found in Steve J. Stern's critique and informative bibliographic essay, "Feudalism, Capitalism, and the World-System in the Perspective of Latin America and the Caribbean," *American Historical Review* 93, no. 4 (1988): 829–72.

48. For two of the better informed and more thoughtful works of this genre, see David E. Apter, *Ghana in Transition* (New York: Atheneum, 1963); and Robert Tignor, *Modernization and British Colonial Rule in Egypt, 1882–1914* (Princeton: Princeton University Press, 1966).

49. Alfred Crosby, *Ecological Imperialism* (New York: Cambridge University Press, 1986).

50. On the challenges posed by the new disease environments the Europeans confronted overseas, see especially Philip D. Curtin, *Death by Migration: Europe's Encounter with the Tropical World in the Nineteenth Century* (New York: Cambridge University Press, 1989).

51. For discussions of these patterns in different colonial settings, see Bayly, *New Cambridge History of India*, esp. pp. 138–44; the relevant contributions to Richard P. Tucker and J. F. Richards, eds., *Global Deforestation and the Nineteenth-Century World Economy* (Durham: Duke University Press, 1983); and E. M. Whitcombe, *Agrarian Conditions in Northern India* (Berkeley: University of California Press, 1972).

52. Richard W. Franke and Barbara H. Chasin, *Seeds of Famine: Ecological Destruction and the Development Dilemma in the West African Sahel* (Montclair, N.J.: Allanheld, Osmun, 1980); and Michel Watts, *Silent Violence: Food, Famine and Peasantry in Northern Nigeria* (Los Angeles: University of California Press, 1983). For an overview of the ecological impact of colonialism in South Asia, see Madhav Gadgil and Ramchandra Guha, *This Fissured Land: An Ecological History of India* (Delhi: Oxford University Press, 1993).

53. A sense of the volume and range of studies devoted to the colonial peasantry can be gained from Allen Isaacman's impressive bibliographic analysis of "Peasants and Rural Social Protest in Africa," *African Studies Review* 33, no. 2 (1990). For colonial India, see the case discussions and references in Sumit Sarkar, *Modern India 1885–1947* (Madras: Macmillan, 1983); and for Southeast Asia, see the extensive bibliography in Joel D. Steinberg et. al., *In Search of Southeast Asia* (Honolulu: University of Hawaii Press, 1985).

54. Respectively, Clifford Geertz, *Agricultural Involution: The Process of Ecological Change in Indonesia* (Berkeley: University of California Press, 1966); James C. Scott, *The Moral Economy of the Peasant* (New Haven: Yale University Press, 1966); and Samuel Popkin, *The Rational Peasant* (Berkeley: University of California Press, 1979).

55. See the contributions to the Scott and Kervliet edited volume cited in note 28; James C. Scott, *Weapons of the Weak* (New Haven: Yale University Press, 1985); Michael Adas, "From Avoidance to Confrontation: Peasant Protest in Precolonial and Colonial Southeast Asia," *Comparative Studies in Society and History* 23, no. 2 (1981): 217–47; Douglas Haynes and Gyan Prakash, eds., *Contesting Power: Resistance and Everyday Social Relations in South Asia* (Delhi: Oxford University Press, 1991); and Allen Issacman et. al., "Cotton Is the Mother of Poverty: Peasant Resistance to Forced Cotton Production in Mozambique, 1938–1961," *International Journal of African Studies* 13, no. 4 (1980): 575–615.

56. See, for examples, Ranajit Guha, *Elementary Aspects of Peasant Insurgency in Colonial India* (Delhi: Oxford University Press, 1983); and the successive volumes of *Subaltern Studies* (Delhi: Oxford University Press, 1982–).

57. This marginalization is, on the surface, less pronounced in the multinational enclaves where women play prominent roles in mass assembly of electronic consumer items or clothing manufacture. But even in these rather limited pools of capitalist growth, women are reduced to laboring in sweatshop conditions at unskilled and poorly paid jobs. See Diane Elson and Ruth Pearson, "The Subordination of Women and the Internationalization of Factory Production," in *Of Marriage and the Market*, ed. Kate Young, Carol Wolkowitz and Rosalyn McCullough (London: Routledge and Kegan Paul, 1984); and Maria Kelly, *'For We Are Sold, I*

and My People': Women and Industry in Mexico's Frontier (Albany: SUNY Press, 1983).

58. Ester Boserup, *Women's Role in Economic Development* (New York: St. Martin's Press, 1970), has proven a seminal work on these themes. For subsequent responses and suggestions for revisions of Boserup's findings based on more recent research, see the essays collected in special issues of *Signs* 3, no. 1 (1977) and 7, no. 2 (1981); and Barbara Rogers, *The Domestication of Women: Discrimination in Developing Societies* (London: St. Martin's Press, 1980).

59. African historians have done particularly useful work on these aspects of gender relations. See, for example, Marjorie Mbilinyi, "Ruanway Wives in Colonial Tanganyika: Forced Labour and Forced Marriage in Rungwe District, 1919–1961," *International Journal of Sociology of Law* 16, no. 1 (1988): 1–29; Maud Muntemba, "Regional and Social Differentiation in Broken Hill Rural District, Northern Rhodesia, 1930–1964," in *Peasants in Africa*, ed. Martin A. Klein, pp. 243–70 (Beverly Hills, Calif.: Sage, 1980); and Michael Watts, "Struggles over Land; Struggles over Meaning," in *A Ground for a Common Search*, ed. Reginald Golledge, pp. 31–51 (Santa Barbara: University of Santa Barbara Press, 1988). For Indian parallels, see Rosalind O'Hanlon, "Issues of Widowhood: Gender and Resistance in Colonial Western India," in Haynes and Guha, eds., *Contesting Power*, pp. 62–108; and Veena Das, "Gender Studies, Cross Cultural Comparisons, and the Colonial Organization of Knowledge," *Berkshire Review* (1986); on the Middle East, see the essay by Judith Tucker in this volume.

60. Judith van Allen, "'Aba Riots' or Igbo 'Women's War'? Ideology, Stratification and the Invisibility of Women," in *Women in Africa*, ed. Nancy J. Hafkin and Edna G. Bay, pp. 59–85 (Stanford, Calif.: Stanford University Press, 1976); Susan Rogers, "Anti-Colonial Protest in Africa: A Female Strategy," *Heresies* 3, no. 4 (1980): 222–25; Luise White, "Separating the Men from the Boys: Constructions of Gender, Sexuality and Terrorism in Central Kenya, 1939–1959," *International Journal of African Historical Studies* 23, no. 1 (1990): 1–25; and Afaf Lufti al-Sayyid Marsot, "Revolutionary Gentlewomen in Egypt," in *Middle Eastern Women Speak*, ed. E. W. Fernea and B. Q. Bezirgan, pp. 261–76 (Austin: University of Texas Press, 1977).

61. For an Indian parallel to the Middle Eastern cases cited by Tucker, see Partha Chatterjee, "Colonialism, Nationalism and Colonized Women: The Contest in India," *American Ethnologist* 16, no. 4 (1989): 622–33.

62. Ramchandra Guha's *The Unquiet Woods: Ecological Change and Peasant Resistance in the Himalaya* (Delhi: Oxford University Press, 1989) provides the fullest account of these struggles. For movements elsewhere in South Asia, see the essays on tribal rebellions in the Subaltern Studies series; and Guha and Madhav Gadgil, "State Forestry and Social Conflict in British India," *Past and Present* 123 (1989): 141–78.

63. *Staying Alive* (New Delhi: Kali for Women, 1988).

64. For a superb summary of the development of oral history techniques, see Jan Vansina, *Oral Tradition as History* (Madison: University of Wisconsin Press, 1985); Vansina is one of the pioneers in this field.

65. See, especially, the seminal essays in Clifford Geertz's *Interpretation of*

Cultures (New York: Basic Books, 1973). Perhaps the most extreme statement of the culture as a system of symbols position can be found in *Negara: The Theatre State in Nineteenth-Century Bali* (Princeton: Princeton University Press, 1980).

66. See Victor Turner, *The Ritual Process* (London, Routledge and Kegan Paul, 1969); Louis Dumont, *Homo Hierarchicus* (London: Weidenfeld and Nicolson, 1970); Pierre Bourdieu, *Outline of a Theory of Practice* (Cambridge, England: Cambridge University Press, 1977); and Jean Comaroff, *Body of Power, Spirit of Resistance* (Chicago: University of Chicago Press, 1985).

67. On these patterns, see especially the essays by Terence Ranger and Bernard Cohn in Eric Hobsbawm and Terence Ranger, eds., *The Invention of Tradition* (Cambridge, England: Cambridge University Press, 1983); Bernard Cohn, "The Census, Social Structure and Objectification in South Asia," *Folk* 26 (1984); and Richard Fox, *Lions of the Punjab: Culture in the Making* (Berkeley: University of California Press, 1985).

68. For a detailed case study of this process that exemplifies the convergence of history and anthropology in recent decades, see Nicholas Dirks, *The Hollow Crown: Ethnohistory of an Indian Kingdom* (Cambridge, England: Cambridge University Press, 1987). For a more general, recent survey of the links between anthropology and colonial administration, see Henrika Kuklick, *The Savage Within: The Social History of British Anthropology* (Cambridge, England: Cambridge University Press, 1991), esp. chap. 5.

69. For studies that best illustrate these contributions, see Mitchell, *Colonizing Egypt*; and Ronald Inden, *Imagining India* (Oxford, England: Basil Blackwell, 1990). For stimulating discussions of the problems of generating and interpreting anthropological data, see the essays in Clifford and Marcus, *Writing Culture*.

70. Especially Edward Said, *Orientalism* (London: Routledge and Kegan Paul, 1978).

71. These gains can perhaps be best seen in the sophistication of recent Marxist-derived approaches to colonial history, exemplified by the writings of, for example, Burton Stein and Claude Meisalloux.

72. For a trenchant critique of postmodernist–poststructuralist approaches to colonial historiography, see Rosalind O'Hanlon and David Washbrook, "After Orientalism: Culture, Criticism, and the Politics of the Third World," *Comparative Studies in Society and History* 34, no. 1 (1992): 141–67. For a more sympathetic treatment of the works of proponents of this approach, see Robert Young, *White Mythologies: Writing History and the West* (London: Routledge, 1990).

Gender, Sex, and Empire

MARGARET STROBEL

The European empires in Africa and Asia have long been the subject of scholarly analysis, initially from the perspectives of the conquerors and later, as the historiography was decolonized following the breakup of the empires, from the perspectives of indigenous peoples.[1] Yet despite the vast changes that the writing of this history has undergone in the past three decades, only recently have women, gender, and sexuality come to be subjects of inquiry.[2]

For substantial time periods, we know little of what indigenous women were doing, much less thinking; the documentary records, be they colonial or indigenous, have left more data about political and economic activity than about the daily domestic lives of individuals. And it is here, in the domestic realm, that much of women's activity has taken place, for women have typically been responsible for reproductive work (childbearing, child-rearing, and the daily maintenance of family members) even when they also were engaged in productive or commercial work.

If indigenous women have been largely absent from our written histories, so too have European women. The empires were thought to be "no place for a [white] woman," and hence the historiography has, with few exceptions, ignored their presence.

The virtual absence of women from the imperial histories is mirrored by the overwhelming presence of men, European and indigenous. Yet these men have rarely been treated as gendered human beings. The notions of masculinity (and femininity) that lay behind the gender divisions of labor in the empire have been largely unexamined until recently. Thus the fact that the European explorers who reached the shores of Africa and Asia were male has not been problematized, with the result that the gendered nature of early cross-cultural contact, and the essential role of indigenous women at those points of cultural contact, is ignored.

If gender has been little explored, so has sexuality, despite the fact that the regulation of sexual boundaries between the communities of the rulers and the ruled came to be a major task of white women in parts of the empire where European communities developed.

The purpose of this essay is to explore these issues, pointing to sites in the historical literature where the study of gender and sexuality, intersecting with race, provides fresh insights into the European imperial dynamic of the eighteenth and nineteenth centuries up through World War I. Because the scholarship is relatively new and its coverage is spotty, the narrative is discontinuous. The areas discussed are primarily British Africa and India, although the essay refers to other imperial powers as well.

The first section takes up European exploration in Africa, examining the rise of wealthy African women in the Semegambia who served as intermediaries for European male traders. Also examined is the phenomenon of "Victorian lady travelers," women who escaped British gender roles to explore parts of Africa.

The next section looks in greater detail at sexual activity in the empires. Interracial sexual relationships were a feature of empire from the start, and official attitudes toward such relationships changed over time and varied by region and imperial power. The arrival of white women and the development of white communities complicated the picture. We critique Ronald Hyam's argument that, for British men, the empire meant enhanced sexual opportunity, drawing on studies of Northern Rhodesia and India. Next we discuss the promulgation of the Contagious Diseases Acts in India to see how sex and race brought imperial tensions to the fore.

If indigenous women were important as actual or potential sexual partners, their treatment was symbolically important as well, as we explore in the third section. In India, the status of Indian women under Hindu law and custom became a major battleground on which colonizers and Indian nationalists and traditionalists fought. If the British Raj used these issues to legitimize its civilizing mission, then white women in India and Britain also used the "plight" of Indian women to define themselves and their mission.

Masculinity, both British and Indian, came under scrutiny as the nineteenth century proceeded. The dimensions of the changes in notions of masculinity, and their relationship to empire, are examined in the essay's fourth section.

The meaning of home and domesticity is the subject of the last section. In terms of white women we look at one of the most persistent myths in British imperial literature: that of the destructive *memsahib*—the wife of the *sahib*, or master. Over time, this myth has acquired considerable stereotypic baggage, with *memsahibs* being blamed for the collapse of the empire and the deterioration of race relations in India. We conclude by exploring the interplay between colonial and indigenous notions of domesticity.

Because this essay ranges widely over time and space, it is important to sketch briefly the historical context. European relations with Africa began with trade and ended, by the late nineteenth century, with formal colonial rule. The early focus on slaves shifted, in the course of the nineteenth century, to commodities—such raw materials as palm oil, rubber, gold, diamonds, and later peanuts, cotton, sisal, and other items needed to fuel Europe's Industrial Revolution. Thus, although Europe's contact with Africa preceded that with India and Southeast Asia, colonialism was firmly entrenched in the latter areas by the time that Europe was establishing colonies in Africa. The British East India Company edged out European rivals on the Indian subcontinent in the eighteenth century and ruled portions of India until the Sepoy Mutiny of 1857 revealed discontent with the company's administration and its ineffectiveness. Thereafter, Britain governed two-thirds of the subcontinent, leaving the rest as somewhat autonomous princely states until, following an extensive struggle, it granted independence separately in 1947 to India and Pakistan.

European Contact with Africa

Although European ships touched the coast of West Africa in the fifteenth century, European exploitation of the continent depended on African intermediaries because of the combination of potent diseases and strong African polities that prevented European penetration.

Along the Upper Guinea coast, in the area of present-day Senegal and Gambia, the institution of *signareship* arose; it reached its peak, according to George Brooks, in the 1780s on the French islands of Saint-Louis and Gorée. Even though the private Senegal Company that controlled trade forbade intermarriage between its employees and local women (and re fused as well to bring French women to Africa), such marriages came to be contracted between African *signares*, generally from among the Wolof and Lebou groups, and European traders, to the benefit of both. The marriages were carried out according to African custom; fidelity on both parts was expected, unless the European left for good, in which case a *signare* was free to marry again. The *signares* provided access to African commercial networks, translated between local languages and French, nursed ailing husbands through a variety of African fevers, and developed a distinctive heterogeneous culture. One of the central features of this culture was the *folgar*, or "ball," that provided an opportunity for displaying wealth and dance as well as making business and marriage contacts. Over time, many *signares* became very wealthy. They had large numbers of domestic slaves, some of whom, as skilled laborers, built impressive multistory stone and brick compounds. The prosperity of these commercial communities can be measured by the size of their slave populations, which are estimated to have been two-thirds to three-quarters of the total population of Gorée and roughly half of that of Saint-Louis by the 1780s.

Thus the establishment of French trade in the Senegambia owes much to the *signares*, who are glowingly described, for example, by the Reverend John Lindsay, who was familiar with both Gorée and Saint-Louis.

> As to their women, and in particular the ladies (for so I must call many of those in Senegal) they are in a surprising degree handsome, have very fine features, are wonderfully tractable, remarkably polite both in conversation and manners. . . . I cannot help thinking, that it was to the benefit of the African company [the French chartered company] in general, and the happiness of those they sent abroad in particular; that, with such promising inhabitants, the French suffered no white women to be sent hither.[3]

Throughout Africa, European males continued to dominate the white end of trade and travel, although largely without the comforts provided by the *signares* of Saint-Louis and Gorée, until the later decades of the nineteenth century. At that time, because of the convergence of a number of features, "Victorian lady travelers" arrived on the African coasts. Not large in number, they came, nonetheless, in a steady stream, and their lives and travels have been documented by Dea Birkett, Billie Melman, and Sara Mills.[4] The painter Marianne North traveled in Latin America, the United States, and Asia, as well as Africa. The Dutch heiress Alexandrine Tinne traveled up the Nile and in the western Sudan. Florence Baker accompanied her famous husband, Samuel, up the Nile. Many of these women were single; they traveled in smaller caravans than male explorers of the period.

They came escaping the confines of Victorian gender norms, which narrowly prescribed domestic and chaste behaviors for middle-class women. The most famous of these female travelers was Mary Kingsley, the self-educated daughter in a family of well-educated men. When her role as dutiful daughter ended in 1892 with the death of her parents, she traveled to West Africa where, over the next eight years, she studied "fish and fetish" and wrote *Travels in West Africa* and *Studies in West Africa*. She died in 1900 from typhoid fever, which she contracted while nursing Boer prisoners-of-war in the Anglo–Boer War in South Africa.

Kingsley was a complex and contradictory figure. Although she traveled to Africa to escape confining gender roles, she nonetheless perpetuated some of them, carefully wearing her corset while she trekked through tropical rains. Although she lectured on Africa, she supported the ban on women's admission to such prestigious scientific societies as the Royal Geographical Society. She opposed women's suffrage. She believed that just as Africans were fundamentally different from Europeans, "a great woman, either mentally or physically, will excel an indifferent man, but no woman ever equals a really great man."[5]

Were such British "lady travelers" different in terms of their attitudes toward their travels and indigenous peoples compared with the British male travelers? The literary critic Susan Blake compares three narratives of traveling from Cape to Cairo—from South Africa to Egypt—and argues that, indeed, women travel writers *were* different. The three narratives she chooses are by Ewart S. Grogan (1900), Frank H. Melland and Edward H. Cholmeley (1912), and Mary Hall (1907).

She concludes that "the relationships of both men and women travel narrators to Africa are functions of their gendered relationships to their own society. Grogan and Melland and Cholmeley represent their relations with Africans in ways that fulfill different aspects of their Victorian concept of manhood." Thus Grogan represents his conquest of Africa in an encounter with a hostile African chief: "In thirty seconds he was prone, and taking a severe dose of hippo-whip before his astonished band of elders; he rose refreshed and brought me flour and fowls. . . ."[6] If Grogan is one expression of Victorian manhood, Melland and Cholmeley are another. Blake explicates: "Where Grogan bags big-game trophies, they collect ethnographic information."[7] More subtle, they nonetheless objectify the African female chief they encounter: They "manage, by the dexterous use of elevated diction and subordinate clauses, to characterize [the female chief] Muchereka as a drunken shrew while simultaneously representing themselves as gentlemanly scientists too well bred to notice a lady's departure from universally accepted standards of decorum, though too thorough to overlook ethnographically interesting evidence of the potency of the local beer."[8] Grogan's brute power is replaced by the gentlemanly colonial officer.

Blake contrasts Mary Hall's narrative with both narratives. Where Grogan is conquering, and Melland and Cholmeley are gathering data, Hall is challenging the notion that Africa is no place for a white woman. Hall pokes fun at herself, granting reciprocity to an angry African chief she encounters. Having successfully cleared up their misunderstanding, she concludes, "I felt I must have impressed him as favourably as he had impressed me."[9] Her ability to grant subjectivity to the African chief, argues Blake, comes from her problematic relationship as a lady traveler to Victorian gender norms. As a woman, Hall can claim neither Grogan's power nor Melland and Cholmeley's colonial officer status; she must succeed by courtesy. In the end, she makes a class identification with the African chief, while rejecting both the racist myth of African savagery and the sexist myth of female vulnerability.

Blake finds similar patterns of irony and the granting of subjectivity to Africans in other European women's travel narratives. Her study highlights the way in which the gender of European male travelers has gone unremarked, when in fact their gender is central to how they experienced Africa and Africans.

Sex and Sexuality in the Empires

Concubinage was a feature of early periods of European conquest and rule in Africa and Asia. Not all African societies were powerful enough to insist, as did the *signares*, that European men conform to indigenous sexual norms and marriages. Hence concubinage was perceived by European commercial firms and colonial offices as an inexpensive way to provide heterosexual release and domestic nurturing to European men, with healthier outcomes than prostitution. Moreover, it resulted in the men gaining some knowledge of local language and customs. Indeed European enterprises, like the Senegal Company, actively discouraged or prevented European women from emigrating to imperial outposts. For example, the Dutch East India Company restricted such emigration for two hundred years, into the nineteenth century, and "the colonized woman living as a concubine to a European man formed the dominant domestic arrangement in colonial cultures through the early 20th century," according to Ann Stoler.[10]

One of the ironies of imperial history is that white women, who are largely absent from the imperial story, come to be imbued with remarkable agency when historians discuss the development of racial boundaries and racist sentiment within emerging European communities in the colonies. They are seen to be jealous of concubines' relationship with European men and quick to delineate social boundaries between European and indigenous peoples. The following example, given by a historian of India, typifies this argument:

> As women went out in large numbers, they brought with them their insular whims and prejudices, which no official contact with Indians or iron compulsion of loneliness ever tempted them to abandon. [They were] too insular in most cases to interest themselves in alien culture and life for its own sake.[11]

In this view, white women were more racist than men and were disinterested in indigenous society. A wife and family distracted a colonial official from his work. In addition, white women had to be protected from the sexual appetites of indigenous men, and they frowned on concubinage, with the result that racial divisions between colonizer and colonized hardened. Where there had been good race relations, tensions now developed. Succinctly put by imperial historians L. H. Gann and Peter Duignan: "It was the cheap steamship ticket for [white] women that put an end to racial integration."[12]

The timing of the arrivals of substantial numbers of white women and the subsequent hardening of racial boundaries varies by colony. In India, European women began arriving in substantial numbers after 1850. The Sepoy Mutiny in 1857 doubtless left in its aftermath increased racial tensions and contributed to the British drawing in among themselves. By the late nineteenth century, imperialist sentiments were strong in Britain, and various ideologies—scientific and medical as well as political[13]—situated whites as the superiors of people of color. All these factors contributed to the increased racism of white women *and* men in India.

It is interesting, however, that historical explanations link the rise of racism to the arrival of white women in widely varying times and places—French and British Africa, British Malaya, Papua New Guinea, Fiji, and the Solomon Islands.[14] Feminist scholars reject the turning of a correlation into a causation. Instead, they see the development of heightened racial hierarchies as a function of the perceived need of European communities to draw together, solidify boundaries, or quell internal splits within the white community. Stoler notes the collusion between European men and women in this refashioning of European space: "The material culture of French settlements in Saigon, outposts in New Guinea, and estate complexes in Sumatra were retailored to accommodate the physical and moral requirements of a middle-class and respectable feminine contingent"; increasingly segregated space joined a tightening of social practices to demarcate European and non-European communities.[15]

The point here is not to absolve white women from their role in the colonial project. Many supported imperialism and benefited from it.[16] The point is to see how, where, and to what purpose arguments about gender and sexuality have been deployed in imperial historiography. In the case of blaming *memsahibs* for the decline of race relations in the British empire, Claudia Knapman charges that such blame

> obscures the realities of the power relationship between ruler and ruled. It protects the actor from the unseen consequences of particular actions and from real accountability. It leaves the imperial idea itself intact, the men who affected it inviolable and, because the argument is male in origin, it excuses men of the ultimate responsibility for what is now both unpopular and assessed as a failure.[17]

Stoler argues that European colonial communities intensified their policing of themselves around issues of interracial sexuality, as "a European family, life and bourgeois respectability became increasingly [into the twentieth century] tied to notions of racial survival, imperial patriotism and the political strategies of the colonial state." [18] Mixed-race offspring from relations of concubinage and marriage came to be an embarrassment and a perceived danger. In the East Indies, notions of eugenics located a propensity to delinquency in the proportion of indigenous ancestry in such children. Rejected by most of their fathers and unable to be supported at European standards of living by the concubine mothers, they counted among the poor population of the Netherlands Indies, as well as other colonies, where orphanages for them became a feature of nineteenth-century colonial life. Racially mixed and poor, they raised disturbing questions of boundaries for Europeans. And the perceived threat they posed was differentiated by gender: Mixed-race women were seen as sexually loose, and mixed-race men as potential political militants. As Stoler notes, concubinage as an imperial strategy "fell into moral disfavor at the same time that new emphasis was placed on the standardization of European administration." [19]

Ronald Hyam analyzes the change in British imperial attitudes toward sexual morality in *Empire and Sexuality*, a recent and explicit contribution to the discussion of gender and sexuality in imperial settings. Dismissing feminist scholarship as impoverished and "fundamentally hostile to sex," Hyam argues that sexual opportunity on the part of the British male imperial elite was critical to the exercise of empire and that the level of opportunity available in the nineteenth century was reduced by the time of World War I through the extension overseas of the domestic "fanatical Purity Campaign." [20] Hyam rejects the earlier interpretation of *memsahibs* single-handedly bringing racism to the Raj. [21] But in place of Stoler's more nuanced discussion of changing sexual mores, Hyam gives explanatory primacy to the actions of social purity mongerers who interfered with European men's sexual access to indigenous women and men. Overall, he argues,

> though sex cannot of itself enable men to transcend racial barriers, it generates some admiration and affection across them, which is healthy, and which cannot always be dismissed as merely self-interested and prudential. For some British men, an introduction to the unabashed sexuality and erotic variation of the Arab and Asian worlds was a liberation and a refreshment, gratefully received. For some, it was the only real contact they had with indigenous peoples. [22]

Although Hyam adds considerably to our knowledge of the sexual practices of British colonial men, his contribution is weakened by the narrowness of his perspective, drawn, as it is, exclusively from the point of view of these men. Although he distinguishes between "perverted" sex based in "domination rather than mutual enjoyment" and the "expression of power rather than sensuality," he asserts and assumes, instead of exploring or proving, that nonperverted sexual encounters were the norm. He does not appear to consider the absence of evidence to be problematic.[23]

Some studies have looked at interracial sexual encounters in the colonies.[24] Here we point to two examples that suggest that sex between the colonizer and colonized may have been more problematic than Hyam suggests. *Distant Companions*, Karen Tranberg Hansen's study of domestic service in colonial Zambia (Northern Rhodesia), ventures into a discussion of colonial sexuality because it is essential to understand why domestic service developed as and remains a male occupation there. By contrast, in the rest of southern Africa, many women have come to be employed as servants. The answer lies not in labor-force demands because the mines of Northern Rhodesia employed large numbers of men. Moreover, the preference for male domestics continued through periods of shortages of male workers and despite colonial government campaigns to hire female domestics. Instead, Hansen locates the evolution of domestic service as a male occupational role in the sexual dynamic of colonial Northern Rhodesia and in colonial white attitudes and beliefs about African female sexuality.

Concubinage (and short-term appropriation) was a feature of nineteenth-century white pioneer society in Northern Rhodesia as elsewhere. The institution of the "cook's woman," that is to say the woman whom the male cook procured for his master, was less open than in neighboring Belgian and Portuguese colonies, but it was common. Stories abound of white men with multiple concubines and many European-African children. In contrast to Hyam's benign view of the empire providing sexual opportunity, Hansen is less neutral in her evaluation: "Most white men took African women in the way they had taken everything else, land and labor, and when it was not forthcoming, then by force. . . . As African men were coerced into wage labor through the tax nexus, so many African women were taken from their local groups at white men's behest and against their wills." The servant would bring African women back to his master; the latter "would then stay at the white man's place for the night, or a few days." Married women were typically avoided, to reduce the possibility of trouble.[25]

Hansen argues that African women in Northern Rhodesia came to be seen as available sexually, in comparison with other areas of southern Africa, because of a combination of factors. Whites perceived African social organization as sexually amoral. They based their beliefs on certain practices found in Zambia and not farther south—for example, matrilineality, polygyny, and polyandry (having multiple wives and husbands, respectively), puberty rites that include instruction in sexual pleasures, and flexible marriage arrangements. Not only did these practices involve a degree of sexual expression and openness that was abhorrent to some white settlers, they also allowed African women options and power in marriage and descent–inheritance that were unavailable to European women. White missionaries and other writers transmuted this threatening combination of empowering customs into evidence of sexual immorality and looseness among African women. The long-term results of this white view of African women as immoral have been significant and have had economic consequences. For, Hansen argues, not only were African women recruited or coerced into liaisons with white men, white colonial women refused to hire African women as domestic servants, fearing their competition as sexual partners. And as African families came to hire domestics, African women adopted the same reservations about employing females. Hence African women were excluded from one of the few areas of wage labor for which they might compete.

Turning to India, the extension of the Contagious Diseases Acts (CDA) there in 1864 provides an interesting opportunity to examine Hyam's approach in comparison with that of various feminist scholars. By the 1860s, sexual relationships between indigenous women and British men occurred less frequently than before, as a result of the combined assault of missionaries frowning upon concubinage, British unease following the Sepoy Mutiny of 1857, and the growth of a more insular community of British women and men. Authorities allowed only a small minority of British soldiers in the Indian Army to marry; they did not favor homosexual relations; and they considered enforced celibacy no option. Alarmingly, one in four British soldiers was found to have venereal disease at the time of the mutiny. In the official mind, the solution was to provide for regulated prostitution. Prostitutes were allowed entry to army cantonments and could become regimental followers (like other Indian support workers) if they had been examined and registered. Under the Indian version of the CDA, prostitutes and soldiers with venereal disease were treated and quarantined in special hospitals. Under pressure from the forces of Josephine Butler, who had fought the CDA in Britain, the Indian regulations were suspended in 1888, although the routine inspection of prostitutes continued until independence in 1947.[26]

Given Hyam's dislike for "Purity-mongers" and "Purity-minded, interfering busybod[ies]" whose actions resulted in governmental interference in private activity, he might be expected to oppose the CDA in India. Instead, he is uncritical and gives reasons the regulations were needed: regimental prostitutes earned "comparatively good money . . . and [were] not generally ill-treated";[27] although regulations had some effect on reducing venereal disease, suspension of regulation resulted in a dramatic increase of the disease between 1888 and 1892. In his concern for the British male's sexual opportunity, he offers only perfunctory concern for the women who provided a sexual outlet (though by no means, as his book demonstrates, the only outlet).

It is fruitful to compare his approach with that of Veena Talwar Oldenburg. Oldenburg searched historical documentary evidence and interviewed women in Lucknow in the 1970s who lived and worked as courtesans, descendants of earlier generations of courtesans. Her research, presented in *The Making of Colonial Lucknow, 1856–1877*[28] and in "Lifestyle as Resistance,"[29] documents an institution of considerable antiquity that offered some women wealth and respite from abusive marital and family circumstances. Under British rule, their profession had declined in status from being an honored one, in which they provided sexual services for rich patrons and promoted Hindu high culture while resisting male domination and building an alternative, socially and sexually women-centered space. As part of the elite of Lucknow and members of the princely court of Awadh, the courtesans had supported the local ruler in the 1857 Mutiny. After the suppression of the rebellion, the British maligned the institution of the courtesans and their salons. Officials were happy to accept them as revenue sources, however; the courtesans were classified as "singing and dancing girls" for purposes of tax collection. Moreover, the British selected the most attractive women and placed them in cantonments to service the army sexually, subjecting them to inspection for venereal disease. The courtesans interviewed by Oldenburg reported their own and their predecessors' experience of governmental regulation, including "the humiliating routine of inspection of their rooms and bodies . . . and incidents where women were abused, insulted, and beaten by [police]. . . . 'All these rules and regulations offended our dignity and sense of pride' [stated one of them]."[30]

Where Hyam assumes that colonial interracial sexual encounters were about mutual enjoyment, Oldenburg provides contrary evidence regarding interracial and intraracial sexual intercourse for a period just after World War I, the end of Hyam's focus. She notes that "almost every one of the [courtesans] . . . claimed that their closest emotional relationships were among themselves, [about one-fourth of the women interviewed] admitted . . . that their most satisfying physical involvements were with other women."[31] They prided themselves on their accomplished deception in dealings with male clients. Rather than describe mutual sexual enjoyment, this sounds like work, an option that provided better chances for economic autonomy for indigenous women than many other avenues in British colonial Africa or Asia.[32]

Antoinette Burton takes a third angle.[33] She sees Josephine Butler's extension of the campaign against the CDA overseas as essential to Butler and her associates' careers once the CDA were repealed in Britain in 1886; they "found themselves in danger of becoming suddenly redundant."[34]

Although Butler was concerned about the reported mistreatment of Indian prostitutes in the course of compulsory examinations, she was motivated significantly by her view of the existence of the CDA in India as a threat of their reintroduction in England. Hence, while Burton does not see Butler as Hyam's "busybody Purity-monger," she is nonetheless critical of Butler's maternalism toward Indian women and appropriation of their realities for her own purposes.

In these various examples, sex, and European attitudes toward sexuality (most especially interracial sexual activity), is seen to be connected to other aspects of imperial rule. In the next section, we explore how British official condemnation of the Indian male's sexuality was linked with the ostensible championing of the Indian woman's plight as a key legitimation of the Raj.

The Raj and the Status of Indian Women

To legitimize intervention and rule, imperial powers often criticized indigenous societies, applying standards derived from Western norms and development. Frederick Cooper, for example, identifies the application of the free-labor ideology to Africa. The concept of free labor, he notes, "was central to the European indictment of African society in the years of the conquest: the antislavery publicists shaped an image of Africa based upon the antitheses of slave and free labor, of tyranny and civilized government, of closed, defensive, subsistence-oriented communities and open market economies, of stagnation and progress."[35] Similarly, in India the nineteenth century witnessed an imperial assault on patriarchal orchestrations of women's behavior: *Sati* was abolished and the age of consent to marriage for girls was raised to twelve. Yet, as recent scholars have argued, the British were contradictory in their approach, and it appears that asserting the barbarity of Indian culture was more salient than alleviating women's hardships.

In 1818, the British Utilitarian James Mill articulated the notion of women's status as a measure of civilization:

> The condition of women is one of the most remarkable circumstances in the manners of nations. Among rude people, the women are generally degraded; among civilized people they are exalted. . . . As society refines upon its enjoyments, and advances into that state of civilization . . . in which the qualities of mind are ranked above the qualities of the body, the condition of the weaker sex is gradually improved, till they associate on equal terms with the men, and occupy the place of voluntary and useful coadjutors.[36]

By this standard, Hindu and Muslim Indian society, which prescribed the social segregation of men and women, failed. The *zenana*, or women's quarters of the household, was, in the words of Janaki Nair, quoting English women writers, "those cavernous depths of 'idolatry and superstition' that the blinding light of reason had not yet reached." Over time, white women saw the *zenana*, variously, as the location of the collective Indian past, a site of potential reform and conversion, female power, and resistance to the civilizing mission of the British.[37]

Mill was writing in the midst of an attack on *sati*, the Hindu practice of a widow immolating herself on her husband's funeral pyre (the term refers to both the practice and the woman herself). The practice was first officially recorded by the British in the 1780s. In 1805 *sati* came under legal scrutiny when a district magistrate stopped the *sati* of a young girl. From then until the abolition of *sati* in 1829, British policy directed officials to ensure that the *sati* was done under conditions that Hindu legal advisers had indicated were acceptable, namely, that it was done voluntarily and not under the influence of drugs and that the widow not have infant children or be pregnant at the time.[38]

The story of the abolition of *sati* became an essential part of the British self-image as champions of Indian women's plight against depraved Hindu tradition, as the beginning of the modernization of Indian society. But recent scholars point to a more complex situation. Lata Mani argues convincingly that the tradition of *sati* was a colonial invention and that the British concern was not for Indian women themselves but for British cultural superiority: "Tradition was . . . not the ground on which the status of women was being contested. Rather the reverse was true: women in fact became the site on which tradition was debated and reformulated. What was at stake was not women but tradition."[39] (This is not to say that *sati* did not exist, but that the *tradition of sati* that the British attacked was a tradition being reinvented as part of the colonial process; it was not an unchanging act, unmediated by history or politics.)

As Joanna Liddle and Rama Joshi point out, the British, in codifying Brahmanic custom into Hindu law in the late eighteenth century, actually enforced on lower-caste Hindu women the restrictions that had been heretofore applied only to upper-caste Hindu women. By this process, Hindu women were prohibited from owning property except for marriage gifts, divorce was not permissible, and marriage was to be monogamous. Although the restrictions on property ownership were not much at issue for poor, lower-caste women, marriage arrangements were typically more flexible among lower castes than among upper-caste Brahmins.[40] Moreover, as Mani notes, Brahmanic interpreters were considerably more tentative regarding the authority and inflexibility of the Brahmanic texts on which the British were relying to shape their notions of legal and illegal *sati* (in the period before 1829). In fact, the scriptural authority for *sati* was highly disputed, with the most ancient texts, the Vedas, mentioning widow inheritance (leviritic marriage) rather than *sati*. The most important of another category of texts, the notoriously misogynist Laws of Manu, similarly did not prescribe *sati*, but called on widows to be chaste.[41]

Mani argues that all the parties to the *sati* debate—the Raj, Hindu reformers such as Rammohun Roy who sought to abolish it, and Hindu conservatives—shared the terms of discourse, which had itself been shaped by colonial intervention. These terms included the notion of a golden age of Hinduism for women, followed by a fall (generally coinciding with Muslim conquest). "This idea of a fall," notes Mani, "grew to be crucial to nineteenth century indigenous discourses, 'progressive' and 'conservative,' and was to intersect with the idea that Britain rescued Hindu India from Islamic tyranny, to produce specifically 'Hindu' discourses of political and cultural regeneration."[42]

In the British view, *sati* was religiously based, and indigenous people submitted themselves to religious custom. The British legal attack focused on revealing to Hindus the proper Brahmanic scriptural interpretation of their own religion: that the texts indeed did not prescribe *sati*. Rather than interfere in local religion to protect women, argues Mani, the "civilizing mission of colonization was thus seen to lie in protecting the 'weak' [women–religious followers] against the 'artful' [indigenous interpreters of Hinduism], in giving back to the natives the truths of their own 'little read and less understood [scripture].'"[43] For this reason, Mani sees women as the ground of debate, but Indian tradition as the true subject of the contest.

In "Whose *Sati*?" Anand Yang seeks to discover something about the women themselves. In actual practice, *sati* was carried out in some regions of India and not others. The martial people whom the British admired had practiced it during the period of the Muslim invasions of northern India so that male warriors could go off to fight assured that, if they were defeated, their widows, having burned themselves, would not suffer the shame of being ravished. In Bengal, where the incidence of *sati* was concentrated at the time of abolition, it had been adopted not only by Brahmins but by lower castes as well. Still, according to Yang's analysis of statistics collected in the years prior to the 1829 abolition, the incidence of *sati* in 1824 was very low in the district that consistently reported the most cases; only 1.2 percent of the estimated number of women who became widows committed *sati*. The highest and lowest castes recorded the comparably high proportions of the cases of *sati*. (This fact casts doubt on the argument by one scholar that adopting the practice of *sati* was, in Yang's paraphrase, "the expression of a rudderless upper-caste Bengali gentry seeking to anchor themselves in a period of flux by resorting to the 'traditional' practice of sati.")[44] More surprisingly, over two-thirds of the *satis* were women over age forty, not the child widows of British propaganda, and a number immolated themselves years after their husbands' deaths. These features, added to the poverty of the *satis*, leads Yang to conclude that women committed *sati* from a combination of factors: the spiritual merit that accrued to them and their families, as well as the reality of continuing a life of poverty, advancing age, and the "cold *sati*" to which Hindu widows were subjected as polluted, marginal, and ostracized members of the community.

In the course of the nineteenth century, the British turned to other women's issues as well. As Mrinalini Sinha argues, the fate of the Age of Consent Act of 1891 reveals much about British motivations and thinking. Indigenous reformers opposed child marriage. Raj officials claimed to be reluctant to interfere in indigenous religion but ended up doing so anyway: Instead of outlawing child marriage, they declared sexual intercourse with a girl under age twelve to be rape. This prohibition based on age contravened Bengali religious custom that prohibited intercourse before a girl's puberty, whether or not that occurred before age twelve. In allowing child marriage but prohibiting intercourse, the British were in fact creating the category of marital rape, a crime committable by Hindu men that did not yet exist in Britain (nor does it exist as a category today in much of the United States).[45]

That the Raj was not single-mindedly pursuing the best interests of Indian women is revealed in two examples in particular: legislation about restoration of conjugal rights and changes in personal laws relating to the Nayars in Kerala Province in the south.

In the case of conjugal rights, the British introduced into Indian law a husband's right to force his wife to return to him. Beginning as early as 1793 in Bengal, claims for conjugal rights were made possible; restoration became part of the Civil Procedure Code in 1859 covering British India as a whole. Hindu custom dealt with a wife's refusal to live with her husband by having her remain with or return to her parents. Hence restoration of a male's conjugal rights clearly had no basis in Hindu tradition. Given child marriage, such refusal by an unhappy wife was an important safeguard, since divorce was not a possibility.[46] The test came in 1885 when Rukhmabai, an educated woman, refused to go to the household of the husband to whom her father had married her when she was a minor. After discovering her in-laws to be unsupportive of her intellectual interests, Rukhmabai left, arguing that she had not consented to the marriage. With considerable support from conservative Hindu men, the illiterate husband successfully sued for restoration of conjugal rights; only an appeal to Queen Victoria led to Rukhmabai's release from jail and from the marriage.[47] In Britain in 1884 there were changes in the law that removed forfeiting of property by the wife, imprisonment of the wife, or both, as punishment for nonfulfillment of conjugal rights. These changes prompted some efforts by an embarrassed British administration in India to alter the Indian law as well. But it remained in place until 1923.[48] Thus, in this example, the British colonizers legitimated the Raj by pointing to the British role in uplifting Indian women by abolishing *sati*, an uncivilized Hindu practice. But the colonial government did not consistently work to improve Indian women's lives; by allowing Indian men to sue for restoration of conjugal rights in a context of women's subordinate legal and social status, the Raj hurt Indian women.

In the second instance, although the Raj often was reluctant to intervene in local custom, the government proved itself willing to alter Indian personal law substantially when it faced certain social norms that empowered indigenous women in ways quite foreign to English sentiments. The Nayars of Kerala practiced matrilineal inheritance and descent and allowed women and men to engage in multiple, informal sexual relationships. Although the matrilineage's collectively held property was administered by the eldest brother, women exercised considerable power and had considerable autonomy, personally and sexually. In a series of legal changes from the 1860s on, the colonial government required men to provide for their biological children, a socially meaningless requirement to the Nayar man, whose responsibility lay with his sister's children (who were members of the same matrilineage as he was) rather than his own biological children. Then marriage was declared monogamous and dissolvable only via law. Over time, men came to hold personal property, the collective property became alienable, and a man's biological children were declared his heirs. Effectively, the social bases for Nayar women's autonomy were severely eroded.[49]

Thus the claims of the British not to wish to interfere in indigenous religious life and custom ring hollow. It is true that the Raj was aware of the dangers of inciting indigenous rebellion (it is argued that a 1856 law allowing Hindu widows to remarry fed the Sepoy Mutiny of 1857).[50] Officialdom was not of one mind, however, and the colonial government on occasion evidenced a willingness to take on indigenous law and custom. Recent scholarship has undercut the claim that British official motivation was rooted fundamentally in their concern for Indian women's lives. Instead, as Mani and others argue, women were the terrain, but the struggle was over something else—the conception of Indian tradition, or Indian moral readiness for self-rule.

Nor was colonial officialdom alone in using the treatment of Indian women as a moral measure. In 1883–84, just before Rukhmabai's court case over conjugal rights, Anglo-Indian women in India (in the nineteenth century, "Anglo-Indian" refers to the British in India, not to Eurasians) raised a considerable stir over a proposed change in the Code of Criminal Procedure. The Ilbert Bill, named after the man who introduced it, sought to give Indian magistrates authority to judge cases involving Anglo-Indian men and women. The bill that eventually passed accorded this authority to Indian jurists, but it included a compromise extracted after British residents registered strong protests: Anglo-Indians were guaranteed a right to trial by a jury at least half of whose members were their racial peers. Mrinalini Sinha's research has probed the gender basis of this protest.[51] Just as the status of indigenous women came to be the site of British reform efforts, so too the battle over the Ilbert Bill was fought with reference to womanhood—Indian and Anglo-Indian.

The attack on the Ilbert Bill was two-pronged. First, Indian magistrates were seen as inappropriate for judging Anglo-Indians because they ostensibly held barbaric attitudes about women. This representative view was articulated by a British magistrate: "Is it likely that time will ever come when Englishmen in India or elsewhere will acquiesce in a measure subjecting their wives and daughters to the criminal jurisdiction of Judges whose ideas on the subject of women and marriage are not European but Oriental[?]"[52] In the heated political climate of the day, Anglo-Indians could choose to ignore the fact that criticisms of Hindu practices of *sati* and child marriage had been articulated by Indian male reformers before these issues became part of the agenda of the Raj. Second, British critics in India and England raised the specter of Indian magistrates using their position to compromise young Anglo-Indian women. For example, an Indian Army officer offered this scenario:

> Many English officers have English servant girls attached to their families; a native Magistrate, puffed up with importance[,] might set eyes upon one of the girls and make overtures to her. If she refused, as she probably would do, what would be easier than for this native, acting under the smart of disappointment[,] to bring a case against the girl to be tried in his court?[53]

In the midst of the debate arose charges of sexual assault on the part of Indian male servants against Anglo-Indian women; these were deployed as evidence of what might occur if Indian men were emboldened by the passage of the Ilbert Bill, despite the substantial class–caste difference between the servants charged with assault and the magistrates who would be empowered by the bill.

The bill became politically controversial within the Anglo-Indian community as well. Although most British men chivalrously rose to the defense of Anglo-Indian womanhood, a few, for example Henry Beveridge, welcomed the racial equity of the bill. Beveridge and his famous wife, Annette Akroyd Beveridge, disagreed. Akroyd joined the anti-bill agitation, lending her reputation as a liberal on racial matters. (She and Beveridge had entertained Indian guests socially in their home, and she had been involved in Indian women's educational reforms.) Echoing other sentiments, she identified the bill as a "proposal to subject civilized women to the jurisdiction of men who have done little or nothing to redeem the women of their race, whose social ideas are still on the outer verge of civilization." [54] She located her opposition in her "pride of womanhood," not her "pride of race," although in speaking for womanhood she went against the Indian women's organizations and individual Indian women who strongly supported the bill. [55]

In organizing politically and socially against the bill, Akroyd and the other Anglo-Indian women challenged the notion of female passivity imbedded in the white womanhood that they and Anglo-Indian men were defending. In addition to boycotting the social season's round of balls and parties, Anglo-Indian women collected 5,758 women's signatures on a petition to Queen Victoria. While Anglo-Indian men were quick to come to the support of their women, they expressed unease at such political mobilization. Comments ranged from patronizing editorials in some newspapers to the *Pioneer*'s position that "the women had 'somewhat unnecessarily joined the fray, . . . [noting that] she is the best woman who is least observed.' " [56]

If Anglo-Indian men were distressed at the political organizing of women of their community, nationalist Indian men welcomed Bengali women's uncharacteristic involvement in overtly political matters. Teachers and students in girls' schools voted their support for the bill. In concurrent and precedent-setting agitation around support for a jailed nationalist leader, the Bengali Ladies Association proclaimed their support, and indigenous women demonstrated in public. [57]

Thus, for women and men, British and Indian, the status of Indian women under Indian tradition and custom became a central issue. Early colonial historiography portrayed, in Gayatri Chakravorty Spivak's terms, white men saving brown women from brown men. [58] Analyzed more closely, the Raj's actions are seen to be serving the imperial mission. If Indian tradition could be characterized as barbaric, then Indian criticisms of foreign rule and claims for self-rule could be dismissed as inappropriate or premature. Moreover, the Raj intervened in personal law and custom with negative, not only positive, consequences for women, at times when such interventions fit its preconceptions and advanced its agenda.

Manliness

These struggles over the status of Hindu women are interwoven with Anglo-Indian notions of masculinity, which are themselves part of the evolution of the British imperial male gender role in the course of the nineteenth century.

As Helen Callaway notes in her study of European women in colonial Nigeria, the idea that the empire was no place for a white woman rested on mutually reinforcing views of the empire and of gender. The early days of empire (characteristic of nineteenth-century Africa, whose interiors were still being explored) required rugged, tough men—the Cecil Rhodes of the world, the sort of man whom Cape-to-Cairo traveler Ewart Grogan emulated. With imperial rule came the more prosaic yet critical establishment of a bureaucracy and an administration. Callaway's representation of the British Colonial Service points to the gendered basis of this administration:

> This male ruling group was assumed to be superior, in India known as the "heaven born," its officers being specially selected for their leadership qualities ideally developed (though not always in practice). . . . The Colonial Service can be viewed as another male institution in the separate sex arrangements of the British middle class of that time—beginning with preparatory schools, continuing through public[59] schools, and then in military establishments or the men's colleges of Oxford and Cambridge, and extending through adulthood (even to senility) in the London [men's] clubs.[60]

Given this sense of imperial space, it is not surprising that one Nigerian colonial servant's wife, when introduced to the local senior British official as late as 1925, was welcomed with the statement, "Mrs. Niven, this is no place for a white woman."[61] Indeed the phrase appears in various memoirs written by British women who lived in colonial Nigeria. The maleness of empire lay behind official encouragement, initially, of liaisons with concubines, official opposition to having colonial servants bring out wives and families, and official reluctance (well into the twentieth century) to appoint women to positions in the Colonial Service.

Hyam traces the changes in British views of masculinity through the nineteenth century:

> A shift from the ideals of moral strenuousness, a Christian manliness, to a culture of the emphatically physical . . .; a shift from serious earnestness to robust virility, from integrity to hardness, from the ideals of godliness and good learning to those of clean manliness and good form. . . . The qualities most unsparingly disparaged by the late-Victorians were sentimentalism and lack of sexual control.[62]

Sports were central to the late nineteenth-century vision of manliness, claims Hyam, and athletics were seen as relevant to empire as well: "The cult of games and the pervading concern with imperial destiny mutually reinforced one another. Football, cricket, and boxing were seen as 'moral agents' in running the empire, capable of weaning subject peoples from unhealthy sexual preoccupations, intertribal warfare and cattle raiding."[63] Along with a shifting construction of masculinity came the constellation of changes in sexual mores associated with the social-purity movement that Hyam bemoans, including increased anxiety about masturbation and homosexuality. A Kenyan settler, Robert Baden-Powell, founded the Boy Scouts in the first decade of the twentieth century in an attempt to instill this vision of masculinity into succeeding generations, to make them "good citizens or useful colonists."[64]

Anglo-Indian disparagement of Bengali masculinity must be seen against this emerging ideal of British masculinity. Mrinalini Sinha notes the unremitting attack on Bengali manliness among nineteenth-century Britons, exemplified in this statement by a colonial official:

> The training of natives from their childhood, the enervating influence of the *zenana* on their upbringing, early marriage, a low moral standard resulting from caste distinctions and the influence of centuries of subjugation all tend to hinder the development in Bengalis of those manly and straightforward qualities which under other conditions are found in Englishmen.[65]

With their slight builds, Bengali men were seen as effeminate.

Sinha views the debate about the Age of Consent Act as a struggle over masculinity. Early consummation of marriage was seen by the British as more evidence of flaws in Bengali manliness: their sexual depravity and their lack of sexual control, which Hyam identifies as key to the British construction of manliness at that time. In comparison, the martial peoples (*real* men) whom the British admired—the Pathans and Sikhs in western and northwestern India—allegedly did not consummate marriage at a young age. Moreover, masturbation was said to be "universal in Lower Bengal," according to a retired British civil servant, and "the marriage of children often with aged males tends to the physical deterioration of the human stock, and physical deterioration implies effeminacy, mental imperfection and moral debility," intoned the *Indian Medical Gazette*.[66]

If the British brought with them to the colonies ideas about masculinity that weighed heavily in their evaluations of colonizing and colonized men alike, they held equally powerful notions of female gender. We have discussed the aspects of femininity linked to sexuality; the domestic domain held powerful meaning as well.

Domesticity

We have seen how *memsahibs* have been credited, misogynously and mistakenly, with the ruin of race relations throughout the European empires. Although the credit, or blame, for a rising sense of racial superiority and desired social distance between colonizer and colonized must be shared by white men and women, it fell to white women to administer the social (as opposed to legal and political) practices through which social boundaries were created and maintained. The creation of a European "home" in the colonies was the ultimate responsibility of *memsahibs*.[67]

The apparent pettiness of social rituals, which were continued in the colonies decades after they had subsided in Britain, belies their importance in articulating a social hierarchy within white colonial society and demarcating the European–non-European boundary. Newly married Sylvia Leith-Ross, who traveled to Nigeria in the early years of the twentieth century, describes the ritual and importance of dressing for dinner on a steel canoe as she traveled up the Benue River:

> Every night, we tied up at the edge of a sandbank and dined—we would not have used a less formal word—[and dressed for dinner]. . . . Between the two of us we had obeyed our code and had upheld our own and our country's dignity. . . . When you are alone, among thousands of unknown, unpredictable people, dazed by unaccustomed sights and sounds, bemused by strange ways of life and thought, you need to remember who you are, where you come from, what your standards are.[68]

Nineteenth-century India, with its substantial European population, held ample opportunity for the social rituals and gossiping through which such standards were defined and redefined. "Calling," formalized by the dropping off of calling cards according to a strict social hierarchy, both marked the social strata of white society and initiated a social relationship.[69] In this context we can appreciate the boycott of the social season called by Anglo-Indian women who opposed the Ilbert Bill; as the guardians of Anglo-Indian social boundaries, they were calling attention to the seriousness of the matter in their eyes.

The domestic realm was not only important to the colonizers but it became contested territory in indigenous society as well. Partha Chatterjee argues that Indian nationalists responded to Anglo-Indian criticisms by envisioning indigenous culture as spiritually superior to the material West. The "material/spiritual distinction was condensed into an analogous, but ideologically far more powerful, dichotomy: that between the outer and the inner."[70] The latter was identified with the home and with Indian women. This formulation made the adoption of Western practices and education highly charged and problematic for Indian women.

The emergence of the *bhadramahila*—respectable female counterparts to reforming Bengali middle-class males—marked the nationalist resolution of this tension. "Formal education became not only acceptable," argues Chatterjee,

> but, in fact, a requirement for the new *bhadramahila* when it was demonstrated that it was possible for a woman to acquire the cultural refinements afforded by modern education without jeopardizing her place at home, that is, without becoming a *memsaheb*. . . . Education then was meant to inculcate in women the virtues—the typically bourgeois virtues characteristic of the new social forms of "disciplining"—of orderliness, thrift, cleanliness, and a

personal sense of responsibility, the practical skills of literacy, accounting and hygiene and the ability to run the household according to the new physical and economic conditions set by the outside world.[71]

Considerable freedom of movement was opened up to the *bhadramahila*, once "the spiritual signs of her femininity were now clearly marked—in her dress, her eating habits, her social demeanor, her religiosity."[72]

In the latter half of the nineteenth century, Indian nationalists became resistant to changes in women's status proposed by the Raj, Chatterjee argues, not because they became more conservative, but because they "refus[ed] . . . to make the women's question an issue of political negotiation with the colonial state."[73] Instead, among the reforming Bengali nationalists, such changes came internally, through redefinition of the *bhadramahila*'s gender role.

European conquest and colonization of Africa involved an agenda of domesticity as well, most often articulated in the nineteenth century by missionaries. Analyzing missionary encounters with the Tswana in southern Africa in the mid-nineteenth century, Jean and John Comaroff identify the domestic ideology as having both a spacial dimension (the redesign of the home and compound) and a gendered dimension (removing Tswana females from agricultural work and enlisting Tswana cattle for plow agriculture under men's hands). Round dwellings were to be replaced by square ones. "The evangelists believed," note the Comaroffs, "the 'houses' literally constructed their inhabitants; that their functionally-specific spaces laid out the geometry of cleanliness and Godliness. By contrast, 'huts' and 'hovels,' undifferentiated within and made of all but raw materials, were brutish and transient."[74] Among the converts, female housebuilders were trained instead to sew and cook, while males were taught carpentry in order to assume their proper tasks as builders.

What made the domestic domain important was its centrality to social reproduction. In the "private domain . . . were contained the elemental relations of gender and generation on which social reproduction depended; in its routines and conventions were vested the signs and practices on which rested the social order."[75]

The Christian ideology of domesticity included features of marriage that initially appealed to some African women. Kristin Mann's study of the Christian elite in colonial Lagos, Nigeria, outlines the tensions between Yoruba and Christian conceptions of marriage. The Yoruba conceived of marriage as between patrilineal kin groups; polygyny was valued; spouses did not inherit from one another; and intimacy came via same-sex friendships rather than companionate marriage.[76] Yoruba elite women initially embraced Christian marriage because it enjoined polygyny and gave them and their children access to their husbands' property. By the turn of the century, however, disenchantment had set in. "It is very much to be feared," wrote a local observer, "that [Christian] marriage brings [women] a false sense of security, and it is because of the disaster it has wrought among so many, that we venture to bring this matter to the public notice." [77] In practice, Yoruba Christian husbands took the customary additional wives in spite of the prescribed monogamy. Furthermore, Christian domesticity entailed women giving up the economic autonomy of traditional Yoruba wives in favor of economic dependence on their husbands, which proved to be unsatisfactory to both spouses. [78]

The colonial project involved the reshaping of indigenous society and beliefs in profound ways. But colonial intentions were not always followed by the expected results. Among the Tswana, the introduction of plow agriculture combined with other economic changes to increase stratification greatly between families and between men and women, as the latter lost control of production. The Bengali middle class, while adopting and modifying aspects of British domesticity, came to form the core of Bengali nationalism. And however much Christianity changed Yoruba society, Yoruba Christian marriage did not evolve into the companionate model prescribed by missionaries. Indigenous norms continued to find expression, alongside Christian structures.

Conclusion

The study of empire in its older form—the actions of great men, famous battles, economic exploitation (or development, depending on one's political persuasion)—has given way in the face of widespread political decolonization since World War II. In the past fifteen years, the developments in the study of social history in the former colonies, as well as subspecialties that focus on women, gender, or both, have shifted the locus to include arenas not earlier covered, among them sexuality and domesticity, resulting both in new information and in reassessments of such earlier concerns as nationalism.

Gender was a significant sociocultural category both for European colonizers and for African and Asian colonized peoples. European gender roles determined that men more than women would travel to the colonies as traders, conquerors, or colonial administrators. European women were at first discouraged from such travel and later, when permitted to travel, were charged primarily with policing the morals and boundaries of the European community. Missionary and secular forces alike prescribed European middle-class domesticity and morals as the ideal for both the European community and parts of the indigenous community. In India, European officials and civilians declared the status of indigenous women to be a measure of "civilization" and evaluated indigenous men in terms of European notions of manliness. The Raj used the law selectively to regulate such customs as *sati*, age of marriage, and conjugal rights. Thus the gender dimension of personal life came to be a significant arena of struggle.

NOTES

1. See, for example, Ronald Hyam, *Britain's Imperial Century, 1815–1914: A Study of Empire and Expansion* (London: Batsford, 1976); V. G. Kiernan, *The Lords of Human Kind: European Attitudes Toward the Outside World in the Imperial Age* (London: Weidenfeld and Nicolson, 1976); C. C. Eldridge, *Victorian Imperialism* (London: Hodder and Stoughton, 1978); D. K. Fieldhouse, *Colonialism, 1870–1945* (London: Weidenfeld and Nicolson, 1981); W. Baumgart, *The Idea and Reality of British and French Colonial Expansion 1880–1914* (Oxford, England: Oxford University Press, 1982); Eric Hobsbawm and Terence Ranger, eds., *The Invention of Tradition* (Cambridge, England: Cambridge University Press, 1983); Ashis Nandy, *The Intimate Enemy: Loss and Recovery of Self under Colonialism* (Bombay: Oxford University Press, 1983); J. M. Mackenzie, *Propaganda and Empire: The Manipulation of British Public Opinion, 1880–1960* (Manchester, England: Manchester University Press, 1984); Dorothy O. Helly, *Livingstone's Legacy: Horace Waller and Victorian Mythmaking* (Athens: Ohio University Press, 1987); Gauri Viswanathan, *Masks of Conquest: Literary Study and British Rule in India* (New York: Columbia University Press, 1989).

2. See Susan Bailey, *Women and the British Empire: An Annotated Guide to Sources* (New York: Garland Publishing, 1987); Cheryl Johnson-Odim and Margaret Strobel, eds., *Restoring Women to History: Teaching Packets for Integrating Women's History into Courses on Africa, Asia, Latin America and the Caribbean, and the Middle East*, rev. ed. (Bloomington, Ind.: Organization of American Historians, 1990).

3. Cited in George E. Brooks, Jr., "The Signares of Saint-Louis and Gorée: Women Entrepreneurs in Eighteenth-Century Senegal," in *Women in Africa: Studies in Social and Economic Change*, ed. Nancy J. Hafkin, and Edna G. Bay (Stanford: Stanford University Press, 1976), p. 26.

4. Dea Birkett, *Spinsters Abroad: Victorian Lady Travelers* (London: Basil Blackwell, 1989); Catherine Barnes Stevenson, *Victorian Women Travel Writers in Africa* (Boston: Twayne, 1982); Billie Melman, *Women's Orients: English Women and the Middle East, 1718–1918; Sexuality, Religion and Work* (Ann Arbor: University of Michigan Press, 1992); Sara Mills, *Discourses of Difference: An Analysis of Women's Travel Writing and Colonialism* (New York: Routledge, 1991).

5. Quoted in Margaret Strobel, *European Women and the Second British Empire* (Bloomington: Indiana University Press, 1991), p. 38; see also Kathleen Frank, *A Voyager Out: The Life of Mary Kingsley* (Boston: Houghton Mifflin, 1986); and Dea Birkett, *Mary Kingsley, Imperial Adventures* (London: Macmillan, 1992).

6. Cited in Susan L. Blake, "A Woman's Trek: What Difference Does Gender Make?" in *Western Women and Imperialism: Complicity and Resistance*, ed. Nupur

Chaudhuri and Margaret Strobel (Bloomington: Indiana University Press, 1992), p. 22.

7. Ibid., p. 24.

8. Ibid., p. 26.

9. Cited in ibid., p. 29.

10. Ann L. Stoler, "Making Empire Respectable: The Politics of Race and Sexual Morality in Twentieth-Century Colonial Cultures," *American Ethnologist* 16, no. 4 (November 1989): 637.

11. Percival Spear, *The Nabobs* (London: Oxford University Press, 1963), p. 140.

12. Cited in Ann Laura Stoler, "Rethinking Colonial Categories: European Communities and the Boundaries of Rule," *Comparative Studies in Society and History* 31, no. 1 (January 1989): 147.

13. Stoler, "Making Empire Respectable."

14. See Strobel, *European Women*, chap. 1, for greater discussion and documentation.

15. Stoler, "Making Empire Respectable," p. 640.

16. Chaudhuri and Strobel, *Western Women*, explores examples of both complicity and resistance on the part of Western women.

17. Claudia Knapman, *White Women in Fiji 1835–1930: The Ruin of Empire?* (Sydney: Allen and Unwin, 1986), p. 175. See also Stoler, "Making Empire Respectable," p. 640.

18. Stoler, "Making Empire Respectable," p. 643.

19. Ibid., pp. 644–51.

20. Ronald Hyam, *Empire and Sexuality: The British Experience* (Manchester, England: Manchester University Press, 1990), pp. 17, 1. For a criticism of Hyam's earlier articles, see Mark T. Berger, "Imperialism and Sexual Exploitation: A Response to Ronald Hyam's 'Empire and Sexual Opportunity,'" *Journal of Imperial and Commonwealth History* 17 (1988): 83–89.

21. Hyam, *Empire and Sexuality*, pp. 119, 214.

22. Ibid., pp. 214–15.

23. Ibid., p. 9.

24. Kenneth Ballhatchet, *Race, Sex, and Class under the Raj: Imperial Attitudes and Politics and Their Critics, 1793–1905* (London: Weidenfeld and Nicolson, 1980), is an early, excellent example. Deborah Pellow, "Sexuality in Africa," *Trends in History* 4, no. 4 (1990): 71–96, surveys the literature for Africa on sexuality in general. For fear of rape by indigenous men, or the "black peril," see Charles Van Onselen *Studies in the Social and Economic History of the Witwatersrand, 1886–1914*, vol. 2, *New Nineveh* (London: Longman, 1982); and Amirah Inglis, *The White Woman's Protection Ordinance: Sexual Anxiety and Politics in Papua* (London: Sussex University Press, 1975).

25. Karen Tranberg Hansen, *Distant Companions: Servants and Employers in Zambia, 1900–1985* (Ithaca, N.Y.: Cornell University Press, 1989), pp. 96–97.

26. Segregation, rather than an African version of the CDA, was the Kenyan post–World War I solution to the VD problem. See Luise White, *The Comforts of*

Home: Prostitution in Colonial Nairobi (Chicago: University of Chicago Press, 1990), p. 46.

27. Hyam, *Empire and Sexuality*, p. 125.

28. Veena Talwar Oldenburg, *The Making of Colonial Lucknow, 1856–1877* (Princeton: Princeton University Press, 1984).

29. Veena Talwar Oldenburg, "Lifestyle as Resistance," *Feminist Studies* 16, no. 2 (1990): 259–87.

30. Oldenburg, *Lucknow*, pp. 140–41.

31. Oldenburg, "Lifestyle," p. 276.

32. The most extensive study of prostitution in colonial Africa, which deals necessarily primarily with the twentieth century, is White, *Comforts of Home*.

33. Antoinette Burton, "The White Woman's Burden: British Feminists and 'The Indian Woman,' 1865–1915," in Chaudhuri and Strobel, *Western Women*, pp. 137–57.

34. Ibid., p. 140.

35. Frederick Cooper, "From Free Labor to Family Allowances: Labor and African Society in Colonial Discourse," *American Ethnologist* 16, no. 4 (November 1989): 745.

36. James Mill, *The History of British India* (1818; 5th ed. 1958; reprinted New York: Chelsea House Publishers, 1968), bk. 2, chap. 7, pp. 309–10.

37. Janaki Nair, "Uncovering the Zenana: Visions of Indian Womanhood in Englishwomen's Writings, 1813–1940," *Journal of Women's History* 2, no. 1 (Spring 1990): 17.

38. Anand Yang, "Whose *Sati*? Widow Burning in Early Nineteenth Century India," *Journal of Women's History* 1, no. 2 (Fall 1989): 8–33.

39. Lata Mani, "Contentious Traditions: The Debate on Sati in Colonial India," in *Recasting Women: Essays in Indian Colonial History*, ed. Kumkum Sangari and Sudesh Vaid (New Brunswick, N.J.: Rutgers University Press, 1990), p. 118.

40. Joanna Liddle and Rama Joshi, *Daughters of Independence: Gender, Caste, and Class in India* (London: Zed, 1986), p. 26.

41. Yang, "Whose *Sati*?" pp. 14–15.

42. Mani, "Contentious Traditions," p. 112.

43. Ibid., p. 95.

44. Yang, "Whose *Sati*?" p. 24.

45. Mrinalini Sinha, "Gender and Imperialism: Colonial Policy and the Ideology of Moral Imperialism in Late Nineteenth-century Bengal," in *Changing Men: New Directions in Research on Men and Masculinity*, ed. Michael S. Kimmel, pp. 217–31 (Beverly Hills, Calif.: Sage, 1987). Barbara N. Ramusack, "Women's Organisations and Social Change: The Age-of-Marriage Issue in India," in *Women and World Change: Equity Issues in Development*, ed. Naomi Black and Ann Baker Cotrell, pp. 198–216 (Beverly Hills, Calif.: Sage, 1981).

46. Dagmar Engels, "The Limits of Gender Ideology: Bengali Women, the Colonial State, and the Private Sphere, 1890–1930," *Women's Studies International Forum* 12, no. 4 (1989): 425–37.

47. Ibid.; Uma Chakravarti, "Whatever Happened to the Vedic *Dasi*? Ori-

entalism, Nationalism, and a Script for the Past," in Sangari and Vaid, *Recasting Women: Essays in Indian Colonial History*, pp. 27–87.

48. Engels, "Limits of Gender Ideology," pp. 429–30.

49. Liddle and Joshi, *Daughters of Independence*, pp. 28–29.

50. Ibid., p. 30.

51. Mrinalini Sinha, " 'Chathams, Pitts, and Gladstones in Petticoats': The Politics of Gender and Race in the Ilbert Bill Controversy, 1883–1884," in Chadhuri and Strobel, *Western Women and Imperialism*, pp. 98–118.

52. Cited in Sinha, " 'Chathams, Pitts, and Gladstones,' " p. 100.

53. Cited in ibid., pp. 100–101.

54. Cited in ibid., p. 110.

55. Sinha, " 'Chathams, Pitts, and Gladstones,' " p. 110; and Barbara N. Ramusack, "Cultural Missionaries, Material Imperialists, Feminist Allies: British Women Activists in India 1865–1945," in Chaudhuri and Strobel, *Western Women*, pp. 119–36.

56. Cited in Sinha, " 'Chathams, Pitts, and Gladstones,' " p. 108.

57. Sinha, " 'Chathams, Pitts, and Gladstones,' " pp. 108–9.

58. Gayatri Chakravarty Spivak, "Can the Subaltern Speak?" in *Marxism and the Interpretation of Culture*, ed. Cary Nelson and Lawrence Grossberg (Urbana and Chicago: University of Illinois Press, 1988), p. 297.

59. Corresponding to private schools in the United States.

60. Helen Callaway, *Gender, Culture, and Empire: European Women in Colonial Nigeria* (Urbana: University of Illinois Press, 1987), p. 14.

61. Cited in ibid., p. 5.

62. Hyam, *Empire and Sexuality*, p. 72.

63. Ibid., p. 73.

64. Cited in ibid., p. 72.

65. Cited in Sinha, " 'Chathams, Pitts, and Gladstones,' " p. 100.

66. Sinha, "Gender and Imperialism," p. 226.

67. Jane Hunter explores this dynamic for American missionaries in China in *The Gospel of Gentility: American Women Missionaries in Turn-of-the-Century China* (New Haven: Yale University Press, 1984).

68. Sylvia Leith-Ross, *Stepping-Stones: Memoirs of Colonial Nigeria, 1907–1960* (London and Boston: Peter Owen, 1983), p. 69.

69. This issue is explored in greater detail in Strobel, *European Women*, chaps. 1 and 2.

70. Partha Chatterjee, "Colonialism, Nationalism, and Colonized Women: The Contest in India," *American Ethnologist* 16, no. 4 (November 1989): 624.

71. Ibid., pp. 628–29.

72. Ibid., p. 629.

73. Ibid., p. 631. For a more detailed discussion, see Meredith Borthwick, *The Changing Role of Women in Bengal, 1849–1905* (Princeton: Princeton University Press, 1984).

74. Jean Comaroff and John L. Comaroff, "Home-Made Hegemony: Modernity, Domesticity, and Colonialism in South Africa," in *African Encounters with*

Domesticity, ed. Karen Tranberg Hansen (New Brunswick, N.J.: Rutgers University Press, 1992).

75. Ibid.

76. Kristin Mann, *Marrying Well: Marriage, Status, and Social Change among the Educated Elite in Colonial Lagos* (Cambridge, England: Cambridge University Press, 1985), chap. 2.

77. Quoted in ibid., p. 87.

78. Ibid., chap. 4.

BIBLIOGRAPHY

Bailey, Susan. *Women and the British Empire: An Annotated Guide to Sources*. New York: Garland Publishing, 1987.

Ballhatchet, Kenneth. *Race, Sex, and Class under the Raj: Imperial Attitudes and Politics and Their Critics, 1793–1905*. London: Weidenfeld and Nicolson, 1980.

Baumgart, W. *The Idea and Reality of British and French Colonial Expansion 1880–1914*. Oxford, England: Oxford University Press, 1982.

Berger, Mark T. "Imperialism and Sexual Exploitation: A Response to Ronald Hyam's 'Empire and Sexual Opportunity.'" *Journal of Imperial and Commonwealth History* 17 (1988): 83–89.

Birkett, Dea. *Spinsters Abroad: Victorian Lady Travelers*. London: Basil Blackwell, 1989.

Blake, Susan L. "A Woman's Trek: What Difference Does Gender Make?" In *Western Women and Imperialism: Complicity and Resistance*, ed. Nupur Chaudhuri and Margaret Strobel, pp. 19–34. Bloomington: Indiana University Press, 1992.

Borthwick, Meredith. *The Changing Role of Women in Bengal, 1849–1905*. Princeton: Princeton University Press, 1984.

Brooks, George E., Jr. "The Signares of Saint-Louis and Gorée: Women Entrepreneurs in Eighteenth-Century Senegal." In *Women in Africa: Studies in Social and Economic Change*, ed. Nancy J. Hafkin and Edna G. Bay, pp. 19–44. Stanford, Calif.: Stanford University Press, 1976.

Burton, Antoinette. "The White Woman's Burden: British Feminists and 'The Indian Woman,' 1865–1915." In *Western Women and Imperialism: Complicity and Resistance*, ed. Nupur Chaudhuri and Margaret Strobel, pp. 137–57. Bloomington: Indiana University Press, 1992.

Callaway, Helen. *Gender, Culture, and Empire: European Women in Colonial Nigeria*. Urbana: University of Illinois Press, 1987.

Chakravarti, Uma. "Whatever Happened to the Vedic *Dasi*? Orientalism, Nationalism, and a Script for the Past." In *Recasting Women: Essays in Indian Colonial History*, ed. Kumkum Sangari and Sudesh Vaid, pp. 27–87. New Brunswick, N.J.: Rutgers University Press, 1990.

Chatterjee, Partha. "Colonialism, Nationalism, and Colonized Women: The Contest in India." *American Ethnologist* 16, no. 4 (November 1989): 622–33.

Chaudhuri, Nupur, and Margaret Strobel. *Western Women and Imperialism: Complicity and Resistance*. Bloomington: Indiana University Press, 1992.

Comaroff, Jean, and John L. Comaroff. "Home-Made Hegemony: Modernity, Domesticity, and Colonialism in Southern Africa." In *African Encounters with Domesticity*, ed. Karen Tranberg Hansen, pp. 45–109. New Brunswick, N.J.: Rutgers University Press, 1992.

Cooper, Frederick. "From Free Labor to Family Allowances: Labor and African Society in Colonial Discourse." *American Ethnologist* 16, no. 4 (November 1989): 745–65.

Eldridge, C. C. *Victorian Imperialism*. London: Hodder and Stoughton, 1978.

Engels, Dagmar. "The Limits of Gender Ideology: Bengali Women, the Colonial State, and the Private Sphere, 1890–1930." *Women's Studies International Forum* 12, no. 4 (1989): 425–37.

Fieldhouse, D. K. *Colonialism, 1870–1945*. London: Weidenfeld and Nicolson, 1981.

Frank, Kathleen. *A Voyager Out: The Life of Mary Kingsley*. Boston: Houghton Mifflin, 1986.

Hansen, Karen Tranberg. *Distant Companions: Servants and Employers in Zambia, 1900–1985*. Ithaca, N.Y.: Cornell University Press, 1989.

Helly, Dorothy O. *Livingstone's Legacy: Horace Waller and Victorian Mythmaking*. Athens: Ohio University Press, 1987.

Hobsbawm, Eric, and Terence Ranger, eds. *The Invention of Tradition*. Cambridge, England: Cambridge University Press, 1983.

Hunter, Jane. *The Gospel of Gentility: American Women Missionaries in Turn-of-the-Century China*. New Haven: Yale University Press, 1984.

Hyam, Ronald. *Britain's Imperial Century, 1815–1914: A Study of Empire and Expansion*. London: Batsford, 1976.

———. *Empire and Sexuality: The British Experience*. Manchester, England: Manchester University Press, 1990.

Inglis, Amirah. *The White Woman's Protection Ordinance: Sexual Anxiety and Politics in Papua*. London: Sussex University Press, 1975.

Johnson-Odim, Cheryl, and Margaret Strobel, eds. *Restoring Women to History: Teaching Packets for Integrating Women's History Into Courses on Africa, Asia, Latin America and the Caribbean, and the Middle East*. Rev. ed. Bloomington, Ind.: Organization of American Historians, 1990.

Kiernan, V. G. *The Lords of Human Kind: European Attitudes Toward the Outside World in the Imperial Age*. London: Weidenfeld and Nicolson, 1976.

Knapman, Claudia. *White Women in Fiji, 1835–1930: The Ruin of Empire?* Sydney. Allen and Unwin, 1986.

Leith-Ross, Sylvia. *Stepping-Stones: Memoirs of Colonial Nigeria, 1907–1960*. London and Boston: Peter Owen, 1983.

Liddle, Joanna, and Rama Joshi. *Daughters of Independence: Gender, Caste, and Class in India*. London: Zed, 1986.

Mackenzie, J. M. *Propaganda and Empire: The Manipulation of British Public Opinion, 1880–1960*. Manchester, England: Manchester University Press, 1984.

Mani, Lata. "Contentious Traditions: The Debate on *Sati* in Colonial India." In *Recasting Women: Essays in Indian Colonial History*, ed. Kumkum Sangari and Sudesh Vaid, pp. 88–126. New Brunswick, N.J.: Rutgers University Press, 1990.

Mann, Kristin. *Marrying Well: Marriage, Status, and Social Change among the Educated Elite in Colonial Lagos.* Cambridge, England: Cambridge University Press, 1985.

Melman, Billie. *Women's Orients: English Women and the Middle East, 1718–1918; Sexuality, Religion and Work.* Ann Arbor: University of Michigan Press, 1992.

Mill, James. *The History of British India.* 5th ed. 1858. Reprinted New York: Chelsea House, 1968. Originally published 1818.

Mills, Sara. *Discourses of Difference: An Analysis of Women's Travel Writing and Colonialism.* New York: Routledge, 1991.

Nandy, Ashis. *The Intimate Enemy: Loss and Recovery of Self under Colonialism.* Bombay: Oxford University Press, 1983.

Nair, Janaki. "Uncovering the Zenana: Visions of Indian Womanhood in Englishwomen's Writings, 1813–1940." *Journal of Women's History* 2, no. 1 (Spring 1990): 8–34.

Oldenburg, Veena Talwar. "Lifestyle as Resistance: The Case of the Courtesans of Lucknow, India." *Feminist Studies* 16, no. 2 (Summer 1990): 259–87.

———. *The Making of Colonial Lucknow, 1856–1877.* Princeton: Princeton University Press, 1984.

Pellow, Deborah. "Sexuality in Africa." *Trends in History* 4, no. 4 (1990): 71–96.

Sinha, Mrinalini. "Gender and Imperialism: Colonial Policy and the Ideology of Moral Imperialism in Late Nineteenth-Century Bengal." In *Changing Men: New Directions in Research on Men and Masculinity*, ed. Michael S. Kimmel, pp. 217–31. Beverly Hills, Calif.: Sage, 1987.

———. " 'Chathams, Pitts, and Gladstones in Petticoats': The Politics of Gender and Race in the Ilbert Bill Controversy, 1883–1884." In *Western Women and Imperialism: Complicity and Resistance*, ed. Nupur Chaudhuri and Margaret Strobel, pp. 98–118. Bloomington: Indiana University Press, 1992.

Spear, Percival. *The Nabobs.* London: Oxford University Press, 1963.

Spivak, Gayatri Chakravorty. "Can the Subaltern Speak?" In *Marxism and the Interpretation of Culture*, ed. Cary Nelson and Lawrence Grossberg, pp. 271–313. Urbana and Chicago: University of Illinois Press, 1988.

Stevenson, Catherine Barnes. *Victorian Women Travel Writers in Africa.* Boston: Twayne, 1982.

Stoler, Ann L. "Making Empire Respectable: The Politics of Race and Sexual Morality in Twentieth-Century Colonial Cultures." *American Ethnologist* 16, no. 4 (November 1989): 634–60.

———. "Rethinking Colonial Categories: European Communities and the Boundaries of Rule." *Comparative Studies in Society and History* 31, no. 1 (January 1989): 134–61.

Strobel, Margaret. *European Women and the Second British Empire.* Bloomington: Indiana University Press, 1991.

Van Onselen, Charles. *Studies in the Social and Economic History of the Witwatersrand, 1886–1914.* Volume 2, *New Nineveh.* London: Longman, 1982.

Viswanathan, Gauri. *Masks of Conquest: Literary Study and British Rule in India*. New York: Columbia University Press, 1989.

White, Luise. *The Comforts of Home: Prostitution in Colonial Nairobi*. Chicago: University of Chicago Press, 1990.

Yang, Anand. "Whose *Sati*? Widow Burning in Early Nineteenth Century India." *Journal of Women's History* 1, no. 2 (Fall 1989): 8–33.

THE CONTRIBUTORS

MICHAEL ADAS, a professor of history at Rutgers University, is currently editor of the American Historical Association's series on Global and Comparative History and co-editor of the Cambridge University Press series on "Studies in Comparative World History." He has published numerous articles and books, including most recently (with Peter Stearns and Stuart Schwartz) *World Civilization: The Global Experience* (1992) and *Turbulent Passage: A Global History of the Twentieth Century* (1993).

JANET LIPPMAN ABU-LUGHOD is a professor of sociology and a member of the Committee on Historical Studies at the Graduate Faculty of the New School for Social Research. She has written extensively on the development of cities in the United States, the Middle East, and the Third World. Her most recently published books are *Before European Hegemony* (1989) and *Changing Cities* (1991). A book on the history and current conflicts in Lower Manhattan in New York City is forthcoming.

ALFRED W. CROSBY is a professor of American studies and geography at the University of Texas at Austin who holds a Ph.D. in history from Boston University. His publications include *America, Russia, Hemp and Napoleon: American Trade with Russia and the Baltic, 1783–1812* (1965), *The Columbian Exchange: Biological and Cultural Consequences of 1492* (1972), *Epidemic and Peace, 1918* (1976), *Ecological Imperialism: The Biological Expansion of Europe, 900–1900* (1986), and a number of articles. A recipient of fellowships and grants from the National Institutes of Health, the National Humanities Institute, the Council for the International Exchange of Scholars, the University of Texas, and the John Simon Guggenheim Foundation, he has also won prizes from the American Medical Writers' Association and the Texas Institute of Letters. His research has concentrated on biohistory.

PHILIP D. CURTIN is Herbert Baxter Adams Professor of History at Johns Hopkins University. He is the author of many books including, most recently, *Death by Migration: Europe's Encounter with the Tropical World in the Nineteenth Century* (1989), *Cross-Cultural Trade in World History* (1984), and *The Rise and Fall of the Plantation Complex: Essays in Atlantic History* (1989).

RICHARD M. EATON is an associate professor of history at the University of Arizona. Trained in the University of Wisconsin's Comparative World History program, he has researched and written in the fields of Indian and Islamic history. He is author of *Sufis of Bijapur, 1300–1700: Social Roles of Sufis in Medieval India* (1978) and of numerous articles on premodern Indo-Muslim history and comparative religious history. He has coauthored a book with George Michell entitled *Firuzabad: Palace City of the Deccan* (1990) and has completed a study of *Islam and the Bengal Frontier, 1200–1760* (1993).

WILLIAM H. McNEILL is professor of history emeritus at the University of Chicago. He has written over twenty books, some of which have treated global themes and long periods of time. The book on which this essay is largely based appeared under the title *Pursuit of Power: Technology, Armed Force, and Society since 1000* A.D. (1983). A past president of the American Historical Association, in 1963 he won the National Book Award in history for *The Rise of the West: A History of the Human Community* (1963).

PETER N. STEARNS is dean of the College of Humanities and Social Sciences, Carnegie Mellon University, and also Heinz Professor of History. He is managing editor of the *Journal of Social History* and has published a wide range of books and articles in social and world history. Stearns has addressed the impact of the industrial revolution, in terms of labor policies, working-class experience, and gender interactions in *Lives of Labor: Work in Maturing Industrial Societies*; *World Civilizations: the Global Experience* (with Michael Adas and Stuart Schwartz); *Be a Man! Males in Modern Society*; and *The Industrial Revolution in World History*. His current research focuses on changes in emotional standards, with a forthcoming book entitled *American Cool: Constructing a Twentieth-Century Emotional Style* and *Jealousy: The Evolution of Emotion in American History* (1989).

MARGARET STROBEL, professor of women's studies and history at the University of Illinois at Chicago, focuses her current research on the Chicago Women's Liberation Union in an attempt to reestablish the Midwest in the history of the women's movement, examine the relationship between local culture and the forms that feminism took, and analyze the interplay of theory and practice as the CWLU developed. She has studied women internationally in *Muslim Women in Mombasa, 1890–1975* (1979, co-winner of the Herskovits Prize of the African Studies Association), *Three*

Swahili Women: Life Histories from Mombasa, Kenya (co-editor, in English and Swahili, with Sarah Mirza, 1989), *European Women and the Second British Empire* (1991), *Western Women and Imperialism: Complicity and Resistance* (with co-editor Nupur Chaudhuri, 1992), and *Expanding the Boundaries of Women's History: Essays on Women in the Third World* (co-editor with Cheryl Johnson-Odim, 1992). She and Johnson-Odim also edited *Restoring Women to History*, vol. 3, a summary of the history of women in Africa, Asia, Latin America and the Caribbean, and the Middle East.

LOUISE A. TILLY is professor of history and sociology at the New School for Social Research and chair of its Committee on Historical Studies. She is currently president of the American Historical Association. Her work focuses on the small-scale effects of large-scale social change in concrete historical settings, especially in France and Italy since 1800, and with emphases on gender and class. She has written extensively and published in a wide range of journals, books, papers, reviews, and symposia.

JUDITH E. TUCKER is an associate professor of history and a director of the Arab Studies Program at Georgetown University. Author of *Women in Nineteenth-Century Egypt* (1985), she is also the editor of *Women in Arab Society: Old Boundaries, New Frontiers* (1993). Her current research is directed to law and gender in seventeenth- and eighteenth-century Syria and Palestine.